Healing Stories

Healing Stories:

The Use of Narrative in Counseling and Psychotherapy

Edited by
Stanley Krippner,
Michael Bova, & Leslie Gray

PUENTE
Publications
Charlottesville, Virginia
2007

Chapter 2, "Just Listening: Narrative and Deep Illness," is reprinted with the permission of *Family, Systems & Health*. Chapter 12, "Style," is reprinted with the permission of Riverhead Books. Chapter 3, "Emplotting the Traumatic Self: Narrative Revision and the Construction of Coherence," Chapter 12, "Vietnam Combat Experiences and Rites of Passage: Healing Through Telling One's Story," Chapter 17, "Psychotherapy: The Art of Experience," and Chapter 18, "Action Stores," are reprinted with the permission of *The Humanistic Psychologist*.

This edition was published as a paperbound book by
Puente Publications
977 Seminole Trail, #299
Charlottesville, Virginia, 22901-2824, USA

ISBN-10: 0-963450-14-X
ISBN-13: 978-0-9634501-4-2

Front Cover designed by Jon Mayer
Back Cover designed by Gérman Aguilera Ampudia of Popete Gráfico
Cover photograph by Ronny Mastrion
Section-separating photographs by Bijan Yashar

Special thanks to Carlos Adrián Hernández Tavares

Printed in Canada

TABLE OF CONTENTS

Dedication

To Jerome D. Frank,
for his numerous contributions to the understanding of psychotherapy,
expanding the frontier of psychiatry,
and for his work in the psychology of conflict resolution.

Acknowledgments

The editors express gratitude to *The Humanistic Psychologist* for permission to reprint the chapters by Stewart and Neimeyer, Paulson, Rosenbaum and Bohart and Serlin.

Editor Michael Bova wishes to extend his thanks to Steve Hart and Sheilah Walsh for their invaluable administrative assistance. He is grateful for the love and support of his beautiful wife Michela, and his loving daughters Alanna and Caitlin. He also wants to acknowledge the support and inspiration of his mother Mary, mother-in-law Jeannine, his siblings, their families and his wonderful extended family. Last but not least, he wants to acknowledge the loving memory of his father Vincent and brother Vincent Jr. His warmest thoughts embrace the memory of his grandmother Anna Rosa Bova.

The Power of Storytelling

Susan Powers

The power of storytelling is perhaps most evident in the story of the *Odyssey*, the epic poem about a king of Ithaca who was a hero in the Trojan War. What we know about Odysseus is based on the narrative given to us by the poet, Homer, as he details this hero's wanderings for a decade subsequent to the Trojan War. Although the *Odyssey* is an exciting literary work, it may be that its true value does not reside in its potential for entertainment. Rather the *Odyssey* is important because of the way in which it functions: this epic poem shows us that history is not simply preserved through stories, it is also shaped.

This insight into the power of storytelling transcends the boundaries of epic poetry. Forming our life experiences into narratives allows us to view our lives in particular ways. Articulating memories and experiences can highlight specific themes, lessons, and personal values. In short, we can make meaning out of the most chaotic or troublesome events by organizing them into narratives.

Healing Stories: The Use of Narrative in Counseling and Psychotherapy presents a comprehensive treatment of the ways narrative can help people make meaning out of their most challenging circumstances. The book is divided into three sections addressing different realms of narrative and meaning-making. Section I, "Narrative Therapy and Trauma," presents the role of narrative in coping with the after-effects of traumatic experiences through stories which range from tales of trauma victims to the challenges of deep illness and loss. Section II, "Personal Mythology," illuminates the ways in which the stories one tells about oneself can imbue a personal history with the power of healing and be formative in attaining a meaningful identity. Finally, Section III, "Narrative and Creative Arts in Therapy," elucidates methodologies that shape one's self-concept through such techniques as drama, art therapy, and writing. In a sense, the human condition is one that requires every individual to partake in an *Odyssey*. Like Odysseus, who finally found his way home, each person must contend with hardships. For example, whereas Odysseus and his men had to struggle with Circe who had the power to turn men into swine, an individual nowadays might find him or herself struggling not to lose sight of personal values and thereby be transformed into some swine-like form. Although Odysseus had to come with a dangerous whirlpool named Charybdis, a contemporary person might be fighting despair as traumatic memories resurface.

Healing Stories: The Use of Narrative in Counseling and Psychotherapy presents the forms narratives can take and their potential for transformation. The stories that Odysseus lived through are what make his tale so interesting. Likewise, understanding our lives in terms of narrative structure can help us become the heroes we want to be in our own personal odysseys.

INTRODUCTION

Constructing Stories:
The Therapeutic Uses of Narratives

Stanley Krippner, Michael Bova, & Leslie Gray

One of the most crucial developments among modern civilizations is their lack of grand narrative schemes to bind their citizens together and help them make sense of their lives. Not only have religious myths lost much of their power, but increasing numbers of people have lost faith in the metanarratives of science, technology, government, and of the very notion of progress itself. On the one hand, this loss can be liberating for people who no longer need to be shackled by constraints that cripple their achievements and self-esteem because of their gender, ethnicity, and sexual preferences. On the other hand, if a culture is "de-storied" it begins to lack external validation for individuals' conduct and values (Parry & Doan, 1994). This absence of covenants often results in alienation, disengagement, and a cultural "balkanization" in which warring cults, sects, and cliques vie for people's allegiance.

An antidote to modern anomie is the articulation of one's personal worldview, one's family myths, and one's community stories. Individuals in therapy can construct and interpret their own tales and use them as a vital part of their healing. However, as Stone (1996) observes, simply repeating negative stories does not free people, but only deepens the pattern of their low self-esteem and perpetuates painful personal myths. When stories lead to these behaviors, it is time "to script a new tale" (p. 208). Hence, clients can play an active role in forming the interpersonal realities to which they will respond throughout the rest of their lives (Neimeyer & Mahoney, 1995).

Along with the demise of political, technological, and religious metanarratives, the once grand psychotherapeutic paradigms are crumbling. Psychotherapists can not simply impose their views of reality upon clients; instead, they must listen carefully to their clients, helping them to clarify, refine, and revise their own stories, ultimately using them as vehicles for change (Mauron, 1962). Kleinman (1988) has presented a number of "illness narratives" not as clinical histories but as moral tales of remorse and regret, social dilemmas, cultural ironies, "as the imperative stuff of myth and tragedy" (Kleinman, 1995, p. 14), even though others have noted that the veracity of these stories often is less important than the strategies they may reveal (Crandon-Malamud, 1991). Kleinman (1995), speaking from an anthropological perspective, observes that it is obvious that these narratives differ from literary stories. Yet "both genres draw upon a sensibility to context" (p. 67), giving their listeners and readers a view particular to a local world that often has more expansive applications because multiple perspectives and divergent interpretations are encouraged.

An increasing number of personality, developmental, psychoanalytic, anthropological, sociological, literary, educational, and clinical scholars and researchers are using narrative methods in their studies (Brooks, 1994; Crossen, 1994; Josselson & Lieblich, 1993; Polkinghorne, 1988; Terkel, 1974). For example, Bettelheim (1976/1977) once suggested that there are stories in each culture that help children traverse various developmental conflict situations. Choi (1973) detected a difference in the content of dream reports from alcoholics who had been sober for more than one year as compared to those who had not been abstinent for a year. Jalongo and Isenberg (1995) observe that most of the practical knowledge that teachers gain through experience is encoded in, and expressed through, stories. Psychotherapists have come to formulate narrative therapies that expressly adopt the metaphors of story, script, and scene to conceptualize such phenomena as identity, personal perceptions, moral development, emotional experiences, and caring relationships. In addition, a variety of personality and psychosocial diagnostic procedures and assessments (such as the Thematic Apperception Test and the Rorschach Inkblots) have been developed in which narratives provide the main data source of information for client appraisal.

White and Epston (1990) ask how the writing of personal and collective stories can liberate and heal, as long as the dominant cultural stories are so problem-saturated. Freedman and Combs (1996) have identified two metaphors to answer this question: (1) narrative and social construction assist people to identify problems in a sociocultural context, to alternative stories, questions, reflections, and plots; (2) the results will help to *spread the news* that there are oppositional ways of viewing reality. Frank (1995) is concerned with ethical issues, noting that psychotherapists who use narratives can help their clients fulfill their need for a voice they can recognize as their own. The use of storytelling helps clients to reclaim their own experience of suffering, making moral sense of their distress, and ultimately, witnessing afflictions that go beyond their own (pp. 18–19).

Pipher (1994) reports successful outcomes based on having adolescent girls write down their angry thoughts in journals and diaries, thus turning their pain outward. Riordan (1996) has used similar techniques to label and describe traumas through writing about them, enabling clients to gain a sense of mastery and control. Kopp (1995) has utilized metaphors to assist clients in the identification and explanation of their underlying belief systems. But are these thoughts, statements, and metaphors based on consensual or idiosyncratic reality?

Recalling Truth

There is evidence that children in the one- to two-year-old age group are able to recall specific events. This type of memory is primarily determined by what children are asked to remember, the number of exposures to that event, and the availability of cues or reminders of that event. Thus, children are able to remember specific events over periods of weeks and even months, but the story must be told and re-told for it to remain accurate and coherent (Bauer, 1996). As a result, these stories allow children, and later adults, to talk about time, space, and place. Some of these stories involve professional knowledge, others are personal experiences of a confidential nature, and others are narratives that are oppositional to the culture's values and traditions.

Clandinin and Connelly (1996) speak of "secret stories" that are usually told to peers in secret places (a bedroom, a business boardroom). But when people move into broader contexts (a dormitory, a clubroom, a business convention), they typically tell "cover stories" in which they portray themselves in ways that they hope will establish or reinforce their desired self-image. There also are "sacred stories" — accounts of extraordinary experiences that may only be told to an intimate friend or respected professional practitioner (in a nature retreat, a church confessional, a psychotherapist's office). These stories can overlap: should someone want to proselytize, the "sacred story" may become a "cover story" and be revealed to multitudes; a "secret story" may become a "cover story" if someone is invited to appear on a television talk show and discuss a personal indiscretion in exchange for fame, money, or both. Needless to say, not all of these stories are life-potentiating; personal, family, and institutional narratives are often intertwined with criminal behavior, substance abuse, sexual promiscuity, misogyny, homophobia, and racism (e.g., Alison, Smith & Morgan, 2003).

Distortion is almost inevitable, especially among people with identifiable personality profiles. For example, "high hypnotizable" individuals tend to close the memory gaps in confabulated fantasies when pressed for details (Ganaway, 1989). When therapists work with individuals who suffer from dissociative disorders, they should be prepared to encounter a mixture of fact and fantasy. There is controversy over whether hypnotic procedures facilitate accurate recall, but there is little disagreement that hypnosis encourages clients to speak about events about which they are uncertain. Spence (1982) asserts that the reconstruction of memory is subject to so much defensive distortion as to require the label of "narrative truth" (or "psychological reality") as opposed to "historical truth" (or "fact-oriented reality").

The term "screen memory" has been coined to describe what happens when a story is used as a shield, or to conceal an unwelcome memory. When a client recalls playing in the basement as a child, but does not remember the nature of the game, he or she may be providing a "screen memory" — a story that "screens" an incident of sexual abuse (Campbell, 1981). When a patient recalls a television program about hostile space aliens and superimposes it on an experience of physical abuse, "screening" may be taking place. A film about incest could evoke a "screen memory" for a poorly-recalled childhood altercation with an adult; hence the resulting incestual story "screens" a very different event. These are some of the ways in which "screen memories" become part of one's "narrative truth," obscuring and distorting one's "historical truth."

The delicate nature of memory is apparent to psychotherapists who work with their clients' dream reports. The dream as directly experienced cannot be used therapeutically, and client reports may be incomplete, poorly remembered, or completely fabricated. Indeed, they may change or undergo revision depending on the social or temporal context. Not only does a dream report represent a dialogue between one's waking and sleeping mentation, it reflects a discourse between the dreamer and the listener. Dreamers may provide one version of the recalled dream to family members, a second version to their friends, and a third version to their psychotherapists (Kramer, 1969). As time goes by, what is disclosed about the dream may vary considerably, depending on how the dreamer forgets, embroiders, or reconstructs different portions of the report. In postmodern terms, serial reports of the same dream are fluid rather than fixed texts. Hence, dreamwork of any type needs to be done with care, with attentiveness, and with modesty.

Schweitzer (1994) has shrewdly analyzed the way in which Joseph Conrad's *Heart of Darkness* and William Faulkner's *Absolom! Absolom!* reached similar unsettling conclusions about the provisional nature of truth, the impossibility of "full utterance," the inevitable obscurity of the past, and the necessity of settling for an incomplete story of the world. Despite these limitations, empowerment through counseling, psychotherapy, and education is helpful for many people if the practitioner is astute. This empowerment is the process by which people, organizations, or groups who are powerless become aware of the power dynamics in their environment, develop skills and capacities that enable them to gain some control of their lives, exercise that control without infringing on the rights of others, and support the empowerment of others in their community (McWhirter, 1991, p. 224). Such empowerment often occurs despite the persistence of an "incomplete" story because it restores agency to survivors and opposes heavy-handed suggestion by therapists (Bowman & Mertz, 1996, p. 628).

For survivors of physical, sexual, and emotional abuse there are several issues, only one of which is whether their stories represent "narrative truth" or "historical truth." They also need to determine at what point the recalled story became interpreted as "abuse." Making a personal connection to a "survivor-of-abuse" narrative is often long-standing, but sometimes does not take place until an individual enters psychotherapy. In the face of the complexities of memory, Friedman (1995) has called for psychotherapy to set aside the authoritative expertise of the therapist in favor of respecting the client as a participant in a relationship based on dialogue. Once a psychotherapist begins his or her work by acknowledging the concrete existence of persons, acknowledging their wholeness and uniqueness, profound healing and change can take place (Friedman, 1992).

Practitioners who use narrative therapies in their practice have not gone unchallenged. Their critics ask how these therapists can pay attention to the uniqueness of each client and, at the same time, preserve a systematic enterprise based on rules and replicability. Critics claim that regarding each client as singular may lead to the rejection of the very categories and diagnoses that could play a vital role in selecting the proper intervention. These commentators often assert that a preoccupation with stories can be a distraction from the fact that there is a fixed reality to be altered or distorted. An over-reliance on narrative by a therapist can do clients a disservice by ignoring the origins of their pathology in favor of transforming their self-narratives (Held, 1995). Other critics claim that the jargon used by some advocates of phenomenological accounts obscure the flow of experience more than they illuminate it (Kleinman, 1995, p. 276).

These are the vital issues that fuel the chapters in this anthology. Despite their limitations, categories are unavoidable and we have classified the contributions to this book into three sections: narrative therapy and trauma, personal mythology, and creative art therapies.

Section One: Narrative Therapy and Trauma

Michael W. Barclay opens the first group of essays by describing how "we tell ourselves stories," contrasting their individual, interpersonal, and societal dimensions. Stories derived from these three dimensions shape people's lives, creating and expressing one's "self."

Arthur W. Frank writes about the stories told by those whom he considers to be involved in those "deep illnesses" — critical or chronic, life-threatening or long-term — which affect virtually all life choices and decisions. Frank works from the position of Arthur Kleinman's (1988) "empathic listening," and from Rachel Naomi Remen's (1996) statement that, for optimal effectiveness, this type of listening is to be seen as a "gift" rather than a "task." For Frank, there are three basic illness narratives: the restitution story, the chaos narrative, and the quest narrative. By grasping the insights these stories offer, therapists can skillfully organize what they hear, providing their clients more than a mechanistic "de-coder," and more than what can be offered by a sympathetic friend.

Alan E. Stewart and Robert A. Neimeyer note that the "constructivism" movement has generated a great deal of theoretical discussion in the mental health fields, but its simplications for clinical conceptualization, assessment, and treatment have been less systematically explored. In this chapter, they attempt to remedy this shortcoming, concluding that a narrative perspective on the traumatic disruption of self-identity holds promise for clinical practitioners.

David Vogel argues that the narrative perspective departs from the clinical perspective in that the latter may label one story "delusional" and another story "reality-based." However, he also contends that the dynamic tension and possible synthesis between these antithetical viewpoints are critical for the future development of psychotherapy and narrative psychology. Vogel's chapter is written from the vantage point of constructivism, giving the reader an outlook that can be used while reading the other authors represented in this book.

In "Cody's Story," Susan W. Schwartz examines transformations of an individual client's conscious awareness through the evolving story of his survival from a life-threatening illness. Through this account, she shows how levels of consciousness may interact in narrative exchange to foster recovery. Research data, dream stories, and internal monologues are among the arenas for the client's healing narratives. Even the medical records of his operation provided information that became an important part of the clarification and refining of his awareness, allowing for a resolution of his internal conflicts.

In "The Truism Metaphor and Positive Age Regression to Experiences of Mastery," D. Corydon Hammond describes how the use of metaphor in indirect hypnotic suggestions can facilitate treatment. In contrast to fabricated metaphoric stories, or metaphors reflecting their therapeutic practice, "truism metaphors" reflect natural processes or life experiences so common that patients cannot easily resist them. Hammond finds that this approach enhances patients' feelings of mastery and self-efficacy, and that it is of special value with trauma survivors.

Section Two: Personal Mythology

Stephen A. Anderson and Sarah E. Holmes explore psychotherapists' and supervisors' personal mythologies to address an additional dynamic within the therapeutic system. Examining the variety of definitions of "self" as they relate to therapeutic identity can be useful in promoting personal growth and wholeness, and differing "self" definitions can be useful in identifying practitioners' unique strengths. In addition, this approach may help practitioners recognize their own emotional blindspots that may hinder therapeutic progress.

David Feinstein outlines a practical program that encourages clients to identify "old myths," "counter-myths," and "new myths." He looks at the mythmaking aspects of the human psyche, the increased personalizing of mythology in recent times, and the mythic structure of psychological development. Client-generated storymaking is described as a tool for uncovering personal myths that operate outside of one's awareness. An application of this program is given in Stanley Krippner's chapter, "Mythic Discord."

In "Story as Personal Myth," G. Frank Lawlis compares one's inner mythology with one's outer experiences, noting that these mythologies provide people with "models by which we measure our lives." But clients who are not aware of their mythologies and how these accounts affect their daily lives need story-telling to search for, and determine, appropriate roles to play in bringing meaning to their lives.

In her chapter, "Style," Rachel Naomi Remen describes how a client's personal symbols were the basis for an imagery program that was used as part of a comprehensive treatment program for a malignant melanoma. Remen's story demonstrates the importance of selecting mental imagery wisely, when it is used therapeutically, because of the idiosyncratic differences from one client to another. In this case, the shift from "shark" imagery to "catfish" imagery proved essential; instead of having the imaginary shark aggressively destroying his cancer cells, the client found it more useful to imagine a catfish lovingly cleansing his body of malignant cells.

Daryl S. Paulson examines narrative therapy's effect on severe psychic trauma, demonstrating how it can be a rehumanizing force for war veterans in the face of the dehumanization of their combat experiences. Using his own experiences in self-healing following his return from Vietnam, Paulson developed a therapeutic program for combat veterans based on the literature in personal mythology and rites of passage.

Section Three: Narrative and Creative Arts in Therapy

In "Dream Drama," Harold R. Ellis reviews the rationale and the procedures for a narrative approach to dreams. A dream report is shared with a group verbally as well as by the kinesthetic cues of body language and nonverbal expression. This process, according to Ellis, helps members of the drama group uncover latent creativity that can be used for healing purposes.

Frederick J. Heide examines structural rather than functional similarities between drama and psychotherapy, using the film *Casablanca* to illustrate these similarities. Several considerations seem to operate in both psychotherapy and theatrical writing, such as conflict and problem development, empathy, motivation, change through crisis, and resolution.

In "Hearing the Body's Story," Stephen R. Koepfer presents clinical examples to demonstrate his use of massage therapy, art therapy, and storytelling in rehabilitation. Koepfer's case studies demonstrate the role that image and emotion often play in mediating mind and body processes.

Patricia Perrine uses the definition of healing — "to make whole" — in support of the sharing of stories as an empowering function for women. Historically, women, like children, were meant to be seen and not heard: "it is this silencing that underscores the importance to women (and to men as well) of being able to tell stories to others." For Perrine, telling a story and being listened to validate the worthiness of the narrator's "self," as well as that narrator's words.

Robert Rosenbaum and Arthur C. Bohart examine the formal aspects of psychotherapy from an esthetic perspective. The formal and stylistic organization of the therapeutic process resembles the organization of artistic productions. Clients' life stories revealed through this process are subject to the same aspects of form, process, structure, and content as are literature, dance, music, and the other arts.

In "Action Stories," Ilene Ava Serlin discusses various capacities of muscular movement as a type of narrative communication. The text for this narrative form is "action language" which bridges inner sensation and outer form. Serlin outlines how action narratives, like verbal narratives, include metaphor, symbolism, and various levels of meaning. Plot (inaction narratives) is not recognizable in content but in dynamic structure; intelligibility is sensed not by rational logic but by kinesthetic imagination. Power, ritual, and the sacred are also aspects of experience that are expressed through action narratives.

Human Action and Change

Each of these chapters provide examples of what Mahoney (1991) refers to as clients' *active roles* create their personal and social realities. Human reason and emotion have neurological and endocrinal bases. The neurosciences that unravel these foundations have yielded data which, in the words of Damasio (1994), indicate that "the most indispensable thing we can do as human beings, every day of our lives, is remind ourselves and others of our complexity, fragility, finiteness, and uniqueness" (p. 252). There is a power in stories that enables them to capture attention and convey meaning (Krumboltz, Blando, Kim, & Reikowski, 1994). According to Rachel Naomi Remen (1996), her collection of "stories that heal" taught her that "wisdom is simply a matter of waiting, and healing a question of time" (p. 345).

In discussing the role of traditional and ethnic storytelling, Kroeber (1992) recognizes that "the arousing of awareness in an audience" is one of its most important features. A characteristic of master storytellers in preliterate societies is their ability to tell a story in such a way that it affects diverse members of its audience differently (p. 60). These factors combine to produce the authority and power that highlight cultural myths, factors that Kroeber finds lacking in most contemporary Western literature.

In Norse mythology, Loki is a trickster deity who confronts the gods and goddesses with their flaws, inconsistencies, and contradictions (Brink, 1995). In much the same way, storytelling confronts people with their flawed memories, their inconsistent recall, and their contradictory life accounts. Sometimes narratives raise more questions than they answer, serving a trickster role that keeps people from becoming complacent, or from jumping to unjustified conclusions about themselves and their world. This "postmodern" sensibility replaces the colonialism of authoritarian psychotherapy in a way similar to the way in which "postmodernity" has replaced "modernity's" colonialism of one truth, one reality, and one voice. Frank (1995, p. 19) describes the "distinctive ethics" of "postmodernism" in psychotherapy as taking responsibility for one's observations, whether the story is purely the clients' or one co-created by the client and the therapist.

Storytelling occurs among individuals, families, and societies. Bynum (1994) reminds us that family consciousness of all kinds moves throughout lives, both darkening and illuminating one's motivations, urges, and dynamics. Like dreams, these familial processes are older and deeper than individualistic consciousness. They send out roots that spiral "into the primordial structure and processes of the human psyche" (p. 12). Jensen (1996) predicts that in the twenty-first century, "storytelling will be a key skill in a wide range of professions, from advertiser to teacher to business entrepreneur to politician to religious leader. ... Each will be valued for his or her ability to produce 'dreams' for public consumption" (p. 10). In the meantime, Pickard (1961) reminds us that "children want good stories and they want them well told" (p. 206) while Warner (1995) realizes that "like a standup comedian, the tale must sense the aspirations and prejudices, the fears and hunger of its audience" (p. 409).

As von Glaserfeld (1995) observes, whatever things we know, we know only insofar as we have constructed them as relatively viable permanent entities in our conceptual world. Storytelling brings to psychotherapy the perspective that clients are more than passive and reactive objects of manipulations (Mahoney, 1996). Instead, clients become proactive agents who are able to participate in the reorganization of their lives. With their therapists, these clients co-create personal realities which evolve into a reciprocity, not only between their environment and themselves but also within different levels of their own activities. In other words, people organize their worlds by organizing themselves. This is reminiscent of John Dewey's (1933) call for "practicing knowledge," because life is much more than a narrative. Once a story provides a vision, that vision must be put to the test by its incarnation into the daily life of the storyteller.

References

Allison, L. J., Smith, M. D., & Morgan, K. (2003). Interpreting the accuracy of offender profiles. *Psychology, Crime and Law, 9,* 185–195.

Bauer, P. J. (1996). What do infants recall of their lives? Memory for specific events by one- to two-year-olds. *American Psychologist, 51,* 29–41.

Bettelheim, B. (1977). *The uses of enchantment: The meaning and importance of fairy tales.* New York: Vintage Books. (Original work published 1976)

Bowman, C. G., & Mertz, E. (1996). A dangerous direction: Legal intervention in sexual abuse survivor therapy. *Harvard Law Review, 109,* 549–639.

Brink, N. (1995). Loki's children: A mythical understanding of hypnosis in the process of change. *Hypnos, 22,* 154–158.

Brooks, P. (1994). *Psychoanalysis and storytelling.* Cambridge, MA: Blackwell.

Bynum, E. B. (1994, July). The African psychological lineage on dream states, family dynamics, the unconscious and beyond. *Psychological Discourses*, pp. 12–14.

Campbell, R. (1981). *Psychiatric dictionary*. New York: Oxford University Press.

Choi, S. Y. (1973). Dreams as a prognostic factor in alcoholism. *American Journal of Psychiatry, 130*, 699–702.

Clandinin, D. J., & Connelly, F. M. (1996). Teachers' professional knowledge landscapes: Teacher stories — stories of teachers — school stories — stories of schools. *Educational Researcher, 25*, 24–30.

Crandon-Malamud, L. (1991). *From the fat of our souls: Social change, political process, and medical pluralism in Bolivia*. Berkeley: University of California Press.

Crossen, C. (1994). *Tainted truth: The manipulation of fact in America*. New York: Simon & Schuster.

Damasio, A. R. (1994). *Descartes' error: Emotion, reason, and the human brain*. New York: G. P. Putnam.

Dewey, J. (1933). *How we think: A restatement of the relation of reflective thinking to the educative process*. (Rev. ed.). Chicago: Regnery.

Frank, A. W. (1995). *The wounded storyteller: Body, illness, and ethics*. Chicago: University of Chicago Press.

Freedman, J., & Combs, G. (1996). *Narrative therapy: The social construction of preferred realities*. New York: W. W. Norton.

Friedman, M. S. (1992). *Dialogue and the human image: Beyond humanistic psychology*. Newbury Park, CA: Sage Publications.

Friedman, M. S. (1995). Constructivism, psychotherapy, and the dialogue of touchstones. *Journal of Constructivist Psychotherapy, 8*, 283–292.

Ganaway, G. K. (1989). Historical versus narrative truth: Clarifying the role of exogenous trauma in the etiology of MPD and its variants. *Dissociation, 2*, 205–220.

Glaserfeld, E. von (1995). *Radical constructivism: A way of knowing and learning*. London: Falmer Press.

Held, B. (1995). *Back to reality: A critique of postmodern theory in psychotherapy*. New York: Norton.

Jalango, M. R., & Isenberg, J. P. (1995). *Teachers' stories: From personal narrative to professional insight*. San Francisco: Jossey-Bass.

Jensen, R. (1996, May-June). The dream society. *The Futurist*, pp. 9–13.

Josselson, R., & Lieblich, A. (Eds.) (1993). *The narrative study of lives*. Newbury Park, CA: Sage Publications.

Kleinman, A. (1988). *The illness narratives: Suffering, healing, and the human condition*. New York: Basic Books.

Kleinman, A. (1995). *Writing at the margin: Discourse between anthropology and medicine*. Berkeley: University of California Press.

Kopp, R. R. (1995). *Metaphor therapy: Using client-generated metaphors in psychotherapy*. New York: Brunner/Mazel.

Kramer, M. (1969). Manifest dream content in psychopathological states. In M. Kramer (Ed.), *Dream psychology and the new biology of dreaming* (pp. 377–396). Springfield, IL: Charles C Thomas.

Kroeber, K. (1992). *Retelling/rereading: The fate of storytelling in modern times*. New Brunswick: Rutgers University Press.

Krumboltz, J. D., Blando, J. A., Kim, H., & Reikowski, D. J. (1994). Embedding work values in stories. *Journal of Counseling and Development, 73*, 57–62.

Mahoney, M. J. (1991). *Human change processes: The scientific foundations of psychotherapy.* New York: Basic Books.

Mahoney, M. J. (1996). Constructivism and the study of complex self-organization. *Constructive Change, 1*, 3–8.

Mauron, C. (1962). *Des métaphores obsédantes au mythe personnel: Introduction á la psychocritique.* [About obsessive metaphors concerning the personal myth: Introduction and psychological criticism]. Paris: Librarie J. Corti.

McWhirter, E. H. (1991). Empowerment in counseling. *Journal of Counseling and Development, 69*, 222–227.

Neimeyer, R. A., & Mahoney, M. J. (Eds.) (1995). *Constructivism in psychotherapy.* Washington, DC: American Psychological Association.

Parry, A., & Doan, R. E. (1994). *Story re-visions: Narrative therapy in the postmodern world.* New York: Guilford Press.

Pickard, P. M. (1961). *I could a tale unfold: Violence, horror & sensationalism in stories for children.* New York: Humanities Press.

Pipher, M. B. (1994). *Reviving Ophelia: Saving the selves of adolescent girls.* New York: Putnam.

Polkinghorne, D. E. (1988). *Narrative knowing and the human sciences.* Albany: State University of New York Press.

Remen, R. N. (1996). *Kitchen table wisdom: Stories that heal.* New York: Riverhead Books.

Riordan, R. J. (1996). Scriptotherapy: Therapeutic writing as a counseling adjunct. *Journal of Counseling and Development, 74*, 265–269.

Schweitzer, H. (1994). Introduction. In P. Brooks (Ed.), *Psychoanalysis and storytelling* (pp. 1–18). Cambridge, MA: Blackwell.

Spence, D. P. (1982). *Narrative truth and historical truth: Meaning and interpretation in psychoanalysis.* New York: W. W. Norton.

Stone, R. D. (1996). *The healing art of storytelling: A sacred journey of personal discovery.* New York: Hyperion.

Terkel, S. (1974). *Working: People talk about what they do all day and how they feel about what they do.* New York: Pantheon.

Warner, M. (1995). *From the beast to the blonde: On fairytales and their tellers.* New York: Farrar, Straus, & Giroux.

White, M., & Epston, D. (1990). *Narrative means to therapeutic ends.* New York: W. W. Norton.

Section I.

Narrative Therapy and Trauma

CHAPTER ONE

We Tell Ourselves Stories: Psychotherapy and Aspects of Narrative Structure

Michael W. Barclay

We tell ourselves stories. We tell our friends and significant others stories. The meanings of the stories are often personal and peculiar. Literature provides (and utilizes) stories by which we measure ourselves or our lives. These measures delineate and bound our world, ourselves. Sometimes the meanings are universal or specifically applicable in our lives. Stories can have a healing effect. In the context of cultural myths, stories soothe people with the analogies that they provide, normalizing, through metaphor, the vicissitudes of life's travails. In the context of religious texts, stories join people together in a common bond of understanding and beliefs. The word religion is derived from the Latin *ligo* which means "tie together." In the context of literature, stories represent our lives and serve as archetypal models and reflections of our lives in art.

In psychotherapy, a person's own story can be the focus of healing. The reauthoring of a person's story, in the context of a psychotherapeutic conversation, can have a restructuring effect on his or her life. What emerges is a new and different story. Such a story can heal. How stories can heal is a question that the following essay attempts to partially answer.

I would like to begin this chapter with a general introduction which discusses the ways in which stories appear to work in peoples' lives. After the introduction, I will present a more philosophical and specifically psychological discussion, structured in terms of the three dimensions of a person's story: (1) individual; (2) intersubjective or interpersonal (including family dyads or triads, and so on); and, (3) societal (regarding the mores or practices of the larger social group).

The first dimension which focuses on the individual is perhaps the most difficult to specify. We often obtain our self concepts from others. But there may be some areas of experience which are individual, at least in one's experience of one's self, notwithstanding the way that this experience has been influenced by history, society (or family) and culture. One might call the relatively individual experience of one's self an experience of agency. Choice and sense of direction are, perhaps, primary aspects of agency.

We interact with others, and in so doing, interact with their stories about themselves and us. The interpersonal relations about which people tend to construct their stories are made complicated by fundamental or personal metaphors. By this I mean that we utilize metaphor in a way that is fundamental to our being in the world. Lakoff and Johnson (1980) write about it in terms of "metaphors we live by." I have suggested (Barclay, 1993) that metaphor has an ontological status. By this I mean that metaphors help to shape our lives. In the interpersonal world of shared stories about shared lives, metaphors abound. The metaphors intersect as people interrelate. The intersubjective or interpersonal section of the chapter will focus on what aspects of narrative structure and metaphor are caught up in personal relations. In this regard, myths or archetypal stories with which people identify are of great importance I suggest that identifying with characters in stories, whether heroes or villains, or creating one's own life on the basis of models provided by others, are key aspects of the narrative structure of a person's experience.

The third dimension of the thesis involved here is the larger arena of social (cultural and historical) influences which come to bear on an individual's story. In some ways, perhaps, the story is constituted by these influences. Were it not for the experiences of agency and choice, such influences might be all encompassing. In fact, some theorists consider that the social construction of our worldview, sense of self, and philosophical or scientific discourse is a primary and unavoidable influence (see Gergen, 1985). Involved in the social construction of one's life story is what I will call the textuality of the social world.

The conclusion of the chapter will discuss ways in which stories are, and can be, used in therapy, drawing on White and Epston's (1990) therapeutic model that has come to be known as "Narrative Therapy." Telling a story is comparable to writing a story; as listening to a story is comparable to reading a story. In some therapeutic situations, an individual might bring in written materials which are autobiographical, or a therapist might write something which narrates a person's successes and send it to the person in the form of a letter (see White & Epston, 1990). These are significant offerings. Like a rebus, these fragments join with what the person says about themselves, forming a life story. The possibility of multiple contributions may make the reframing of a life story by the individual a viable therapeutic focus for the clinician. In the discussion, it is hoped that such concepts support the notion that stories are involved in psychological healing and suggest ways of thinking about how that can happen in therapy.

Introduction to Narrative

Consider narrative structure. By this I mean consider both the format or formulation of a story as well as the effect that a story has on people: that is, the way in which people can change in the sway of the metaphors that make up their own stories. A personal story intersects with the stories of other people and with the story of a society. I think the relationship of these intersecting stories, on multiple levels, defines the idea of a text which is not merely the series of printed pages of a book, but is also the theme, argument, discourse, or sermon embodied in the pages. Moreover, a text is formed, metaphorically speaking, as a weave of ideas and concepts. The roots of the word, text (from the Latin *texere*, meaning weave), tie it to such words as "textile" or "texture." The text is a sort of broadcloth, combined of elements, strands, forming a whole. There are etymological roots of the word "whole" which tie it to "heal." These relations in words are not insignificant or merely semantic. It is often through words that people can reach a sense of wholeness. At the very least, the way in which a person puts their experience into words — the way they tell their story — can give an impression of how they feel, whether they feel whole (complete or healed in some measure), or whether they feel disjointed, disappointed or, as it were, diseased.

In the work of psychotherapy, the way in which people tell their stories can be significant in their sense of wholeness, thus in their healing. A story might need rewriting, if individuals tend to de-emphasize their successes in light of overwhelming disappointments. Their futures might depend upon a renewed account of themselves — a story which can heal a life that feels fragmented. Some stories (such as myths) have a healing effect. Some stories (life stories) may need to be made more whole.

The direction I would like to go in trying to form a partial answer to the question, "How do stories heal or get healed?" is dependent on a particular sort of philosophical perspective. In esoteric terms, this philosophy is called hermeneutics. But that name is not necessarily remote from the experience of stories. It is derived from the Greek god, Hermes, who was also known as Mercury. Hermes was the messenger of the gods. He was also known as the "trickster." From this philosophical perspective, meaning (of a story, for example) is a central feature. But there is a tricky aspect to meaning. What a story means to me may be different from what it means to you. As a result, from the hermeneutic point of view, interpretation is a crucial practice. Examining the way in which meanings shift and differ is, then, in this view, an important exploration.

Interpretation of meaning is central to understanding one's own story, the story of another person, or a universal (mythological or archetypal) story. In psychotherapy, the meaning of someone's story to that person him- or herself is clearly very important. As an individual tells his or her story, both the therapist and the individual become *present* to its meaning. The narrative itself takes on a significance which is developed in the context of a therapy. That is, therapy itself is a story. There are expectations and disappointments involved in the unfolding of that story as well as hidden meanings, prejudices and biases, and situations — subtexts, pretexts, or contexts. Particularly, the way in which a person's story functions in his or her life has a relationship to the way stories work in general.

In the context of narrative structure, stories contain characters, situations, plots, sequences of actions and events, climaxes, a denouement (or the "tying up"), and endings. These aspects of narratives relate directly to persons, contexts, plans, life events, crucial moments, resolutions, and death. These correspondences are either imaginary, symbolic, or perhaps, real. The correspondence of one's life to a particular story is also an important aspect of this chapter.

When I asked my children about their favorite stories, one (when he was ten years old) told me a tale from *The Hobbit* (Tolkien, 1937/1966) and the other (when he was four) recounted a chapter from The *World of Pooh* (Milne, 1957/1985). The tale of the Hobbit was important because of the quest involved and the treasure which was the object of the quest. And, in Pooh, the story of the Woozle involved Pooh and Piglet who follow their own footprints thinking that it is another animal they are tracking. In each case, a quest was involved. In the first, the quest was for material goods and the returning of them to the rightful owners. In the second, the quest was for the revelation of the sort of mysterious animal which appeared to be frequenting the area. The journey or quest is often a central aspect of a story, especially in psychology. It is also central to a chapter like this. When we ask such a question as, "How do stories work in the psyche?" we are on a quest. The word "quest" is buried in the word "question." The quest seems to represent a universal practice. The reason that the story of a journey or quest can apply to so many peoples' lives is that it reflects our experience in a way that we can share. It is, albeit, simplistic, but its universality is somehow uniting or healing. Other stories have healing capabilities or uniting functions.

For example, people can be united by religious stories, as noted above. Or, as seen in the Greek culture, myths are stories that, in many ways, are lived in the practices of a society. Science utilizes stories as well, and in some ways competes with other major dimensions of human culture. A classic example of this competition is the opposition of the story of "creation" to the theory (story) of "evolution" in the famous Scopes "monkey" trial. Interestingly, this competition is still at work. The fundamentalist creation story still vies with the scientific story of evolution. In fact, stories of how people heal, or become whole, compete similarly in psychological literature as methods of healing. Stories work on, or in people, in specific ways. A particular story or character in a story will communicate with a person at particular stages of his or her life.

Each of my children chose a story that was typical of their developmental age. The ten-year-old chose a story about material goods and the (moral) return of them to rightful owners. A quest for such goods represents an exploration of both morality and economics. These sorts of topics are paramount to a child of ten. My four-year-old daughter chose a story in which the characters are fooled or confused by their own quest. The quest involved is a quest of knowledge of a more general sort — "who am I?" The characters sought the identity of the animal they followed, when in fact, the animal was a sort of reflection of themselves in that they followed their own footprints. This, too, is typical of a child of four to whom identity is paramount, especially as separate from a primary caretaker.

Metaphor and Narrative

Narratives depend on fundamental metaphors. The metaphor that underlies the quest story can be identified. Consider examples utilized by metaphor theorists, Lakoff and Johnson (1980), who examine many metaphors which they think we "live by." One of these metaphors is *"Love Is a Journey"* (emphasis in the original, p. 44). Different ways in which we speak about our experience of love relationships, for example, emanate from this metaphor. They note a few: "We're stuck; It's been a long, bumpy road; This relationship is a dead-end street" (p. 45). These descriptions have a certain "coherence" that is determined by the fact that they fit together under the umbrage of the "basic metaphor ... of a *Journey*" (emphasis in the original, p. 45). Lakoff and Johnson elaborate on the way in which we understand our experience:

> For the most part, our comprehension of love is metaphorical, and we understand it primarily in terms of concepts for other natural kinds of experience: *Journeys, Madness, War, Health,* and so on. (Italics in the original, p. 119)

I would like to extrapolate from Lakoff and Johnson's idea of the basic "journey" metaphor in suggesting that the experience of travel can contribute also to the idea of another metaphor: Life is a journey. I would surmise that, in a similar way as the *"Love Is a Journey"* metaphor works in helping us structure our experience of love, the "Life is a journey" metaphor helps us get a handle on what it is to experience the quests upon which we embark. That is, the metaphor, "life is a journey," is basic to the concept of the quest.

Lakoff and Johnson also identify what they call a "conventional" metaphor, *"Life Is a Story"* (emphasis in the original, p. 172). They note that "this is a metaphor rooted deep in our culture" and "it is assumed that everyone's life is structured like a story, and the entire biographical and autobiographical tradition is based on this assumption" (p. 172). This conventional metaphor not only provides an underpinning to the theme of this chapter and volume but also provides a foundation for our thinking about ourselves. Lakoff and Johnson note that metaphor affects the conceptual level of human experience, and that concepts themselves are metaphoric (pp. 6–7). A concept is structured in terms of other concepts. This interaction of concepts is definitively metaphoric. Lakoff and Johnson note:

> The most important claim we have made so far is that metaphor is not just a matter of language, that is, of mere words. We shall argue that, on the contrary, human *thought processes* are largely metaphorical. This is what we mean when we say that the human conceptual system is metaphorically structured and defined. (Italics in the original, p. 6)

The upshot of the metaphoric nature of the conceptual system is that narrative structure, containing metaphors in abundance, is intimately connected to our fundamental concepts about ourselves. Thus in terms of the relationship of one's concepts and experience to one's ease or disease, narrative and metaphor are fundamentally important. Although illness, as, for example, Sontag (1978/1979) notes, is "not a metaphor," the world of the ill is replete with metaphors (p. 3). Sontag seeks elucidation of, and liberation from, "the lurid metaphors with which [the kingdom of the sick] has been landscaped" (p. 3). I would argue, in contrast, that it is exactly the metaphors she identifies that constitute our experience of illness, particularly illness of a psychological sort. In an important way, illness is metaphoric because our concepts of illness are metaphoric, or affected by metaphor, as Sontag notes. Implicit in concepts of illness are concepts of "self." In the next section, we can examine the relationship between these two conceptual domains. Given Lakoff and Johnson's argument that our conceptual system is metaphoric, we might consider the concepts of both illness and the self as constituted by metaphor.

The Individual and The Story

Consider first the relationship of an individual and his or her life story. There are many theories of development which might impact this discussion. One which is somewhat controversial is Lacan's concept of the "Mirror Stage" (1966/1977). Lacan postulates the advent of the ego in this stage of infant development. Infants, according to Lacan, views themselves in a mirror (or, in a metaphoric mirror) and come to experience themselves in a fundamentally different manner. The infant's ecstatic contact with his or her own reflection takes place around the ninth month. He writes:

> This jubilant assumption of his specular image by the child at the infant stage, still sunk in his motor incapacity and nursling dependence, would seem to exhibit in an exemplary situation the symbolic matrix in which the I is precipitated in a primordial form, before it is objectified in the

dialectic of identification with the other, and before language restores to it, in the universal, its function as subject. (1966/1977, p. 2)

My understanding of Lacan's comment is that the infant's relation to his or her "specular image" exemplifies the symbolic arena in which we all live in some measure; specifically the arena wherein the ego of the infant takes shape. This development of the ego occurs before the infant has hold of the experience of his or her objectification as a "person" or a "personality" or an "individual." Lacan goes on to point out "that this form situates the agency of the ego, before its social determination, in a fictional direction" (p. 2). What makes fiction important at this level of self development, in my reading of Lacan, is that the child is a fragmented being (as we all are, to some measure, perhaps) who senses a wholeness in their specular image. The imagination is stimulated by the confrontation with the reflection in the mirror. Jubilation is produced, according to Lacan's theory. This invigoration of happiness or jubilance comes from the imagined sense of completeness that infants can experience in seeing themselves, as reflected by the mirror, appearing to be a whole entity. This vision contrasts with the incompleteness of the infant's motor skills and his or her dependency upon others to move about and understand the world. The theory suggests that the imagination is engaged in a fantasy about the self as reflected in the mirror image. In fact, the image itself is imaginary in the basic sense of the word.

Thus it is useful to think in terms of the "fictional direction" of the ego. That is, I would suggest, the ego of the infant is "set off," before social influences have had determining effects, on the path of a "life story" which is fictional. This is not to say that the story is purely illusory or a mere fantasy. But such a conceptualization does point out the difference between what we might consider our historical experiences and the ways in which these experiences come together in a coherent narrative (see also, Spence, 1982). This difference is most easily understood, I think, when we consider a person who is said to have a "big ego," an inflated view of him- or herself. Those of us who make this judgment about someone consider the story that person tells to be blatantly fictional. In a similar way, our stories about ourselves contain fictional elements — if only in terms of the structure in which the stories are told.

The fictional aspect of the ego contributes to a life story at a fundamental level, the level of agency. It involves subjective choices based on feelings about the self. Lacan's notion of the fictional direction in which the ego begins may be a way of understanding how a person's imagination comes to have an effect on their choices. Perhaps fantasies best illustrate how this fictional element of the ego's sense of direction comes into play in the world. There is a relationship, it seems, between fictional aspects of the ego and stories that we tell ourselves. In this view, it might be possible to understand both psychological illness and therapy to be bound up in personal narratives which have fictional aspects that transcend historical events, per se.

Hillman (1983), in his book *Healing Fiction*, suggests convincingly that fiction lies at the root of therapy. He thinks that in the therapeutic conversation "two authors are now collaborating in a mutual fiction of therapy" (p. 16). Hillman notes:

> Successful therapy is thus a collaboration between fictions, a revisioning of the story into a more intelligent, more imaginative plot, which also means the sense of mythos in all the parts of the story. (p. 18)

The story, in Hillman's thesis, is raised to a level of import that is significant in joining art and healing. Hillman argues that the imagination is an essential aspect in the therapeutic process. He thinks that "psychotherapy encourages the musing, that activity which frees memories into images" (p. 42). The imagination, thus engaged, begins to serve a move from fact to metaphor, from history to story:

> As we muse over a memory, it becomes an image, shedding its literal historical facticity, slipping its causal chains, and opening into the stuff of which art is made. The art of healing is healing into art. Of course, not literally ... (p. 43).

The story is foundational. That is, according to Hillman, one "founds" oneself in one's story:

> I need to remember my stories not because I need to find out about myself but because I need to found myself in a story I can hold to be "mine." I also fear these stories because through them I can be found out, my imaginal foundations exposed. (p. 42)

Hillman clarifies his argument when he notes that "for psychology, the healing power of image lies not in a literal, magical effect: if your ear hurts, paint it or hang a tin ear-shaped replica on a shrine" (p. 73). Rather, he suggests that this idolatry is ineffectual, particularly because of its literal nature, for psychological healing. Hillman emphasizes the image as central to healing because of its fictional quality: "This kind of healing process by means of image-work depends on a fictional sense: one is in attentive service (*dulia*) within an imaginational reality" (p. 73). He thinks that "the healing, if it comes, is first of all of our fictional sense, giving a fictional sense even to our ailments. Imagination itself must be cared for since it may well be the source of our ailing" (p. 73). The fictional image of the self or the fictional sense in a story about one's self provides not simply insight into one's self, but more importantly provides a foundation of the self. The fiction, foundational to one's life, forms a story that goes beyond the history of the events of a person's life. The imaginal aspects of the psyche are central to envisioning historical events as significant, as meaningful in a symbolic, metaphoric, and directional way. Hillman notes:

> From the viewpoint of narrative, the visions and voices are an unfolding
> story without end. Active imagination is interminable because the story
> goes into death and death is endless — who knows where it has its stop?
> From the viewpoint of narrative, self-understanding is that healing fiction
> which individuates a life into death (p. 80).

From the psychological point of view, Hillman suggests, ailments are imaginal at root because the significance of a story is located not in its historical value,
but rather in its fictional value. Fiction heals. It heals because it individuates a
life in meaning. From birth to death, the plot — the series of events — take on
meaning and significance because of the imagination of both the main character
of the life story and the ancillary characters. In the therapeutic conversation, the
main character and the therapist take on significant roles as co-authors of the
fiction of the individual's narrative, according to Hillman. The narrative is
timeless; it outlives the protagonist. The narrative is foundational. An individual
is individuated by its imaginal aspects. The history is secondary to the fiction of
the foundational narrative. This fiction depends upon the imagination which
lends itself to the pliability of the narrative — to its suppleness and its capacity
to transform and bend. The supple nature of the fictional, meaningful aspect of
the story has an effect on the history. It restories a history by reconfiguring the
meaning of past events in terms of present consciousness of meaning and
metaphors that arise from the past, yet are construed (and refigured) in the
present. The narrative sets up a future by reauthoring a plot through imaginal
intention.

We come to understand ourselves in our stories. Kerby (1991) focuses on the
idea that a person's sense of self is constituted in and by the narrative about their
life. The life story becomes not only reportage but more importantly an effective
means of both expressing and creating the "self." Both the stories told about the
individual and the story told by the individual come to bear on who the person
is, on how the person understands himself or herself. Kerby describes the
experiences of our lives as "prenarrative." He suggests that when we tell our life
story we begin to put a cohesion to events. They form a plot. Kerby argues that
"it is as a character in our (and other people's) narratives that we achieve an
identity" (p. 40). He suggests that narrative is a means of collecting events to
make them more comprehensible. But the central point, I think, is that we
understand ourselves in virtue of our stories. Kerby notes:

> Implied in this statement is that the self is generated and is given unity
> in and through its own narratives, in its own recounting and hence
> understanding of itself. The self, and this is a crucial point, is essentially
> a being of reflexivity, coming to itself in its own narrational acts. ... The
> self is not some precultural or presymbolic entity that we seek simply to

capture in language. In other words, I am, for myself, only insofar as I express myself. (p. 41)

Kerby supports his argument by involved discussions about time and succession which lie outside the scope of this chapter. But an essential point is that prenarrative experience, in the context of human culture, demands narration and emplotment. Where this has particular concern for the therapist can be, perhaps, understood in Kerby's conception:

> Lived time already has a quasi-narrative character, and this is why it is not amenable to just any telling. One fabricates one's past at one's risk — at the risk of one's self. Involved in such narrations can be both psychologically harmful factors associated with self-deception and repression and socially harmful ones associated with lying to and deceiving other people. (p. 43)

It may be that Kerby's concept of the narrative mode of being can be augmented with the idea of an ego which begins its journey in a fictional direction. The focus on the individual in both Lacan's conception of the ego of the infant and Kerby's notion of a narrative self elaborates a perspective in which the agent, ego, or self of a person is storied. The life story is not merely a rhetorical creation. It is constitutive of the sense of self and is likely to be, at least in part, a fiction. People lie to themselves. And, of course, people lie about themselves to others. There are, clearly, both positive and negative aspects of the fictional sense that is involved in the narrative world of the self. As a result, the life story — fictional in part yet meaningful as a result — can take on a significance that can make it central to therapeutic focus.

Oneself as Another

The self, it might be said, is a character set in a story about life events. Kerby draws upon the work of Ricoeur in developing his thesis about the self. Ricoeur (1990/1992) analyzes narrative as it functions in the lives of human beings. He emphasizes the narrative means of identity by which the self establishes its own continuity as well as character. Ricoeur writes:

> The person, understood as a character in a story, is not an entity distinct from his or her "experiences." Quite the opposite: the person shares the condition of dynamic identity peculiar to the story recounted. The narrative constructs the identity of the character, what can be called his or her narrative identity, in constructing that of the story told. It is the identity of the story that makes the identity of the character. (p. 148)

Moreover, Ricoeur also emphasizes the role of imagination when he suggests that a mediating "function performed by the narrative identity of the character between the poles of sameness and selfhood is attested to primarily by the imaginative variations to which the narrative submits this identity" (p. 148, emphasis in the original). Narrativity and its imaginative variations form the identities of people in the contexts of stories.

Let us consider the way in which a "self" is involved in relationships with others. I noted earlier that there is a correspondence between characters, situations, plots, sequences of actions — events, climaxes, a denouement (or the "tying up"), as well as endings and persons, contexts, plans, life events, crucial moments, resolutions as well as death. Intersubjectivity is implicit in the inter-actions of characters (persons) in their stories (lives). The reciprocal dyadic relation, Ricoeur's focal point of "oneself as another," is relevant to describing relations to our heroes or simply to other people with whom we identify. We are constituted in and by these relations which are inescapable and which occur at a different level or in a different dimension than the level of individuality, thus utilizing a different metaphor. Ricoeur's (1990/1992) title, *Oneself as Another*, is a simile. Underlying the simile is the metaphor: oneself is another. Although this may seem peculiar on the surface, it requires us to consider the ways in which we are others, how we take on the styles of others and make them our own. Identification, projection, and introjection depend upon this feature of our lives and thus, in a fundamental way, on stories.

Ricoeur's contribution to narrative theory in his most contemporary work leads to a view of the identity or character of a person in terms of his or her relationship with others. Ricoeur suggests that we consider "the work of other-ness at the heart of selfhood" (p. 318). Although he cautions against the idea that the Other is identifiable with other people, Ricoeur specifies that "the Other is not only the counterpart of the Same but belongs to the intimate constitution of its sense" (p. 329).

The idea at the heart of this section is that in a relationship with another, as in one's relation to one's own story, one finds oneself. That is to say, the ontology or constitution of one's self is in some fundamental way dependent upon others. Ricoeur turns our attention to the way in which language exchange points this up by noting that "this intertwining is expressed on the grammatical plane by the omnipersonal character of the self, which circulates among all the pronouns" and "the affection of the self by the other than self is the basis for this ordered exchange between the grammatical persons" (p. 329). Further, on the topic of fiction, Ricoeur writes:

> It thus appears that the affection of the self by the other than self finds in fiction a privileged milieu for thought experiments that cannot be eclipsed by the "real" relations of interlocution and interaction. Quite the opposite, the reception of works of fiction contributes to the imaginary

and symbolic constitution of the actual exchanges of words and actions. Being-affected in the fictive mode is therefore incorporated into the self's being-affected in the "real" mode. (p. 330)

The fictions which constitute our stories about ourselves are effective in development of, and understanding of, the self. So are the stories that we come into contact with as told by others about us. At the intersubjective level, then, the self is perhaps not as distinct from others as might appear on the surface. Perhaps, a more adequate way of understanding the self can be telegraphically communicated in Ricoeur's simile: oneself as another. My sense about the "subject" is that the subject becomes him or her "self" in the context of intersubjectivity — that is in relationships. Gergen (1995) elaborates this view. He thinks that we do not necessarily need to view "individuals as originary sources of their own actions (an assumption that casts us in the image of God)" but rather we might abandon "the entire free-will/determinism binary" (p. 79). Implications of the intersubjective/relational view, for psychotherapy, suggest that relationships constitute a significant dimension in which a person experiences unhappiness or disease. If relations represent an overarching context within which we experience our enjoyment and distress, and if the stories (narratives) that form our self knowledge also occur within the context of relationships, then we may find that the relations and stories which arise within them are the focus for treatment of distress. Gergen suggests:

> On this account, to experience happiness or sadness is to manifest forms of relationship. My moment-to-moment sense of the real is premised on my history within the culture; in effect, there would be no experience of "happiness" save through a particular array of coordinated practices within the culture. (Relationships, for example, in which we come to agree that happiness exists and these are the conditions in which we feel it.) (p. 78)

Gergen suggests that, in this view, we are invited to consider our subjectivities as part of relational interactions, and not isolated necessarily "beyond the comprehension of others." "Rather," he notes, "we sense ourselves as both constituted by, and constituting, the other. In a certain sense, we are each other, our consciousness born of each other" (p. 78). His view, as a "social constructionist," does not fall far from Ricoeur's hermeneutic viewpoint. Personal interactions involve typical functions of identity. Children identify with one another in ways that they clearly exchange roles, character and operations. As we have seen, the interactions which characterize relationships can be understood theoretically in the context of the metaphor which lies beneath the simile: oneself as another. This simile, provided by Ricoeur, involves persona, characters, and interlocution. A means of understanding the language exchanges of persons in which characters switch roles — as do children in play (sometimes called transitivism) — is found in Jespersen's (1922/1959) concept of "shifters" which identifies the way in which personal pronouns shift. "I" becomes "you" in conversations. These interpersonal shifts of character, identity, and pronominal "grammatical" persons point up the way in which the basic metaphor (oneself is another) works on the grammatical level. We can extrapolate from that grammatical level to social interactions. Gergen's idea is that "we are each other" in a particular sense. I am my hero when I do what he does. In a sense, I am Willy Mays when I chase a fly ball. In a sense, I am Eric Clapton when I play the guitar. These identifications take place in the imagination, but they have an applicability to one's own story because of the ways in which that story is founded in a fictional sense. I know I am not really Willy Mays, but in my imagination I emulate his looking over his shoulder for the ball; bring the glove up at the precise moment; make the catch. In a fundamental way, I am the Other in order to accomplish what I have seen him model for me.

In the same way, my kids identify with the characters of the stories they appreciate. It is complex (self-constituting) play in which my daughter calls me Tigger and reenacts scenes from the Pooh stories. She becomes Roo. The story of the Woozle is the best, according to her, because of how the characters get fooled. In some ways, her search for self is identified with Pooh's and Piglet's tracking the Woozle. She becomes Pooh and Piglet as I read her the story before sleep. Her character is formed around the characters in the books she reads in a palpable way, evidenced in her play. It is constitutive play which forms a sense of "self" out of the unlikely and fictional characters in the narratives.

The metaphor, oneself is another, is fundamental in the context of personal interrelations. Relationships which involve the identities of characters and persons also operate in a third dimension, the social dimension, much in the same way as in the intersubjective dimension. It may be that the distinction between the intersubjective and social dimension is ultimately difficult to make. But, in the interest of understanding character, person, and relationship on a broader scale, consider social interactions in narrative terms.

The Textuality of Social Life

A means of understanding the way in which narrative functions on the social level is to consider the story that society develops about itself which is comprised in its practices and background operations. By this I mean that art (including fine art, music, drama, literature), rituals, ceremonies, work-related behaviors, play, and other operatives in social interactions form a discourse. Peoples' life stories intersect, in the discourse of social operations. The constitutive effects that social operations have upon individual life stories has been identified as "social construction" and the psychological or sociological scrutiny by discourse theorists and social constructionists has been articulated by Gergen (1985) among others. The constitution of a narrative self is not necessarily at odds with the social constructionist point of view. In that view, the self as bounded or "masterful" can be critiqued as perhaps only a purely Western conception (see Cushman, 1990). Concepts of self are historically ones that have evolved from the Enlightenment to imbue even our contemporary notions of child development (Cushman, 1991). The idea at the root of Cushman's observations of the history of concepts of self is that social practices and discourse establish the way in which we conceive of having selves. Moreover, the social legacy of the concept of self emerges from the way in which parents engage with infants and children, in which current notions of selfhood are perpetuated.

The view of "self" in narrative terms is consistent with a social constructionist perspective in that what is said about selves or an individual's self, particularly in stories about the individual (or by the individual), constitutes or constructs the self. What this means is the "self" is not necessarily an entity which is strictly identifiable apart from the social context in which the individual story unfolds. Cushman, (1991) examining Stern's (1985) theory of the development of the "self" in the infant, suggests that treating the mother-child dyad as exclusive of culture and historical influences (such as social conditions) "seems impossible from an ontological perspective":

> The activities that parents and infants participate in, the language they use, and the meanings imputed to them, consist of everyday habits, songs, games, and stories that are embedded in a culturally-transmitted heritage. (p. 216)

The basic idea which arises from social constructionism, at least in my view, concerns the construction of a worldview at the root of a person's life story by means of social and historical influences. This implicates relationships as fundamental entities in the constitution of subjectivity, as Gergen has said. But, further, it implicates social practices as influencing people's concepts of themselves.

The upshot of this perspective is that our stories about ourselves are influenced by a more general story, the story of our society. Brown (1987), in his book, *Society as Text*, considers the textuality, narrative structure, and context which comprise the story of social life. I noted above the concept of text as an interweaving. The fabric of the social story has its influence in the social construction of individual worldviews which are metaphorized in characterizations and identities at the level of individual stories.

Brown (1987) suggests, with Ricoeur (1981/1982), that human action can be understood as text. Brown takes the notion into sociological realms by analyzing cultural practices (like the institution of marriage or even a mental institution). He sees them as formed within language, within discourse. He argues that society understood as text is, at root, dependent upon the codes of language which structure the behavior of people within the communications which occur between people. Brown (1987) notes:

To see the polity as text is to understand it as a process of communication in which each new item of information is interpreted in terms of other messages already pronounced, as well as in terms of the reciprocal reaction it engenders on the part of the political addressee. The grammar in which the text is written guides perception and establishes the range of what will be taken as a real or possible fact. In this way, happenings are organized into events through the attribution of meanings. (p. 129)

Brown argues for the concept of "social reality as narrative text" by which he means to identify what is "real or possible fact" in terms of what I call the grammar and textuality of social life. He suggests that "textual analysis of society not only reveals that received forms of knowledge are determined by the structures of language; it also shows them to be invented through acts of speech" (p. 141). By this, Brown means, I think, that society operates within a shared sense of reality by means of speech acts and narrative. The power of the word is the creation of a narrative social world. It is this creation that I call the textuality of social life. Brown considers narrative fiction "as social text." He writes that "as society can be seen as a factual text, so fictional texts can be viewed as social-symbolic acts, as representations of possible selves and societies" (p. 143). The significance of this concept, in my view, is in the notion of possibilities for selves and social groups. The textuality of social life represents a dimension in which narrative functions by representing possibilities. We invent stories and we share them in the interest of constructing shared meaning and cultural continuity. Brown concludes:

Narrative enables us to understand the actions of others and endow them with meaning, because it is through narratives that we live and understand our own existence. (p. 165)

Part of the fabric of our social life is woven by the metaphors in the stories that, somehow, have become stories of universal choice. Consider the story my daughter chose as her favorite. Milne's tales have become classics by social contract. Disney appropriated them into cartoons and products. The Disney products in turn reify Pooh and Piglet. In some ways, this reification destroys the potential for an imagined Pooh and Piglet. The images which a child might construct have been preempted by the already existing images which the products foists upon the imagination of the children. My daughter likely imagines the Disney Pooh and Piglet as performing the actions of the story characters. Although this might be judged negatively, the point is that society appropriates the stories and recycles them in new ways — including new images. The new images exemplify the influences that the broad text and discourse of "Poohness" might have on a child. Moreover, the plight of Pooh (certainly reflective of our own problems and quests) constitutes the broader metaphor of "plight." It does so by means of the textuality of social life. The stories and images, in part, create the world in which quests and plights exist.

Text, Narrative, and Psychotherapy

In the present discussion, I have suggested that at the individual, relational, and societal level, it is possible to interpret human action and events as a narrative text. (see Ricoeur, 1981/1982) When people interact, or choose to act on their own as individuals, they do so within a particular context. The general context is constituted by subtexts, pretexts, and palpable texts. By this I mean, the dimension within which people interact (context) is constructed by unspoken codes of ethics or morality (subtexts), prejudices or at least prefigured anticipations of responses by others (pretexts), and by the books and documents (texts) that surround them.

If, in the context of psychotherapy, one takes the textuality of individual, relational, and societal life seriously, a focus on the patient's narrative mode of being might be more easily brought into view. A therapist can begin to formulate what is customarily understood as interventions from a narrative perspective. In doing so, the textuality of an individual's life can become more apparent. The stories that contribute to that textuality become more important. The pretext — or perhaps mind-set, in a cognitive sense — can be understood more clearly in its contribution to the life story of the patient. The context — or background of family relations and history — will emerge in its narrative dimension as contributing to the story of the person's life. The subtext — or perhaps unconscious motivations — also become part of a personal or family narrative. The personal narrative has meaning in the three dimensions outlined above. In each dimension, the life story intersects with other life stories and with sociolinguistic codes of morality.

Certain key stories will develop, in the textuality of individual, relational, and social life. These stories have the capacity to affect the person in emotional terms. That is, in the context of relations as narrative structures, happiness and sadness become understandable themselves as narrative structures. A story can come to bear on a person's sadness or distress in the context of a person's narrative because the emotions that define sadness or anxiety are imbued with, and constitute, intersecting individual, relational, and societal stories. Thus, in their stories, a person can feel whole or fragmented, anxious or settled, hopeless or hopeful. Stories bring the affective states of an individual into view. Therapeutic interventions can be situated in the context of the life story and its subtexts of contributing stories. Reframing stories that contribute to a life story is one method of effecting a sense of wholeness in a person. Supporting a person's reinterpretation of the event structure of their own story in comparison to classic myths or contemporary novels may help the person find themselves in a context of both pain and pleasure which becomes bearable by that comparison. When a story or myth works to support a person in the context of their own life story, we can understand it as a healing story — especially if it helps the person experience their life as less fragmented and more whole. The healing story contributes to the reauthoring of the story of the narrative self.

The personal life story can become a focal point for therapy. Approaches to this focal point can be made, perhaps, with the narrative structure of our collective lives in view; or with the narrative structure of a person's family background in view; or with the narrative structure of the individual decisions that come to form the plot (or event structure) of the person's life story in view. Scrutiny can be directed to the way in which particular stories with which the person identifies come to affect the person's life story.

Narrative methods of psychotherapy should, I suggest, situate the individual in the context of the textuality of social life. White and Epston (1990) have developed a method which takes the life story of the individual seriously. In describing "a storied therapy," the authors note that they believe "that persons generally ascribe meaning to their lives by plotting their experience into stories and that these stories shape their lives and relationships" (p. 79). White and Epston suggest attributes of a narrative method such as "externalizing the problem" which helps to separate the person from a problem-saturated story; or finding "unique outcomes" which are triumphs over the problems that arise in the context of the person's story. They suggest helping a person to reauthor their own story. This is perhaps the most direct way in which a story can be seen to heal. When the life story can change, the experience of the individual can change. Any number of subtexts contribute to the life story. These are perhaps other stories that change and develop in conversation and eventually make shifts in a life story which is dominated by a particular problem. White and Epston suggest eight concepts that help define their method of therapy:

> A therapy situated within the context of the narrative mode of thought would take a form that: 1. privileges the person's lived experience; 2. encourages a perception of a changing world through the plotting or linking of lived experience through the temporal dimension; 3. invokes the subjunctive mood in the triggering of presuppositions, the establishment of implicit meaning and in the generation of multiple perspective; 4. encourages polysemy and the use of ordinary, poetic, and picturesque language in the description of experience and in the endeavor to construct new stories; 5. invites a reflexive posture and an appreciation of one's participation in interpretive acts; 6. encourages a sense of authorship in the telling and retelling of one's story; 7. acknowledges that stories are coproduced and endeavors to establish conditions under which the "subject" becomes the privileged author; [and] 8. consistently inserts pronouns "I" and "you" in the description of events. (p. 83)

The suggestion of multiple perspectives and polysemy (that is, multiple meaning) in the context of therapy creates a multiplicity of possibility for an individual's story. With possibilities for change, the feeling of being "stuck" can be overcome. In order to obtain meaning from a story, interpretation is a key feature. Drawing the effects out of the story implicates the therapist as the listener/reader and the client as the teller/writer. Interpretation is necessarily present in both.

Interpretation, especially from the hermeneutic point of view, occurs on multiple levels. The focus on individual, relational, and social dimensions emphasizes multiplicity of perspective and meaning. Meaning is fundamental to the narrative structure of experience. A story of a quest, or a life as a journey, has different but complimentary meanings in all three of the dimensions discussed above. A story heals by its impact in a person's life on multiple levels in its telling and retelling, especially when the story is at least identifiable in some mythic, analogous, or metaphoric way with a person's life story. White and Epston summarize:

> The narrative mode locates a person as a protagonist or participant in his/her world. This is a world of interpretative acts, a world in which every retelling of a story is a new telling, a world in which persons participate with others in the "reauthoring," and thus in the shaping, of their lives and relationships. (p. 82)

From the narrative perspective, we are characters in our own stories. Other (relational and social) stories and incipient metaphors come to bear on our life stories. I understand my own experience by virtue of stories. A metaphor such as "life is a journey" helps me understand my quest for both self knowledge and the treasure of positive experiences, as well as, perhaps, the confusions and problems that arise. At the individual level, the interpersonal level, and the societal level, narrative gives meaning to, and structures, events. In the context of experience that is often understood and communicated narratively, stories have palpable impact. Stories can heal. Moreover, stories can be healed.

References

Barclay, M. W. (1993). The echo phase. *Journal of Phenomenological Psychology, 24,* 17–45.

Brown, R. H. (1987). *Society as text: Essays on rhetoric, reason and reality.* Chicago: University of Chicago Press.

Cushman, P. (1990). Why the self is empty: Toward a historically situated psychology. *American Psychologist, 45,* 599–611.

Cushman, P. (1991). Ideology obscured: Political uses of the self in Daniel Stern's infant. *American Psychologist, 46,* 206–219.

Hillman, J. (1983). *Healing fiction.* Barrytown, NY: Station Hill Press.

Gergen, K. J. (1985). The social constructionist movement in modern psychology. *American Psychologist, 40,* 266–275.

Gergen, K. (1995). Postmodernism as a humanism. *Humanistic Psychologist, 23,* 71–82.

Jesperson, O. (1959). *Language: Its nature, development, and origin.* London: George Allen & Unwin. (Original work published 1922)

Kerby, A. P. (1991). *Narrative and the self.* Bloomington, IN: Indiana University Press.

Lacan, J. (1977). *Ecrits: A selection.* (A. Sheridan, Transl.) New York: W. W. Norton. (Original work published in 1966.)

Lakoff, G., & Johnson, M. (1980). *Metaphors we live by.* Chicago: University of Chicago Press.

Milne, A. A. (1985) *The world of Pooh.* New York: Dutton Children's Books. (Original work published 1957)

Ricoeur, P. (1982). *Hermeneutics and the human sciences.* (J. B. Thompson, Transl.) New York: Cambridge University Press. (Original work published 1981)

Ricoeur, P. (1992). *Oneself as another.* (K. Blamey, Transl.) Chicago: University of Chicago Press. (Original work published 1990)

Sontag, S. (1979). *Illness as metaphor.* New York: Vintage Books (Original work published 1978)

Spence, D. P. (1982). *Narrative truth and historical truth: Meaning and interpretation in psychoanalysis.* New York: W. W. Norton.

Stern, D. N. (1985). *The interpersonal world of the infant: A view from psychoanalysis and developmental psychology.* New York: Basic Books.

Tolkien, J. R. R. (1966). *The hobbit: Or there and back again.* New York: Ballantine. (Original work published 1937)

White, M., & Epston, D. (1990). *Narrative means to therapeutic ends.* New York: W. W. Norton.

CHAPTER TWO

Just Listening:
Narrative and Deep Illness

Arthur W. Frank

*For seven days and seven nights [Job's friends] ...
sat beside him on the ground, and none of them
spoke a word to him, for they saw that his suffering
was very great.*

Job 2:13

This essay is about the stories told by those whom I have come to call the "deeply" ill. Deep illness may be critical or chronic, immediately life-threatening or long-term. Levels of functional impairment vary: some of the deeply ill are seriously disabled, in pain, and require intense and constant medical treatment. Others are in stable remission, with their illnesses effectively invisible to strangers and even to work associates. What counts is the person's own perception of illness: Illness is "deep" when perceived as lasting, as affecting virtually all life choices and decisions, and as altering identity. The essence of deep illness is to be *always there* for the ill person, and the person believes it always will be there. If illness moves temporarily to the background of awareness, that shift is only provisional.

For as long as one is deeply ill, there is no end in sight. Deep illness is lived in the certainty that it will be permanent and with the fear of this permanence. Some of the deeply ill have every assurance that they will be ill for the rest of their lives. Others have some chance of recovery, possibly a good chance, but illness is deep as long as any light *they* can see at the end of the tunnel is, at best, flickering. Whether someone remains deeply ill while in remission from cancer or while enjoying a good prognosis following successful heart surgery is a matter of that person's subjective interpretation of her or his situation. Between two and three years after my own treatment for cancer ended, I realized I was referring to myself as someone who had *had* cancer, rather than someone living *with* cancer. I had imperceptibly moved out of deep illness, and the shift bore little relation to a medical definition of remission.

The Need for Stories

Several recent studies have described the ill as storytellers (Frank, 1995; Good, Brodwin, Good, & Kleinman, 1992; Hawkins, 1993; Kleinman, 1988). The clinical importance of ill people's stories can be framed between two quotations. The first is from psychiatrist and medical anthropologist Arthur Kleinman. After noting that "physicians do not routinely inquire into the meanings of illness," Kleinman (1988) argues that "a powerful therapeutic alternative is at hand":

> There is evidence to indicate that through examining the particular significances of a person's illness it is possible to break the vicious cycles that amplify distress. The interpretation of illness meanings can also contribute to the provision of more effective care. ... This key clinical task may even liberate sufferers and practitioners from the oppressive iron cage imposed by a too intensely morbid preoccupation with painful bodily processes and a too technically narrow and therefore dehumanizing vision of treatment, respectively. (p. 91)

Kleinman emphasizes "empathic witnessing ... of the patient's and family's stories of the illness" as central to clinical work (p. 10).

Kleinman's emphasis is strategically placed on clinical efficacy. As a professor of medicine, he seeks to convince his colleagues and his students to allocate time, first in the curriculum and then in practice, to attending to the stories in which patients reveal the meanings they attach to their suffering. My own concern is less with the *patient* — the object of medical attention and intervention — and more with the *ill person* — the one who is struggling to negotiate a life lived in deep illness. Thus I balance Kleinman's statement with a different voice, that of the physician Rachel Naomi Remen.

Remen works with persons who have cancer, offering them not medical treatment but empathic attention. Kleinman advocates attending to stories as a functional part of clinical work. Remen moves outside her physician role self-consciously placing herself as another who is wounded (see Remen, 1994, 1996). She makes attention an end in itself:

> Being here [in the Commonweal retreat program] opens up opportunities for people to be listened to, and heard, and validated. They're not stuck anymore. If you ask, "How does that happen?" I have to say I'm not sure — but it does, and I trust that. I think the greatest thing you can ever give someone else is your attention — not with judgment, but just listening. (Quoted in Moyers, 1993, p. 345)

No great distance divides these two quotations. Both Kleinman and Remen clearly emphasize that stories count not just for the ill person but also for the healthcare professional who, as Kleinman states so powerfully, also suffers within an "iron cage" of reductive concerns.[1] Those who care for the ill also have their own stories (Hunter, 1991; Kleinman, 1988, pp. 209–226; Williams, 1984). In the most interesting and recent of these narratives (Campo, 1997; Hilfiker, 1994), physicians suggest that their capacity to know their own stories depends on the extent that they can hear the ill. For professional care-givers to be persons to themselves, they must first see and attend to the persons who are their patients.[2]

On the benefits of attending to the voices of the deeply ill, let me add a third voice — my own. I study the stories of the ill because when I was in the midst of my own period of deep illness — first heart attack, then cancer (Frank, 1991) — I longed for healthcare professionals who would "audit empathically" (Kleinman, 1988, p. 17) the story that *I could not tell unless they listened.* A story needs a listener. I needed their gift of listening in order to make my suffering a relationship between *us*, instead of an iron cage around *me*. Thus I first came to the concerns expressed in this essay by seeking to express what I needed when I was ill.

Professional Use of Narratives

The importance of listening to ill people's stories should be qualified by a reservation about professionals taking up listening as a routine task. When listening becomes a task, instead of what Remen calls a gift, then I believe much of its therapeutic efficacy is lost. When "narrative" becomes another professional technique for assessment, diagnosis, and intervention, then what Kleinman and Remen value in listening becomes part of a routine and is experienced as such. Narrative reduced to *clinical technique* leaves both clinician and patient inside Kleinman's iron cage of reductionism.

What Kleinman and Remen point toward, and what I wanted when I was ill, is a mutual relationship of persons who are also clinician and patient. Stories that are shared among persons can open mutual relationships; narrative reduced

---

1. Non-social scientist readers may miss Kleinman's allusion to the German historian Max Weber who, in 1905, concluded *The Protestant Ethic and the Spirit of Capitalism* with the condemnation that capitalist acquisition had become an "iron cage" in an age of "specialists without spirit." This allusion broadens Kleinman's critique to how society has created an institution of medicine that mirrors its own values.
2. On physicians' narratives, see Frank, 1997b.

to clinical technique may or may not be an improvement over biomedical reductionism.

When I as an ill person offer someone my story, I reach out as one human being to another. Stories certainly have content: they reveal the meanings that the ill have constructed around their illnesses. But telling the story also implies a *relationship* that I desire with those who care for me. For others to respond as if my story has not touched their personal core separates the content of my story from my desire for a relationship. Content then becomes "clinical material," and the gesture toward relationship is implicitly refused. Clinicians who attend to the meanings that stories reveal while rejecting the relationships that telling offers adopt a contradictory stance that will affect any future therapeutic relation.

The potential of narrative is to reorient our understanding of therapeutic relationships, but until this reorientation is effected, "therapy" can be a misleading word when coupled with narrative. Exchanging stories fractures the asymmetrical, dualistic assumptions of most doctor/patient or therapist/client relationships. Clinical relationships are too often between subjects-who-know and objects-who-are-to-be-known. The story, to be worth that name, is a ground on which subjectivities meet in *mutual* knowing. This fundamental human need is to know and to be known. Parker Palmer (1993) adapts a line from *1 Corinthians 13* as the title of his book on educational relationships: *To Know As We Are Known*. This title could serve equally well as an ideal of clinical practice and a basis for revising clinical training.

Physicians and other professionals — I include myself as a university teacher — do not routinely take seriously our own *need to be known* as part of the clinical relationship. Yet unless the professional acknowledges this need, the client remains the object of the professional's privileged subjectivity; there is no relationship in the sense of reciprocated feeling for the other, only an interaction.[3] The pressure of being the one who is supposed to know is, of course, as enormous as it is isolating. By contrast, knowing and being known each supports the other.

The rest of this essay will describe the stories told by the deeply ill, with the understanding that these stories are *not* being attended to as objects for chart notation or as justifications for interventions. Instead, professionals hear stories to know as they are known. An inextricable relation exists between knowing the other, being known by the other, and knowing oneself. When this relation is

---

3.   In a period of "managed care," professionals' motivation to know the other in a way that excludes being known by that other may have less to do with professional socialization or with personal desires for control and distance, and more to do with institutional demands for "productivity." Clinical encounters are overdetermined by institutional, professional, and personal factors.

forgotten, attention ceases to be a gift and becomes reduced to instrumental necessity; both parties find themselves back inside the iron cage.

One last loop needs to be thrown into the argument. Having argued for the necessary mutuality of storytelling — that it is a gift relation, not a professional technique — I need to add that, within the clinical relationship, a *hierarchy of needs* exists. The deeply ill person is the immediately needy one, and this person's story deserves primary attention. Clinicians may share parts of their own stories, but they do so in response to the ill person's story. Reciprocity is sustained in the appreciation with which the clinician receives the patient's stories. To give the gift of listening is to appreciate receiving the gift of a story. Not just understanding this reciprocity but *embracing* it seems to me to be the beginning of clinical work.

What stories, then, do the ill tell? I propose three basic *narrative types* of illness stories. These are not specific stories but types of stories. Folklorists throughout this century have pointed out the basic narrative structures that underlie many particular tales. Children learn these narrative forms without knowing they know them, and they then use them both to make sense of new stories and to improvise stories of their own. Folk tales require a hero, or more accurately, a protagonist, who will become a hero in the course of the story. The hero then seeks something, and the seeking is blocked by some antagonist. The eventual defeat of the antagonist is often made possible by a helper who at first appears minor and ineffectual but eventually provides the hero with an essential resource. On the bare bones of such narrative skeletons, many different stories are fleshed out. Oral storytelling in particular requires some recognizable narrative structure if listeners are to find their way through the story.

What I present below are three recognizable narrative structures — the skeletons on which many stories of illness are fleshed out. To grasp the uniqueness of stories as they are told, it helps to be able to place a story in relation to others: how does the immediate story build on the skeleton(s) it shares with other stories? These three narrative structures also help to hear what is not being told in any particular story. I propose these three narratives not as privileged professional categories for decoding and classifying stories. Again, stories are not material to be analyzed; they are relationships to be entered. But staying with a story can be like finding a usable pathway through a thicket. I intend these three narratives to be such usable pathways. As others leave my pathways and find their own, they and those they listen to will be served all the better. But these pathways can at least be ways of entering.

The Restitution Story

The narrative of illness that is culturally preferred in North America tells of getting sick, suffering, being treated, and through treatment being restored to health.[4] When the ill person's answer to "How are you?" is to repeat everything that treatment has already done, is doing, and will be able to do if the present efforts fail, then a restitution story is being told. On closer listening, it is possible to hear an absence: the subjectivity of the ill person who is telling the story has been displaced by others. The clinicians — physicians, nurses, and therapists of all sorts — are the heroes, the active players in the story; their subjectivities determine the course of the action. Restitution stories are told by ill people who narrate from the sidelines.

Restitution stories predominate in the talk of the recently diagnosed, and the ideal of restitution recedes farthest into the background of stories of chronically ill persons. Few published illness stories follow the restitution narrative: in the logic of restitution, illness is nothing in particular to talk about once one is cured. The conventional pejorative label for such talk is "dwelling on it." Restitution stories are better told by physicians themselves, in their own journals.[5]

Restitution stories are expected and encouraged by the most scientific (and "heroic") versions of medical practice. Because disease is an enemy and cure is a version of conquering that enemy, the notion of talking about illness as *meaningful* experience seems superfluous — even vaguely subversive — to biomedicine. In the biomedical model, patients' talk *should be* second-hand medical talk: close enough to the physician's version to insure compliance with medical orders, but not so close as to suggest patients might make their own treatment decisions.

Because most illness conditions will end in the restoration of health, for most ill people the restitution narrative is adequate. Problems arise as soon as restitution is no longer perceived as forthcoming: when the persistent cough turns out to be lung cancer or the problem of balance is diagnosed as multiple sclerosis. My own testicular cancer was first diagnosed as a urinary tract infection and

---

4. The three types of narrative — restitution, chaos, and quest — are described with extensive examples in Frank, 1995, chapters 4–6. In this essay, I have minimized examples in favor of a more programmatic exposition.

5. I retain this paragraph even though the Internet seems to be providing a venue for the proliferation of written, if not published, stories that are strongly oriented toward cure and medical intervention. When ill people use their own web sites to marshal medical information and resources, they become the protagonists of their own restitution stories. Physician dislike of patients' posting their medical progress — and bringing the responses they get back to the clinic with demands for treatment — remains anecdotal (see McLellan, 1997).

treated with antibiotics; for the weeks until my symptoms intensified, restitution stories made good sense. But when those drugs failed to have any effect, I had no narrative I could use to tell the story of my deterioration.

My lack of a narrative that could make sense of my decline into deep illness was not a personal shortcoming of mine nor of my physician. North Americans are culturally deficient in narratives to tell after the restitution narrative no longer applies. What Kleinman calls the "vicious cycles that amplify distress" are cycles of *narrative lack*: when people have no story to tell, they are isolated in their suffering; they can achieve no critical distance from their pain. Other narratives — those described below — are available, but too many healthy people — and too many clinicians — do not attend to them. These other narratives are disregarded until we need them, which for those who are ill means needing them yesterday.

I hardly want to deprecate restitution stories. The restitution narrative represents the triumphant optimism of medical science — a science that has saved my own life — and commitment to the idea of cure deserves to be honored. The problem occurs when we love the idea of restitution to the point of demonizing illness. When we believe that no other narratives are legitimate, we then pathologize other stories as depressing (a lay epithet) or as symptoms of depression (the professional analog). The deeply ill, whose immediate reality does not include restitution, are further marginalized. Those who have no story that society judges worth telling feel they have no place in society.

The Chaos Story

Diametrically opposed to the restitution narrative is the chaos narrative. Here is deepest illness: disability can only increase, pain will never remit, physicians are either unable to understand what is wrong or unable to treat it successfully. Medical problems proliferate into social problems: persistent ill health means job problems, which mean loss of income, which leads to inadequate medical care. The ill person is shuffled between bureaucracies, each claiming that they need something from somewhere else before they can provide any benefits. Stress exacerbates medical problems. Family responsibilities cannot be fulfilled: social ties are lost, and the ties that remain are often more demanding of the ill person than they are supportive.

Chaos stories can be heard most clearly in the responses they elicit in listeners: when the listener feels sucked into a whirlpool and only wants to get away from the story, then a chaos story is being told. If the dominant verbal style of restitution stories is quotation from the clinician, the dominant style of chaos stories is a series of incomplete sentences. Actions end with a shrug, not an object of the verb. To complete a sentence is to imply a world in which subjects can act on objects and have some effect. The world of the chaos story is devoid of effective action. The passive voice reigns: "it" affects the teller. Events take place in a perpetual present tense punctuated by "and then" constructions: "and then" the physical problem, "and then" the family problem, "and then" the bureaucratic hassle, and then how each of these makes the others all the more unresolvable.

Chaos stories reflect life lived at the bottom of the funnel of these problems. People live chaos, but chaos cannot in its purest form be *told*. To talk from the position of chaos is to be unable to render one's life as a story with any narrative ordering of beginning, middle, and (anticipated) end: the story perpetually trails off in a formless sequence of "and then" contingencies. To tell enables achieving a coherent stance as to what took place and why. The coherence that stories give to lived reality, along with the effect of sharing the story with a listener, offers the teller some distance from his or her life. The chaos talk that cannot become a story induces claustrophobia in the listener because of its lack of any distance from immediate events. Chaos talk is submerged, gasping for air, and it soon leaves the listener gasping.

To turn a life lived in chaos into a story *about* that chaos would effect a transitory escape: at least a crack of light shines into a room that was entirely dark. Paradoxically then, the chaos story that can be told is no longer total chaos, and in that paradox lies a therapeutic opening. The clinical problem is not to push toward this opening prematurely. The chaos narrative is already populated with others telling the ill person that "it can't be that bad," "there's always someone worse off," "don't give up hope," and other statements that ill people often hear as allowing those who have nothing to offer to feel as if they have offered something.

If our culture loves the restitution narrative that any illness can be cured, it fears the chaos narrative that, with illness, troubles multiply. The chaos narrative (that cannot be told) is about how thin the ice is upon which we skate, and how cold and deep is the water into which we can suddenly sink. In my undergraduate medical sociology course I show a film about a young man who discovers he has a rare adrenal cancer. In response to the film a student wrote that he had never before realized how suddenly he himself — anyone — might have a life-threatening illness. By keeping the recognition of serious illness out of his conscious awareness, my student had enjoyed what might be called *deep health*. The chaos narrative — with its vision of how awful life can get — threatens deep health.

To deny the living truth of the chaos narrative is to intensify the suffering of those who live this narrative. The problem is how to honor the telling of chaos while leaving open a possibility of change; to accept the reality of what is told without accepting its fatalism. Sustaining this delicate balance requires, at minimum, not being overwhelmed by the need to *do* something for the ill person. If it were easy to change that person's situation, others probably would have done so. Any change will take time; thus, with the deeply ill, change is a problematic goal. What kind of change may be appropriate is a difficult issue on which the professional must be constantly guided by the ill person and his or her family. The first thing a person in chaos needs is someone who will just listen, without attempting any change. Too quick offers of help may show the listener's own dis-ease with what is being told; compassion means, literally, to suffer *with* the other.

Job's three friends first sat with him in silence for seven days and nights. They became less useful when they began asserting their own answers to his question of why he suffered. When Job eventually finds an answer to his suffering, it is not one that admits articulation. The measure of his wisdom is his new capacity for silence.[6]

As a society, our problem is how to honor the suffering that the chaos narrative implies without accepting the remediable conditions — the lack of care — that perpetuate this suffering. Primary among these remediable conditions is the professional and lay tendency to pathologize chaos: to label the ill person as "depressed" rather than to accept depression as a legitimate response to an awful life. Everyone prefers to treat the symptom as labeled rather than attend to the life. Compassion means just listening.

The Quest Story

When restitution can no longer be imagined, a life can be fashioned in which illness is neither "accepted," a word that is too passive, nor is it "welcomed," a word that romanticizes illness. Illness is lived as a quest: as a condition from which something can be learned (although not in a didactic sense), and this learning can be passed on to others. The line I hear and read most often from people who have had cancer is that they are certainly not glad they had it, but they are grateful for how it changed them and their lives.

Quest stories are being told when the teller claims new qualities of self and believes illness has been responsible for these changes. Quest stories are about illness leading to new insights. They are based on a claim that the ill person now sees *in* to a depth that illness has made visible. As I read the title of William Styron's (1990) memoir of suicidal depression, *Darkness Visible*, Styron's text not only makes the darkness of mental illness visible to readers; Styron also acknowledges that illness has made an aspect of his own life's darkness visible to him. Perhaps the key phrase in quest stories is some version of "I can now ... " — although the expression of this phrase is usually muted. If, by the time the quest story can be told, illness is no longer chaos, if suffering now has some meaning and even value, the reality of chaos is still recognized and respected. The quest

---

6.   Professional education emphasizes articulate answers, which is another reason why professionals have trouble hearing the wisdom of the ill. Professionals gain their status through their capacity to articulate what others cannot say; articulation becomes a standard of wisdom.

story fears being heard as a triumph over chaos; part of the lesson of deep illness is that victories are always provisional.

A subtle and therefore powerful example of the quest narrative is found in the life and work of Kay Toombs.[7] Toombs suffers from a progressive, degenerative multiple sclerosis. At first she seems to repudiate the idea of illness as quest. She writes of giving a speech about her illness experience and being asked by audience members "to state explicitly those things that I find 'good' about my situation. Is it 'enabling' rather than 'disabling?' Has the experience caused me to 'grow' in certain ways?" To these questions Toombs answers, "Harsh though the reality may be, there is nothing intrinsically good about chronic, progressive multiple sclerosis. Nothing" (Toombs, 1995, pp. 19–20).

Yet Toombs also writes of how she found, without noticing exactly when, that she had begun "to reclaim my life" (p. 21). This reclaiming is not a sudden epiphany but a slow, gradual process. Toombs writes of what she has gained through illness — empathy for others' suffering, friendships, and "a clearer view of what is really important in my life" — but she is equally clear that these "do not, however, make me glad that I have M. S." (p. 20).

Gladness, at least about illness, has little place in the quest narratives; "reclaiming" figures largely. What Toombs does not state explicitly, but what her writing and speaking enact, is what illness has given her to teach. Summarizing someone else's quest is a precarious matter, but I would presume to say that Toombs' quest is to tell others about a world that illness has made her uniquely prepared to articulate. Illness has not given her a voice, but she has given a voice to illness. Another harsh truth is that I cannot imagine her writings having the force they have if she were not ill; the quality of witness could not be present. Toombs' quest is to testify, and ultimately the quest narrative is testimony.[8]

The audience members who press Toombs to put a more positive spin on her experience of illness do not want her testimony. They want her reassurance that, if they become ill, they can find something "good" and "enabling" themselves. In my interpretation, they want not a quest story but a restitution story. They realize Toombs will not have her physical health restored, short of a miracle. Thus she embodies every healthy person's fear of illness without restitution. But the audience members' commitment to their own deep health can still be preserved by imagining a restitution in like measure. The audience wants to believe that what Toombs has lost in one aspect of her life, she has gained elsewhere. The quest story refuses this fantasy, even as it acknowledges what has

---

7. Toombs' writing was not available to me when I wrote *The Wounded Storyteller* (1995). See also Toombs, 1992.
8. See Frank, 1995, Chapter 7, "Testimony."

been gained. Toombs calls her response of "nothing intrinsically good" harsh, but I read her whole story as imbued with a wisdom that can only come from such harshness.

This wisdom is a matter of being exactly where one is, yet grateful for that. Reynolds Price (1994) expresses this gratitude at the end of his story of being rendered paraplegic by a malignant tumor inside his spine:

> I write six days a week, long days that often run till bedtime; and the books are different from what came before in more ways than age. I sleep long nights with few hard dreams, and now I've outlived both my parents. Even my handwriting looks very little like the script of the man I was in June of '84. Cranky as it is, it's taller, more legible, with more air and stride. It comes down the arm of a grateful man. (p. 193)

I have heard Price say, in a radio interview, that at least once a day he wishes he could stand up for just a moment and stretch, but then he realizes his life will be spent in his wheelchair. The quest story is cranky but grateful. If Price is more explicit about his gratitude than Toombs, in part this may be because his disability is not deteriorating while hers is. Or perhaps Toombs is even more wary — Price is wary enough — of how much a healthy audience wants to dilute the harsh realities of the illness. She knows how easily the quest story can be read or heard as a restitution story, and she fears betraying (to use another harsh word) the suffering that illness is.

Quest stories express an unflinching view of the reality of illness. In the face of this reality, they look not to restitution but rather to what can be reclaimed of life: what can be learned, and how this lesson can be passed on to those who have not made their journey. Those who tell the quest story are ancient mariners, returned to tell a tale that others need to hear but may resist hearing. If the teller of the quest story is rarely pathologized in the way that the exemplar of the chaos narrative often is — even society honors the quest storyteller — people will rarely embrace quest stories. Why?

Listeners resist the quest narrative because they still need to believe in a restitution that the teller has had to work to give up; much of the quest concerns renunciation as a preface to reconstruction. Nancy Mairs (1996) writes of how living with advanced multiple sclerosis requires her to give up comparison to "The 'her' I never was and am not now and never will become," lest she "make myself mad with self-loathing" (p. 47). No one living in even moderately good health, much less living in deep health, wants to imagine ceasing to be the person they enjoy being; it is far preferable to imagine that breakdowns can be fixed. Physicians and patients reinforce each other's commitment to restitution as the only speakable eventuality. But quest stories carry the unavoidable message that the restitution narrative will, one day, prove inadequate to what experience has in store for many of us. Because, as Kleinman notes in the quotation above, physicians prefer to concentrate on cure and do not routinely find meaning in illness, they are not often disposed to listen to patients' attempts to reconstruct selves beyond restitution. I myself want a physician who concentrates on trying to cure me; but because that cure may be unavailable, I also want a person with whom I can share my story.

Thus listeners resist quest stories because of these stories' assertion, sometimes implicit and sometimes explicit, that the ill person has become what Price calls a new self. Deep illness requires giving up the old self, "the person you used to be" (Price, 1994, p. 182). Price's advice is to "find your way to be somebody else, the next viable you" (p. 183). He is clear that this quest will meet with the best intentioned resistance:

> Your mate, your children, your friends at work — anyone who knew or loved you in your old life — will be hard at work in the fierce endeavor to revive your old self, the self they recall with love or respect. ... At the crucial juncture, when you turn toward the future, they'll likely have little help to offer; and it's no fault of theirs (they were trained like you, in inertia). (p. 183)

Price hints at the subversive quality of quest stories — a subversion that complements the chaos story's subversive display of how bottomless despair can be. Those living in "deep health" value objects, including themselves and those they love, in ways that are often far more instrumental and conditional than they are willing to acknowledge. Quest stories are about being forced to accept life unconditionally; or, in the stories of Price, Mairs, or Toombs, finding a grateful life in conditions that the previously healthy self would have considered unacceptable.

Not all ill people are oriented to these authors' level of introspection, nor do all have the physical capacities that allow such articulate tellings of their stories; rather, their stories have to be heard in how they live their lives. Physician and journalist Lonny Shavelson tells the story of Pierre Nadeau, a trapeze artist, dying of AIDS. Pierre's illness was marked by a series of "lines in the sand" that he is certain he would rather die than cross: getting AIDS, being plugged into oxygen, having chemotherapy and losing his hair, wearing diapers. Yet he does cross each of these lines (Shavelson, 1995, p. 55). As Shavelson describes him, Pierre does not tell many stories, yet Shavelson quotes a hospice nurse who speaks of his "amazing spiritual change" (p. 56). She seems to have heard, somewhere, a quest story.[9] Perhaps this story is told most eloquently in Pierre's willingness to cross those lines he had said he would not cross.

---

9.   Of course, we do not know what is interpreted as Pierre's "spiritual transformation." We know Pierre chose to continue to live, but was this choice motivated by a dread of dying,

The Pierre who draws his lines in the sand is closer to the values of healthy society than the Pierre who crosses those lines and in the process undergoes spiritual change. It seems a cliché to conclude that the skeleton underneath quest stories is the unconditional acceptance of life, yet perhaps the notion of unconditional acceptance has become a cliché because of its profound and unattainable value. Although quest stories are the narrative structure that is most eloquently told in prose, perhaps the most moving quest stories are those, like Pierre's, that are lived (see Frank, 1997a). In finding terms to live with illness — not grateful for illness, but grateful for a life that includes illness — those telling quest stories show the healthy how they too could be living.

Just Listening

The three types of stories I have described are not intended to classify tellers of particular stories. If they are diagnostic of anything, it is the culture and relationships within which people create their stories. But these types are not designed to diagnose. Rather they are listening devices: tools to help those who attend the ill to understand — not to decode — what they hear. For those who use these narrative types in their clinical work, three additional caveats are worth making explicit.

First, all three narratives *intertwine* in most stories told by any deeply ill person; few individual stories have only one skeleton. Often in a particular story, at a particular time, one narrative type is foreground and the others are background. Shifts in foreground and background map changes in illness experience. When listeners attend to which type of story seems more important than others, they can hear where the ill person is. Knowing *where* someone is, is important, but equally important is recognizing why they have to be where they are. I want to arouse clinicians' suspicions of assumptions that the ill person as teller ought to be in some other narrative space than where he or she is.

Second, although strong cultural and personal preferences exist for one type of story over another, all three types have their necessary places in all trajectories of illness experience. Each deserves to be *honored* in its time of telling; I will

---

or did Pierre find some value in life that he had not anticipated? The hospice worker's observation, as much as I would like to credit it, could be more a projection of her own need to find value in her work than it is an observation of Pierre's reality. But matters become more complex still: even if the quest story began as her projection, her story may still have become his reality and given him a resource to continue living. What counts is not who told which story first, but that, in a relationship with such intensity and duration of care, each person's story becomes the other's. Unfortunately, within contemporary medicine, hospice care is singular for its intensity and duration of personal care relationships.

discuss why and how in the following section. Because of this importance of honoring the immediate story being told, my narrative types are the opposite of a developmental theory that predicts ill people "moving through" stages of narrative, pathologizing the failure to keep moving. The quest story is not a goal toward which ill people ought to move, nor does the chaos story represent personal or social failure.

Third, listeners will certainly have distinct *preferences* for one type of story over another. I believe the proper initial use of the narrative preferences that we all have is to pose questions about oneself as a listener. If listeners find themselves wanting the ill person to move from one narrative type to another, that desire may say more about the culture (professional and social) of the listeners, their own anxieties and narrative commitments, than it says about the ill person.

My strong assumption is that *people tell the stories they need to tell in order to work through the situation in which they find themselves.* As long as a story continues to be told, the work of that situation continues to need doing. This assumption hardly obviates the desirability of change. It does suggest that, for the deeply ill, change cannot be hurried by external intervention; if anything, the processes that nurture change may become confused and set back. The corollary for clinical practice is that, when time is limited by "managed care" and other constraints, it is generally preferable to accept less change than to seek to hurry change by pressing a patient toward a new story. Better yet, rather than the pejorative implication of accepting less change, clinicians might think of change occurring after, perhaps long after, their work of listening has finished. In Tim Brookes' story of his mother's hospice care, he recounts a hospice physician telling him that often the value of their work is not apparent for twenty years (Brookes, 1997, p. 276). I believe the truth of that statement, and I find very moving the clinical conviction that allows this physician to conceptualize his work in that time span.

Change happens. Telling one's own story can help move a person through a particularly difficult situation by providing some critic*al distance.* When a story is well heard, it becomes something that teller and listener can talk about and reflect on. When experience becomes an object for what is now a mutual involvement, the teller gains some distance between what is being lived and what is being told. Only at this distance can actions — including interpretations — be perceived as possibly having alternatives, thus making change imaginable. This critical distance is the key to any "movement" that may occur.

Clinicians, especially those who trade most in the therapeutic value of clients reinterpreting their reality, may find it frustrating to remember how many restrictions illness imposes, and how difficult change is within these. Impositions are both external (by jobs, families, and "helping" systems themselves) and internal (originating in the body's pains and disruptions, moving to the mind's fears of these). These impositions may have to be told over and over before the ill person begins to sort out what can be reinterpreted, what can be endured, and perhaps what can be materially changed (quitting the job, getting improved pain-medication). Out of retellings some critical distance *may* emerge, and *perhaps* some aspect of suffering can be assimilated to some "higher" scheme of meaning. But, as I will emphasize in my concluding comments on intervening in people's stories, any higher assimilation of the meaning of present troubles can only be discovered by ill people themselves in their own storytelling.

More than Just Listening

Richard Zaner's (1993) work presents the hospital ethicist as one who primarily listens to patients and helps them to sort out the ethical issues that are already inherent in their stories, if not yet reflected upon. He wonders whether, in doing this work, is he "any different from any good friend?" (p. 21). Clinicians reading this essay may have the same question. How is the role of "just listening" a *professional* role, making use of extensive training and — in a time of cost-cutting — justifying financial remuneration?

I have argued throughout that one listens to ill people's stories not in order to fix them by doing something "therapeutic," but rather to honor them. Again, people tell the stories they need to tell in order to work through the situation they are in. Efforts to change the person's story, however well-intentioned, are so easily mistimed or misguided. Toombs, quoted above, exemplifies resistance to narrative intervention when she reacts against the questions posed by her audience; questions that presuppose what sort of narrative ("enabling") she ought to be telling and coerce her to get it right.

The point of listening to Toombs is coming to realize that she *already* has it right. But does every ill person have it right in every story they tell? The paradoxical response is that every teller does have his or her own story right just as that story is: not fair, not necessarily accurate in a medical or sociological sense, but right as an expression of who and where they are. But — here's the paradox — what's right can still change, and that change may also be right and welcome. The resulting clinical problem could be called the nonelicitation of change. How to do this nonelicitation returns us to Zaner's question: What does the clinician do that the good friend may not be able to do?

My first response to this question is to want to rescue clinicians, as professional listeners, from imagining their role as dichotomously opposed to that of the friend. Instead, I understand the clinician as one who may enact certain "friendship" roles using different resources. A common experience for the deeply ill is to have many of their former friends disappear. In the world of deep illness, friends die or become physically unable to visit with greater than average frequency. Healthy friends defect from the tensions and demands of being with the ill. Friends who do not disappear outright may be uncomfortable with talk about deep illness: their own fears of illness admit only restitution stories. Thus, friends may be the least willing to sustain the ill person through struggles over decisions that admit no "good" resolution: for example, whether to opt for debilitating therapies that offer a small chance of remission, or whether to choose palliative care with a better quality of life in the short term but no chance of remission.[10] Friends may be too threatened by the suffering involved in either "option" to be useful in talking through this "choice." The first requirement for professionals is to have control of their own sense of threat. This control should not preclude empathic sharing of the sorrow involved in having to make such a choice, but such empathy cannot be weighed down with the clinician's own fears and regrets.[11]

Long-standing, personal friends may also be poor listeners to stories of personal change because, as Price predicts in the quotation above, they want to steer the ill person back to being the self who was. Friends are often least willing to watch an ill person's painful groping toward the self who may yet be; they cannot hear the stories in which that new self assumes an increasingly real identity. The clinician has the advantage of having no stake in the ill person continuing to be who she or he was before illness. The clinician should neither be threatened by changes that illness can precipitate, nor be overly invested in seeing the ill person change. Anything beyond just listening is not directed at fixing the story, but rather is about *nurturing* it.

Let me be honest about having my own preferences and ideals. When I encounter ill people, I have to question whether I am nurturing *their* story or fostering my own preference. Perhaps I have too many exemplars of illness in my head — too many quest stories — and I have to work to separate what I might hope for the person who is with me from that person's own trajectory of meanings of illness. Most therapies agree that people must *discover for themselves* that change is possible; therapies begin to differ over how to instigate or facilitate that discovery, and how fixed an idea the therapist should have of what change ought to occur. In both respects, the instigation of change and the content of change, therapeutic work that attends to people's stories is far at the nondirective end of the spectrum. As I suggested earlier, stories are not told as "clinical material" in order to keep a "therapeutic process" moving.

Stories are told to cultivate relationships. In a relationship, we come to know ourselves as we are known, and we may change with that knowledge. For either person in a relationship, change is something that is allowed to happen. If I as a listener welcome certain stories more than others because they fit my ideal of self-knowledge, I limit my relationship with the person telling the story; I render his or her story instrumental to some "higher" goal that is mine, not necessarily

---

10. I draw this example specifically from Timothy Quill's famous "Diane" case (Quill, 1993), although the scenario is a common one.

11. On empathy in medical relationships, see Spiro, Curnen, Peschel, and St. James, 1993, especially the papers by Rita Charon, Jodi Halpern, and Stanley Joel Reiser.

the other's. Relationships, and friendships, seem to require that the story be an end in itself, although stories do change, and friends change with them.

Personal discoveries of meaning take place at unpredictable moments when — tautologically — people are prepared to make that discovery. I can advance the theoretical propositions that change occurs when the restitution narrative is no longer viable and when the chaos narrative is no longer necessary, yet these propositions have the unhappy effect of setting up the quest story as the kind of narrative *telos* that I have been working to avoid. In practice, no one can say when these moments of change will occur for any ill person, only that they do happen as both ill people themselves and their caregivers attest. How then can change be nurtured, without being directed?

My first suggestion for nurturing change is to hold the utterly sincere belief that the story you are hearing *needs no change*. The ill person's whole life has brought him or her to this story, and deep illness is no time for anyone to repudiate how that life was lived. The ill person himself probably has sufficient regrets and self-reproaches. The best opening to change may be the recognition that the story the person is now telling is a perfectly adequate representation of his or her experience, *which it is*.

Again, this message has to be entirely sincere. Sincerity depends on the listener's willingness to accept both regret and suffering as part of life, both inevitable *and* remediable. I believe that clinical work becomes uncertain at best, and evasive at worst, when clinicians lack their own beliefs — philosophical or spiritual — about suffering. My own belief is that humans do have to suffer; call it our existential destiny. But there are better ways to suffer; call those ways grace. Whatever the clinician's own beliefs, as a listener, she or he should assume an attitude diametrically opposite to that of Toombs' questioners, who want to see only the remediable side of suffering.[12] The clinical attitude I recommend may reject the chaos narrative's supposition that suffering is *only* inevitable, but it honors chaos as a necessary part of life.

To work with the deeply ill, I believe a clinician must be able to honor suffering. Honoring suffering shapes the spirit of helping. The helper who honors suffering can accept the "dark night of the soul" but also offers the immediate, practical help others need. Part of this help is recognizing that people are telling the story they need to tell, for a while, before they can move on.

A second aspect of nurturing is to help the ill person *hear exactly what story* she or he is telling. Everyone is a storyteller, but few of us are sufficiently reflective

---

12. Even worse is the attitude of Job's friends, who want to believe that suffering must be deserved. Believing that suffering is an inevitable part of human life seems to free us from believing that any individual's suffering is deserved, while allowing us to see how individuals continue to make choices that affect how they suffer.

about what stories we tell, in our lives and words. Only through reflection can storytelling, and life, become truly ethical. To hear the story being told, my three types may be useful. Does the hope of restitution leave open other possibilities? Can the chaos story be told until the teller can feels its claustrophobia as part of the tale, outside of how life is being lived? And how is the present story turning illness into a quest? Any actual story should include elements of *all three* narratives, because each of these questions deserves reflection. Sorting out the three narrative skeletons in any actual story does not direct the story away from one story and toward another. The point is to show the ill person that the story *already* contains different, immanent narrative directions: a direction that is now mostly in the background could become foreground.

The third aspect of nurturing is that listening carries the message, which is not self-evident for the deeply ill, that they are living *a story that is theirs to tell.* Everyone else seems to have a story *about* the ill person, but few people have an interest in that person's own story. Very soon the ill person begins to doubt the interest of his own perceptions. Nurturing begins and ends in the message that no one knows their stories better than the ill themselves, that their stories matter not just for themselves but for others, and that their stories can be told, and lived, differently. Noting a change between what is said one day and the next, without interpreting that change, affirms to the ill person that it's *his* or *her* story, to tell as he or she will.

The situation of the ill changes rapidly: the body's condition changes; the conditions of treatment and care change; professionals move to new jobs; friends and family members get sick themselves, or defect, or reengage with the ill in strengthened relationships. These changes require new stories, and every type of story has its day.

But what if the ill person's story seems to be overstaying its day? It is seductively easy to observe that ill people get stuck in one narrative when they would do better to have greater narrative flexibility. Flexibility is a popular value.[13] Less popular is the idea that people may need time and repetition to work through all the possibilities of a narrative they have relied on throughout their lives. Before flexibility comes the importance of learning what one's own inflexible narrative has meant for all these years: how this narrative was shaped by one's circumstances even as it shaped those circumstances, how it was once the person's best possible response to what life offered, and how much the person owes to this narrative. Words like "stuck" fail to honor the stories that have been a person's life. If some stories now seem to limit their tellers, let us not forget that the ability to tell these stories may have once been hard-won.

---

13. For a brilliant analysis of the increasing status of flexibility as a cultural value, see Martin, 1994.

Many stories do need to change. Letting people tell their story repeatedly, gently noting changes in that story, can help. Most significant to the process of change, the person who is so attended is no longer alone.

Anatole Broyard (1992), when he was dying of prostate cancer, wrote that his "first instinct was to try to bring [cancer] under control by turning it into a narrative." He describes stories as "antibodies against illness and pain" (p. 20). Broyard's ideal relationship to a physician was based in narrative: "I want to be a good story for him, to give him some of my art in exchange for his" (p. 45).

Fortunately, most ill people have some art to exchange for their care. The greatest clinical gift to the ill is to appreciate them as the "good stories" they are. In these stories there is nothing to fix, only a great deal to listen to.

References

Brookes, T. (1997). *Signs of life: A memoir of dying and discovery.* New York: Times Books.

Broyard, A. (1992). *Intoxicated by my illness: And other writings on life and death.* New York: C. Potter.

Campo, R. (1997). *The poetry of healing: A doctor's education in empathy, identity, and desire.* New York: W. W. Norton.

Frank, A. W. (1991). *At the will of the body: Reflections on illness.* Boston: Houghton Mifflin.

Frank, A. W. (1995). *The wounded storyteller: Body, illness, and ethics.* Chicago: University of Chicago Press.

Frank, A. W. (1997a). Enacting illness stories: When, what, and why. In H. L. Nelson (Ed.), *Stories and their limits: Narrative approaches to bioethics* (pp. 31–49). New York: Routledge.

Frank, A. W. (1997b). The virtuous professional: Doctors healing themselves. *Christian Century, 114,* 1158–1165.

Good, M. D., Brodwin, P. E., Good, B. J., & Kleinman A. (Eds.). (1992). *Pain as human experience: An anthropological perspective.* Berkeley: University of California Press.

Hand, S. (Ed.) (1989). *The Levinas reader.* Oxford: Blackwell Publishers.

Hawkins, A. H. (1993). *Reconstructing illness: Studies in pathography.* West Lafayette, IN: Purdue University Press.

Hilfiker, D. (1994). *Not all of us are saints: A doctor's journey with the poor.* New York: Hill & Wang.

Hunter, K. M. (1991). *Doctors' stories: The narrative structure of medical knowledge.* Princeton: Princeton University Press.

Kleinman, A. (1988). *The illness narratives: Suffering, healing, and the human condition.* New York: Basic Books.

Mairs, N. (1996). *Waist-high in the world: A life among the nondisabled.* Thorndike, ME: G. K. Hall.

Martin, E. (1994). *Flexible bodies: Tracking immunity in American culture from the days of polio to the age of AIDs.* Boston: Beacon Press.

McLellan, M. F. (1997). *The electronic narrative of illness: Computer mediated communication, Internet, World Wide Web.* Unpublished doctoral dissertation, University of Texas, Graduate School of Biomedical Sciences, Galveston, Texas, USA.

Moyers, B. (1993). *Healing and the mind.* New York: Doubleday.

Palmer, P. J. (1993). *To know as we are known: Education as a spiritual journey*. (2nd ed.) San Francisco: Harper San Francisco.

Price, R. (1994). *A whole new life*. New York: Atheneum.

Quill, T. E. (1993). *Death and dignity: Making choices and taking charge*. New York: W. W. Norton.

Remen, R. N. (Ed.). (1994). *Wounded healers*. Mill Valley: Wounded Healer Press.

Remen, R. N. (1996). *Kitchen table wisdom: Stories that heal*. New York: Riverhead Books.

Shavelson, L. (1995). *A chosen death: The dying confront assisted suicide*. New York: Simon & Schuster.

Spiro, H., Curnen, M. G. M., Peschel, E., & St. James, D. (Eds.). (1993). *Empathy and the practice of medicine: Beyond pills and scalpel*. New Haven: Yale University Press.

Styron, W. (1990). *Darkness visible: A memoir of madness*. New York: Random House.

Toombs, S. Y. (1992). *The meaning of illness: A phenomenological account of the different perspectives of physician and patient*. Dordrecht: Kluwer.

Toombs, S. Y. (1995). Sufficient unto the day: A life with multiple sclerosis. In S. K. Toombs, D. Barnard, & R. A. Carson (Eds.), *Chronic illness: From experience to policy* (pp. 3–23). Bloomington, IN: Indiana University Press.

Williams, W. C. (1984). *The doctor stories*. New York: New Directions.

Zaner, R. A. (1993). *Troubled voices: Stories of ethics and illness*. Cleveland: Pilgrim Press.

CHAPTER THREE

Emplotting the Traumatic Self: Narrative Revision and the Construction of Coherence

Alan E. Stewart & Robert A. Neimeyer

This book is premised on a view of human beings as inveterate narrators, constructors of personal, familial, and cultural stories that punctuate, organize, and attribute meaning to experience. Seen in this light, stories serve both a mnemonic and a performative function, consolidating a sense of who we are as the protagonists of our accounts, and scripting the ways we engage in our lives with others. This deepened understanding of narration suggests that it does more than simply represent human experience; it literally constitutes human experience, as well as our identities as social beings. Thus, anything that frustrates our efforts to "story" experience serves psychologically to destroy human life. In this chapter, we will explore one set of all-too-prevalent experiences that defy narration — the encounter with traumatic events — and sketch the outlines of an emerging constructivist conception of both the impact of trauma and its treatment. This chapter is therefore part of a broader attempt to understand distress as a breakdown in the human "effort after meaning," and to articulate the concrete implications of this constructivist perspective for the helping professions (Neimeyer, 2001; Neimeyer & Raskin, 2000; Neimeyer & Stewart, 1999).

We will approach this task first by noting the frequency of traumatic stress in contemporary society, briefly describing its symptomatic expressions. We will then consider the dominant normative approach to its conceptualization and more idiopathic alternatives, the latter of which are more coherent with a constructivist perspective. This will provide a springboard into a more extended discussion of narrative models of knowing and their applicability to the phenomenon of posttraumatic stress, which not only radically challenges survivors' ability to cope in conventional social contexts, but also undermines their very sense of self-continuity. Finally, we will conclude with an extended case study that exemplifies this narrative model and illustrates its possible relevance for clinical assessment and psychotherapy.

Prevalence of Traumatic Stress

Traumatic experiences exist in an abundant supply, encompassing such events as physical or sexual assault, natural catastrophe, random violence or murder, genocide, and complicated bereavement, such as that associated with the suicide of a loved one, or with an unexpected and mutilating death through motor vehicle accidents (Neimeyer, 1998; Stewart, 1999). Yet not everyone who experiences a traumatic event manifests the psychological symptoms of posttraumatic stress disorder or other anxiety disorders (American Psychiatric Association, 1994). In a sample of low income and urban-dwelling young adults the lifetime prevalence rates of exposure to traumatic events (such as being assaulted or witnessing murder) was 39.1%. Of these individuals, the rate of PTSD was 23.6% (Breslau, Davis, Andreski, & Peterson, 1991). Snow, Stellman, Stellman, and Sommer (1988) estimated PTSD prevalence rates of 1.8% to 15% in a sample of 2,858 American Legion members who served in Southeast Asia, depending upon how traumatic experiences and combat exposure were defined. Summarizing a national study of Vietnam veterans, Hyer (1994) cited point prevalence estimates of 13% to 17.4%. The American Psychiatric Association (1994, p. 426) estimates 1% to 14% of all persons experience clinically significant symptoms of PTSD some time during their lives. And finally, studies of complicated grief, in which the bereaved struggle with traumatic distress in the wake of profound loss, place its incidence at 10% to 20% (Neimeyer, Prigerson & Davies, 2002). Despite the variability in incidence within these studies and across various populations, it is clear that exposure to traumatizing events is all too common even in technologically-advanced western societies, and it is probable that such experiences are still more prevalent in societies that are undergoing civil turbulence, where natural catastrophes are more frequent and uncontrolled, and where widespread disease is unchecked by the availability of modern medical services and public health programs.

Normative and Idiopathic Perspectives of Trauma

When response to a traumatic event is marked by posttraumatic stress disorder, three primary symptom clusters characterize the survivor's adjustment. The first involves persistent reexperiencing of the traumatic event through dreams, intrusive recollections, or behaving as if the traumatic event were recurring. The second symptom cluster involves the avoidance of stimuli associated with the trauma. This may entail a general numbing of responsiveness as well as detachment from others. The third cluster of symptoms includes sleep and concentration difficulties, hypervigilance, impulsiveness, and heightened physiological reactivity (American Psychiatric Association, 1994, pp. 424–426).

Until recently, the development of normatively-defined PTSD was considered to be related to the objective significance of the experienced event. Thus, earlier editions of the *Diagnostic and Statistical Manual* (American Psychiatric Association, 1987, p. 247) stipulated that the traumatizing event was "outside the range of human experience and ... would be markedly distressing to almost anyone." In the current revision of the DSM, a wider range of distressing events and experiences have been recognized as phenomena that potentially could result in PTSD symptoms. The framers of the current DSM also have emphasized the subjective effects of the trauma on the person. As a result, "trauma" is defined largely in terms of its impact on the survivor, rather than by features intrinsic to the instigating event itself. Nonetheless, the emphasis is on responses of the survivor that presumably follow directly from the traumatizing event.

Anchoring the basis of a psychological reaction primarily in the actual event experienced by the individual obscures what the person of the victim brings to the traumatic event as an active meaning-making participant. Such an exclusively realist and objectivist emphasis does not reflect the person's "premorbid" personality, life experiences, and core ways of construing people, things, and events in life. Hyer's (1994) case formulation model has expanded the definition of trauma beyond classes or categories of events themselves. In his specification, the lifestyle or essence of the person is a function of core ordering processes (schemata) used to organize the world. Lifestyle also stems from personality traits, beliefs, and symptoms. Hyer (1994) maintains that trauma disrupts integrated functions of both the personality and core ordering processes such that the person becomes influenced by the "overwhelming pull of symptoms" (p. 12).

Sewell (1996) and Sewell, Cromwell, Farrell-Higgins, and Palmer (1996) have developed a constructivist model of trauma focusing on how the victim defines his or her experiences. Sewell (1996, 1997) maintains, consistent with personal construct theory (Kelly, 1955), that individuals make meaning of events by processing them in the context of phenomena previously experienced. As novel experiences are encountered, overarching constructs are created to relate these experiences to the existing construct system. In this way the individual's meaning system is extended and elaborated as new experiences are encountered and then construed.

Sewell (1996) has demonstrated empirically that traumatic events preclude such elaborative processing which is at the core of meaning-making. The traumatic event remains as an isolated and unprocessed collection of fragmented memories. Unelaborated traumatic experiences have the effect of biasing the anticipation of future events in an extremely enduring and polarized way. For any new experience that may possess minor threat, the construct system of the victim predicts the occurrence of the full traumatic experience. By failing to elaboratively process the trauma, the person's core identity structures become compromised. This, in turn, leads to the symptoms of depression, anxiety, depersonalization, and dissociation that were discussed above.

From Sewell's constructivist perspective, therefore, a traumatic experience could be anything that results in the aforementioned type of polarized and fragmented construing. This perspective acknowledges the very individualized nature of both the traumatic experience as well as the person's attempt to cope with it.

The Narrative Nature of Existence

Sewell's constructivist account of trauma resonates with narrative descriptions of life experiences. Emplotment, the activity and operation of a narrative, organizes the events and experiences of life into a coherent, ever-evolving life story (Polkinghorne, 1991; Terrell & Lyddon, 1995; Vogel, 1994). These stories help a person to understand and respond adaptively to the occurrences and events of life. Some regard narrative to be the basic way in which life experiences are organized meaningfully over time (Atkinson, 1995; Bruner, 1986; Mair, 1988, 1989; Polkinghorne, 1988, 1991; Russell & Van den Broek, 1992; Sarbin, 1986; Terrell & Lyddon, 1995; Wigren, 1994). Sarbin (1986) asserts that events in the world, or historical acts, are understood in the context in which they occur. This process of contextualizing historical acts in an ongoing way comprises a narrative. Such narrative, Sarbin maintains, is a root metaphor for psychology. The possibilities of the narrative metaphor have inspired numerous researchers.

Narrative conceptualizations of psychological processes provide more than apt analogies or intriguing clinical heuristics. Empirical research in domains that are central to self-definition (autobiographical memory and language use) have supported the hypothesis that human meaning systems are organized in narrative terms. Concerning autobiographical memories, there is evidence of narrative structure in both memory patterns themselves, and in the ways autobiographical episodes are recalled (Barclay, 1996; Howe & Courage, 1997; Rubin, 1998; Russell & Van den Broek, 1992). Regarding the former, Linton (1986) and Barsalou (1988) have observed that, as similar events are repeated over time, they become stored in large scale structures in memory known as "event structures" or "extendures." These fundamental units tend to integrate thematically-related material over time and could underlie the narrative structure of the human memory (Robinson & Swanson, 1990).

Language also plays a critical role in the way meaning is attached to the self and to one's lived experiences (de Shazer, 1994; Shotter & Gergen, 1989). The person's particular "languaging" of a narrative can indicate the ways that she or he relates to it. For instance, the use of the first person "I" in narratives suggests both more vivid autobiographical memories and a greater level of agency or involvement (Rubin, 1998). Conversely, the predominant use of the second person "me" in the narrative might convey a more passive or observational involvement. The use of different verb tenses in a narrative also can reveal the person's temporal relationship to a particular experience or role (Pillener, Desrochers, & Erbanks, 1997). Finally, the use of imagistically rich and detailed language in establishing the setting of a story and the motives of its central characters enhances its fictional plausibility, while also opening the narrative to new and different tellings (Neimeyer, 2000). Thus, appreciation of narratives as organizing schemes implies a need to understand their style, as well as their structure.

Narrative Conceptualizations of Problems in Living

While there have been some attempts to characterize life problems as stemming from "broken," "decomposed," or "gapped" narratives (see Neimeyer & Stewart, 1998, for a brief review), an adequate taxonomy of life problems from a storied perspective has yet to emerge. Although a more elaborate scheme for understanding narrative "breakdown" could take many forms, we believe that a clinically useful taxonomy, minimally, should focus on the following: (1) the person's role or self-characterization in the story; (2) the extent to which the person is able to emplot lived experiences adequately in terms of organizing life themes; (3) the entry and exit of significant characters, settings, or themes; (4) the explicit or implicit goals towards, or away from, which the emplotted events move; and (5) the person's sense of authorship over the resulting narrative.

Numerous "narrative diagnoses" could be framed along these dimensions. For example, a client's immersion in a new geographic setting, or the appearance of significant new characters in his or her emotional life, may temporarily challenge the client's ability to incorporate them meaningfully into an existing narrative, and force modification of a once familiar "story line" for life. Some clients may have little sense of authorship of their lives, and instead feel compelled to live out a dominant (and sometimes oppressive) narrative "written" by others in their family or culture (Monk, Crockett, Winslade, & Epston, 1996). Still other clients may grieve the loss of principal persons, places, projects, or even parts of the self, necessitating a profound revision of a once meaningful life script, which must now be reauthored along different thematic lines (Neimeyer, 1998, 2001).

Narrative Conceptualizations of Trauma

Several constructivist clinicians have begun to work toward a narrative conceptualization of traumatizing life events (Neimeyer & Stewart, 1998). Almost by definition, traumatic experiences fragment a client's narrative structure for organizing and anticipating life events, while presenting the survivor with urgent experiences that resist integration into his or her pre-established meaning system (Neimeyer, 2004). Perhaps even more dramatically, such events as being sexually assaulted, witnessing the murder of a loved one, surviving a combat "fire fight," or watching one's home and family be washed away by a flash flood, can disrupt the consolidation of the sensory and autobiographical memory processes that comprise narratives (McNally, Litz, Prassas, Shin, & Weathers, 1994; Siegel, 1995). That is, the sights, sounds, smells, and sensation experienced during the event, along with the person's felt experiences of fear, horror, or shock, are often "bundled together" and become the trauma memory.

Because these memories were encoded in an intense, unelaborated, and primitive form, they resist assimilation into one's ordinary declarative memory, which is implicated in the construction of narrative (van der Kolk & van der Hart, 1991). Such traumatic memories may be so poignant and isolated that they give rise to a "traumatized self," which is unrelated to the survivor's previous sense of identity, but which can itself provide the person with an identity as a "victim," "refugee," "widow," "crash survivor," and so forth (Neimeyer & Stewart, 1998). In severe cases of combat trauma, for example, this role constriction can take the form of nearly exclusive self-characterization as someone with PTSD, a role that carries fixed implications of being irreparably damaged and alienated from mainstream society (Klion & Pfenninger, 1996). Although preemptive identification with this constricted role may have had understandable survival value at an earlier point, inflexible identification with the traumatized self can set in motion a vicious circle of social validation for this reduced script, as others avoid or marginalize the survivor.

As an essential part of the person, the traumatic self constrains the other possible selves. That is, as long as the traumatic self exists in its original, unelaborated form, the cognitive, perceptual, and emotional processes invoked during its creation will place limits on the psychological resources that are available for maintaining and enhancing the premorbid selves (Klion & Pfenniger, 1996). The narrative, meaning-making processes of the former selves become more like those of the traumatic self. The subjective experiences of such a constrained and fragmented existence may give rise to the often-repeated lamentations that "I am not the person that I once was" or that "I lost part of my self that day and I haven't been the same since."

Psychotherapy

This conceptualization stresses two issues that should be considered in providing psychotherapeutic interventions for trauma victims. First, the conceptualization places primacy upon the victim's selfhood and how basic psychological processes of the person may be temporarily or permanently altered by the traumatic experience. During and after the traumatic experience, a person's "symphony of selves" becomes discordant and incoherent with the introduction of the traumatic role and self. Therapeutic interventions should be responsive to the fundamental challenge to the "psychological embodiment" of the person following traumatization.

A second and related implication of the above conceptualization is that psychotherapy with the traumatized person involves not only diagnosing the way the person's primary narrative is incomplete or damaged, but also finding ways to join the traumatic self and associated narrative with the pre-existing selves and primary narrative. That is, psychotherapy involves weaving the traumatic self and premorbid selves together in the present, in a way that fosters not only the retelling of the past, but also the performance of a new narrative in the future (Neimeyer & Arvey, 2004).

The narrative conceptualization of trauma presented above can inform many types of interventions for the treatment of trauma. In considering the diversity of available approaches, it may be helpful to remember that many different therapeutic interventions can affect the narratives people construct. In this way, narratives are treated as objects of psychotherapeutic intervention. For example, in the early stages of treatment, therapists can assist trauma survivors in managing acute symptomatology through anger management training, or graded task assignments, to overcome tendencies toward social isolation (Sewell, 1997). Viewing these cognitive-behavioral interventions through the lens of narrative theory, the therapist can then ask, "What does this say about you that you were able to take control of a previously uncontrollable rage, or face the fears that were holding you hostage in your home?" "As you continue to move forward in this self-assertive direction, what does this imply about the form your life might take a year from now? Five years from now?" Such questions can help consolidate concrete progress made using techniques arising in other perspectives, by assisting survivors to integrate the gains not only into their repertory of coping skills, but also into their expanded narrative of self.

As a psychotherapeutic method, a number of narrative or constructivist techniques can have more general therapeutic effects than just narrative repair or reconstruction. We will briefly discuss a few of these narrative methods, and then selectively exemplify their use in actual cases of trauma therapy.

Regarding general approaches to treatment, a consensus is emerging that psychotherapy of PTSD may be both multimodal and multiphasic (Hyer, 1994). During the active phases of treatment, psychotherapy optimally occurs on at least two general levels (Stewart, 1995). The first level involves intense emotional exploration of the sequence of traumatic events and of their impact on the victim's life. In many respects work at this level involves the exploration and expression of the victim's traumatic self. The second tier of treatment involves more reflective and integrative work. Here, the person may move in and out of his or her experience of the trauma to weave together the traumatic self identity with other identities. The activity of experiencing and subsequent reflecting is particularly consistent with Guidano's (1995) "movieola technique," in which the therapist slowly pans the "camera" of therapeutic attention over the scene of the traumatizing event, in order to help the client first articulate, and then attribute meaning to the experience. Narrative therapy techniques and therapeutic work on narratives may be focused on either or both of these levels.

Constructivist practitioners have developed several specific narrative approaches to psychotherapy and to the treatment of trauma. Stewart (1995), for example, helps combat trauma victims deconstruct their traumatic memories and develop a more integrated set of selves through the construction of character sketches, values clarification exercises, and drawings that have as their goal the development of consistency across situations. She further helps victims develop a sense of continuity across their lifespans through the completion of an autobiographical repertory grid, lifegraphs, and construction of autobiographies. Similarly, Neimeyer (1995) believes a client's narrative activity in psychotherapy (such as storytelling and/or journal writing) serves the vital intrapersonal function of helping establish a continuity in his or her lived experience. Such narrative techniques as loss characterizations, meaning reconstruction interviews, metaphoric stories, and memory books can be especially relevant to the task of assimilating loss, effectively reauthoring a story of self and others that has greater wholeness and perspective (Neimeyer, 1998). The use of such techniques can help trauma victims understand themselves in ways that are more integrated, flexible, and self-aware, with a greater sense of control over their life experiences.

A hallmark of constructivist narrative interventions concerns their emphasis not only upon ameliorative goals (such as the reduction of symptoms) and restorative goals (for example, the return to premorbid functioning), but also upon elaborative goals (such as the construction of new, possible selves) (Harter & Neimeyer, 1995). Attention to the traumatic past is supplemented with helping the individual develop beyond the point at which the trauma was encountered. This emphasis is also evident in Sewell (1996) and Sewell *et al.* (1996) in describing how growth of the combat victims beyond the trauma is accomplished by having the victims actively and elaboratively process their traumatic memories along with memories of other events (and selves) that did not involve this trauma. Such outcomes are consistent with a growing body of evidence that post-trauma adaptation can promote greater maturity, empathy, and spiritual or philosophic development in a substantial minority of people whose lives have been shaken by profound losses of many kinds (Tedeschi & Calhoun, 2004).

Many of the aforementioned narrative techniques share a common change ingredient. First, by writing, drawing, explaining, or comparing life events, narrative techniques induce more extensive cognitive processing (memory recall and attention) of these phenomena. Second, once such a processing focus is established for disparate experiences that previously were unbound by a common narrative, then the interrelationships, commonalities, and discrepancies of the experiences may be incorporated into new, overarching narratives. Narrative therapeutic techniques foment the processing of experiences at multiple levels so that meaningful relationships are created where no relationships, or less meaningful ones, existed previously.

In summary, constructivist and narrative theorists are beginning to offer a novel set of concepts and procedures that hold promise for shedding new light on the experience of trauma and its aftermath. Several of these emphases are illustrated in the case studies below.

Case Study One: How Did This Happen, and Who are We Now?

Barry F. was a forty-eight-year-old teacher, who contacted one of the authors (RAN) for therapy at the advice of a friend.[1] He described his concern about the adjustment of his fifteen-year-old stepson, Matt, following a "crisis in the family," and asked if I could see him in therapy "just to assess the situation." When I asked that the whole family accompany him to this first session, Barry was audibly silent, then noted tersely that the family consisted only of himself and his son, and that he would gladly accompany him to the meeting. Sensing that there was much more in this response that deserved to be unpacked in session, I established a time for them to come in for an initial consultation.

When we met, the unspoken words behind his laconic telephone response were quick to emerge in the form of a controlled account of a traumatic event that unfolded in their home only six weeks before. As his stepson sat silent, staring at the floor, Barry related how, coming home early and unannounced from work, he heard his wife, Lisa call their four-year old daughter, Valerie, back to the bedroom. Suddenly, as Barry walked to the refrigerator for a beer, two gunshots rang out from the back of the house, and Barry froze for a moment, unable to comprehend what was happening. The subsequent minutes were a blur of horror for him: his running back to the bedroom which was filled with the smell of gunpowder; seeing the crumpled body of this little girl on the floor, her blood seeping out into the gray carpet; his fiercely turning on his wife, only to be knocked back against the wall by a gunshot to his chest; his stepson's entering the room as he staggered forward again, the two of them finally wresting the gun from the wife's grasp; and his wife's collapsing to the floor and dying, the second shot before he entered the room having been to her own chest. The last thing he remembered before losing consciousness was their somehow getting him and his daughter into the car, as Matt drove them to the emergency room. He awoke seven hours later, having survived surgery, to learn that two of his family members were dead, and the third was in police custody under suspicion of murder.

---

1. Identifying information has been altered to preserve the client's anonymity.

Needless to say, the murder/suicide decimated not only Barry's family, but also his assumptive world. Although he acknowledged his marital tensions with Lisa and her increasingly "paranoid" behavior in the months preceding the deaths, he had continued to believe that things would somehow work out, and that "God would take care of things." The killings cruelly cut these threads of consistency in an otherwise stormy life and relationship, and left him and Matt alternating between posttraumatic numbness and aching, avoidance, and flash-back to the terrible event. As the tale unfolded, Barry's tears were met by Matt's apparent stoicism, although both acknowledged struggling desperately with the question of "why" this had happened to them, and how they could move ahead with lives that seemed to have ended with those of Lisa and Valerie.

At this early point in therapy, my role was that of a respectful and deeply concerned listener, an audience to a tale of terror too traumatic to share except in sharply abridged form to anyone else. Thus, rather than attempting to "package" the account or move quickly toward a forced resolution or solution to their anguish, I helped them "unpack" the setting of the story further, going over it in slow motion detail, each augmenting the other's perceptions with his own. Using this "movieola" method (Guidano, 1995) in the fourth session, we soon began to encounter vivid sensory images that had been edited out of their earlier tellings. Two in particular stood out to Barry: the impassivity of his wife's expression as she leveled the gun at his chest and pulled the trigger, and the feral mask of rage that twisted her visage moments later as her son ran into the room to assist his stepfather. Shifting from setting to theme, we then wondered together about the possible meaning of these two contrasting images. Barry shivered, and ventured an interpretation: Lisa had planned coldly to kill her daughter (and Barry, too, as the opportunity arose) to punish him for his alleged "sexual abuse" of her, and became enraged when confronted with the son who failed to support her view of his father's culpability. With this painful but plausible plot structure forming the skeleton of a new, if agonizing narrative of the family's history, we began to weave a more coherent account of Lisa's motives, and what her "meltdown" meant for each of the survivors.

As this provisional explanation crystallized for Barry, he began to feel his way through the torn fabric of his life for those strands of meaning and identity that remained viable (such as his relationship to his adolescent stepson), and those that were no longer sustainable (such as his career as a teacher, which daily confronted him with the painful reminders in his young students of the daughter he no longer had). Guilt, understood as dislodgment from his core identity constructs associated with being a husband and father (Kelly, 1955), emerged as a predominant issue, as Barry attacked himself for having "turned a blind eye" to his wife's escalating anger and accusations, rather than press the two of them to "get help" for the family. A thematic focus on his insufficiency as a partner opened old wounds from previous failed marriages, in which Barry enacted the script of a kind of fairy tale gone wrong — romantically falling in love at first sight, only to have his seemingly childlike trust in his spouse degenerate into controlling suspicion of her infidelity. As we examined this procrustean narrative pattern, Barry began to link the reenactment of this script with Lisa to the cycle of sexual estrangement in the marriage that planted the seeds of her distrust about his sexual involvement with their daughter, an involvement that he and Valerie continued to deny. The tearful exploration of his role in the tragic drama of Lisa's final months prompted several individual sessions, in which he reflected on who he had been, and who he wanted to be, as a man, a parent, and (perhaps) a husband.

Not surprisingly, the gradual reconstruction of a life story took a different form for Matt, who struggled initially to bridge his view of the mother who had always "been there for him" with the image of the woman who had seemed bent on taking the lives of everyone in the family. His "solution" was to construct two different "mothers," one before, and one after the "mental illness" that he blamed for her murderous actions. Likewise, he tended to compartmentalize the story of the trauma, and instead elaborate other subplots in his life, especially those concerned with his friends and girlfriend. The most useful therapeutic moments for Matt came in joint sessions with his stepfather, as they renegotiated their respective roles in relation to each other, in a way that gave each the support he wanted from the other. Although the discussion and facilitation of their connection was often poignant for both, it also was frequently practical, as they jointly "rewrote the script" of mundane household scenarios (such as preparing dinner together) in light of their loss.

In summary, Barry and Matt's case illustrates mainly the heuristic use of narrative as a metaphor for the rebuilding of lives shattered by trauma, a metaphor that sensitized us to their shared and separate struggle to make sense of not only the trauma itself, but also the larger life stories in which it was embedded. In this work, their stories were often also the object of our attention, and therapy consisted of gentle encouragement to explore the gap between their account of their experience and the horrific elements of plot and motive it struggled to contain. Occasional use of explicit narrative methods (for example, the movieola technique) advanced this "effort after meaning," although the stories that took shape provided no simple reassurance that their lives or selves would ever again be the same. Ultimately, however, both father and son were able to allow the image of their shared trauma to recede, at least occasionally, permitting them jointly, and individually, to reflect on the possible futures that remained open for them both.

Case Study Two: Where Does this Fit?

Mark W. was a forty-two-year-old man referred to therapy with one of the authors (RAN) by a regional managed care organization for the treatment of a cluster of personal, occupational, and relational problems, following a violent and traumatic assault he had suffered approximately one year earlier.[2] At the time of the attack, he was working with a state utility company repairing electrical lines, a job he had held successfully for fourteen years. While making a residential call, he was approached by four young men who demanded his wallet, and when he reached into his pocket, pistol whipped him to the ground and proceeded to beat him savagely until he lost consciousness. As a result of the assault he suffered extensive damage to his abdomen and, especially, to his head, requiring a total of seven facial and dental reconstructive surgeries to restore a normal appearance.

In his own terms, Mark reported feeling "just confused" by his post-assault adjustment. He noted that he was "pissed off all the time," particularly feeling an urge to "want to hurt people who harass others." This sense of barely suppressed rage at interpersonal situations that he viewed as involving victimization had become a primary concern, both of Mark himself and of those involved with his treatment. The significance of this issue was underscored by his report of an incident in which he "blanked out" and physically accosted a belligerent customer in a drugstore who he viewed as "attacking" an undeserving sales clerk. Despite his generally congenial and cooperative demeanor in therapy, Mark noted that he always felt "a fire burning inside" that only needed the kindling of an encounter with someone he viewed as a "predator" to leap into full blaze.

Although Mark's vivid anger and its potential for physical expression clearly commanded therapeutic attention, he also complained of a number of other symptoms that were consistent with the diagnosis of posttraumatic stress disorder that he had received during several weeks of inpatient psychiatric treatment following his medical stabilization. These included intrusive recollections of his assault, often accompanied by spontaneous crying and elevated anxiety, marked sleep disturbance, chronic physiological activation (which he described as "shaking inside"), and general avoidance of social situations. Mark also reported difficulty in concentrating on reading, television, and other activities for extended periods of time, in part because of intrusive "daydreams" regarding the assault and his fantasized revenge against his assailants. Psychological testing confirmed his difficulties with elevated anxiety and depression, and uncontrolled anger. It was not surprising, therefore, that Mark's already distant marriage had disintegrated into a formal separation under the further pressure of his immobilization and unpredictability, and that he had been placed on indefinite medical leave from his job out of concern not only for Mark, but also for those with whom he would come into contact.

---

2.   Identifying information has been altered to preserve the client's anonymity.

History of treatment

Following his brief inpatient treatment, Mark was discharged to the care of a respected psychiatrist and psychologist, who followed him for several more months in outpatient treatment. Mark reported no real gains from the antidepressant medication he was prescribed from the physician, an impression that was corroborated in the psychiatrist's own treatment summary. Moreover, the cognitive behavioral strategies employed by Mark's psychotherapist (such as relaxation training, response prevention, and rational disputation of his self-defeating thoughts) had produced only transitory symptom relief. Thus, after nearly a year of marginal therapeutic progress, Mark was referred to me for more specialized outpatient treatment of his posttraumatic adjustment.

As Mark recounted his story in our first session, I was struck by his statement that "I don't know myself anymore; I feel like I'm losing my mind. It's like I've lost who I was." As I encouraged him to elaborate on this remark, he stated that "I don't know if I can get back to who I was, but I don't like what I am. It's like I can't remember the piece that has consumed me." This theme of disrupted identity and lost memory had apparently been neglected in previous therapy, which was more focused on symptom relief than on helping Mark reconstitute a viable new sense of self that accommodated the trauma while not being confined to it.

Jigsaw memories

As a first step toward an exploration rather than elimination of the trauma memories, I metaphorically described Mark's recollection of the assault in our second session as a "jigsaw puzzle from which some of the pieces seemed to be missing." He resonated to this image, saying he could recall isolated fragments of the attack and its aftermath, but "the whole picture didn't come together." This suggested a collaboratively designed homework assignment, which consisted of Mark's writing these fragmentary memories, sensory details, and so on, on separate index cards, and then adding new details as any came to mind. He was then to reconstitute a more coherent narrative of the attack sequence by arranging the cards in chronological order, concentrating on any gaps in an attempt to bridge the fragments in a plausible fashion. Because I anticipated that this reimmersion in the trauma would likely be distressing to him, we constructed a list of "time out" strategies he could use to "break the tension" associated with the task (among them, in his case, listening to classical music, and walking). Engagement in this metaphoric "solving" of the "jigsaw puzzle" of Mark's assault represented one means of exploring the sequence of traumatic events, as recommended in constructivist accounts of treatment (Hyer, 1994; Stewart, 1995).

Mark faithfully tackled the assignment, in spite of his self-consciousness about his writing — something he had done relatively little of since completing high school at age eighteen. He brought in the completed narrative the following week, scrawled in red ink on a series of index cards. He began with, "Walking toward the pole with the transformer, noticed four men [here he crossed out "men" and substituted "things"] under streetlight. ..." The remainder of his unedited prose appears below.

> When I got to pole they came running toward me spread out where I couldn't run. They came up to me and put a 9 mm Ruger Automatic to my head. Said what you got raised my hands said take it. When they got what they wanted they hit me in the head with the gun and I went to the ground. He said you motherfucker before he hit me on the ground. Remember flashes of bright light it was so bright I couldn't see anything. All these guys were kicking me in the head. But one in particular was running back and jumping on my face. I remember feeling intense rage mostly at the one jumping on me. I was thinking how I could hurt him easy if I could get up. I decided it would be worth getting shot just to get one good shot to his nose with the palm of my hand with an upward thrust. I decide was going to do this no matter what but every time I raised up I would get knocked back to the ground. I tried many times to do this, I would guess, 20 times.

In discussing his construction of this account in our subsequent session, Mark noted that he "remembered things I couldn't before," as new recollections "came to me every day" he worked on the narrative. In particular, he became aware of a number of sensory details of the attack, as well as his efforts to resist his assailants. For example, he described how he "just remembered the heel of the cowboy boot [worn by his most vicious assailant] coming down. The heel is very vivid. ... I'll never forget it as long as I live." The only feeling he could recall during the attack was rage, though he acknowledged, "I should have been scared."

As we considered together the fragmentation of memories associated with the trauma, we gradually broadened the discussion to include his continuing sense of fragmentation in his life. Mark connected this with his subsequent disruption of interpersonal relationships, and recognized that his tendency to "hole up inside himself" was in fact an old, familiar pattern, anchored in childhood events that flashed vividly to mind. This sort of "serial accessing" of "emotional truths" can unfold rapidly in response to a therapy that examines the client's disowned "need" to maintain the symptom (in this case, his seclusiveness), despite the pain associated with it (Ecker & Hulley, 1996). This suggested that an exploration of his broader life narrative, beyond the assault per se, would be an important aspect of his therapy.

Biographical Grid

Although Mark acknowledged that "rehashing and figuring out the incident with somebody else almost made him feel good," it was clear that more than a reconstruction of the trauma event itself was necessary to give Mark a greater sense of wholeness and meaning. I therefore introduced a second strategy, the Biographical Grid (Neimeyer, 1985), as a means of both assessing and focusing therapeutic attention on the broader life narrative of which the trauma episode was part.

As a variant of repertory grid technique (Kelly, 1955; Neimeyer, 1993), the administration of the Biographical Grid includes three distinct steps: (1) identification of significant life events or stages; (2) elicitation of life themes or personal meanings; and (3) weaving events through with themes. Here, we will briefly summarize its use with Mark, deferring to other publications for a more detailed exposition of the procedure and its interpretation (Neimeyer & Stewart, 1998).

As a first step in the procedure, I discussed with Mark particular autobiographical memories that anchored his sense of self at various points in the life trajectory. I began my inquiry with the question, "From your early childhood, what events stand out for you in shaping your identity in important ways, or representing who you were at that time?" Mark immediately responded by recounting a vicarious trauma that occurred when he was seven years old, in which his father was nearly electrocuted in an industrial accident. As a result of this injury, his father was removed to a medical facility in a distant city for nine months, accompanied by his mother. Mark wept as he recalled this experience of being functionally "orphaned," left in the custody of a little-known aunt and uncle. Other significant anchor points for his construction of self included his participation in Little League baseball, a proud early childhood experience when he independently rode his tricycle home from the neighborhood swimming pool to the chagrin of his worried parents, and the persistent abuse by bullies during his high school years, which Mark finally overcame by positioning himself as a "crazy" and unpredictable "loner" who would "go down swinging." Finally, as we moved into Mark's adult life, he nominated still other episodic memories that included the "proud moment" at age twenty-six when his son was born, the attack that precipitated his treatment, and (at my prompting) a present self, future self, and ideal self that conveyed who he now was and might yet become.

As a second step in the Biographical Grid procedure, we sought to tease out the themes that Mark used to organize the important events of his life narrative. This involved my asking him to systematically compare and contrast the self-defining moments elicited earlier, describing ways that they were alike and different. For example, presented with images of himself at the time his father was injured, when his son was born, and his ideal self, Mark distinguished the latter two elements, which he associated with "liking himself," from the former, which he associated with "hating himself."[3] In response to other comparisons, he discriminated between the Little League years and high school, on the one hand, and his assault at age forty-one, on the other, because at the first two points in time, he was "able to keep what was his," whereas during the attack, he was "violated." Likewise, he differentiated his present and future self, which he associated with "a fire always there," from his self-image while in Little League when he was "able to reason." Thus, in the span of a single session, we were able to evoke a number of emotionally resonant themes that defined both his senses of continuity and discontinuity over time.

Although a picture of the significant shifts and continuities in the respondent's life experience begins to emerge in the above two steps, the third step in the Biographical Grid procedure explicitly invites the person to weave autobiographical memories through with interpretive constructs. This may be done qualitatively in the course of the interview (for example, by asking, "In which of these other times did you experience yourself as violated?"), although it can also be done in more precise, quantitative form, in keeping with repertory grid methods in general (Fransella & Bannister, 1977; Fromm, 2004). Several features of Mark's responses were of clinical interest. First, it became clear that his narrative was organized into two diametrically-opposed clusters of self-images, one of which contained his positively-valenced self elements — on the tricycle, when playing baseball, when his son was born, and even in high school, when he successfully struck back at his persistent bullies until they "steered clear of him." This tight grouping of self-identities closely approximated his ideal, and was woven through with constructs implying control, ability to reason, liking himself and others, happiness, and keeping what was his. In sharp contrast, both his current, posttraumatic self and his projected future self were tightly linked, recapitulating in virtually every detail the themes he associated with his experience at age seven in the aftermath of his father's injury. Now, as then, Mark viewed himself as hating others as well as himself, as having lost control, and as disgusted, sad, and violated. Moreover, all three identities were linked to his experiencing a "fire inside," as well as with anger and chaos. No life events bridged or articulated these two opposing clusters of situated self identities, suggesting an instability in self image associated with vulnerability to depression and other forms of distress.

---

3.   This same "triadic sort" method of construct elicitation has been used and documented for other forms of grid technique, as discussed by Fransella and Bannister (1977), Fromm (2004) and others. Although I employed this procedure in the more intimate context of a clinical interview, a host of computer-based grid elicitation and analysis programs could also be employed with the Biographical Grid procedure (Bringmann, 1992; Sewell, Adams-Webber, Mitterer, & Cromwell, 1992).

In summary, the Biographical Grid suggested that Mark had assimilated the experience of his recent assault into the meaning structure associated with an earlier trauma in his life, namely, the multiple losses tied to his father's injury. Both left him contemptuous of self and others, both triggered a smoldering rage and impotence associated with a sense of violation. But in neither case could he find ways to accommodate these traumatic selves into the larger texture of his primary narrative, leaving him isolated in a regressive identity that was radically discontinuous with his pretraumatic self. The result was a life story that was painfully incoherent, with no clear way of integrating his experience of loss into the preexisting structure of his life. While speculative, it is tempting to conjecture that the isolation of his previous traumatic identity in the text of his life posed a vulnerability factor for his later development of PTSD in response to the assault, providing a ready-made but fragmentary template within which to give meaning to his subsequent attack.

Discussion of these patterns with Mark in the next session was powerful, for him as well as for me. For example, when I asked him to reflect on the striking parallel between his construction of his life at age seven and following his attack, he replied, "I never thought about it, but it makes good sense. It's a real eye-opener. It's like I'm at the same place in life as when I was in first grade. Hmm. ... I never put that together before." Likewise, asked to consider the polarization of his situated identities into two non-overlapping groupings, Mark responded, "I often thought that there was no in-between, life was either good or it sucks. I kind of always thought this way, even before the attack happened. It just came to me now, I don't think I ever realized it. I just thought everyone was that way."

The results of Mark's Biographical Grid were instructive in identifying Mark's resources as well as his liabilities. This was illustrated by his response to my question concerning "what strengths he had at age seven that let him re-engage the world at age nine." Mark hesitated for a moment, and then noted that he "just made myself do it," because he "was going downhill and had nothing to lose." He went on to observe that he was "procrastinating now, avoiding people because I was so uncomfortable with them." We further considered the facilitative role of organized baseball in "drawing him out of himself" and giving him a safe way of "reconnecting with others." Indeed, it was the upward life trajectory established by his Little League and Pony League years that buoyed him into his more turbulent late adolescence, and gave him the conviction that he could resist, rather than submit to the bullying of his high school peers.

My remaining nine sessions of therapy with Mark first explored, then enacted, and finally consolidated the potential for reconstruction suggested by our discussion of the Biographical Grid. Mark surprised me in the fifth session by proudly announcing his stiffness from having played a "pick-up game of baseball" in his neighborhood, his first in over fifteen years. With genuine astonishment and excitement, I validated the powerfully symbolic importance of this "unique outcome," which represented an enacted form of resistance against the oppressive influence of the "dominant narrative" of his identity as a trauma victim (White & Epston, 1990). By session eight Mark had begun to envision an alternative future, one predicated on his gaining additional training in mechanics at the community college level. This ability to orient toward a possible future that was different than the traumatic past was itself a remarkable achievement, one that he followed with concrete exploration of job retraining as an alternative to accepting long-term psychiatric disability. Naturally, the road to reconstruction of his primary sense of self was not an unswerving one, and he occasionally reported "getting sidetracked" by traffic confrontations, abrasive interactions with his in-laws in the course of his divorce, and other events that once again cued up his urge to retaliate against the "attacks" of others. Gradually, however, we were able to identify self-monitoring strategies that enabled him to "enter" and "leave" this traumatic self identity more easily, although this required considerable fortitude for him to develop.

How can we understand Mark's experience of "rebiographing" (Howard, 1991) in the context of psychotherapy? At the most general level, he appeared to have restored his elaborative meaning making about the events surrounding his victimization, literally and figuratively rewriting a coherent story of the assault that encompassed his previously fragmentary recollections of it. As he did so, and subsequently reinstated this powerful but isolated sequence in the script of his life, he was better able to move from it to more empowering self-identities that engaged the world and other people less stereotypically and more adaptively.

At another level, he seemed to have recovered the threads of his more optimistic primary narrative, the one that was instantiated in his earliest childhood, his baseball years, and his young adulthood. In other respects, however, his reconstructed identity did not simply recapitulate the thematic structure of these simpler times. Indeed, for some weeks he grieved the "loss of innocence about life" that he associated with them. He felt partially compensated for this loss, however, by his enlarged capacity to "be empathic with others who are hurting or crazy," and by his greater ability "to deal with anger openly, rather than passively, the way he used to."

In summary, Mark's case illustrates the use of several explicit narrative methods (for example, jigsaw memories and the Biographical Grid), while also adopting narrative as a conceptual framework for therapy. By first immersing himself in the fragmented story of his assault and working toward a more adequate account of the experience, Mark began to scaffold the trauma in thematic, as well as sensory terms. This thematic exploration was considerably extended by our elicitation of significant self-defining moments from his biography, whose careful discussion permitted us to glimpse the ways in which his response to the attack had recapitulated his response to earlier adversities in his life. Likewise, these narrative methods prompted him to recognize and reengage his own strengths in response to these events, allowing Mark to move beyond posttraumatic stress, to posttraumatic growth (Tedeschi, Park, & Calhoun, 1998).

Conclusion

Obviously, the broad range of constructivist psychotherapies (Mahoney, 1995; Neimeyer & Bridges, 2003; Neimeyer & Mahoney, 1995, Neimeyer & Raskin, 2000) is too rich in theory to be conveyed in a discussion of a single disorder, and too multifaceted in practice to be illustrated in one or two brief case studies. But as a relatively new field of research and practice, the area of trauma and loss invites novel conceptualization, and we have tried to respond to this invitation by extending a constructivist account of posttraumatic stress and providing concrete examples of its application. In doing so, we are aware that the narrative model we have found compelling on a heuristic level is only beginning to be evaluated empirically, just as its concrete ramifications for the helping professions require further elaboration and refinement. We hope that the present chapter makes a modest contribution to this effort, and that the reader will join us in exploring the implications of constructivism for helping clients rework the sometimes fragmentary and entangled themes of their life narratives.

References

American Psychiatric Association. (1987). *Diagnostic and statistical manual of mental disorders* (3th ed., revised). Washington, DC: American Psychiatric Association.

American Psychiatric Association. (1994). *Diagnostic and statistical manual of mental disorders* (4th ed.). Washington, DC: American Psychiatric Association.

Atkinson, R. (1995). *The gift of stories: Personal and spiritual applications of autobiography, life stories, and personal mythmaking.* Westport, CT: Bergin & Garvey.

Barclay, C. R. (1996). Autobiographical remembering: Narrative constraints on objectified selves. In D. C. Rubin (Ed.), *Remembering our past: Studies in autobiographical memory* (pp. 94–125). Cambridge, England: Cambridge University Press.

Barsalou, L. W. (1988). The content and organization of autobiographical memories. In U. Neisser & E. Winograd (Eds.), *Remembering reconsidered: Ecological and traditional approaches to the study of memory* (pp. 193–243). Cambridge, England: Cambridge University Press.

Breslau, N., Davis, G. C., Andreski, P., & Peterson, E. (1991). Traumatic events and posttraumatic stress disorder in an urban population of young adults. *Archives of General Psychiatry, 48,* 216–222.

Bringmann, M. W. (1992). Computer-based methods for the analysis and interpretation of personal construct systems. In R. A. Neimeyer & G. J. Neimeyer (Eds.), *Advances in personal construct psychology* (pp. 57–90). Greenwich, CT: JAI.

Bruner, J. S. (1986). *Actual minds, possible worlds.* Cambridge, MA: Harvard University Press.

Ecker, B., & Hulley, L. (1996). *Depth-oriented brief therapy: How to be brief when you trained to be deep — and vice versa.* San Francisco: Jossey-Bass.

Fransella, F., & Bannister, D. (1977). *A manual for repertory grid technique.* New York: Academic Press.

Fromm, M. (2004) *The repertory grid interview.* Munster, Germany and New York: Waxman.

Guidano, V. F. (1995). Self-observation in constructivist psychotherapy. In R. A. Neimeyer & M. J. Mahoney (Ed.), *Constructivism in psychotherapy* (pp. 155–168). Washington, DC: American Psychological Association.

Harter, S. L., & Neimeyer, R. A. (1995). Long term effects of child sexual abuse: Toward a constructivist theory of trauma and its treatment. In R. A. Neimeyer & G. J. Neimeyer (Eds.), *Advances in personal construct theory: Volume 3* (pp. 229–270). Greenwich, CT: JAI.

Howard, G. S. (1991). Culture tales: A narrative approach to thinking, cross-cultural psychology, and psychotherapy. *American Psychologist, 46,* 187–197.

Howe, M. L., & Courage, M. (1997). The emergence and early development of autobiographical memory. *Psychological Review, 104,* 499–523.

Hyer, L. (1994). The trauma response: Its complexity and dimensions. In L. Hyer & Associates (Eds.), *Trauma victim: Theoretical issues and practical suggestions* (pp. 27–92). Muncie, IN: Accelerated Development.

Kelly, G. A. (1955). *The psychology of personal constructs.* New York: Norton.

Klion, R. E., & Pfenninger, D. T. (1996). Role constriction and Vietnam-era combat veterans. *Journal of Constructivist Psychology, 9,* 127–138.

Linton, M. (1986). Ways of searching and the contents of memory. In D. C. Rubin (Ed.), *Autobiographical memory* (pp. 50–67). Cambridge, England: Cambridge University Press.

Mahoney, M. J. (Ed.). (1995). *Cognitive and constructive psychotherapies: Theory, research and practice.* New York: Springer.

Mair, M. (1988). Psychology as storytelling. *International Journal of Personal Construct Psychology, 1,* 125–138.

Mair, M. (1989). Kelly, Bannister, and a story-telling psychology. *International Journal of Personal Construct Psychology, 2,* 1–14.

McNally, R. J., Litz, B. T., Prassas, A., Shin, L. M., & Weathers, F. W. (1994). Emotional priming of autobiographical memory in posttraumatic stress disorder. *Cognition and Emotion, 8,* 351–367.

Monk, G., Crockett, K., Winslade, J., & Epston, D. (1996). *Narrative therapy in practice: The archaeology of hope.* San Francisco: Jossey-Bass.

Neimeyer, R. A. (1985). Personal constructs in clinical practice. In P. C. Kendall (Ed.), *Advances in cognitive-behavioral research and therapy* (pp. 275–329). San Diego, CA: Academic Press.

Neimeyer, R. A. (1993). Constructivist approaches to the measurement of meaning. In G. J. Neimeyer (Ed.), *Constructivist assessment: A casebook* (pp. 58–103). Newbury Park: CA: Sage.

Neimeyer, R. A. (1995). Client-generated narratives in psychotherapy. In R. A. Neimeyer & M. J. Mahoney (Ed.), *Constructivism in psychotherapy* (pp. 231–246). Washington, DC: American Psychological Association.

Neimeyer, R. A. (1998). *Lessons of loss: A guide to coping.* New York: McGraw Hill.

Neimeyer, R. A. (2000). Narrative disruptions in the construction of self. In R. A. Neimeyer & J. Raskin (Eds.), *Constructions of disorder*. Washington, D.C.: American Psychological Association.

Neimeyer, R. A. (Ed.) (2001). *Meaning reconstruction and the experience of loss*. Washington: American Psychological Association.

Neimeyer, R. A. (2004). Fostering posttraumatic growth: A narrative contribution. *Psychological Inquiry, 15*, 53–59.

Neimeyer, R. A., & Arvey, M. J. (2004). Performing the self: Therapeutic enactment and the narrative integration of traumatic loss. In H. Hermans & G. Dimaggio (Eds.), *The dialogical self in psychotherapy* (pp. 173–189). New York: Brunner Routledge.

Neimeyer, R. A., & Bridges, S. (2003). Postmodern approaches to psychotherapy. In A. Gurman & S. Messer (Eds.), *Essential psychotherapies* (2nd ed.) (pp. 272–316). New York: Guilford.

Neimeyer, R. A., & Mahoney, M. J. (Eds.). (1995). *Constructivism in psychotherapy*. Washington: American Psychological Association.

Neimeyer, R. A. & Raskin, J. (Eds.). (2000). *Constructions of disorder*. Washington, D.C.: American Psychological Association.

Neimeyer, R. A., Prigerson, H & Davies, B. (2002). Mourning and meaning. *American Behavioral Scientist, 46*, 235–251.

Neimeyer, R. A., & Stewart, A. E. (1998). Trauma, healing, and the narrative emplotment of loss. In C. Franklin & P. S. Nurius (Eds.), *Constructivism in practice: Methods and challenges* (pp. 165–184). Milwaukee, WI: Families International.

Neimeyer, R. A., & Stewart, A. E. (2000). Constructivist and narrative psychotherapies. In C. R. Snyder & R. E. Ingram (Eds.). *The handbook of psychological change: Psychotherapy processes and practices for the 21st century* (pp. 337–357). New York: John Wiley & Sons.

Park, C., Calhoun, L., & Tedeschi, R. (1998). *Post-traumatic growth: Positive changes in the aftermath of crisis*. Mahwah, NJ: Erlbaum.

Pillener, D., Desrochers, A., & Erbanks, C. (1997). Remembering the past in the present. In C. P. Thompson, D. Hermann, D. Bruce, J. Read, D. Payne, & M. Toglia (Eds.), *Autobiographical memory: Theoretical and applied perspectives* (pp. 145–162). Mahwah, NJ: Erlbaum.

Polkinghorne, D. E. (1988). *Narrative knowing and the human sciences*. Albany, NY: State University of New York Press.

Polkinghorne, D. E. (1991). Narrative and self-concept. *Journal of Narrative and Life History, 1*, 135–153.

Robinson, J. A., & Swanson, K. L. (1990). Autobiographical memory: The next phase. *Applied Cognitive Psychology, 4*, 321–335.

Rosen, H., & Kuehlwein, K. (Eds.). (1996). *Constructing realities: Meaning-making perspectives for psychotherapists*. San Francisco: Jossey-Bass.

Rubin, D. C. (1998). Beginnings of a theory of autobiographical remembering. In C. P. Thompson, D. Hermann, D. Bruce, J. Read, D. Payne, & M. Toglia (Eds.), *Autobiographical memory: Theoretical and applied perspectives* (pp. 47–67). Mahwah, NJ: Erlbaum.

Russell, R. L., & Van den Broek, P. (1992). Changing narrative schemas in psychotherapy. *Psychotherapy, 29*, 344–354.

Sarbin, T. R. (1986). The narrative as a root metaphor for psychology. In T. R. Sarbin (Ed.), *Narrative psychology: The storied nature of human conduct* (pp. 3–21). New York: Praeger.

Sewell, K. W. (1996). Constructional risk factors for a posttraumatic stress response after a mass murder. *Journal of Constructivist Psychology, 9,* 97–107.

Sewell, K. W. (1997). Post-traumatic stress: Towards a constructivist model of psychotherapy. In G. J. Neimeyer & R. A. Neimeyer (Eds.), *Advances in personal construct psychology 4* (pp. 207–235). Greenwich, CT: JAI Press.

Sewell, K. W., Adams-Webber, J., Mitterer, J., & Cromwell, R. L. (1992). Computerized repertory grids: Review of the literature. *International Journal of Personal Construct Psychology, 5,* 1–23.

Sewell, K. W., Cromwell, R. L., Farrell-Higgins, J., & Palmer, R. (1996). Hierarchical elaboration in the conceptual structure of Vietnam combat veterans. *Journal of Constructivist Psychology, 9,* 79–96.

de Shazer, S. (1994). *Words were originally magic.* New York: Norton.

Shotter, J., & Gergen, K. J. (1989). *Texts of identity.* Newbury Park, CA: Sage Publications.

Siegel, D. J. (1995). Memory, trauma, and psychotherapy: A cognitive science view. *Journal of Psychotherapy Practice & Research, 4,* 93–122.

Snow, B. R., Stellman, J. M., Stellman, S. D., & Sommer, J. F. (1988). Posttraumatic stress disorder among American legionnaires in relation to combat experience in Vietnam: Associated and contributing factors. *Environmental Research, 47,* 175–192.

Stewart, A. E. (1999). Complicated bereavement and posttraumatic stress disorder following fatal car crashes: recommendations for death notification practice. *Death Studies, 23,* 289–321.

Stewart, J. (1995). Reconstruction of the self: Life-span-oriented group psychotherapy. *Journal of Constructivist Psychology, 8,* 129–148.

Tedeschi, R. A., & Calhoun, L. G. (2004). Posttraumatic growth: Conceptual foundations and empirical evidence. *Psychological Inquiry, 15,* 1–18.

Terrell, C. J., & Lyddon, W. J. (1995). Narrative and psychotherapy. *Journal of Constructivist Psychotherapy, 9,* 27–44.

Van der Kolk, B. A., & Van der Hart, O. (1991). The intrusive past: The flexibility of memory and the engraving of trauma. *American Imago, 48,* 425–454.

Vogel, D. (1994). Narrative perspectives in theory and therapy. *Journal of Constructivist Psychology, 7,* 243–261.

White, M., & Epston, D. (1990). *Narrative means to therapeutic ends.* New York: Norton.

Wigren, J. (1994). Narrative completion in the treatment of trauma. *Psychotherapy, 31,* 415–423.

CHAPTER FOUR

Fact and Knowledge:
A Construction of Delusions

David G. Vogel

As I have tried to elaborate a narrative based approach to delusions, I have confronted some fundamental questions regarding the essence of my endeavor: Isn't the whole movement towards a narrative perspective also a movement away from the idea that we can label one story "delusional" and another story "reality-based"? Does the judgmental diagnostic approach that speaks of reality and delusion belong in a discussion that embraces a narrative approach which honors and respects the great variety of stories, perspectives, and realities which people express? How could anyone attempt to build a bridge across the chasm which lies between the language of narrative and the terminology of clinical and medical assessment?

Ultimately, I came to the conclusion that the same questions apply to any attempt to link a narrative perspective with a clinical one. The dynamic tension and possible synthesis between these two antithetical orientations (I'll call them "narrative" and "clinical") are critical for the development of psychotherapy and narrative psychology.

The title of this book, *Healing Stories: The Use of Narrative in Counseling and Psychotherapy*, refers to both perspectives and implies the possibility for constructive integrations of the two. I am hopeful that the development of narrative psychotherapies will entail a dramatic transformation of our understandings of both narrative and clinical-diagnostic concepts. However, in the pages that follow I will be focusing on the tensions between the clinical and the therapeutic.

Healing and Narrative

A case can be made for viewing the narrative and the therapeutic as distinct and incompatible orientations to human experience. Generally speaking, a narrative perspective is constructivist (Howard, 1991; Mahoney, 1988; Neimeyer, 1995; Vogel, 1994). In other words, a narrative approach to human knowledge runs directly contrary to simple (or "naive") realism. At the core of realism is what Nietzsche (1969b) called the "dogma of immaculate perception" (p. 145), the deeply-held belief that reality can bear forth information untainted by bias, interests, or desire. Realists hold that those who seek knowledge can and must faithfully, objectively, and precisely reflect information as it is received (or taken) from the world. For constructivists, knowledge about the world is not copied or discovered, but invented or constructed (Efran, Lukens, & Lukens, 1988).

For the realist, the struggle for perfect objectivity is essential to the scientific endeavor so as to more perfectly reflect reality. The human propensity for creating meaning and the particularities of any individual or group perspective is seen as something like a taint or a crack in the lens of the scientific microscope. Scientific realism entails the pursuit of ever more flawless lenses, free from the taints of human subjectivity. Objective facts are pursued through such means as controlled experiments, falsifiable claims, and the precise and careful collection of data.

On the other hand, narrativists and other constructivists view knowing as an active creative process, and see the creation of meaning as essential to our ability to think about the world. From a narrative perspective, views of reality are composed of stories (see, for example, Howard, 1991), and there is no one true story about reality, or about any set of events in the "real world." Narrativists do not seek after objective factual truth, but a good and useful story. Although we may try to compare stories, there is no one privileged perspective nor is there a vantage point from which we can transcend all perspectives (the so called "view from nowhere"). Because there is no objective definition of a good or accurate story, all of us speak with equal "authority."

For some narrative purists, any attempt to discriminate between stories or any assertion that one story is better or more accurate than any other story is merely a power play. At a day-long symposium on narrative, I heard one such narrative "purist" position clearly enunciated by a speaker who asserted that "questions about accuracy are always and only a cover for issues of power and entitlement to speak."

Narrative and Health

There is no health as such, and all attempts to define a thing that way have been wretched failures. Even the determination of what is healthy for your body depends on your goal, your horizon, your energies, your impulses, your errors and above all on the ideals and phantasms of your soul. (Nietzsche, 1969a, pp. 176–177)

Notions of health, psychotherapy, and healing often conflict with a "purist" approach to narrative, because these notions necessarily involve some ranking of stories, some preference for certain stories over others. I see two reasons for this.

First, the very notion of health carries with it ideals and values. Without some discrimination between a state of relative illness and a state of relative wellness, the very idea of healing or therapy is meaningless.

Although some might argue that such conditions as cancer, diabetes, and AIDs are so obviously unhealthy that failure to acknowledge the objective nature of health and illness in some cases is pure sophistry. Yet, there are clear value commitments implicit in this observation. One such value commitment is that prolongation of individual human lives (or the elimination of suffering for particular human individuals) is the ultimate measure of health. However, from a definition of health that is planetary in scope and places great value on biodiversity, anything that reduces or reverses the rate of human population growth might be considered healthful.

Whether we see therapy as resulting in healing, growth, personal development, self-actualization, spiritual evolution, or the restoration of some normal or natural state, we are admitting a value-laden distinction between healthier and sicker, progression and regression, transcendence and entanglement, liberation and enslavement, self-actualization and self-destruction, or some other distinction(s) that orients us towards desirable states of affairs and away from other, less desirable states.

Natural science terms like "health" can deflect attention away from political and philosophical values. Nonetheless, it is important to note that, without an implicit or explicit reference to some ideal state, notions of healing and psychotherapy have little meaning. It is only with reference to some notion of how a person ought to be experiencing the world, or functioning in it, that we can speak of someone becoming healthier or less healthy. Without such values, we cannot differentiate between good therapy and bad, failed treatment and successful treatment, or pathology and progress.

Second, the ideas of therapy and healing contain clear if rudimentary narratives involving a sufferer and a healer and some interaction between them through which the sufferer is changed and his or her functioning is improved. Therapists orient their actions according to their stories about illness and healing. Indeed, I would suggest that to be a therapist is to embrace some "personal" or "professional" stories about health and healing and, most likely, about the development and sources of pathology as well.

A simple exercise might illustrate this point. Consider several theories of psychotherapy, or several case studies with which you are familiar. It shouldn't be very difficult to categorize them as representative of specific genres, or archetypal tales, of therapy.

Biological psychiatrists often present therapeutic romances about finding the potion which will cure disease, or heroic tales of overcoming irrational beliefs about mental illness, so that the patient will accept a scientific cure. Behaviorists tell stories about pairings of stimuli and incompatible responses, and often speak of irrational explanations offered by unscientific therapists for simple learned behaviors.

One romance popular among many therapists, particularly narrativists, constructivists, and humanists is as follows: the therapist bears witness to the unfolding story of another person. Through exercises, or through the process of conversation with an open and careful listener, the client has a chance to reorganize his or her story, to find coherence and to become more whole. The client's true story is recovered in the presence of a warm non-judgmental witness. It is the client who contains some vision, some seed of health, and the healing process allows clients to align their being with that vision. Through therapy, clients grow or develop and become what they already were. In other words, the client is able to realize/actualize their potential which existed before the therapy.

One common version of this is the story about the therapist who helps voiceless patients find their voices and speak their truths. Often this involves a process by which the therapist gently helps the patient explore the dark and terrible secrets of his or her past or psyche. Ultimately the journey into this darkness ("the dark night of the soul") results in the uncovering of truth. Then, the patient finds self acceptance and uncovers his or her true inner orientation towards growth.

This last professional story is one in which the conflict between psychotherapy and narrative might seem to be eliminated. The healing is non-directive; it merely releases the client's potential. But the very notion that an ongoing conversation with a psychotherapist could simply restore the patient in a way that did not reflect the influence of the therapist is really untenable for a constructivist. Can we observe a person without influencing him or her? If our perception is not immaculate how could our therapy be? Is it possible to empower a person in all possible directions at once, or is therapeutic empowerment directional? If there is no one true story about any event, how can there be one true story about a person? If reality is created, not discovered, how is self discovery, especially self-discovery in the context of an intimate conversation, possible?

For a constructivist to claim to be merely a witness to change, or to merely reflect the patient to himself or herself, is to embrace a dogma that constructivists have rejected. We cannot simply reflect reality. There is no immaculate perception of reality, of stories, or of individuals.

It seems to me that if we are to make value commitments, we need to label them as such. If we make truth claims and talk about matters of fact, then we need to embrace the methods and rules of evidence appropriate to these types of claims. In other words, we need to validate our claims about facts through the tangible data of the everyday physical world and the world of biomedical knowledge. It would make little sense to reject these kinds of data as somehow constructed and arbitrary and then claim knowledge of intangible essences such as "real self," "true voice," or even "self esteem" as if these were matters of fact.

In my personal conversations with psychotherapists of many stripes, from psychoanalysts to constructivists, I am struck by how many of them have rejected or ignored the realist truth claims of science with its strict rules of evidence and argument only to embrace realist truth claims based on intuition or special insight. I am led to wonder if truth claims based on intuition and insight are most attractive because they are far less vulnerable to compelling contradiction. These topics were recently addressed by Robyn Dawes (1994) in a book remarkable for its anger, angst, and thoroughness.

Those who use constructivist or narrative methods also need to take great care about claims to knowledge about their clients. Therapists are not mere elicitors, recoverers, or respecters of stories. Therapists do not simply recover stories or help patients find their voices. Therapists are also literary critics who hear, read, and interpret texts. For me, this is not only true for those psychoanalytic therapists who see in every life the workings of a finite number of core themes and conflicts, it is also true of narrative therapists. Narrative therapists hear stories and differentiate adequate stories from inadequate ones, locate discontinuities and problems in the narratives, and open doors to alternate ways of constructing biographical stories.

Some therapists purport to differentiate the patient's authentic stories from those which have been imposed on them by others. There is realism present in any claim to "recover" one's voice or one's story — as if this voice or story was an artifact lying nicely preserved underneath so many layers of sediment. Through actions and inactions, a therapist conveys a great deal about her or his healing stories healing, and about the way he or she perceives the stories told by the client.

Many of us may have taken for granted notions regarding the pathways that lead to health and the pathways that lead to illness. We may not see the values and the goals (and, often, the social and political visions) which underlie our ideas of health. As we hear the many voices of the patient, we often construe some as authentic and others as imposed. To perform any kind of therapy with a human being is to pursue some vision of health and some notion of how human beings ought to function. Even the most ostensibly non-directive therapy carries with it powerful values. For example, the concept of self-acceptance involves a complex set of value laden notions about the nature of the true self and the illusions which may obscure it, as well as some degree of rejection of available frameworks for negative self-judgments.

To be a narrative therapist entails some ordering, or some integration of two very different impulses, one being an egalitarian impulse regarding the willingness to listen to stories, to hear many voices without ranking or silencing any, and another impulse to guide others toward some ideal state we call health. In pointing out this tension between impulses, I am not insisting that we should abandon either narrative or therapy.

What I am suggesting is that therapists are deeply involved in the criticism and analysis of stories. Active participation in human conversations entails, in some sense, becoming literary critics who edit and critique stories and do so within the context of the vast web of stories which we inhabit. To be a therapist, especially a narrative therapist, is to specialize in this kind of literary criticism. Such criticism is analytical, but it is also creative. People will often change the telling of their stories in response to audience reaction and criticism.

If I belabor this point, it is because I believe that the fantasy that therapists do not influence the stories told by clients is dangerous. It can lead to something like ventriloquism, a process in which our speech and our stories come out disguised as stories told by the patient.

A paradigm for the dangers of this process is Facilitated Communication (FC), a process by which a sensitive, empathic, and supposedly non-directive helper was to enable people with severe difficulties in communication (usually autistic or brain-injured) to communicate in words (e.g., Biklen, 1993). This was usually done by helping the patient type or touch letters on a keyboard or pad. Many of the stories which were communicated were often exciting and moving, revealing surprising levels of intelligence and sensitivity. Also startling to many was that in an initial sample described by the leading American exponent of Facilitated Communication (Biklen, 1993), thirteen percent of those who "spoke" using this new medium made allegations of sexual abuse.

Ultimately many children were removed from class work designed to teach autistic children basic skills (especially basic language skills) and placed in mainstream and mainstream content classes in which they participated and demonstrated their learning through FC (Biklen, 1993). Jacobsen (1993) estimated a rate of 132 million dollars per year were spent on expenses related to FC. Although the barrage of empirical evidence against facilitated communication has probably kept expenses far below that level, Levine, Shane and Wharton (1994) noted a shift of time and resources away from proven means of communication augmentation and towards FC. Numerous allegations of sexual abuse were made on the basis of FC, and parents, children, and providers have been removed from the home (Botash, Babuts, Mitchell, O'Hara, Lynch, & Manual, 1994; Pendergrast, 1995; Rimland, 1992). Testimony using facilitated communication has been allowed in court (Randall, 1993). Thompson (1994) describes the case of one father who was incarcerated for seven months on the basis of a facilitated accusation before the charges were dismissed.

Although it is not impossible for FC to work for someone who cannot communicate through language in any other way, this has yet to be demonstrated. However, it has been shown repeatedly that, in case after case of "FC," it was facilitators, not patients who were telling the stories, and that the facilitators were often speaking inaccurately (Smith, Haas, & Belcher, 1994;

Regal, Rooney, & Wandas, 1994; Vasquez, 1995). In other words, most FC can be understood as a form of ventriloquism. Nonetheless, as interviews with former facilitators seem to show, facilitators believed quite passionately that they had been allowing the patient to speak for herself or himself (Pendergrast, 1995, p. 564).

In many of the various schools of psychotherapy, patients achieve "insight" by telling biographical stories which fit the "insight" stories prominent in that school of psychotherapy. In this sense, patients end up speaking the psychotherapist's truths in what I see as a form of ventriloquism.

In speaking to a variety of therapists it seems interesting that depending on who I speak to I may hear stories of patients from all walks of life who realized in therapy that their suffering was caused by fears of inadequacy, incest, ritual abuse, unresolved Oedipal desires, disowned dependency needs, lack of self acceptance, "irrational oughts," undiagnosed biomedical conditions, undetectable brain lesions, or a crisis in spiritual development. Regardless of how closely the stories seem to match the therapists' own theories, I often hear the same certainty that the stories were revealed by the patients. The therapists just listened and provided a context in which the patients' truths could emerge.

In the course of my current work, I occasionally review a person's inpatient psychiatric records over several decades. I have been amazed at how many different and conflicting insights and revelations the same patient is purported to have had over the years with differing therapists. If you know therapists with markedly different orientations you might consider for a moment: given a very brief biographical sketch of a patient, could you predict the kinds of "insights" or "understanding" and the kinds of illness and healing narratives that might result from psychotherapy with each of these therapists?

Controversial New Narratives

The tendency towards "ventriloquism" combined with the willingness to claim knowledge of historical facts on the basis of creative narrative techniques is highly significant. These issues take on great urgency as they play a role in two of the most divisive controversies in psychotherapy today. Our understanding of these issues may have an impact on the future of psychotherapy and the lives of many therapy clients and their families. The most significant of these controversies is probably the recovered memory versus false memory debate. Still important is the debate over the nature, prevalence, and diagnosis of Multiple Personality Disorder (or Dissociative Identity Disorder), especially as related to alleged ritual cult abuse.

Ellen Bass and Laura Davis (Bass & Davis, 1988; Davis, 1990) are arguably the most influential of recent proponents of the recovery or de-repression of abuse memories through such creative narrative techniques as visualization, light trance induction, automatic writing, and creative/exploratory writing exercises.

Judging from the self report of many survivors of long remembered sexual abuse, *The Courage to Heal* (Bass & Davis, 1988) has helped many people who had experienced childhood sexual abuse to come to create an integrated life story which allowed them to confront their abuse and integrate it into an empowering tale of survivorship.

I am troubled by *The Courage to Heal* to the extent that it is used to "recover" memories of abuse. To begin with, any momentary inkling that one might have been abused is treated as the "true voice" of the reader. Every bit of narrative, every "voice" which contradicts or doubts this voice is to be silenced as thoroughly as possible. Thus, in the introduction Bass and Davis write:

> Often the knowledge that you were abused starts with a tiny feeling, an intuition. It's important to trust that inner voice and work from there. Assume your feelings are valid. So far, no one we've talked to thought she might have been abused, and then later discovered that she hadn't been. The progression always goes the other way, from suspicion to confirmation. If you think you were abused and your life shows the symptoms, then you were. (p. 22)

The feelings and the inner voice that one must trust are the feelings that say you are abused. Beliefs to the contrary are to be ignored (pp. 86–91). Counselors are told to "believe that your client was sexually abused, even if she sometimes doubts it herself" (p. 347), even as they are told "the client is the expert in her own healing" (p. 346). A process has begun by which a "tiny feeling" can be amplified to the point of certainty, while beliefs to the contrary become dissociated from the client.

Also, please note that while the reference to "symptoms" in the quotation above may seem reassuring, there is no specific set of symptoms listed. Any noteworthy experience or behavior can be tied conceptually to some story of abuse and thus be considered a symptom.

Bass and Davis (1988) suggest a number of ways in which an abuse narrative can be constructed for a woman who does not remember and/or believe that she was abused. For example, they recommend the technique of hypnotic age regression as a way "to regain memory" (p. 73) of the facts of the abuse. Davis (1990) recommends the use of techniques such as "automatic writing" to find out about what happened.

Bass and Davis (1988) also encourage the use of creative imaginative writing in two slightly different exercises. In the section "Healing Process" there is a writing exercise called "Reconstructing Family History":

> Irena Kepfisz ... developed an exercise that enables you to piece together things you can't possibly know about your history or the history of your family. This form of "remembering" which she calls imaginative

reconstruction" can be a valuable tool in coming to terms with people and patterns in your family. Although you write about things you couldn't realistically know, the result often seems chillingly realistic:

> Take an event in your family history that you can never actually find out about. It could be your father's childhood or the circumstances in your mother's life that kept her from protecting you. Using all the details you know, create your own story. Ground the experience or event in as much knowledge as you have and then let yourself imagine what actually might have happened. (p. 154)

This exercise is acknowledged to be a "reconstructing" exercise. It is not represented as a way to reveal historical "facts." Indeed, phrases such as "seems chillingly realistic" and "actually might have happened" make it clear that it is not a technique for discovering facts. This exercise seems like it could be a wonderful narrative tool which could be used to explore and come to terms with one's past and one's feelings about it.

On the other hand, a very similar technique is offered in the section entitled "Remembering." This exercise is called "what happened to you" and is presented as a method for uncovering facts. The instructions begin with the injunction to "write about your experience of being abused as a child," but the writer is also told:

> If you don't remember what happened to you, write about what you do remember. Recreate the context in which the abuse happened, even if you don't remember the specifics of the abuse yet. Describe where you lived as a child. What was going on in your family, your neighborhood, in your life. ... Start with what you have. When you utilize that fully, you usually get more. (p. 83)

This exercise does not does not call for the writer to "imagine." To do so, could undermine belief in the historical accuracy of the written accounts produced by this exercise. Instead a creative exploratory mood is called for, in which the writer is to write down just about whatever comes to mind:

> If you go off on tangents, don't pull yourself back too abruptly. Sometimes what may look irrelevant leads us to something more essential. Although you want to stay with the subject, do so with lose reins (p. 83). ... As with all writing exercises, try not to judge or censor. (p. 84)

Thus, the writer is told to write freely, to disengage from critical thinking, and to expect to "get" repressed memories of actual abuse.

Through the use of creative narrative techniques, the system provided by Bass and Davis can result in a narrative which has been created, guided, and shaped through readings, exercise and, often, psychotherapy. This narrative is treated as a repressed or concealed memory of actual events located elsewhere in time. Bass and Davis suggest that the objective reality of these new memories be fully embraced and that these memories form the basis for grieving and mourning (pp. 118–121), anger, and rage (pp. 122–132), disclosures, accusations and confrontations regarding the remembered abuse (pp. 133–148), and an emergency phase in which apparently happy functional lives become severely disrupted for prolonged periods of time (pp. 65–69). They also approve of a "weeding out" of relationships with family and friends depending on their willingness to support and confirm the new abuse narrative (pp. 68, 101). It is the real world consequences to the "survivors," the accused and their families which is at the heart of the intense controversy that currently surrounds their work and the idea of recovered abuse memories (Pendergrast, 1995; *Family Therapist Networker*, 1995).

Self-defined narrativists and constructivists have also made this sort of confusion between discovery and creation of narratives, with respect to multiple personality disorder (MPD) and recovered memories. Please note, I am using the term "multiple personality disorder" as opposed to "dissociative identity disorder" (DID) because it is the term used by the authors with whom I am concerned.

For example, Keen (1995) treats multiple personality disorder as a real disorder and the diagnoses of MPD as often involving the recovery of a true narrative of multiplicity which lies hidden beneath a false narrative of unity. Multiple personalities are uncovered through "a respectful hearing to discover the narrative dimensions of their lives" (p. 251, emphasis added). Keen also believes in the uncovering of factual, but unavailable memories, thus he refers to the "fact that people with MPD are often amnestic for their enactments" (p. 250).

McCann and Perlman (1993) offer a "constructivist self-development theory" in which they embrace the fundamental constructivist notion that "individuals construct and construe their own realities" (p. 188). McCann and Perleman hold the position that the formation of multiple personalities is often the consequence of ritual cult abuse.

Widespread belief in secret ritual abuse cults is a recent phenomenon, despite some similarities to earlier phenomena such as the Salem Witch trials, the inquisition and the era of the *Malleus Malificarum* (Victor, 1993). Belief in ritual abuse cults has been greatly fueled by "recovered" memories such as those related in *Michelle Remembers* (Smith & Pazder, 1980). Despite the attention given to ritual cult abuse, there is little evidence for their existence independent of recovered memories of cult activity (Pendergrast, 1995; Victor, 1993).

Within their constructivist framework, McCann and Perlman proceed to speak as if true memories of cult-organized ritual abuse and "real" pre-existing alters are discovered in therapy. Thus they speak of "the emergence of traumatic memories" (p. 191) and of alters, with scant evidence of any skepticism regarding the reality of such claims.

Summary and Conclusions

Narrative perspective and narrative techniques have a great deal to offer. This should be apparent from most of the chapters presented in this volume. I have argued elsewhere (Vogel, 1994) that by looking at all sorts of representations of the world (from scientific text, to descriptions of personal experience) as varieties of narrative we can view knowledge and claims about knowledge in a new and interesting light. Therapeutically, narrative techniques can be used to find new perspectives on life and life's problems, to see the way our stories affect us and to envision new stories.

But a narrative perspective comes with limitations that many theorists and therapists may not want to accept. Within a narrative perspective, we cannot establish discriminations between health and illness as a matter of fact, although we can make a case for certain notions on the basis of shared meanings and value commitments.

It is also inconsistent with a narrative perspective to claim to have immaculately recovered another person's true story or true voice. Furthermore, we can get into serious trouble when we attempt to establish historical facts on the basis of narrative techniques. I want to stress that these warnings apply equally to those who would reject recovered memories and to those who would "uncover" or de-repress them.

Nonetheless it is difficult (at least for me) to listen to people's stories about themselves and about the world without having a strong sense that many of us — not just those who are said to be clinically deluded — get into great trouble with our stories. It certainly seems that we can inhabit stories which make our commerce with the world far more confused and chaotic than some alternate stories would.

This leads to a clear problem. If I abandon realism how can I make these assertions without resorting to intuitionism or claims of special insight? For me, part of the solution is that we need to gain some humility about our abilities to know.

For me, this leads to a method which is closer to literary criticism than to science and which must necessarily forgo some of the claims to knowledge, proof and expertise which exist within a scientific discourse. What we need to build is a framework for the critical analysis of narrative, a sort of literary criticism which can be applied to belief narratives.

I imagine such literary criticism to be fully reflexive: it can be applied to the narratives of those sufferers who come for treatment, as well as to those who are practically or theoretically concerned with the process. My struggle to develop such a framework is incomplete. In the meantime, it is heartening to see that so many people with far more experience and knowledge than I have are involved in the fruitful and promising field of narrative.

References

Bass, E., & Davis, L. (1988). *The courage to heal: A guide for women survivors of child sexual abuse.* New York: Perennial Library.

Biklen, D. (1993). *Communication unbound: How facilitated communication is challenging traditional views of autism and ability-disability.* New York: Teachers College Press.

Botash, A. S., Babuts, D., Mitchell, N., O'Hara, M., Lynch, L., & Manuel, J. (1994). Evaluations of children who have disclosed sexual abuse via facilitated communication. *Archives of Pediatric Adolescent Medicine, 148,* 1282–1287.

Davis, L. (1990). *The courage to heal workbook: For women and men survivors of child sexual abuse..* New York: Perennial Library.

Dawes, R. M. (1994). *House of cards: Psychology and psychotherapy built on myth.* New York: The Free Press.

Efran, J. S., Lukens, R. J., & Lukens, M. D. (1988). Constructivism: What's in it for you? *Family Therapy Networker, 122,* 27–35.

Family Therapy Networker (1995). Special issue, "Fallen from Grace," entire.

Howard, G. S. (1991). Culture tales: A narrative approach to thinking, crosscultural psychology, and psychotherapy. *American Psychologist, 46,* 187–197.

Jacobson, J. (1993). *Worldwide perspective on facilitated communication: Parental research and theory.* Paper presented at the annual convention of the American Speech-Language and Hearing Association.

Levine, K., Shane, H. C., & Wharton, R. H. (1994). What if … : A plea to professionals to consider the risk-benefit ratio of facilitated communication. *Mental Retardation, 32,* 300–304.

Mahoney, M. J. (1988). Constructivist metatheory I: Basic features and historical foundations. *International Journal of Personal Construct Psychology, 1,* 1–35.

McCann, L., & Perlman, L. A. (1993). Constructivist self-development theory: A theoretical model of psychological adaptation to severe trauma. In D. K. Sakheim & S. E. Devine (Eds.) *Out of darkness: Exploring Satanism and ritual abuse.* New York: Lexington Books.

Neimeyer, R. A. (1995) Constructivist psychotherapies: Features, foundations, and future directions. In R. A. Neimeyer & M. J. Mahoney, (Eds.) *Constructivism in psychotherapy* (pp. 231–246). Washington, DC: American Psychological Association.

Nietzsche, F. (1969a). *The gay science.* (W. Kaufmann & R. J. Hollingdale, Transl.) New York: Random House.

Nietzsche, F. (1969b). *Thus spake Zarathustra.* (R. J. Hollingdale, Transl.) Harmondsworth, UK: Penguin Books.

Pendergrast, M. (1995) *Victims of memory: Incest accusations and shattered lives.* Hinesburg, VT: Upper Access Books

Randall, G. (1993, March 30). Disabled boy gives landmark testimony. *The Wichita Eagle,* pp. 1a, 8a.

Regal, R. A., Rooney, J. R., & Wandas, T. (1994). Facilitated communication: An experimental evaluation. *Journal of Autism & Developmental Disorders, 24,* 345–355.

Rimland, B. (1992). Facilitated communication: Now the bad news. *Autism Research Review International, 6,* 3.

Smith, M. D., Haas, P. J., & Belcher, R. G. (1994). Facilitated communication, the effects of facilitator knowledge and level of assistance on output. *Journal of Autism & Developmental Disorders, 24,* 357–367.

Smith, M. D., & Pazder, L. (1980). *Michelle remembers.* New York: Gongdon & Lattes.

Thompson, T. (1994). Review of *Communication unbound. American Journal of Mental Retardation, 98,* 670–673.

Vasquez, C. A. (1995). Failure to confirm the word-retrieval problem hypothesis in facilitated communication. *Journal of Autism & Developmental Disorders, 25,* 597–610.

Victor, J. S. (1993). *Satanic panic: The creation of a contemporary legend.* Chicago: Open Court Press.

Vogel, D. (1994). Narrative perspectives in theory and therapy. *Journal of Constructivist Psychology, 7,* 243–261.

CHAPTER FIVE

Cody's Story:
Transformations in Healing

Susan W. Schwartz

Each atom of this universe, conscious of its sickness,
procures for itself within or without, a means for its restoration.

Hazrat Inayat Khan, Sufi master

"Those who have ears to hear, let them hear." So bespoke a master storyteller of healing, Jesus of Nazareth, according to the biblical gospels. Yet Jesus preached in parables; his language imparted directives, indirectly. Possibilities for transformation were portrayed in tales that instructed but did not impose. Listeners discerned meaning commensurate with their predisposed abilities to perceive and receive. The choice was theirs to respond as they would, as best they could, reflective of their natures (Campbell, 1968).

This chapter will focus on a narrative of personal healing with respect to the capacity of the genre to serve as therapeutic device for self and others. It is posited that the endeavor to reconstruct lived experience into narrative form promotes organization of consciousness and thereby inherently advances healing even if, paradoxically, one's response suggests avoidance or denial. For, despite appearances, in any given moment of a lifespan, three consequences of shaping challenging events into storied structures often result: insight, inspiration, and liberation. These are considered for their value in healing.

As the opening comments imply, a story might assist healing and yet not patently address the topic. Conversely, an explicit account of healing may for some simply tell a tale. Quintessentially, then, it is the interaction between a listener's consciousness and a story that allows it agency as a restorative means. It has been said we often do not know our thoughts until we hear ourselves speak — a reminder that a creator-narrator is concomitantly a listener and therefore an active recipient as well. Outward communion, as in shared narrative, may generate connections that further refine awareness of a given matter and expand perspectives on it. For exclusive of dialogue, external verbalization provides another listening mode for the speaker. This, in itself, can make prominent what internal monologue may overlook, helping to approach situations anew.

In recent decades, the tremendous outpouring of personal accounts on myriad experiences of healing (Angelou, 1970; Biro, 2000; Brinkley, 1994: Broyard, 1992; Carter, 1993; Duff, 1993; Harvey, 1991; Middlebrook, 1996; Rollin, 1976; Sacks, 1984; Schneider, 1987; Sizemore & Pitillo, 1977) reflects recognition that this manner of expression holds appeal. Desire to inform, support, inspire, and shape community are among the stated motivations (Cousins, 1979; Frank, 1991; Moss, 1981; Sattilaro, 1982; Simpson, 1982). Presumably, listeners respond in kind. Stories can likewise engender sensibilities of kindred and/or novel experience. Either may enhance one's perspective, fostering lucidity that confers greater coherence and depth of understanding. Thus, there is perhaps a quiet hope, as well, that the openness which narratives of personal lived experience assume to embrace can heal collective wounds and advance societal well-being (Delany & Delany, 1993; Graham, 1997; Mandela, 1994; McNamara, 1995; Palmer, 1987; Rosenbaum, 1988; Van Devanter, 1983).

Relatedly, Lightfoote (1992) acknowledged illness narratives as a distinct category worthy of exploration. Investigation of these testimonies, she observed, might further biomedicine's purported ideal of achieving the highest levels possible for individual health. Kleinman (1988) appreciated the illness narrative as a multi-task organizational tool. It enables meaningful structure of one's salient illness events; thereby provides an effective means to communicate them, and thus richly assists the clinician in strategizing therapeutic supports and treatments. Likewise of import, "over the long course of chronic disorder, these model texts shape and even create experience" (p. 49). Hunter (1991) presented a superb exposition on the narrative form as the actual basis for all biomedical knowledge, theoretical and applied. Indeed, most healing systems rely on elements of narrative discourse to discern diagnosis and treatment, although the exchange may not necessarily be vocalized or take place between healer and healee (Eliade, 1972; Harner, 1980; Krippner & Villoldo, 1976).

Moreover, the stories we tell ourselves and others, and the mind-sets from which we speak, are increasingly understood to impact individual and collective realities (Bateson, 1991; Bly, 1990; Campbell & Moyers, 1988; Church, 1996; Deveare Smith, 1992, 1994; Eisler, 1987; Feinstein & Krippner, 1988; Gray, 1992; Larsen, 1976; Pennebaker, 1995; Tannen, 1990). The power of consciousness to create has long been declared in spiritual and metaphysical traditions (Bailey, 1960; Leadbeater, 1978; Nhat Hahn, 1987; Thurston & Fazel, 1992). Advances in high technology eventually prompted consideration of this view in diverse scientific and medical fields (Achterberg, 1985; Beck & Beck, 1987; Bohm, 1980; Borysenko & Borysenko, 1994; Capra, 1984; Chopra, 1990; Dossey, 1993; Flowers & Grubin, 1993; Hunt, 1996; Isenberg, Lehrer, & Hochron, 1992; Jasnoski & Kugler, 1987; Locke & Colligan, 1986; Pelletier, 1977; Pert, 1997; Rider & Achterberg, 1989; Shealy, 1999; Tart, 1993). These realizations signal the importance of attending to what we construct in consciousness for the welfare of all creation, human and otherwise.

Storied Sources

Sample material was drawn primarily from data gathered for a doctoral dissertation (Schwartz, 2003). Research participants were asked, via taped, in-person interviews, for detailed descriptions of their lived experiences of healing when dealing with life-threatening illness. The resulting transcripts were then studied with attention to the transformations of consciousness undergone. Of note, each person had previously shared aspects of their illness-healing journeys with others. Two respondents had told extensive versions to select audiences via oral presentations. They were further portrayed in published accounts — either their own (Tate, 1989, 1991) or as part of another's inquiry into healing. (For reasons of confidentiality, the latter, out of print work, is not cited.) Despite these prior tellings, each respondent reportedly still found fresh benefit in the comprehensive telling required for this study.

Although the primary speaker was the respondent, the research narratives developed in the context of dialogue. Thus the interviewer, through directives, probing, and presence, had substantial impact on the form and content of data. Each participant's healing pilgrimage was dense with relevant, intriguing episodes. However, the material of only one respondent, Cody, will be focused upon here. For in the course of data-gathering, incidents transpired which in microcosm presented compelling, mutlifaceted examples of how realms of consciousness may interplay through narrative exchange to foster healing.

Modifications

To preserve the natural force of the events, much of the material is offered in Cody's voice. This approach reiterates belief in the personal narrative as a prime didactic tool. I hope it will also allow the reader the pleasure of discovery in the transformations that developed, comparable to that appreciated by Cody and myself.

Ellipses denote omission of text: (…) for one or several words, (….) for lengthier segments. An underline (___) denotes a brief pause; extended pauses are noted in parentheses. Quotes from the raw data were occasionally edited in a limited manner to increase readability. For instance, utterances such as "uh" have been deleted. These adjustments were not thought to alter the meaning of content nor to impinge upon the integrity of the speaker's expression. Because the material derives from unpublished research data, citations are limited to Cody's initial ("C") and the transcript pages.

As prelude, a limited recounting of early events in Cody's tale is provided for background. Perforce, many incidents are excluded and much of the complexity is deleted from those included.

Cody's Story

Cody was in his mid-thirties, with a wife and infant daughter, when he left his white collar office job, one day, to receive a regularly scheduled allergy shot. His treatment regimen had been standard for almost a decade, with no apparent negative effects. However, this routine had been interrupted for several months due to extra demands on his time as a result of his newborn. To accommodate the disruption, Cody received shots reduced in strength. On this occasion, uniquely, there was a painful reaction to one of them, and it appeared to precipitate degenerative nerve damage. Cody rather quickly began to experience loss of motor control. Early biomedical evaluation suggested a demyelinating episode was occurring, with multiple sclerosis indicated.

Medication appropriate to this disorder was prescribed. Cody did not take the medication initially, though once started, it did not lessen the numbness. A progressive loss of sensory feedback continued to spread throughout his body despite interventions with other medications. Biomedical assessment was also ongoing. Cody was now diagnosed as having a rapidly growing tumor in his spinal cord. Because of the severity of this condition, emergency surgery was scheduled. It was the day before Thanksgiving. Cody was led to believe he would either die on the operating table, or survive as a quadriplegic. He prepared for his death psychologically, and took practical measures to arrange financial and emotional support for his family after his demise.

The operation was performed: Cody's spinal cord was exposed. No tumor was found! Instead, the cord was revealed to be massively injured. But Cody neither died, nor did he become paralyzed. Post-surgery, sensory feedback returned. Although it was unclear which was most contributory to this outcome, the operation itself, or the increased level of medication he had received during it, Cody was often in excruciating physical pain as he recuperated from surgery. Various strategies for pain control were employed, including imagery — a technique Cody found intellectually captivating and physiologically very effective. He sought and received assistance from family, friends, health care providers, and people knowledgeable about multiple sclerosis. Cody's brother (an occupational therapist) and one biomedical intern proved to be especially supportive. Cody's demyelinating episode was idiopathic; its etiology remains unknown (as is presently the case for multiple sclerosis as well). An experimental dosage of steroid medication was tried and found successful.

> And just as this neurologic thing had crept upon me, I could feel it creeping away. I was discharged two weeks later—walking under my own

power. Tipsy and…beginning to taper off the steroids. It would take two years. I've now been off them for ten months. And…I'm quite well [despite] problems with heat, and other things that are typical of multiple sclerosis. The point that thwarts the typical diagnosis is that's the only lesion they ever found. There hasn't been any additional occurrences. So it's technically single sclerosis. But there is no such disease. Therefore, they call it a demyelinating episode. Acute atypical demyelinating episode is the technical diagnosis. (C, p. 14)

Days in the Life

Cody found his initial research interview (the only one anticipated by him or myself) engaging. "It's been a very moving experience … I hope you'll track me for the rest of my life" (C, p. 38). Unexpectedly, four months later, a form of tracking did indeed begin. Cody, sounding desperate, called with an urgent request for me to come over immediately and bring my tape recorder. At the outset of this encounter, aware of his predicament, Cody asked if our research relationship could serve as therapy. This option had likewise not been antici- pated. It was now an issue for the respondent because, in his moment of need, the impulse was to *talk it out* in narrative exchange, in a setting which seemed safe and amenable.

Cody was offered the choice of speaking outside the scope of the research — taped or not. For, if he decided to operate within it, whatever he chose to share would become data. Participants were regularly cautioned in this regard. When- ever I felt prompted to issue a reminder, I did. In the heightened intimacy that typically develops in this interview context, sensitive revelations may leave one quite vulnerable. Regardless of the research benefits such disclosures can provide, protection of a respondent remains paramount. Cody decided to proceed in the research mode. " … somehow the officialness helps me" (C, p. 40). For all my earlier pronouncements, events took on a life of their own — often of a decidedly therapeutic turn. (Too, taping was stopped when material was judged not to be recounting phenomenological experience relevant to healing.) Cody introduced his reasons for requesting this meeting by stating why his outlook on our initial interview, and his perception of our connection had unexpectedly, and signifi- cantly, altered.

> There was nothing at stake. And this is___ something really important here. I was describing something that happened. It was pleasant___to have the opportunity to carry on at length. I was surprised when sud- denly___I needed___some solution. And I didn't know where to turn. Suddenly the stakes went way up. I was on the precipice of something. And I didn't know what. It's clear to me, that's the minute that___our

relationship changed from researcher and whatever I am called in such a thing, to___you know, patient and___clinician, therapist, counselor. (C, p. 62)

The discussion which had followed was extremely powerful for the respondent and riveting for me as the researcher. The session was transformative. Later, Cody cited elements of its form that he believed enabled healing.

The particular thing about the research that made it right___I don't think enough can be stressed on the personality of the person that I'm talking to. I either feel like talking with you or I don't. I…I can open it up to you, or I can't. But it's also that___we don't get a set half hour and then it's all done. And it's supposed to be fixed…by then. There's something about the research that, you know, obviously you're here to capture all that there is to be captured. And that gives me a great opportunity to let it all out. Regardless of how much time it takes to let it out.…As I said, if this is gonna take two or three hours___here's a person I can take it with. We got the rapport. We have the mechanism. And I don't have to worry about being told___time's up. That gave me safety. I said: "We can do something with this." And, you know, it's taken three years, really, to get to this point.

Once you were in my apartment (little laugh/sigh) I didn't want to let you out. Because I knew we could do this now.…I was in a very needy state. I mean, I wasn't calculating in my mind, anything. Other than___take a chance, call Susan. Tell her that there's a healing thing about___somewhere. Get your tape recorder. I gotta say somethin.' And it was all emotion. It was a very affective day…You know, I can't tell you what it is about the research [in] particular, other than you were available. And___we have a rapport. I mean you have, you have a way…And clearly there's an agenda to this research that brought me___to the emotions. That's the part that worked. (C, p. 51)

To my dismay, however, the majority of the session was not caught on tape. (While not recommended, this is another way to safeguard respondents' privacy!) Difficulties with the equipment, indiscernible at the time, prevented recording beyond the first several minutes. The mishap was discovered within hours. Within days Cody and I met again, not to reenact what had occurred, but to discuss the lost data for research purposes. That content dealt with several recent incidences which had created conditions Cody found untenable.

I learned that my neighbor, two houses down, who's my age, passed away___from a tumor, two nights ago, leaving behind two children the age of my daughter, and a wife who I've met—and…established a short, small rapport [with] when my daughter played with…her children, some year ago. I've noticed that they've been absent from the street, over the last year. And I made some comments___about that (clears throat) to my wife. And….the other night when the…rescue squad came, around midnight, I noticed that they came and left the house within minutes—ten minutes total. And I said to myself and to my wife: "Gee, the only time…when I was a rescue person, that I ever came and left the house that quick, was when somebody passed away—usually somebody old."…And I went to bed that night thinking about___those times…years ago. The next day I learned that it wasn't an old person at all. That it was the husband of the woman I had met___whose children played with mine. (C, p. 39)

I got the news from a neighbor that this other fellow died and almost immediately I___this big cement block went up around me. And I didn't know what to do with it. And…went into that night and had this dream. I, I woke at 3:00 in the morning___almost hyperventilating. And I woke my wife and told her I had a nightmare. And couldn't she, would she please make it better for me___I needed some soothing words. And she gave me a few, and we all went back to sleep. Or at least I tried to. In the morning the dream remained vivid. It does to this day. (C, p. 42)

Lobster Dream

Cody and his wife were on a beautiful, sparsely inhabited tropical island, similar to the place where they had spent their honeymoon. They were walking on the beach. All of a sudden Cody noticed hundreds of lobsters. The dream scenes were all in blacks, whites, and grays. But one lobster was vivid — in red and yellow stripes. Cody felt the lobster to be an ominous presence. Cody pretended he wanted to view the other islands, playing the interested tourist. But really he knew he wished to escape that lobster. Even when Cody was safely away, he periodically would look over his shoulder, half anticipating the lobster to be in hot pursuit. Then Cody was somehow back with the lobster, which was now clinging to someone's pants leg, around the calf. Cody felt frightened by the pincers of the lobster, envisioning they could shred him, or somebody, to death. To his surprise, when he peered more closely, Cody realized the lobster had a face he recognized — it was the face of Jacqueline Onassis. While staring at this lobster, which maintained its grip on another's leg as it stared back at him, Cody felt he had to decide whether to stay or flee. He chose to flee. Cody awoke from the dream terrified and in a cold sweat.

In the lost session, when reminded of his decision to flee, Cody had had a strong response. He addressed it in the review session:

I just didn't know I was feeling that way. But it's when I said that, in describing this dream, I…I feel tearful even now thinking of that moment. I burst into tears. Hearing those words in my ears made it obvious to me, at that minute, that this was what the real problem was___with the news I heard down the street. (extended pause) And the…the message of my dream was I didn't know whether to flee, or stay. I don't know how to help the family. I feel that I should. Because the fellow who died was my age. He has two children. I'm about to have two children. (extended pause) That could have been me. (extended pause) And I don't know what to do about that. (C, p. 44)

That's really the dream. And the realization that it brought me to by talking about it. And…just to reflect for a minute, it's a very difficult place to know when___what to do with the feeling of wanting to run, or wanting to help. (extended pause) I don't think I've ever had that quandary, ever. I've never hesitated to help—even when my life was in some physical danger. From the days of my rescue squad…and days after that, when I've placed myself in peril…to physically help an injured person. But to actually have the rescuer___come to a moment of being afraid. Gee, you know, it kind of destroys my entire sense of identity—at least for a minute. (extended pause) And I don't want to admit that I'm afraid. That's why I think…I just didn't know how to immediately deal with the news that a man down the street had died from a tumor. (C, p. 45)

The narrative exchange fostered by the research mediated some of Cody's avoidance and resistance to this situation. The terror regarding the lobster figure dissipated once he acknowledged his fear as triggered by this recent death. Cody's tearful release and insight brought immediate cessation to his sense of being encased in cement. It "lifted___lifted right away" (C, p. 46). (Once he removed his blockage in consciousness, the kinesthetically-felt block was no longer experienced.) Moreover, when asked to recall the moment right before he burst into sobs (during the lost session), Cody reconsidered the image of the lobster and received another insight.

Well, I remember it very well. And I remember the distaste I had in myself, over fleeing. It felt wrong all the time. And at the same time I remember being afraid, you know, for my life. This lobster looked like it was going to shred me to pieces….But when I looked more carefully, and a little bit longer (extended pause) instead of acting to save the person to whom the lobster was attached, I saw this lobster looking hurt___clutching___ looking for nurturance, sustenance. And I thought: Oh, here's something that needs my help….I, I better reach down. Maybe I should hold it, and cradle it. Then I thought: Don't get too close. It'll…it'll pinch you. Its razor sharp claws will shred you to pieces. (C, p. 54)

There was a lobster with the face of Jacqueline Onassis on it. And I didn't know whether to be terrorized by it…or___help it or run away. And that was a very blubbering moment for me. To admit that I didn't know whether to help or run. (C, p. 56)

Yet the fearful ambivalence felt in the dream state toward the lobster figure, and the cognitive dissonance (Festinger, 1957) it generated, no longer lingered in the waking state once Cody's horror of it was gone. Providing further narrative on the lobster, moreover, had given birth to a new perspective. Not only did the person seeming attacked need help, so perhaps, did the attacker: the emblem of wounding at once embodied woundedness. Still, puzzlement remained about the ambiguous symbolism in his dream and continued to absorb Cody. Unaware that his efforts to comprehend it had extended beyond his musings in ordinary reality, he was delighted and surprised when his consciousness produced answers from other quarters.

The engagement of dreams to problem-solve for the waking state — consciously intended or not — has yielded many innovative responses, as the literatures on dream work, creativity, and problem-solving demonstrate (Faraday, 1972; Krippner, 1990; Vernon, 1971). Over the last century, attention to dreams has fluctuated historically as a source of interest between scientific and popular domains in the United States and Europe. In recent decades, however, this rich resource is increasingly being explored in both arenas (Krippner, 1993). LaBerge and Rheingold (1991) crossed the divide. They offer the populace methods to induce lucid dreaming — that striking phenomenon in which one is conscious and alert while in the dream state — as a means to research its possibilities and enhance the quality of ordinary reality. For Cody, it was less common to have a waking state response serve as a resolution to his dreams. Several weeks after the review session, Cody yet again requested a meeting to discuss exactly that occurrence.

I think there's sort of been three phases to this research. The first is when you called me and said: Hey, you wanna do something? The second was when I told you: Something has just happened in my mind. I need you.…And unfortunately, as you already recorded…that___recording process failed. Although the healing process took a giant leap forward. And the third one is this moment. In a word…there comes a moment when something really terrible happens. And you say to yourself: Uh oh! I'm in trouble. And.…that's when I called you.…And that was, as I described in the rehash of that lost session, that my neighbor had passed away. It was bothering me greatly, in some___unknown way. And I had

had a dream....with (sigh) things in it that meant something. They were representative of what I was thinking and feeling. And I just didn't know what they were. And I needed some help to get it___all sorted out. And you offered some___perspectives.

Well, now in this third phase, something else has happened. I put the pieces together. They just fit. (extended pause) The solution has everything to do with an item in that dream....It was (sigh) that this face on this lobster was Jacqueline Onassis. And I just couldn't figure it out. And it's been haunting me ever since. Why exactly? I mean, although she represents a hurt fawn in our society. But, really, why exactly? And that's just been a loose piece floating out there. That I never really knew was going to come and fall into place. Boy, did it fall into place....And the specific is...that the pieces have fallen together. They've connected with something that I grew up with. And something that happened. (extended pause) I read in an obituary___that my neighbor passed away. And that night or a day later had the dream. I'd like to give you that obituary. And I'd actually like to have you read it....And I have no doubt that you're gonna get a revelation about how dream process can work to confound people—but also to free them up. (C, p. 56)

I read the obituary, quickly grasped the relevant point, and confirmed it with Cody.

I don't know why that escaped me for so long. When it came to me, I was driving down the road. I don't know where I was. And my mind has been constantly musing that situation, that dream, that intense need to release the guilt I felt about not being able to help. But seeing myself as a helping person. It was an identity crash. And suddenly....when I reviewed the obituary in my mind—not reading it, but in my mind—I suddenly realized the woman's name was Jacqueline. (C, p. 57)

This gift from Cody's unconscious was presented when he was actively seeking to resolve a problem. It is unclear whether he was actually pondering his dream concerns at the instant of his insight or whether, his concerns having incubated, this lucid solution appeared unexpectedly, out of context. Either way it was a collaboration of consciousness realms in a kind of conversation. Although functioning in ordinary reality (driving a car), an altered state of mind was also operant. Reportedly unaware of his physical surroundings, Cody was perhaps intensely focused, or the reverse, somewhat meditative. Nevertheless, his states of mind were seemingly conducive to enabling this cognitive connection, which produced his strong sense of consonance. Cody's attained answer conjoined with these either/or possibilities for its delivery, corroborate the multiform and seamless flow of consciousness (although the conscious self may experience boundaries), and its propensity for meaningful, coherent constructs.

Expressions of consciousness are not always accessible to, or understood by, the conscious mind. Still, when there is comprehension one can, at times, retrospectively, trace synchronistic events that seemed to abet resolutions, and discern what had registered in attention, despite apparent unawareness. For instance, the obituary had mentioned the first name of the deceased's wife. I reminded Cody how unvarying he had been in referring to Onassis as Jacqueline, never any of the names more commonly used by the mainstream media. He had been so consistent about this, that I had silently observed it at the time, and thought it, perhaps, a sign of respect. The obituary also stated the family's surname, which began with "K." I now commented on this fact (although at this juncture I had had no idea of its significance).

> Yeah, and in fact her name isn't Jackie. It's Jacqueline. And all the time I'm thinking to myself why Jacqueline Kennedy, Jacqueline Onassis, Jacqueline___whatever her last name is? But it was clearly her face. What I still haven't resolved, and may never, is___why a lobster? And why a red and yellow striped (little laugh) lobster? But those are some of the details that matter much less than figuring out this…you know, Fellini film running in my dreams — that puts these___representations and meanings together like that.

> ….Why should I choose Jacqueline Onassis as the icon? Why not the real Jacqueline, down the street, for the face of this lobster? And I dug a little bit back into my mind. And I remember that there have been times that I've watched my father—at significant moments of political history coming across our television set—very, very upset. And I never quite knew why. In a word, when___Jack Kennedy was killed, my father cried for days. (extended pause) I remember him crying in front of the radio. When Robert Kennedy was killed, I remember seeing my father crying in front of the television set. As though something personal had happened to him. And I had inferred from that, that well, when politicians are killed, it affects American fathers. [Cody was a young boy at this time.] But I hadn't seen many American fathers affected like that, really, since then. Something didn't compare.

> And I recently received an autobiography from my father. With some things in it that I never knew before. That he grew up in the political circle of Washington, D.C.___watching these politicians. [Socializing in the White House and Congress were part of Cody's father's childhood.] And had always wondered if he would be one of them. He took it as a personal thing—not just as a national trauma. But to see Jack Kennedy

killed, on television, was something that affected my father deeply. And, of course, I watched my father. And I was affected deeply by my Dad. A connection comes full circle. That's why Jacqueline Onassis. She is the broken fawn....But not of my nation—of my father. The connection comes very clear to me. That (extended pause) Jacqueline Kennedy meant something to my Dad. And through him, she meant something to me.

That's the point of this reading. And I guess my point of this is, isn't it interesting how healing works? There can be floating pieces, puzzles that don't come together. They can last a lifetime. Or suddenly, if you're lucky, the pieces fit. And my goodness, the feeling of wholeness that you have. I felt the need to tell you this. And to document this....I'm very glad this research exists. I...don't know how to say that stronger. I don't think I would have had the opportunity to sort this out. And to, and to declare victory. That's what I wanted to do. The last time we went on tape, I was declaring trauma. And now I'm declaring victory. And I've held this now for___I haven't described this connecting with this obituary to anyone...I wanted to keep it fresh in my mind. Because I wanted it to...sort of spill out emotively right here. And also because I think you've seen, and shared with me, that moment when I felt so traumatized by that dream. I also wanted you to share with me, for the first time, the description and the letting out of the victory...I've sort of held this party in abeyance. And now it's time to toss the balloons. Do you understand? (C, pp. 57–58)

Cody's choice to save his moments of illumination as contributions to the research suggests not just a generosity of spirit, but also tribute to the process of shared narrative (here ostensibly in the research interview mode). This medium cultivated understanding in both participants — for the form as well as the content.

I think in particular___[it was] the way in which you___you proceeded on your line of questioning and challenge___when we were in that session. If I came to an interpretation about the dream___you weren't afraid to say: "Gee, I'm not so sure. I think, for example, Jacqueline Onassis is a hurt being in this life, in this time." And I, I didn't think of that. You know, I thought of___gee, I don't know why she was on the face of the lobster....I couldn't figure it out. And you challenged my interpretation...I thought, for example, that because she was wealthy, and the lobster was, was a mean and nasty device come to attack me that___I feel bad about not being wealthy enough to protect my family. That made as much sense to me at the time. But___it didn't feel entirely right. And I know that. Because when you challenged me with this hurt___suddenly___I was in the world of hurt. This was a hurt lobster. Jackie Onassis is a hurt person. (C, p. 53)

I had remarked that for all Jacqueline Onassis' social position and material wealth, she was not protected from experiencing deep hurt in her life. (And, as later became apparent, she seemed to experience her greatest trauma as Jacqueline K. rather than as Jacqueline O.) I also commented on the lobster being a crustacean with a hard outer shell and soft innards — seeing a parallel with Cody's vulnerability when part of his protective vertebra had been removed to access his spinal cord. I had likewise reminded us that lobsters molt, noting this as a transformative quality. Clearly, I felt quite free to share my own associations and insights. Delaney (1993), in a brief overview of several contemporary methods of dream interpretation, observed that theoretically the approaches show growing respect for the dreamer of the dream, with deference to that person's conscious "thoughts and feelings" (p. 8) about them. However, clinical observation suggested that, in practice, despite those intentions, when assisting interpretation, dreamworkers tend to be a bit more imposing. The research *interview/dream discussion* noted here tends to support Delaney's comments. Realizing this in response to his remarks, I laughingly conveyed to Cody that by guiding him I had further deviated from the kind of interview I was supposed to be conducting. The session had long since moved into an interactive counseling mode. Fortunately, nonetheless, Cody's responses suggest that he felt himself to have benefited from the deviations.

Well you, you had to follow my lead if this was gonna give to me what I needed. [Or]…we wouldn't have accomplished___facing pain. (extended pause) I wouldn't have___gotten in touch with, with this hurt that I was feeling. I (sputters a bit)___even thinking about Jacqueline Onassis as, as a person deserving of compassion—as I said, I___she's always had money. [It] allowed me to realize___wait, you know, she's not an icon of wealth. She's an icon of hurt. And, and suddenly I could, I could face it. (C, p. 53)

Discussion prompted insights that inspired Cody to further efforts, and furthered cognizance. When Cody had the realization which induced an awareness of wholeness, it came with distinct sensibilities.

A feeling happened, when I recov[ered], when I realized___why—I…was driving down the road. It was almost as though I had a physical sensation of being___I,…how do you say it? (extended pause)….Like a mind-body integration, or something like this. But___I felt whole. And I hadn't been feeling whole since I heard the news about my neighbor dying from a tumor, leaving two children. And suddenly it came together. And I felt—this is what a healing feels like. Healing has a feeling. Just like traumatizing has a feeling. And they're in the same bucket. But they're somehow profound, life-changing, threatening, consuming. Everything you think and do, from the moment after a trauma, is always compared with the trauma. And so after a healing. (C, p. 57)

It has a physical sensation. It feels___physically light—as opposed to heavy. And I think anybody knows what heavy feels like. (C, p. 59)

Truly, for Cody, this narrative research approach had brought about significant change.

I just feel a whole lot less needy today. And…you know, this…process of being able to talk about this stuff, in itself, has brought about___healing. That's___you know…that's just___the only point I can make. How? I don't know. It just has. The by-product of this research is not just data. Data for you—but I've employed you, here. And I've come out of this. (pause/sigh) And I don't think I would. I had nowhere to turn, really—other than this. I mean, I would have carried this kind of sick feeling in the pit of my belly. Hiding, even more—and even longer. I had nowhere to go with it. (C, p. 54)

I suggested that we do not know that, for certain. But I was glad to have been of service. Often the ramifications of acts are not known, for certain. Like the proverbial pebble thrown into water, incidents create ripple effects. When Cody first learned of his neighbor's death, it was extremely unsettling. A marked connection in consciousness was forged.

And when I heard that he died of a tumor___something happened in my mind. I…became afraid___I went back to that place that___was scary. That moment at the desk at the hospital when I signed the paper that had the…diagnosis on it for intramedullary tumor. There was that word again. It's the second time I've heard it now in three years___in a real situation. And suddenly that piece of paper came to my mind. I have to have it. This is important. People do die from this. It's not in my imagination.…And to put that word behind me—or in a place that I can manage it—I need the paper. I need the instrument___of the message. (C, p. 40)

Salaman (1982), the Russian novelist and biographer, perceived a distinction between *involuntary* and *conscious* memories. Observation of her own and other writers' work led her to notice that the former seems to appear when an intense focus in attention relates to them. As if waiting to be revealed, they are drawn into conscious awareness. Too, "an involuntary memory has this in common with the solution of an artistic, mathematical, or any other problem: it is a swift and usually unexpected contribution of the unconscious mind, while the conscious mind is taking infinite pains, yet almost immediately one recognizes its validity, and claims it as one's own" (Salaman, 1982, p. 59). She also noted that an involuntary memory of an event brings emotions of the past strongly and directly into the present. The sensibility is that *then* becomes *now*. For Cody, involuntary memory of a particular moment on admission to the hospital created a reaction that started churning in him as other events unfolded.

> This sort of came in a revelation to me yesterday....[which] has to do with___a missing___piece of paper at the hospital that___stated the diagnosis in stark terms. The only time I saw that diagnosis. And a diagnosis___that has the connotation of imminent death attached to it. The paper said___an operation being laminectomy for intramedullary tumor. I knew what the word tumor meant. But I didn't know laminectomy. And I didn't know intramedullary. Within the hour I got on the phone to someone and I asked them what it meant...And (clears throat) it came very real to me that we weren't just biopsying for___a small little lesion to see what it looks like. They were going to cut my spinal cord in half. I didn't see any way that this was going to result in anything other than___eventual death. And some great trouble___painful___paralyzed trouble—with everything___being effected....And that moment I became___hypervigilant to my situation. Everything hinged on every second from that moment forward....By a process of this research, I've been attempting to produce that paper. Not even thinking that it was important to me. [Documentation of the specific problem(s) in need of healing had been requested.] And that, in itself, is becoming a problem for me, emotionally. (C, p. 39)

Cody intuited what he needed to help himself heal.

> The piece of paper, itself, sort of glows in my memory. And I'd like to see that very piece of paper___sort of looking like so much pulp on the table with no glow to it at all (catch/laugh in voice) in, in this time, far away from when I was in the middle of facing this___very intrusive surgery...I'd like to see those words again. And realize how unempowered they are. How...they can't affect me anymore. And yet at the same time to piece that together with the fact that this fellow down the street died of a tumor. How do I reconcile the problem that this paper, with this diagnosis, has no power? And yet, that diagnosis does have the power to kill. It's a problem in my mind. It's a problem in my emotions. It's a problem in my dreams. (C, p. 41)

Seeing that piece of paper would help me realize, yup, in fact it did happen. And looking at it lying there on the table, powerless, with me sitting there with all of my, my hair combed and everything, that___I lived. For three years—and I'm sure of it—for three years I've been convinced that I dropped dead. And that I'm not here….There was some sort of surrealistic thing that said: "I'm finished. This is it." I've never quite exactly said, since then: "Hmm, maybe I actually lived." Well this guy died down the street. He's gone. And I'm here. That juxtaposition, between us, sort of woke me up. (extended pause) And…I don't know, I kinda feel like___gee, maybe there's still things to be done. And not just sweeping the floor. That's, that's more healing than I've done__in a while. I mean, I got a future. (C, p. 47)

After several attempts by phone and two visits to the hospital, Cody and I finally obtained his medical records. Additional conscious connections were formed, and transformed — to promote coherence and salience.

In a word, we found the paperwork. The missing paperwork from that hospital that___stated the admitting diagnosis—which was intramedullary tumor. Certainly something that spells death. No matter how you define it. And [that] I could put them (the words of the diagnosis) in their place, too, is___not only liberating—it's connecting. And that's the, the other, I think, major word of the day. We found those___surgical reports. And I, you know, I was so afraid. I didn't even know why that paperwork was missing. We found out it was just misfiled. But I thought maybe somebody was pulling something over on me. They didn't want to admit their mistake. I was looking for a rat in every hole. What's wrong with these missing words? Because the stigma that came with those words was absolutely terrorizing. I had to see those words in written form again. So I could connect them___with my experience, my history. And now I can tuck 'em away. They don't carry the, the force in my memory. Because I've just seen them again. They are now part of my memory, again. And now my memory says: "It's okay. It was okay." As opposed to the last time I saw those words in my memory—I was done for. Now I'm not done for. I'm ready for tomorrow. So it's to desensitize those words—and the memory. When I see those words photographically in my mind, I laugh at them. Ha, ha, ha. They're meaningless. (C, p. 59)

Cody was reminded that when we left the hospital and traveled around on various errands, he put that packet of papers right over his heart.

And occasionally, just to make sure, I'd…sort of grab my chest and rub them on me. There was a minute there when I thought I had misplaced the papers. I didn't know what I did with them. And I, I suddenly felt___a fear. I have to have that document. So I don't___still know why. Maybe tomorrow it will all be different. But if I had left those documents on the subway, or on a table top somewhere___still, somehow, I'd be shattered.

Because, you know, I'm in this, what I call this dither. I'm euphoric....When all this is over with, I wanna look at the paper___and then (sigh) put it in the file. And that's where it goes. But I have to make sure the paper stays with me during this euphoria period. And rub myself on it. And know that it's true...It validates the memory. It validates the fear. I did, in fact, have something to be afraid of. I didn't invent this fear. That's something I had to know. I don't know of too many other people—I don't know anybody that's gone through this. I say to my doctor: "Did I really have anything to be afraid of? Or am I nuts?" That's something you wonder about. Because you are nuts. Your whole life is upside down. And you don't know if it's manufactured, or very real. 'Cause it's just totally weird. (C, p. 60)

Within Cody's medical records were surgical reports that contained information new to him. Yet again connections were forged — this time with substantial impact to his self-esteem. On reading the reports, Cody discovered that a procedure he had been led to believe would not be performed by a particular means had, in fact, been accomplished by precisely that means.

That's part of the___thing where___pieces fall into place. I've known that my neck hurts me. In a way that they told me it would hurt if they did the procedure in a certain way. Which is a very bad way to do it___I don't know if that's clear? Well, my neck does hurt me. And I couldn't understand why it hurts me if they didn't___ do it___that way they said would be very difficult. Not a bad way, but___obviously they did it. So it's, you know, I assume it's the way they had to do it. The procedure itself creates___symptoms which are very unpleasant. Well, I have those symptoms....Well this tells me: Hey___this pain that I've got in my neck isn't___ me being a wimp. It's real. That's validating. (extended pause)

It feels funny, sometimes, to sit there and say: "What—am I concentrating on my pain? What am I, a wimp?" I feel like I have—my body hurts. There must be something wrong with me psychologically. I'm—it's all in my mind. It's not in my neck. Well I just found out, in fact, it is (laugh in voice) in my neck. And I can relax. I'm not a wimp. I'm not a jerk. I'm, I'm...a reasonable person. And I haven't known that....I didn't bring this on myself. And, and the pains and agonies that I keep to myself___do take effort. And they'd take anybody effort.

I don't know if you can understand the self-doubt that goes___along with___surviving a mortal problem with severe injury. And I don't mean accident injury. I mean, you know, surgical injury. But, whenever you fill out disability paperwork, you wonder: Am I really disabled? Or am I faking it? Because your self-esteem says: I'm a worker. I'm a producer. But why do I feel bad about filling out this paperwork? Well, it's because somebody told me I wouldn't be feeling that bad. But I do. Now, to find out it's because the procedure did create___a structural instability. Well, next time I fill out the paperwork I won't feel so bad....These are concrete things about injury, trauma, feeling, and healing. And that's why___I really wanted to get this on tape. This is no longer what do I think about healing. This is the healing. I hope, I hope you understand. I think you do. (C, p. 60)

The desire to be heard and understood by another person was strong. But the need to hear and understand oneself was even more palpable. In this research context, shared narrative tended to facilitate both aspects. For his efforts to impart experience brought Cody more deeply into his own. Provocatively, as well, it was Cody's responsiveness to the experience of another, and his need to understand it, which evoked even greater self-awareness.

One of the first emotions that come to mind is that I've lived my life for three years___frozen. Afraid to encounter___anything that might cause a relapse, physically. I'm afraid to die. I'm afraid to leave my family behind. I'm afraid to die in pain. (extended pause) And the terror that___became real was, you know, to see that somebody did die — somebody young....I don't want...to cause anything that's gonna create harm to myself, psychologically or physically, by, by...having a lesion reappear. I was told by doctors that the first one was so atypical that if it were to happen again it would certainly be...my death bell....You know I can't say that my neighbor's death is my gain. But it's causing me to face myself. And the issue of, of being afraid of___what's happened. And whether or not it's ever gonna happen again to me. (C, p. 46)

On further consideration of himself vis-à-vis his deceased neighbor, a contradictory view was given voice.

Poignantly, he's the instrument of change. That___what happened to me is okay. And I haven't been sure of that. Somehow, I was afraid of what happened to him. And at the same time___something has clicked in me. In the week___that I've taken the process since then...(extended pause), it sounds cruel—but his demise is my gain. I've learned that___living with what happened to me is okay. And that actually now, more than before, I can go on. And I really haven't been going on. I've been doing a great deal of hiding, a great deal of hiding. I can maybe take some risks now. I don't know exactly why that is, with the exception that he made this, this death issue, this pain issue, this leaving family behind issue so real. How real can you get?....It's not in the "fear" bucket. It's in the "it happened" bucket. That I was brought to having to face it....I got a feeling that I know what the issues are. I got my fingers firmly wrapped around them. I know what happened to me. I don't have to say that it didn't. And I don't have to say that it did. (C, p. 47)

The more Cody considered the flow of events, the more mindful he became of his belief that the changes wrought had brought him back to himself: his restoration was an outcome of healing. In perceiving his enhanced reintegration, Cody credited newly attained cognitive and emotion-based connections as significant transformative factors. They were facilitated by the narrative process of monologue and dialogue.

The analogy that I feel...really illustrates where I am is that___we plugged in the oven the other day, and got some stuff cooking that was shelved___for years....I feel better. Things make sense to me. And, and I think being able to face some things that were up on the shelf___and pull 'em back inside of me___and put 'em together and...put some heat to them (extended pause)....I'm different today—I know that—than I was a week ago....I sort of feel all put together....I feel like I have access to myself....And somehow by putting some heat to these issues, you know, the parts came together in the oven, and cooked up a nice pie...extended pause) It's nice to be back. It really is. (sigh/laugh) I...ask myself: Where was I all this time? Hiding someplace in the refrigerator?___These cute little phrases like: "I was on ice" (little laugh) or "we got something cooking," or whatever. But, you know, it's very real. Just having access to my, to my emotions about being afraid...of the parts...that...terrify me....I don't feel afraid of that now. You know? I guess that means I'm gonna get up and do something. And I feel like I got all my parts together to do it, whatever that may be.

If that's not healing, I don't know what is. But it's not hiding anymore....I mean, I just___somehow, I don't know if it was the research, or whether it was you___but I knew I couldn't get where I am now___with someone else. And I knew I could [get there]. It was before me. The time is right. The opportunity is right. (extended pause) And___thanks. (C, p. 50)

From the outset, Cody had been stimulated by this research endeavor. The focus on healing held his attention long after the actual moments we spent in the first interview. As noted, it was only due to Cody's request that a second meeting occurred. The interim of several months was an apparently fertile time for Cody, as he indicated:

> Despite the real time, the mental time has given me___an opportunity to think...and feel about things that we've talked about—things that I've shared in this research....The more I think about what we're doing here, the more I get an opportunity to think about it. (C, p. 39)

His thoughts suggested heightened sensibilities of reintegration were manifesting in both waking and dream states, and yielding increased awareness about the research topic.

> Healing is sort of this process....but healing isn't something that's done. Healing is something...you're doing. It's ongoing. And you're either on track, or you're off. If you're off, healing is knowing that—and getting back on. And if you're not healed, you ignore it. (C, p. 37)

> It's, you know, the liberate___part is the healing part. Maybe up until now I've always thought of healing as eating right...and encountering good encounters. But, when something's happened___and you get old enough to realize that people do hide from things, and that you gotta get, you gotta get 'em out___off the shelf and present, so that you can work on 'em and make 'em go away. It's liberating. It's very liberating. (C, p. 51)

> I know there's been things I haven't been liberated from for three years—some very intense fear. I've been having recurring nightmares for years....Here I decided I would talk to you about this, this very severe nightmare. I've had other severe nightmares (extended pause) and they've been getting___more real, you know? Somebody comes to, to my room when I'm sleeping, in one___one dream. But I never see their face. They simply tell me it's time to go. Who are they? What, what do they mean?....[And] where are we going? And, you know, you wake up with a big question in your mind. But more recently, you know, prior to last week, I saw the face of the person in the dream. It wasn't the surgeon___coming to me saying it's time to go. And I've always wondered if it was. It was, it was a man who raped me. When I was a young teenager — if that old. (extended pause)

> Finally I could see who was in the dream. I've been having that dream for three years—didn't have it before. Something about surgery

and___that other thing (makes little breathy sound)—the, the, the two plates fell on top of each other. And I couldn't___take 'em apart. And then one day I did. I found that___it allowed me to face some really early issues that were very painful and___Jeez, I'm starting to get faces to these dreams. And...that's liberating. That's — what's healing? Healing is being liberated. It's being able to...to be—to have access to myself, to all my parts. (C, p. 52)

Cody had consciously employed the research format as a means for therapeutic intervention. The narrative construction of his lived experiences, formulated in that setting, had triggered reactions which altered his thoughts and feelings of self and specific, traumatic events. Cody attributed this reorganization as leading to his eventual sense of emancipation. These were deemed outcomes of healing. But the process of healing entailed the transformations, themselves. Reflecting on this, Cody referred to a beloved possession, a wall-hanging of a musical movement: *Tod und Verklärung* (Death and Transfiguration) in Opus 24 by Richard Strauss. Cody loves this symphonic depiction.

It reminds me that there are___transformations. And that transformations___aren't particularly terrible. They feel terrible....but [the far] side of a transformation is really a pleasant place to be. Despite the, the hard ___ everything difficult that goes into the transformation. When you, when you actually put out (extended pause) the finished piece, it's beautiful. (C, p. 55)

In the initial interview, Cody spoke of healing as analogous to a symphony.

It's almost...a creative process. The most creative things in the world will speak to something different to you next week than they did last week. The best symphonies don't sound the same. (C, p. 38)

He later elaborated on this view, using the work by Strauss.

It moves___from one end to the other. It's going all the time. And it has all these pieces. And it can be pretty hard to put the pieces together. And if you look at this (Opus 24 movement) there's 15___instruments playing simultaneously across the orchestra—for 10, 15 stanzas....It's one of the busiest pieces of work I've ever seen. And it's no less busy than what it takes to heal. To put the pieces together—to liberate. A bad orchestra is not very liberating. You have to work and work and work...to get the notes right, the pieces right....But that's sort of an intellectual looking at what healing is. Because the middle of healing is this gut-wrenching, emotional place. It's fear. It's terror. It's relief. It's___tension. It's relaxation....And, suddenly, when it's all done, you're different. Because you can react accessibly. When this orchestra plays this piece, the world listens. And pays tickets to hear it...They go: "Wow that was great." And that's a lot what it's like going through a healing transformation. One that takes you from pain___to relief. You're left with not only the relief, but an understanding. (C, p. 55)

Many people yearn for this kind of knowledge. It is a hunger of the soul which the use of narrative, fed from multiple realms of consciousness, can nurture. For instance, as Faulkner (1932) observed: "Memory believes before knowing remembers" (p. 88). When healing is needed, some domain of consciousness already has an understanding.

Narrative Organization

Findings from diverse research topics and modes of investigation have tended to make it a given that people routinely, often unconsciously, integrate and alter new information, as well as memories, to promote a comfortable sense of coherence and current salience as life evolves (Bartlett, 1932; Hudson, 1975; Klatzky, 1975; Linton, 1982; Neisser, 1982; Neisser & Fivush, 1994; Wells, 1999). Blossoming literatures on autobiographical memory, narrative truth in recollected personal events, and the dynamics of self and society as influential constituents, present a stunningly exciting array of the inherent complexities in functions most of us not only take for granted but also credit, in tacit confidence, with validity that is not necessarily warranted (Bruner, 1994; Gergen, 1994; Reed, 1994; Ross & Buehler, 1994; Wagenaar, 1994; Winograd, 1994). It is likewise becoming common for investigators concerned with varied facets of human memory, autobiographical and otherwise, to presuppose premises Barclay (1994) articulated: "My position is that the self is not remembered because the self does not exist as something to be remembered. ... The self is not an entity whose existence becomes separate from and controlling of the dynamics of perception, interpersonal relationships, and cognition; and remembering is an adaptive process through which the constructed and reconstructed past serves present psychosocial and cultural needs" (p. 71). The spectrum of state-of-mind conditions influences structural and functional content of what is remembered and forgotten (Goethals & Reckman, 1982; Loftus & Palmer, 1982; Neisser & Winograd, 1988). Moreover, as Bruner (1994) remarked: The self is "'storied,'or narrative, in structure" (p. 43) and "... notoriously, stories have a way of changing with circumstances and, notably, with the interlocutor to whom they are being told" (p. 46).

Therefore variance in what may emerge as constituent and/or prominent is assumed — further shaped in part by modification from such narrative elements as phrasing and tenor of expression. The flow of Cody's consciousness exemplified all these factors, as he dealt with the constructions and reconstructions of both trauma and healing. There also tends to be the common acceptance that an account of a lived event repeated verbatim, time after time, suggests rehearsal and a reason to question the trustworthiness of the statement. This may appear counterintuitive, although lived experience easily verifies its authenticity. As Cody's recollections demonstrate, the intent to relate phenomena faithfully (events or any form of realization) results in neither undeviating cognizance nor report. Yet this incongruity is so routinely discernible that it often seems invisible. However its implications about consciousness are profound.

Consciousness is fluid (James, 1950). Although this characteristic is readily ascribed to conceptually, its real life outcomes are not. Intelligibility may be lost or misconstrued because the flow of consciousness is inadvertently jammed by limitations placed on the scope and boundaries of its individual and collective operations. Efforts to seek meaning may lead one to confuse the appearance of constancy as manifestation of clarity. Nonetheless, as the aphorism affirms: One cannot stand in the same river twice. Regardless of the fact that one may seek to repeat an expression of consciousness, it never precisely duplicates. Even an exact repetition of stimuli will not produce a replicate response. Yet it is precisely in the discrepancies, of intentional and unintentional alterations, that the textures of experience may be more fully nuanced and revealed. Existence, by nature, is transformative. The power of narrative comes with its ability to capture that existence and, itself, transform it.

Story as Healer

Cody's accounts appeared to do just that. Instances of his illness-healing journey manifested in multiple narrative arenas from seemingly distinct realms of consciousness. There are the stories he told in ordinary awareness as internal monologues and research data dialogues, as well as the stories from altered states, such as dreamtime nightmares or daytime involuntary memories. The workings of unconscious states bestowed lucid moments in conscious states, to further sensibilities of cogency and consonance. Cody increasingly realized that his past medical records, oral and written material regarding his deceased neighbor, and the autobiography recently received from his father, were all incorporated by him in highly selective fashion, to assist his healing needs. These items constituted key ingredients from which Cody perceived revelations that led him to experience emancipation and restoration in body, mind, and spirit.

"Stories are medicine," as Estes (1992, p.16) amply illustrated, and their treatments can be potent. Therapists of many persuasions customarily rely on the examination of storied creations to aid therapeutic processes (Baur, 1994; Bollas, 1995; Garfield, 1995). Research evidences that narrative acts of disclosure can facilitate healing in cognitive, emotional, and physical domains (Pennebaker, 1995). As vehicles to organize, clarify, and refine consciousness, stories can awaken insight, inspiration, and liberation (Canfield & Hansen, 1993; Fields,

1994) to result in healing as process with outcomes of restoration and/or actualization. Yet for consciousness to inhabit wholeness, and manifest healing, it must be allowed to transform — which enables abilities to perceive and receive. Sufficient refinement of consciousness may bring healing, wholeness, perhaps a sense of the holy. A resurgent interest in the mainstream culture for diverse literature on spiritual matters suggests a widespread yearning to encounter our deepest nature (Bennett-Goleman, 2001; Breathnach, 1995; Capra, Steindl-Rast, & Matus, 1991; Evans, 1993; Kübler-Ross & Kessler, 2000; Krippner & Welch, 1992; Kurtz & Ketcham, 1992; Moody, 1993; Moore, 1992; Tart, 1997; Williamson, 1992).

This comes from disclosing our natures — telling our stories. We look not only to ourselves but also to the evolved souls among us for revelation. Historically, across cultures worldwide, we have continually sought guidance from spiritually enlightened beings whose consciousness appear most illuminated, to help us become both more conscious and more adept at fostering healing. Narratives on the evolved being — whether fictionalized such as *Sidhartha* (Hesse, 1971), reputed historical fact, such as the *King James Bible* (1977), autobiography (Yogananda, 1974), or mystical texts such as the *Tao Te Ching* (Lao Tzu, 1988) — convey myriad expressions of the potentials for life embedded within the appearances of life. As with all true spiritual Masters, the stories they tell us, we enternally long to hear.

References

Achterberg, J. (1985). *Imagery in healing: Shamanism and modern medicine.* Boston: Shambhala.

Angelou, M. (1970). *I know why the caged bird sings.* New York: Random House.

Bailey, A. A. (1960). *A treatise on the seven rays. Vol. 5: The rays and the initiations.* New York: Lucis Publishing.

Barclay, C. R. (1994). Composing protoselves through improvisation. In U. Neisser & R. Fivush (Eds.), *The remembering self: Construction and accuracy in the self-narrative* (pp. 41–54). New York: Cambridge University Press.

Bartlett, F. C. (1932). *Remembering: A study in experimental and social psychology.* Cambridge: Cambridge University Press.

Bateson, G. (Ed.). (1991). *A sacred unity: Further steps to an ecology of mind.* San Francisco: HarperCollins.

Baur, S. (1994). *Confiding: A psychotherapist and her patients search for stories to live by.* New York: HarperPerennial.

Beck, D., & Beck, J. (1987). *The pleasure connection: How endorphins affect our health and happiness.* San Marcos, CA: Synthesis Press.

Bennett-Goleman, T. (2001). *Emotional alchemy: How the mind can heal the heart.* New York: Harmony.

Biro, D. (2000). *One hundred days: My unexpected journey from doctor to patient.* New York: Parthenon.

Bly, R. (1990). *Iron John: A book about men.* Reading, MA: Addison-Wesley.

Bohm, D. (1980). *Wholeness and the implicate order.* London: Ark Paperbacks.

Bollas, C. (1995). *Cracking up: The work of unconscious experience.* New York: Hill & Wang.

Borysenko, J., & Borysenko, M. (1994). *The power of the mind to heal.* Carson, CA: Hay House.

Breathnach, S. B. (1995). *Simple abundance: A daybook of comfort and joy.* New York: Warner.

Brinkley, D. (with P. Perry). (1994). *Saved by the light: The true story of a man who died twice and the profound revelations he received.* New York: HarperPaperbacks.

Broyard, A. (1992). *Intoxicated by my illness: And other writings on life and death.* New York: C. Potter.

Bruner, J. (1994). The "remembered" self. In U. Neisser & R. Fivush (Eds.), *The remembering self: Construction and accuracy in the self-narrative* (pp. 41–54). New York: Cambridge University Press.

Campbell, J. (1968). *The hero with a thousand faces.* Princeton: Princeton University Press.

Campbell, J., & Moyers, B. (1988). *The power of myth.* New York: Anchor Books.

Canfield, J., & Hansen, M. V. (Compl.), (1993). *Chicken soup for the soul: 101 stories to open the heart and rekindle the spirit.* Deerfield Beach, FL: Health Communications.

Capra, F. (1984). *The Tao of physics: An exploration of the parallels between modern physics and Eastern mysticism.* (rev. ed.). New York: Bantam.

Capra, F., Steindl-Rast, D., & Matus, T. (1992). *Belonging to the universe: Explorations on the frontiers of science and spirituality.* San Francisco: Harper.

Carter, G. (1993). *Healing myself: A hero's primer for recovery from tragedy.* Norfolk, VA: Hampton Roads.

Chopra, D. (1990). *Quantum healing: Exploring the frontiers of mind/body medicine.* New York: Bantam.

Church, K. (1996). *Forbidden narratives: Critical autobiography as social science.* (vol. 2). Williston, VT: Gordan & Breach.

Cousins, N. (1979). *Anatomy of an illness as perceived by the patient: Reflections on healing and regeneration.* New York: Bantam.

Delaney, G. (1993). The changing roles of dream interpreters in the understanding of dreams. *International Journal of Psychosomatics, 40,* 6–8.

Delany, S. L., & Delany, A. E. (with H. A. Hearth). (1994). *Having our say: The Delany sisters' first 100 years.* New York: Dell.

Deveare Smith, A. (1992). *Fires in the mirror: Crown Heights, Brooklyn and Other Identities.* New York: Anchor.

Deveare Smith, A. (1994). *Twilight: Los Angeles, 1992. On the road: A Search for an American character.* [Berkeley Repertory Theatre production].

Dossey, L. (1993). *Healing words: The power of prayer and the practice of medicine.* San Francisco: Harper.

Duff, K. (1993). *The alchemy of illness.* New York: Pantheon.

Eisler, R. (1987). *The chalice and the blade: Our history, our future.* San Francisco: HarperCollins.

Eliade, M. (1972). *Shamanism: Archaic techniques of ecstasy.* Princeton, NJ: Princeton University Press.

Estes, C. P. (1992). *Women who run with the wolves: Myths and stories of the wild woman archetype.* New York: Ballantine.

Evans, D. (1993). *Spirituality and human nature.* Albany, NY: SUNY Press.

Faraday, A. (1972). *Dream power.* New York: Berkley Books.

Faulkner, W. (1932). *Light in August.* New York: Random House.

Feinstein, D., & Krippner, S. (1988). *Personal mythology: Using ritual, dreams, and imagination to discover your inner story.* Los Angeles: J. P. Tarcher.

Festinger, L. (1957). *A theory of cognitive dissonance.* Stanford: Stanford University Press.

Fields, R. (Ed.). (1994). *The awakened warrior: Living with courage, compassion, and discipline.* New York: Tarcher/Putnam.

Flowers, B. S., & Grubin, D. (Eds.) (1993). *Healing and the mind, Bill Moyers.* New York: Main Street.

Frank, A. W. (1991). *At the will of the body: Reflections on illness.* New York: Houghton Mifflin.

Garfield, P. (1995). *Creative dreaming: Plan and control your dreams to develop creativity, overcome fears, solve problems, and create a better self.* (Revised ed.) New York: Fireside.

Gergen, K. J. (1994). Mind, text, and society: Self-memory in social context. In U. Neisser & R. Fivush (Eds.), *The remembering self: Construction and accuracy in the self-narrative* (pp. 78–104). New York: Cambridge University Press.

Goethals, G. R., & Reckman, R. F. (1982). Recalling previously held attitudes. In U. Neisser (Ed.), *Memory observed: Remembering in natural contexts* (pp. 178–188). San Francisco: W. H. Freeman.

Graham, K. (1997). *Personal history.* New York: Alfred A. Knopf.

Gray, J. (1992). *Men are from Mars, women are from Venus: A practical guide for improving communication and getting what you want in your relationships.* New York: Harper Collins.

Harner, M. (1980). *The way of the shaman: A guide to power and healing.* New York: Bantam Books.

Harvey, A. (1991). *Hidden journey: A spiritual awakening.* New York: Penguin.

Hesse, H. (1971). *Siddhartha.* New York: Bantam Books. (Original work published 1946)

Hudson, L. (1975). *Human beings: The psychology of human experience.* Garden City, NY: Anchor.

Hunt, V. V. (1996). *Infinite mind: Science of the human vibrations of consciousness.* (2nd ed.). Malibu, CA: Malibu.

Hunter, K. M. (1991). *Doctors' stories: The narrative structure of medical knowledge.* Princeton, NJ: Princeton University Press.

Isenberg, S. A., Lehrer, P. M., & Hochron, S. (1992). The effects of suggestion and emotional arousal on pulmonary function in asthma: A review and a hypothesis regarding vagal mediation. *Psychosomatic Medicine, 54,* 192–216.

James, W. (1950). *The principles of psychology.* (Vol. 1). New York: Dover. (Original work published 1890.)

Jasnosk i, M. L., & Kugler, J. (1987). Relaxation, imagery and neuroimmunomodulation. *Annals of New York Academy of Sciences, 496,* 722–730.

King James Bible (1977). Nashville: Thomas Nelson.

Klatzky, R. L. (1975). *Human memory: Structures and processes.* San Francisco: W. H. Freeman.

Kleinman, A. (1988). *The illness narratives: Suffering, healing, and the human condition.* New York: Basic Books.

Krippner, S. (Ed.). (1990). *Dreamtime and dreamwork: Decoding the language of the night.* Los Angeles: J. P. Tarcher.

Krippner, S. (1993). A centenary of dreams: Introduction to the symposium. *International Journal of Psychosomatics, 40,* 4–5.

Krippner, S., & Villoldo, A. (1976). *The realms of healing*. Millbrae, CA: Celestial Arts.

Krippner, S., & Welch, P. (1992). *Spiritual dimensions of healing*. New York: Irvington.

Kübler-Ross, E., & Kessler, D. (2000). *Life lessons: Two experts on death and dying teach us about the mysteries of life and living*. New York: Touchstone.

Kurtz, E., & Ketcham, K. (1992). *The spirituality of imperfection: Storytelling and the journey to wholeness*. New York: Bantam.

Lao Tzu (1988). (S. Mitchell, Transl.) *Tao te ching*. New York: HarperPerennial.

LaBerge, S., & Rheingold, H. (1990). *Exploring the world of lucid dreaming*. New York: Ballantine Books.

Larsen, S. (1976). *The shaman's doorway: Opening the mythic imagination to contemporary consciousness*. New York: Harper & Row.

Leadbeater, C. W. (1978). *The inner life*. Wheaton, IL: Theosophical Publishing House.

Lightfoote, M. J. (1992). On patients, patience, and impatience. *Advances: The Journal of Mind-Body Health, 8,* 88–90.

Linton, M. (1982). Transformations of memory in everyday life. In U. Neisser (Ed.), *Memory observed: Remembering in natural contexts* (pp. 77–91). San Francisco: W. H. Freeman.

Locke, S., & Colligan, D. (1986). *The healer within: The new medicine of mind and body*. New York: New York American Library.

Loftus, E. F., & Palmer, J. C. (1982). Reconstruction of automobile destruction. In U. Neisser (Ed.), *Memory observed: Remembering in natural contexts* (pp. 109–115). San Francisco: W. H. Freeman.

Mandela, N. (1994). *Long walk to freedom: The autobiography of Nelson Mandela*. Boston: Back Bay Books/Little, Brown.

McNamara, R. S. (with B. van De Mark). (1995). *In retrospect: The tragedy and lessons of Vietnam*. New York: Random House.

Moody, R. (with P. Perry). (1993). *Reunions: Visionary encounters with departed loved ones*. New York: Villard.

Moore, T. (1992). *Care of the soul: A guide for cultivating depth and sacredness in everyday life*. New York: HarperPerennial.

Moss, R. (1981). *The I that is we*. Millbrae, CA: Celestial Arts.

Neisser, U. (1982). John Dean's memory: A case study. In U. Neisser (Ed.). *Memory observed: Remembering in natural contexts* (pp. 139–159). San Francisco: W. H. Freeman.

Neisser, U. , & Fivush, R. (Eds.). (1994). *The remembering self: Construction and accuracy in the self-narrative*. New York: Cambridge University Press.

Neisser, U., & Winograd, E. (Eds.). (1988). *Remembering reconsidered: Ecological and traditional approaches to the study of memory*. Melbourne: Cambridge University Press.

Nhat Hanh, T. (Ed., Transl.) (1987). *The sutra on the eight realizations of the great beings: A Buddhist scripture on simplicity, generosity, and compassions*. Berkeley, CA: Parallax Press.

Palmer, L. (1987). *Shrapnel in the heart: Letters and remembrances from the Vietnam Veterans Memorial*. New York: Random House.

Pelletier, K. R. (1977). *Mind as healer, mind as slayer*. New York: Delta/Dell.

Pennebaker, J. W. (Ed.) (1995). *Emotion, disclosure, and health*. Washington, D.C.: American Psychological Association.

Pert, C. (1997). *Molecules of emotion: Why you feel the way you feel*. New York: Scribner.

Reed, E. S. (1994). Perception is to self as memory is to selves. In U. Neisser & R. Fivush (Eds.), *The remembering self: Construction and accuracy in the self-narrative* (pp. 278–291). New York: Cambridge University Press.

Rider, M. S., & Achterberg, J. (1989). Effect of music-assisted imagery on neutrophils and lymphocytes. *Biofeedback and Self-regulation, 14,* 247–257.

Rollin, B. (1976). *First, you cry.* New York: Signet Press.

Rosenbaum, E. E. (1988). *A taste of my own medicine: When the doctor is the patient.* New York: Random House.

Ross, M., & Buehler, R. (1994). Creative remembering. In U. Neisser & R. Fivush (Eds.), *The remembering self: Construction and accuracy in the self-narrative* (pp. 205–235). New York: Cambridge University Press.

Sacks, O. (1984). *A leg to stand on.* New York: Summit Books.

Salaman, E. (1982). A collection of moments. In U. Neisser (Ed.), *Memory observed: Remembering in natural contexts* (pp. 49–63). San Francisco: W. H. Freeman.

Sattilaro, A. J. (with T. Monte). (1982). *Recalled by life.* New York: Avon Books.

Schneider, M. (1987). *Self-healing: My life and vision.* New York: Routledge & Kegan Paul.

Schwartz, S. W. (2003). *Closing the divide: Phenomenological perspectives on transformations of consciousness evoked during healing in the context of life-threatening illness.* Unpublished doctoral dissertation, Saybrook Graduate School, San Francisco.

Shealy, C. N. (1999). *Sacred healing: The curing power of energy and spirituality.* Boston: Element.

Simpson, E. L. (1982). *Notes on an emergency: A journal of recovery.* New York: W. W. Norton.

Sizemore, C. C., & Pittillo, E. S. (1977). *I'm Eve.* Garden City, NY: Harcourt Brace Jovanovich.

Tannen, D. (1990). *You just don't understand: Women and men in conversation.* New York: Ballantine.

Tart, C. T. (1993). Mind embodied: Computer generated virtual reality as a new dualistic-interactive model for transpersonal psychology. In K. Rao (Ed.), *Cultivating consciousness: Enhancing human potential, wellness and healing* (pp. 123–137). Westport, CT: Praeger.

Tart, C. T. (Ed.) (1997). *Body Mind Spirit: Exploring the parapsychology of spirituality.* Charlottesville, VA: Hampton Roads.

Tate, D. A. (1989). *Health, hope, and healing.* New York: M. Evans.

Tate, D. A. (1991). *In the matter of Billy K.* New York: M. Evans.

Thurston, M., & Fazel, C. (1992). *The Edgar Cayce handbook for creating your future.* New York: Ballantine Books.

Van Devanter, L. (with C. Morgan). (1983). *Home before morning: The story of an army nurse in Vietnam.* New York: Beaufort Books.

Vernon, P. E. (1971). *Creativity.* New York: Viking/Penguin.

Wagenaar, W. A. (1994). Is memory self-serving? In U. Neisser & R. Fivush (Eds.), *The remembering self: Constrcution and accuracy in self-narrative* (pp. 191–204). New York: Cambridge University Press.

Wells, G. L. (1999, August). *The law's role in causing mistaken eye witness identifications.* Paper presented at the annual meeting of the American Psychological Association, Boston, MA.

Williamson, M. (1992). *A return to love: Reflections on the principles of "A Course in Miracles."* New York: HarperCollins.

Winograd, E. (1994). The authenticity and utility of memories. In U. Neisser, & R. Fivush (Eds.), *The remembering self: Construction and accuracy in the self-narrative* (pp. 243–251). New York: Cambridge University Press.

Yogananda, P. (1974). *Autobiography of a yogi.* Los Angeles: Self-Realization Fellowship. (Original work published 1946)

CHAPTER SIX

The Truism Metaphor and Positive Age Regression to Experiences of Mastery

D. Corydon Hammond

Interspersal of Suggestions and the Use of Metaphors

Research and clinical experience suggests that persons who are highly responsive to hypnosis will respond somewhat better to suggestions offered in hypnosis, but they also often remain quite responsive to the same suggestions when they are offered without a formal hypnotic induction (Barber, 1969, 1978; Brown, Scheflin, & Hammond, 1997). Thus, in working with a patient with postsurgical pain, a physical therapist or nurse may in casual conversation offer some of the same suggestions that a physician or mental health professional might offer in formal hypnosis, and assist the patient in obtaining many of the same benefits, or in reinforcing hypnotic suggestions given previously. There are many types of hypnotic suggestions (Hammond, 1990). Two of the styles of suggestion central to this book on healing stories are the use of metaphors and the idea of interspersing suggestions within stories or conversation.

The interspersal of suggestions is one of the techniques of indirect suggestion used by Milton H. Erickson (Erickson & Rossi, 1979). Indirect suggestions may be subtly interspersed within stories, anecdotes, hypnotic deepening techniques, or conversation. This is done by including words or phrases, often set apart by very brief pauses or slight changes in vocal tone, that may convey the desired suggestion. For instance, if I am working with a patient with chronic pain, I may brainstorm ideas and phrases that convey the desired ideas of comfort. I often begin by consulting a comprehensive thesaurus to identify synonyms and phrases such as "for comfort," or "pleasure." I then contemplate how these words and phrases may be interspersed within analogies, examples, metaphoric stories, or hypnotic deepening techniques. Those interested in metaphors and the interspersing of suggestions should consult Erickson's (1966) classic paper on this topic, illustrating its use with cancer patients, as well as his collected papers (Erickson, 1980).

Metaphors are simply one form of hypnotic suggestion and interpersonal influence that I believe should ideally be used along with other forms of suggestion (Hammond, 1990). One may think of metaphors as a method of utilizing the hypnotic principle of repetition of suggestion without using identical words or phrases. Through their use you may bring up a topic and use words or phrases that "seed" an idea, focus attention, and indirectly suggest something to a patient. Metaphors or anecdotes may be used to illustrate a point or tag a memory, indirectly to suggest or model solutions, to foster self-reflection and insight, to increase positive expectancy or motivation, to bypass resistance, to reframe or redefine a problem, and to intersperse suggestions while bypassing defenses (Zeig, 1980). They are used, like other styles of suggestion, to facilitate behavioral, affective, or cognitive-perceptual changes.

I personally conceptualize three basic styles of metaphors. Some therapists tell metaphoric stories out of their personal background of experience, from their earlier life or work with patients (Erickson & Rossi, 1979). Other therapists (see, for example, Gordon, 1978; Lankton & Lankton, 1989) construct and fabricate metaphoric stories to fit a patient problem or situation, often seeking to create characters and components that are parallel to aspects of the patient's circumstance. Still another type of metaphor is the *truism metaphor*. These are metaphors that are commonly about nature or the kind of life experiences that are so universal that the patient cannot deny them. Thus, they establish a "yes-set" or "acceptance-set" in patients as they listen, and thereby may facilitate the acceptance of subsequent ideas. In example, is there anyone who has not had a scrape or cut that developed a scab? Therefore, I may describe to a patient the process, following an injury, of a scab forming for protection, while natural and internal healing processes take place. Later, a scar may be left, as a small reminder of a hurt, long ago, but which doesn't have to remain painful anymore. I have used this metaphor (Hammond, 1990, pp. 536–537) to convey ideas to a patient who has experienced trauma, incest, rape, or divorce.

It is my personal preference to use metaphors out of my own background of experience or truism metaphors, although no research exists about differential effectiveness. For me, making up stories risks being perceived by the patient as not being genuine or authentic — qualities consistently found to be one of the important "nonspecific" ingredients of successful therapy and relationships (Hammond, Hepworth, & Smith, 1977; Truax & Carkhuff, 1967). Making up a tale with the "once upon a time" quality has come across as condescending to patients I have seen who previously worked with therapists who used this metaphoric style. Thus, it seems possible that the use, or at least the over-reliance, on such stories may risk impairing the therapeutic alliance with the patient.

Erickson, who often serves as a model for therapists emphasizing a metaphoric orientation to hypnosis or psychotherapy, seems to have almost always used metaphors from his own life experience or truism metaphors. I think it is also important to emphasize that close and long-term colleagues who actually observed Erickson's therapy, as well as some of his patients, have emphasized that metaphors were only occasionally used by him (Hammond, 1984), probably not representing any more than twenty percent of his hypnotic work (Hammond, 1988). It is my position that metaphors clearly have a place in our therapeutic armamentarium, but we are wise to keep a balanced perspective and realize that therapy is more than storytelling. Metaphors and healing stories are one valuable therapeutic technique to be themselves interspersed along with other psychotherapeutic techniques in a multidimensional treatment approach, rather than primarily relied upon as "the one true light" or the only medium of influence in a unidimensional approach to therapy.

These things being said, in the remainder of this chapter I will describe my use of two narrative techniques. First, the construction and use of truism metaphors. Second, I will discuss the use of positive age regression to personal or fantasized experiences of mastery — something that I not only believe is valuable in therapy in general, but particularly with trauma survivors. In this technique, I will illustrate how a therapist may use historic material that may be accurate, partly accurate and partially confabulated, or even simply imagined "memories," quite possibly lacking in historic accuracy, as a method for ego-strengthening, therapeutically altering perceptions, and increasing feelings of self-efficacy.

Truism Metaphors

One may introduce a metaphor by simply saying, "And let me give you an example," or "You may remember," or "Can you remember a time when ... ?" Therapeutic metaphors do not always have to be long and involved to make an important point. Thus, one may talk about the serendipitous discovery of penicillin when Fleming noticed mold on a culture plate. Instead of throwing out the contaminated plate, he examined it and found that the bacteria he was studying were being destroyed by the mold. Barker (1996) used this metaphor to convey the idea that we should not always take things at face value.

During the middle east Gulf War, I prepared some suggestions for use with a child suffering with anxiety about having a parent in the war. Naturally such suggestions should be edited for the individual experiences of a child, and they may be used with even more questions (Hammond, 1990) as a type of suggestion, to make the experience even more interactive. Several truism metaphors were used as part of these suggestions.

> Maybe you can remember the first time that you were going to sleep over, at a friend's house overnight [an almost universal experience]. Even though you were happy and excited about it, you were probably really nervous, and kind of scared. What you were afraid of, was the unknown — because you'd never done it before, and you didn't know what to

expect, or what it would be like. It's natural to have a fear of the unknown [accepting and normalizing the child's fear]. But once you've slept over with a friend a couple of times, you know what it's like, and it isn't so scary anymore. Now you smile when you think of sleeping over, and it's a happy, enjoyable thought.

The first day you went to school or pre-school, or stayed with a new teacher, I'll bet it was kind of scary too, wasn't it? We had a fear of the unknown, and just didn't know what to expect. But pretty soon you felt more comfortable about school, and were familiar and relaxed with it, weren't you, and you had fun playing with your friends, and didn't worry anymore.

It's like being afraid of the dark — when it's dark we can't see everything, and so we can imagine all sorts of scary things, like monsters or big spiders that might be there in the dark. [The trance experience could be made interactional at this point, eliciting personal experiences from the child.] But when someone turns the lights on, we relax, and see that what we were afraid of and worrying about, wasn't really there. But when it's the unknown and its dark, we can imagine all sorts of terrible, frightening things — but they are just made up in our own mind, and aren't real. We imagined them.

Sometimes we can imagine things and scare ourselves, and make ourselves nervous. Some people worry about flying on an airplane, and get very scared. They know that once in a very great while an airplane does crash. So they imagine crashing, and they really frighten themselves. But airplanes *almost never* crash. Some people worry like that about driving in their car. Only a *very few* people die in car crashes, but some people imagine their cars crashing, and they make themselves so nervous, that they're afraid even to drive to the store, or go to a movie. That's sad! Instead of picturing all the scary things in their heads, they could relax, and picture happy things, like the fun they'll have when they get to the movie theater, and the popcorn and candy, or how much they'll enjoy getting an ice cream cone.

I know that you're worried, because your Daddy [or Mommy] has gone to help with the war [a truism, accepting the child's experience]. You worry because it's the unknown, and you don't know what to expect and what will happen [a bridging association to previous metaphoric examples]. Just like sometimes a car crashes or an airplane crashes, sometimes people can get hurt in a war too. But that usually only happens to a few of the people who go away to help. I don't think Daddy would want you scaring yourself, by imagining terrible things every time he drove to the store to buy bread or cookies, would he, because bad things usually don't happen? And concerning the war, instead of picturing scary things in your mind, you can picture how fun and happy it's going to be, when he comes home, and imagine what presents he might bring home to you [giving the child mastery over imagery]. Do that right now. [10 second pause] While you rest, you can picture and imagine the fun things you'll do together. [15 second pause] While you rest back quietly, you can even imagine the fun things you can write to him about, [5 second pause] and the interesting or fun things, like maybe pictures or drawings, that you can send while he's away, to make him laugh and smile. [10 second pause] And you can imagine the look on his face when he sees it, [5 second pause] and what his laugh and smile is going to look like [3 second pause], and what he's going to say when he sees what you sent him. [5–10 second pause] Instead of scaring yourself, when you hear about the war, imagine the fun times you're going to have with him before long, and imagine what you can do and send to him, to make him smile and laugh.

Truism Metaphors in the Working Through of Trauma

Some patients have experienced emotional upheavals or personally traumatic events in their lives. One aspect of the resolution and integration of such memories consists of helping the patient to cognitively reinterpret this material. Metaphors are one of the useful methods for facilitating this working through process.

Can you imagine anyone who has not felt miserably sick in his or her life? Thus, this has been the basis for a metaphor that I prepared on sickness and immunity (Hammond, 1990) for use in reframing negative life events (such as grief, divorce, past trauma). The patient is reminded of a time when she had the flu — how miserable she felt, how her body felt, and how it dragged on and seemed endless. In the process we may discuss how with a fever, perceptions can become altered and distorted, we don't think clearly, how slowly times passes, and even how frightening it sometimes feels:

> And at those times, we can feel so alone, can't we — cut off from the world. And sometimes we cut ourselves off when we're sick, because of feeling so rotten and not wanting to make others feel sick, and because we can't imagine anyone wanting to be around us. And so, because of that, the world can seem rather uncaring and not understand how really sick you feel, even though this is the time we really need tender loving care and some attention. But, as utterly miserable and bad as that was, you got over it, and it ended. And it wasn't very long before you began

forgetting how miserable that was. At the time it seemed torturous and endless, but you lived through it, and before long, forget how bad it was. And later, you rarely ever think about it, because it was just something that happened long ago, and so many other interesting and wonderful things happened later, that they kind of obscure and outweigh that brief period long ago, that really doesn't have to continue to influence you now.

Talking in this manner accesses a person's memory of the event, particularly in a focused state of hypnosis. We then make a bridging association to the patient's current problem:

And with regard to *this* pain that you've been through, even though it was much worse than the misery of the flu, and although recently you've been miserable and preoccupied with it, it also, will seem this way. And later, it will be hard to remember how bad it was.

Such a metaphor may even be expanded further, discussing how life experiences (such as having the measles or chickenpox), can actually have a hidden benefit:

Through the process of suffering, without any conscious awareness, we *inwardly change*. We develop some immunity, and have been influenced in such a manner that in a sense we've grown stronger, much stronger, internally. It's as if, because of the suffering and adversity — even though we seldom recall the experience later — we've been made *stronger*, more immune to some things, for having lived through it. And we also change, in that we also have a greater sense of empathy and compassion for others, who suffer. And we can appreciate, that without unpleasant experiences in life, you wouldn't be able to so fully enjoy and appreciate how wonderful the beautiful, happy times are. And as you reflect for a moment about the suffering *you've* been through, you can feel a sense of *inward strength*, realizing that *you* survived this. As the saying goes, a smooth sea, never made a skillful sailor. And this pain and struggle *have made you stronger*, like a tree strengthened by the winds. Those painful experiences have formed a foundation of strength. And therefore, deep inside, you can have an inner sense, that having survived the pain of *this*, you have the strength to cope with *anything*, that comes along.

Other challenging and painful experiences that the patient has lived through may form the basis at times for this kind of metaphoric reframing; for example, a best friend moving away. Sometimes you may have already asked about whether the patient ever had certain experiences. In other cases, one may spontaneously ask the hypnotized patient, "As you were growing up, did you ever break your arm or leg?" If the answer is "yes," details may be obtained, and consideration given to facilitating an informal regression to the event, or of at least referring to it in relation to some painful event that is now being worked through.

Positive Age Regression:
Accessing Resources for Ego-Strengthening

When many people think of age regression, they think of exploring abuse or trauma. Perhaps this is because much of our training as therapists teaches us to be pathologists who focus on problems and weaknesses rather than assets and strengths. Hypnotic age regression to problematic material, and subsequent reframing and integration of memories is a legitimate phase of therapy (Brown et al., 1997; Hammond, Garver, Mutter, Crasilneck, Frischholz, Gravitz, Hiber, Olson, Scheflin, Spiegel, & Wester, 1995). But, ego-strengthening is also typically involved in either the stabilization phase preceding therapy with past trauma or abuse and/or following work on negative life events. Thus, it is important to emphasize that age regression may also be positively focused. It seems reasonable to wonder, in fact, if we should not be doing as much positive age regression as we do memory work that is focused on themes of suffering. Many patients already spend too much time mentally reviewing negative life experiences.

Thus we may perceive the patient's history (and, just as importantly, help the patient perceive his or her own history) as not only possibly having unfinished business to be resolved, but as also being a repository of inner resources that may be accessed with age regression. For instance, we may ponder what feelings and qualities a patient needs more of in his current life. Perhaps a patient needs to experience more feelings of confidence, tenderness, enthusiasm, playfulness, trust, or joy. Virtually all of us have been in situations in life in which we experienced these feelings. Thus, we may access them, or some imagined version of them, through age regression, thereby assisting our patients to experience more of these feelings currently.

Similarly, virtually all of us have struggled and accomplished rather amazing things that initially seemed overwhelming and impossible (such as learning to walk, to feed ourselves, to read, to do arithmetic, to print and write, or to ride a bicycle). Most of us have also lived through painful events and overcome them (a childhood friend moving away, the death of a pet, a broken arm or leg, or as already described, being miserably sick, getting well, and then forgetting about it). Have you ever had an adult patient who needed to learn how to laugh again, and who may infrequently grin or chuckle, but who has forgotten how to really have fun, laugh and enjoy life? Would not this patient benefit from age regressions that allowed him to re-experience the freedom of his own uninhibited laughter as a child? In addition to exploration of unresolved negative life experience, we also need to use hypnosis to look for resources, strengths, and joys within the patient.

Example of Ego-Strengthening
Through Eliciting Recall of Experiences of Mastery

An example such as the one which follows may consist of informally facilitating hypermnesia, or of an age regression to childhood experiences of mastery in some patients. In other patients, it may simply facilitate an imagined experience of what the past may have been like, quite possibly lacking in substantial historic accuracy for details, but which may nonetheless serve as an experiential method for reframing perceptions and increasing feelings of self-efficacy. Because historic accuracy is unimportant in this usage, having the patient initially engage in free recall, without the use of questions (or leading questions) (Hammond et al., 1995) is not a concern. In this example, I am using with a person in hypnosis his or her narrative, undeniable past experiences as truism metaphors, to make our point — in this case, that frustrating, overwhelming current life problems or new skills can be mastered, and the changes can become automatic and taken for granted.

Therapist: When you were a boy, did you enjoy riding a two-wheeled bike?

Patient nods affirmatively.

Therapist: Then, I'd like you to remember back to when you were much younger and smaller, when you were first wanting to learn to ride a bike. [Pause] Did you see other children who were riding bicycles?

Patient nods.

Therapist: And I'll bet you wanted to do that, did you not? [A negative to discharge resistance.] And just remember the time when you very first tried [implies a memory of when he "tried" but failed] to ride a two-wheeled bike. [Brief pause] Where are you? [Note use of present tense.]

Patient: On the driveway of our apartments.

Therapist: And is there anyone with you?

Patient: A bigger boy from up the street, who has a bike.

Therapist: And have you been watching him ride his bike?

Patient: Um hmm. He can ride it good.

Therapist: And I want you to just tell me, what's happening?

Patient: He's letting me get on his bike. I'm touching with both my tippy toes and trying to start, but it's too wiggly. He tells me to pick up my feet and push on the peddles, and he pushes on the back of the bike. I'm starting to go, but it's going over and I'm falling. Oww! I skinned up my leg, and he's saying, "You can't even do it."

Therapist: And how do you feel?

Patient: Stupid. I don't know how he can ride it like that. I can't make it stay up.

Therapist: It kind of feels impossible, huh?

Patient nods "yes" to the expression of empathy.

Therapist: Now allow your mind to move ahead in time, to the very next time that you tried to ride a bike. And when you're there, nod your head, and describe to me what's happening.

Patient recounts another experience with the same boy, of trying several times, and falling down, failing each time.

Therapist: And I'll bet that really hurt your feelings. The frustrations of that, and the pain and discouragement of that, must have been enormous. You must have wondered if you would ever learn to ride like other people.

Patient nods.

Therapist: But you didn't give up, did you?

Patient shakes his head "No."

Therapist: And let your mind move ahead further, beginning to remember times when you tried again. And I wonder, did someone else, who was kind, help you?

Patient nods.

Therapist: And before long I'll bet you could go a little further before you lost your balance, couldn't you?

Patient nods.

Therapist: That's right, and enjoy experiencing that. [Brief pause] And then a little further. [Brief pause] And finally, remember what it was like when you really sailed along on that bike, and then, stopped it, under your own control. [Pause] And was there a smile on your face?

Patient nods affirmatively, and begins to grin.

Therapist: Yes! Because what had seemed impossible, and insurmountable, you just did! And can you feel that sense of triumph right now?

Patient nods "yes."

Therapist: [Brief pause] And yet, you know, it wasn't very long after that, before you began to forget how challenging and difficult that was. In the years ahead, you just began riding that bike automatically, spontaneously, instinctively, didn't you?

Patient nods.

Therapist: And without remembering the very complex neuromuscular coordination it required, without thinking about how many times you made mistakes and fell, in learning to ride that bike. It was such a challenge! There was a time when it seemed impossible and overwhelming! And yet you came to take it for granted. And that wasn't the first time, and it most assuredly wasn't the last experience you had, of discovering that what may seem impossible and overwhelming, can be accomplished, and taken for granted. There was a time, I'm sure, when you were even younger, when it felt impossible for you to be able to get up and walk, like you saw other people do. And maybe you can imagine, or reexperience that for a few moments again, now. [Brief pause] And how frustrating it was when you fell down, so many times, in initially trying to learn to walk. [Brief pause] But you didn't give up! And maybe there was someone you turned to for help. And after a while, you mastered it. But, at one time I'm sure it must have felt like you'd never learn to walk like others. [Brief pause] And it was the same with learning to feed yourself, [Brief pause] and with learning to read. [Brief pause] And so you've really had a lifetime of experiences of discovering, that what can seem insurmountable, can be accomplished, and taken for granted. And with regard to [Citing a current skill or problem the patient is seeking to master], this also will be mastered, and taken for granted. And a time will come, when you'll seldom even remember how difficult it seemed or what a struggle it was. From all of your learnings of the past, and the things you've mastered that were difficult, there will be an abiding sense of confidence, deep inside you, that you will finally triumph over and accomplish this too.

Considerations in Using Hypnosis With Trauma Victims

Recently, hypnosis has been unfairly singled out for criticism by persons in the false memory movement. New myths, as outrageous as the old historical myths about hypnosis, are now being perpetuated — for instance, that hypnosis creates false memories. Although the research in this area is exhaustively reviewed elsewhere (Brown et al., 1997), the scientific literature on hypnosis and memory basically finds the following.

Hypnosis, while not magical in producing hypermnesia, has definite potential for enhancing the recall for personally meaningful or emotional material (for example, over standard interviews), without increased potential for confabulation. However, hypnotically elicited memories cannot be assumed to be accurate without independent corroboration. Suggestive influence may mildly increase someone's confidence in either accurate or inaccurate recollections, including memories recalled in hypnosis. However, the allegations that hypnosis concretizes someone's memories, making them immune to subsequent cross-examination (and that, therefore, hypnotically refreshed testimony should not be admissible in a court of law), has been disproven. Hypnotic influence on confidence in recollections has been found to pale in comparison with the usual pretrial preparation done by an attorney.

It can also now be definitively stated that hypnotic procedures do not encourage the development of false memories any more than may occur in an interview situation, and that social influence (such as the use of leading questions and undue suggestion) is the most influential variable in creating false recollections. It is one's style of interviewing (or telling anecdotes or metaphors), not whether or not hypnosis is used, that may distort recollections or beliefs. Furthermore, it appears that most of the very simple false memory reports elicited in hypnosis experiments do not represent actual alterations in memory at all. Instead, the vast majority appear to only represent false memory reports that seek to meet the experimenter's expectations. Furthermore, giving suggestions for hypnotic age regression has not been found to increase the possibility of obtaining false memories. Nonetheless, in hypnotically-facilitated psychotherapy, or any form of therapy, there appears to be an increased risk for pseudomemory production when: a person comes to therapy with pre-existing beliefs compatible with a recollection that is obtained later (so that the event has a high perceived likelihood to the patient of having occurred); when the person lacks memory and is uncertain what occurred; the person possesses higher hypnotic ability (an intrapersonal quality independent of whether hypnosis was used); and when contaminating social influence is then brought to bear (from a twelve-step or therapy group, reading, parents, friends, lawyers, documentaries, therapists). But, to reiterate, when used in an appropriate manner, hypnotic techniques are no more likely to contaminate memory than other routine psychotherapy and interviewing techniques (Brown et al., 1997; Hammond et al., 1995; Kanovitz, 1992).

Although metaphors may be utilized without the formal use of hypnosis, it is vitally important for clinicians treating trauma survivors to be aware of current research and guidelines for treatment in order to offer a high standard of care (Brown et al., 1997; Hammond et al., 1995). For example, a hypnotic-like procedure (such as guided imagery, "deep relaxation") may be judged in legal proceedings to have constituted the use of hypnosis. The use of hypnosis or hypnotic-like procedures, particularly without following forensic guidelines (Hammond et al., 1995), with someone who may subsequently have to testify in a court of law (for example, about a rape or molestation) may disqualify their testimony (Scheflin & Shapiro, 1989), and incur liability for the therapist who has not conducted informed consent prior to using the procedure (Hammond et al., 1995).

In 1994, I served as an expert witness in a case in which a young therapist with limited hypnosis training responded to a seriously disturbed and unstable patient's desire to be hypnotized so as to recall the man who raped her many months before. Previously, the patient indicated that the rapist had been someone known to a certain relative. Later, the therapist alleged that she had not used hypnosis. However, a tape recording was made of the session. My analysis of the tape found that an induction procedure was used and suggestions made for some hypnotic phenomena. Subsequently, the therapist offered several therapeutic metaphors (read to the patient from a book), many of which conveyed the theme that things which have seemed to be one way, and which we believed were one way, can be discovered to actually be quite different. After this hypnosis session, the patient changed her story and now accused an in-law of raping her. There was no independent corroborating evidence for this allegation, and, in fact, evidence existed that the accused was hundreds of miles away at the time. Although we may never know with assurance the identity of the rapist, I had to testify in an evidentiary hearing that the procedure was, in fact, hypnosis (which the embarrassed therapist afterwards admitted in court, although referring to it as "Ericksonian hypnosis"), and that undue suggestion had been used which represented a potential contaminant. In keeping with state statutes, the woman's testimony was not allowed, and the case dismissed.

Too often, clinicians without thorough training (certification through the American Society of Clinical Hypnosis,[1] experience, or diplomate status from a *legitimately recognized* hypnosis board), may begin to use hypnosis or "guided imagery" with abuse or trauma cases without proper preparation. It is recommended that even when hypnosis is not being used in trauma treatment, that therapists are wise to either elicit hypnotic phenomena of known difficulty level, or preferably, to formally administer a scale of hypnotic responsivity such as the Hypnotic Induction Profile, the Stanford Hypnotic Clinical Scale, or the Harvard Group Scale of Hypnotic Susceptibility. This recommendation is

---

1. For information on systematic, high quality training, certification in clinical hypnosis, and guidelines on hypnosis and memory, contact: American Society of Clinical Hypnosis, 140 N. Bloomingdale Road, Bloomingdale, IL 60108, USA; http://www.asch.net.

offered because research (summarized in Brown et al., 1997) suggests that the intrapersonal quality of moderate to high hypnotic capacity likely makes a person more vulnerable to suggestive influence and the possible creation of pseudomemories, irrespective of whether traditional talking therapies or hypnosis is used. Thus, assessing the level of hypnotic responsivity demonstrates awareness of these issues in the current litigious environment of false memory allegations, and provides important information to the clinician. With my patients with potential abuse issues, I also now administer the Gudjonsson Scale of Interrogative Suggestibility (Gudjonsson, 1984, 1987) which evaluates how easily a patient's recollections in a non-hypnotic interview are vulnerable to social influence (leading questions). These procedures, along with a written informed consent document, help assure both a high standard of care for patients and provide added liability protection for therapists working with patients with potential abuse (Brown et al., 1997; Hammond et al., 1995).

Other recommendations for using hypnosis include prehypnotic assessment of the patient (including evaluation of potential sources of previous contamination in new patients who have beliefs that they have been abused, and yet do not recall it, or who have previously recovered memories of being abused); eliciting patients expectations concerning the nature of hypnosis, and then educating them concerning hypnosis, hypnosis and memory, the imperfect nature of memory processes, the existence of confabulation, and the need for corroboration before one may know for sure the veridicality of new memories; obtaining written acknowledgment of this informed consent process; seeking to create neutral expectations in patients concerning both whether any new information may be forthcoming if hypnotic exploration techniques are used, and concerning the possible accuracy or inaccuracy of any such information that is elicited; suggestions on the importance of allowing free recall and for how hypnotic exploration should be conducted; careful chart documentation; and the importance of maintaining supportive neutrality concerning the accuracy of any recovered memories.

Conclusions

Metaphors are one of the suggestive techniques that may be valuable in communicating with patients in psychotherapy, perhaps particularly when their attention has been focused on the ideas through the formal or informal use of hypnosis. In particular, truism metaphors and the use of formal or informal age regression to positive life experiences or metaphoric experiences of mastery seems to elicit an acceptance-set in the patient. Such techniques are invaluable in facilitating perceptual change. However, it is vitally important for anyone working with potential survivors of trauma or abuse, and especially when using suggestive techniques or hypnosis, to have an awareness of research in this area and to incorporate the latest guidelines into their practice.

References

Barber, T. X. (1969). *Hypnosis: A scientific approach.* New York: Van Nostrand Reinhold.

Barber, T. X. (1978). Hypnosis, suggestions, and psychosomatic phenomena: A new look from the standpoint of recent experimental studies. *American Journal of Clinical Hypnosis, 21,* 13-27.

Barker, P. (1996). *Psychotherapeutic metaphors: A guide to theory and practice.* New York: Brunner/Mazel.

Brown, D. B., Scheflin, A. P., & Hammond, D. C. (1997). *Memory, trauma treatment, and law.* New York: W. W. Norton.

Erickson, M. H. (1966). The interspersal hypnotic technique for symptom correction and pain control. *American Journal of Clinical Hypnosis, 8,* 198–209.

Erickson, M. H., & Rossi, E. L. (1979). *Hypnotherapy: An exploratory casebook.* New York: Irvington.

Erickson, M. H. (1980). *The collected papers of Milton H. Erickson on Hypnosis.* (4 vols.) (E. L. Rossi, Ed.) New York: Irvington.

Gordon, D. C. (1978). *Therapeutic metaphors: Helping others through the looking glass.* Cupertino, CA: Meta Publications.

Gudjonsson, G. H. (1984). A new scale of interrogative suggestibility. *Personality and Individual Differences, 5,* 303–314.

Gudjonsson, G. H. (1987). A parallel form of the Gudjonsson Suggestibility Scale. *British Journal of Clinical Psychology, 26,* 215–221.

Hammond, D. C. (1984). Myths about Erickson and Ericksonian hypnosis. *American Journal of Clinical Hypnosis, 26,* 236–245.

Hammond, D. C. (1985). An instrument for utilizing client interests & individualizing hypnosis. *Ericksonian Monographs, 1,* 111–126

Hammond, D. C. (1988). "Will the real Milton Erickson please stand up?" *International Journal of Clinical and Experimental Hypnosis, 36,* 173–181.

Hammond, D. C. (Ed.) (1990). *Handbook of hypnotic suggestions and metaphors.* New York: W. W. Norton.

Hammond, D. C., Garver, R. B., Mutter, C. B., Crasilneck, H. B., Frischholz, E., Gravitz, M. A., Hibler, N. S., Olson, J., Scheflin, A., Spiegel, H., & Wester, W. (1995). *Clinical hypnosis and memory: Guidelines for clinicians and for forensic hypnosis.* [Seattle, WA]: American Society of Clinical Hypnosis Press.

Hammond, D. C., Hepworth, D., & Smith, V. G. (1977). *Improving therapeutic communication.* San Francisco: Jossey-Bass.

Kanovitz, J. (1992). Hypnotic memories and civil sexual abuse trials. *Vanderbilt Law Review, 45,* 1185–1262.

Lankton, C. H.., & Lankton, S. R. (1989). *Tales of enchantment: Goal-oriented metaphors for adults and children in therapy.* New York: Brunner/Mazel.

Scheflin, A. W., & Shapiro, J. L. (1989). *Trance on trial.* New York: Guilford

Truax, C. B., & Carkhuff, R. R. (1967). *Toward effective counseling and psychotherapy: Training and practice.* Chicago: Aldine.

Zeig, J. (1980). Erickson's use of anecdotes. In J. Zeig (Ed.), *A teaching seminar with Milton H. Erickson, M.D* (pp. 3–28). New York: Brunner/Mazel.

Section II.

Personal Mythology

CHAPTER SEVEN

Personal Mythologies:
A Framework for Dealing with
Therapeutic and Supervisory Impasses

Stephen A. Anderson & Sarah E. Holmes

Few interpersonal encounters outside of our own family and close personal relationships have the potential to consistently unleash such powerful emotions and personal responses as therapy. The often urgency of clients' needs, the seriousness of their situations, the intensity of their interpersonal conflicts, and their ambivalence over making necessary changes can leave therapists feeling overwhelmed, pressured, and highly reactive. At such times, clinical supervision can either become an important source of support and guidance, or another source of stress. Although the field of marriage and family therapy has made significant advances in delineating the critical conceptual, intervention, and relationship skills needed for effective family therapy (see, for example, Anderson, 1992; Barton & Alexander, 1977; Cleghorn & Levin, 1973; Piercy, Laird, & Mohammed, 1983; Pulleyblank & Shapiro, 1986; Myers, Avis, & Sprenkle, 1990), only recently have family therapists begun to examine how therapists deal with intense affect as it occurs in therapy (Kiser, Piercy, & Lipchik, 1993; Kleckner, Frank, Bland, Amendt, & Bryant, 1992). Yet to be explored is how supervision can help therapists to manage these intense emotions when they arise.

In this chapter, we will present a brief review of the literature on the role of affect in marital and family therapy. This will be followed by a review of the supervision literature on this topic. We will then outline our own mythological perspective and describe how it can be used in supervision to facilitate therapists' work with clients around emotionally-loaded issues. We will then provide a case illustration that will highlight the role of supervision in facilitating affective expressions in the therapeutic system.

Affect in Marital and Family Therapy

Marriage and family therapists who emphasize the role of affect in their therapeutic work tend to operate within the general domain of experiential and systemic approaches. Experiential models highlight the importance of the immediate, moment-to-moment encounter. Systemic approaches, in contrast, emphasize the role of communication and how redundant interactional patterns maintain relational problems. In affective approaches to therapy, couples and family members are encouraged to interact directly with one another in sessions and to examine and disclose their underlying feelings and needs as they arise in the current moment (Dandeneau & Johnson, 1994). Change is thought to occur as a result of clients being helped to access key emotional experiences which bring to light new aspects of the self. Increased access and responsiveness to repressed, denied, or unexpressed feelings can alter a person's presentation of self to significant others who are then, in turn, able to alter their responses to the person (Greenberg & Johnson, 1986; Johnson & Greenberg, 1988). The outcome of such interactions is often a greater sense of shared intimacy between family members (Weingarten, 1991).

For instance, a spouse who has refrained from expressing his anger and frustration at his wife after finding out that she is pregnant again, distances himself, spending increasing amounts of time away from home in new projects. As his anger and underlying hurt is disclosed, the couple is able to address the conflict between them more directly. The wife's anger at her husband for being unavailable to her, and her suspicions that he is having an affair, subside as her view of him changes from a callous, unfeeling cad to a man who feels disappointed and betrayed. The therapeutic goal here is not to increase insight or facilitate ventilation, per se, but rather to help individuals achieve a greater level of self-acceptance and to enhance the flexibility in spousal and family interactions. Affective expression is viewed as a vehicle by which new perceptions of self and other, and new definitions of the relationship, become possible (Johnson & Greenberg, 1988).

Dealing with Affect in Supervision

As noted above, little attention has been given in the family therapy field to the supervisor's role in helping therapists deal with clients' emotional experiences. The one notable exception has been symbolic-experiential supervisors who use such concepts as "co-transference," "battle for initiative," and "non-rational experience" to highlight the importance of helping therapists to tolerate their own and clients' anxiety, to develop the courage necessary to face difficult problems, and to trust their own unconscious and creative impulses (Boylin,

Anderson, & Bartle, 1992; Connell, 1984; Connell, Whitaker, Garfield, & Connell, 1990; Whitaker & Keith, 1981). Here, co-therapy teams often comprised of the supervisor and supervisee struggle with one another and with their own personal imperfections, fantasies, and irrational impulses in front of clients who learn to struggle with similar issues as a result of the therapists' encouragement and modeling behaviors. Awareness of, and attention to, the needs of self and others is encouraged. The therapist's active participation in the process of self-examination and disclosure can lead to a sense of shared intimacy between clients and therapist (Weingarten, 1992; Whitaker, 1989).

Although the symbolic-experiential model of therapy and supervision is extremely helpful in eliciting intense affects, the focus is primarily upon what emerges in the therapy room, in the here-and-now. The model does not systematically address the connections between therapists' in-session experiences and their broader familial and interpersonal experiences. Most notably absent is attention to the therapist's/supervisee's family of origin experiences and the history of their own significant relationships. The integration of one's therapeutic self with other definitions of self is not a focus of supervision.

It is our contention that examining these other definitions of self as they relate to one's therapeutic identity can be useful in several respects. First, the integration of differing definitions of self can promote personal growth by contributing to a greater sense of wholeness. Second, these differing self-definitions can be useful in identifying therapists' unique therapeutic strengths. Third, such information can be useful in helping therapists to identify any of their own "emotional blindspots" that may be interfering with their clients' therapeutic progress. We have found a narrative approach, or what has been referred to elsewhere as a mythological perspective, to be extremely useful in helping therapists integrate different definitions of self, and in identifying intense affects that can either facilitate or inhibit clients' therapeutic progress (Anderson & Bagarozzi, 1989; Bagarozzi & Anderson, 1989).

A Mythological Perspective

The perspective taken here relies heavily upon earlier writings in which a model of therapy with individuals, couples, and families was developed (Anderson & Bagarozzi, 1983, 1989; Bagarozzi & Anderson, 1982, 1989). The model integrates unconscious, symbolic, and metaphorical elements of individual human experience with the narrative and interactional dimensions of human relationships.

The concept most relevant to the present discussion is *personal mythology*. Personal myths are those cognitive structures that serve the function of explaining, sacralizing, and guiding the individual in a manner analogous to the role played by cultural myths in society (Feinstein, 1979). They are symbolic reconstructions of past experiences (biological, familial, social, cultural) which infuses them with psychological order and meaning for the individual (Anderson & Bagarozzi, 1989). Personal myths are the stories we create to explain our past, give meaning to our present, and guide our future. The family of origin is where one's personal mythology has its genesis. Personal mythologies are complexes of three basic structural components: the self, the self-in-relation-to-others (interpersonal style), and the internalized ideals we hold of significant others.

The *self* is defined as a superordinate personal structural system having cognitive and affective components operating at both conscious and unconscious levels of awareness. The self attempts to bring order and meaning to one's life and existence. Although the self strives for wholeness and completeness, traumatic experiences during critical periods of an individual's development often impede or prevent full integration and actualization. One's personal behavior and the behavior of others are perceived, experienced, interpreted, and responded to according to how these experiences are cognitively organized and viewed by the self.

Interpersonal styles evolve as one confronts and attempts to master the various developmental tasks and interpersonal conflicts with significant others that occur during each stage of the life cycle. The more difficulty one has in mastering a particular developmental task, the more this unresolved task will persist as a motive throughout one's life. *Such unresolved issues with significant others continue to resurface as major themes in one's personal mythology.* Major themes tend to develop around unresolved issues of loss, separation, abandonment, individuation, nurturance, and deprivation (Anderson & Bagarozzi, 1983).

We contend that one way persons attempt to rework unresolved conflicts with significant others is through the selection of personally meaningful fairy tales, folk stories, nursery rhymes, novels, short stories, motion pictures, television programs or other favorite stories and recollections. The story becomes a screen memory for significant (traumatic) events. Much like the manifest content of a dream, it can be viewed as a symbolically disguised wish or attempt to solve an important relationship conflict or developmental task that is pressing for expression and successful resolution. These stories can also offer new solutions to interpersonal problems, or re-edited versions of one's personal mythology.

As we recollect our family of origin experiences, significant persons with whom we came in contact become associated symbolically with specific characters in our stories through such processes as projection, introjection, transference, or modeling. When we recall our significant relationships, what we actually remember are reconstructions of events and experiences with idealized versions of these persons.

Truth or accuracy can have little to do with how these persons and one's relationship with them are recalled. These reconstructed relationships between and among significant others can become models for our contemporary marital or familial role expectations and relationship themes.

The term *"ideal"* as we use it, does not connote perfection. It simply represents an enduring, fairly stable, internal, cognitive image of one's desired mate, child, friend, client, therapist or supervisor that becomes a standard against which all prospective relationships are compared and judged. The discrepancy between one's ideal image and the actual behavior of the significant other can become a source of unfilled expectations, frustration, and interpersonal conflict.

The development of personal themes depicting the self, the self-in-relation-to others and the idealization of others is illustrated in the case of a young woman who was raised by punitive, authoritarian parents. A central theme in this young woman's personal mythology was, if translated concretely, "I am an unworthy person who can easily disappoint those to whom I am close. I have little to offer those who have given the most to me. They would be better off without me. Therefore, I will not impose myself upon the people with whom I am close, but rather, I will keep to myself and in so doing not risk disappointing or failing them." This theme: (1) organized the woman's memories of her earlier experiences; (2) defined her sense of self (unworthy); (3) prescribed the present and future behavior of the self-in-relation-to-significant others (stay away from them so as to not fail them); and (4) idealized significant others (as easily disappointed in her and deserving better). Such a theme could easily lead to conflicts in this young woman's adult personal relationships with regard to self disclosure, intimacy, or even chronic anxiety about disappointing others. It might predict a history of broken relationships which would reinforce her feelings of failure. It might even predict a future career of "helping others" to "prove her parents wrong" or to "make up for the disappointments she has given to significant others."

In our approach to clinical supervision, the therapist's own personal origins, mythologies, and symbolic and affectively-laden themes play a critical role in the development of the therapeutic system. We assume that therapists will perceive, define, and respond to others (clients, supervisors, colleagues) in ways that are congruent with their own preconceived cognitive schemata, attributions, values and beliefs, and that they will reenact their own familiar scripts, roles, and personal themes within the therapeutic system. For this reason, we believe that it is essential to understand the therapist's view of himself/herself, the functioning of that self-in-relation to significant selves (members of the family of origin, spouses, children, the supervisor) and the internal ideals the therapist has regarding significant others. The central elements of the therapist's personal mythology alert us to potential unresolved conflicts within the self, or in relationships with significant others which may resurface in the therapist's personal encounters with clients. The essential question is "Who does the client (or perhaps the supervisor) represent in the therapist's own personal mythology?"

As we have worked with the model, we have isolated four indicators which are helpful in identifying ones' personal themes. Although they were first developed as an aid to clinical assessment in therapy, we have found that they are equally applicable to supervision. These are:

1. Recurrent topics of concern. We pay particular attention to the content of topics that supervisees continue to express during supervision. For example, one therapist consistently brought up the topic of clients not making rapid enough progress in therapy. This might have been nothing more than a by-product of inexperience and a lack of familiarity with the process of therapeutic change. However, it turned out to be an element of a central, life-long theme of feeling valued by others only when one can demonstrate "hard effort, quick results, and visible success in whatever one undertakes."

2. Redundant interaction patterns. Here we are interested in assessing whether family members' interactions, or the interactions between therapist and family members, or between supervisee and supervisor have taken on a rigid, inflexible pattern. Have, for instance, therapeutic sessions taken on a pattern in which the therapist reinforces dysfunctional interactions or have supervisory sessions taken on a predictable pattern of sameness? In the example noted above, the therapist would typically press clients to formulate their goals and then press for concrete progress before establishing sufficient trust and safety in sessions. When clients were reluctant to comply with the therapist, she would become frustrated with them for their "lack of progress."

3. Repeated surfacing of specific, affect-laden conflicts. This indicator focuses upon whether similar conflicts surface in a variety of clinical cases or whether the same conflicts surface consistently during supervisory sessions. In the above example, a great deal of supervisory time was devoted to the impasse this therapist was experiencing with clients. The more she would push them to change, the more "resistance" she would encounter. Underlying this therapist's frustration and anger at her clients were her own feelings of inadequacy and self-doubt. As long as she focused on her "frustrations" with her clients, she was unable to examine her own personal feelings. Furthermore, she was unable to decenter and take the perspective of her clients whose own feelings of mistrust, anxiety, and fear hindered them from following the therapist's lead.

4. The supervisory session's predominant affective tone. Here we are especially interested in how working with a particular supervisee makes us feel. We use our own experience to underscore the central affective tone that may characterize an entire therapeutic system of supervisor, therapist, and clients. In this example, the supervisor's affective experience was one of anxiety. When the supervisor's experience was openly acknowledged, a discussion ensued as to whom else in the therapeutic system (clients, therapist) might also be feeling anxious. This, in turn, made it possible to examine the origins of the therapist's anxiety and to begin to explore the content and origins of the theme of "hard effort, quick results, and visible success in whatever one undertakes."

We have found these four indicators to quite helpful in identifying significant themes that we assume to be operating at multiple levels of the therapeutic system. The therapeutic system is a powerfully charged, fluid, dynamic patch-work of contributions from clients, therapist, and supervisor. We believe that the themes that predominate at one level of the system are generally operating at other levels as well. They have the potential to both hinder or facilitate therapeutic progress. If we can help the therapist to tap into and understand his or her own predominant themes, he or she will be able to use this information as a therapeutic resource for clinical work. Those themes that have the potential to hinder therapeutic progress when understood, have the equally powerful potential to facilitate personal growth and development for both therapist and clients alike. They facilitate a greater sense of wholeness and self awareness and sensitize the therapist to the connections between their in-session behaviors (therapeutic self) and their broader familial and interpersonal experiences (other definitions of self). Furthermore, they provide the therapist with a greater sense of freedom, spontaneity, flexibility, and creativity in responding to clients' needs.

Personal Myths Assessment Guidelines

Central themes in the therapist's personal mythology can be also be identified with the aid of the Personal Myths Assessment Guidelines (Bagarozzi & Anderson, 1989). The fourteen questions that comprise the guidelines, when combined with basic information about the supervisee's family of origin history, provide rich information about the central conflicts, themes, and relationship dynamics that the therapist may bring to the therapeutic system. The questions follow:

1. What is your favorite fairy tale, book, short story, play, movie, or television show, and why do you like this particular story? Please give a summary of the story in your own words. It is important to let supervisees tell the story in their own words without interference. Truth or accuracy in reporting the story is not important. It is the person's version of the story that is important.

2. Who is your favorite character in the story and why do you like this character so much? One's favorite character is not necessarily a significant other with whom one identifies, it may also represent an aspect of the self. And, it may change over time, depending upon external circumstances, or in response to some reorganization in one's personal mythology. Frequently, the person's favorite character and the character he or she would like to be (# 13) are one in the same, but this is not always the case.

3. How is this character treated by others in the story? This question is helpful in identifying salient relationship conflicts and interpersonal themes.

4. What important things does the character do in the story? This question can help one learn more about the person's drives and motives and highlight developmental tasks that may not have been successfully mastered.

5. What important things happen to the character throughout the story? Significant, sometimes traumatic events are often described in response to this question.

6. What happens to this character at the end of the story? In many instances, the end of the story offers a solution to the character's central problem or provides a resolution to an interpersonal conflict between various characters.

7. What character in the story do you dislike the most? Why do you dislike this character? In our view, each character identified in one's story symbolically represents not only significant persons in one's life (or a least aspects of these individuals), but also significant aspects of the self. For example a hero may represent one's ego ideal whereas a harsh, demanding character may represent one's super ego or sense of self worth. Animals or monsters may represent instincts, drives, or motives. Villains or sinister characters may represent denied, repressed, and projected shadow aspects of the self that are totally unacceptable to conscious awareness.

Questions eight, nine, ten, and eleven correspond to numbers three, four, five, and six but they are focused on the disliked character rather than on the favorite character. They are used to gain additional depth, breadth, and insight into central conflicts, motives or themes, and to unearth additional ones.

8. How is this character treated by others in the story?

9. What important things does this character do in the story?

10. What important things happen to this character in the story?

11. What happens to this character at the end of the story?

12. How does the character you dislike treat your favorite character? What is their relationship like? This question usually crystallizes the major dynamic of a central conflict. However, the conflict may or may not be one in which the individual participated directly. It may be one the individual observed peripherally between significant others which, nonetheless, produced a traumatic impact that has been internalized.

13. If you could be any character in the story, who would you be and why? This question is important because it underscores the person's conscious identifications and brings to light some of the beliefs, expectations, attributes, values and attitudes that the person consciously holds concerning his or her role in resolving interpersonal conflicts or mastering pressing development tasks.

14. If you could change any part of the story, what changes would you make and why? This question enables us to see the person's desired outcome from his or her own perspective.

When we contrast supervisees' responses to these questions with: (1) their family of origin history; and (2) the topics of concern and affective responses that recur in their work with clients, the parallels are often striking. Once the therapist has been able to make these connections on a conscious level, new solutions to therapeutic impasses with clients often follow. The following case is presented to illustrate how this information can be applied to clinical supervision.

Case Example

This case example is about Stacy, a twenty-three-year-old white female in a marriage and family training program. In response to the Personal Myth Assessment Interview (Bagarozzi & Anderson, 1989), Stacy identified Cinderella as her favorite fairy tale. As she described a brief summary of this fairy tale, she stated that everything was wonderful in Cinderella's life before her mother died. She was in a happy family with two parents who took very good care of her. When her mother died and her father remarried, Cinderella's life turned into a nightmare. Her needs were ignored, she was severely punished for no apparent reason, and she had to work excessively hard at doing housework.

Stacy continued retelling the story by describing how the King decided that his son, the Prince, needed to find a wife. So, the king held a ball to which every eligible woman in the kingdom was invited to attend. Of course, her mean step-mother decided that Cinderella could not attend the ball. But, thanks to a fairy godmother, she was able to attend. She and the prince fell in love and were tragically separated due to the magic spell running out. Even though her step-mother tried to keep her trapped in the home, she was able to escape and run into the arms of the Prince. After finding that the glass slipper did indeed fit, she and the Prince left and were married. And of course, she lived happily ever after.

When Stacy was filling out the Personal Myth Assessment Interview, she had a difficult time deciding which was her favorite character in the story. She finally decided on two characters, Cinderella and the Fairy Godmother. Following is her description of why she liked each of them and what happened to them in the story. She liked Cinderella because, "she was a real fighter. She had a good heart and never gave up on her dreams. Because she was such a good person, good things happened to her that helped her make her dreams come true" (escaping her mean step-family and marrying the Prince).

Stacy described the obstacles in Cinderella's way (the mean step-mother and step-sisters) and the unfair things that happened to her. Stacy thought that Cinderella's step-mother and step-sisters were selfish, self-centered and not interested in what Cinderella wanted. Stacy thought that those characters stood in Cinderella's way of happiness. She also liked the fact that Cinderella triumphed in the end. Stacy described Cinderella as persevering in the end, with the help of her friends (the animals and fairy godmother). She was able to leave behind those who stood in her way of happiness and escape to a life of happiness. Stacy described the last scene of the fairy tale as one of her favorites. That is the scene in which Cinderella and the Prince are in the carriage, going down the road after just being married.

Stacy's other favorite character was the Fairy Godmother. She liked this character because she had the magic to make everything alright for Cinderella. The fairy godmother came to her rescue, fixing everything so that she could go to the ball. Stacy remembered feeling in awe of the power of the Fairy Godmother. She simply appeared out of nowhere and transformed Cinderella's life. Stacy also described her as "old, plump, kind, and generous, just as a Godmother should be." According to Stacy, "this was one character who was trying to take care of Cinderella and had her best interests in mind."

Stacy's least favorite characters were the stepmother and the stepsisters. Stacy recalled one scene in which the step-mother promised that Cinderella could go to the ball. Of course, Cinderella did not have a dress, so she made one out of scraps that her stepsisters had thrown away. When Cinderella came downstairs, ready for the dance, her step-sisters became jealous of how good she looked. They became very angry and began tearing her dress apart, saying that Cinderella could not have the material that they had previously discarded. So, bows and sashes were torn off her dress until nothing was left but rags. Stacy described the step-mother as standing there laughing at Cinderella instead of protecting her. Stacy thought that they were incredibly cruel and unfair to Cinderella.

When asked about what Stacy would change about the fairy tale, she responded by saying that she would have Cinderella's step-mother and step-sister "accept her and treat her well." She would have Cinderella become part of a "normal and happy stepfamily instead of having to escape from a terrible situation." She also would have written a more nurturing role for Cinderella's father, instead of having him absent from the story.

In examining Stacy's responses to the questions from the Personal Myth Assessment Interview, several themes emerged. First, Stacy consistently described Cinderella's life as unsafe. Because of the erratic mood swings of her step-mother and step-sisters, Cinderella had to be constantly on guard. Any little thing might send the step-mother into a rage, according to Stacy. Therefore, the theme that *"intense emotions were not safe"* emerged as an important part of this fairy tale.

The second theme to emerge was *"I must make the other person happy."* Stacy described how Cinderella tried to placate both her step-mother and step-sisters by doing whatever they wanted her to do. If Cinderella made them happy, she could remain safe. Clearly, these two themes were intertwined. If Cinderella could "appease others," she could remain "safe" and avoid anything that would cause an intense emotional reaction.

The third theme that emerged as a consequence of the first two themes was, *"family members do not meet your needs."* By placating others and trying not to upset anyone, Cinderella was not able to ask for anything that she needed. Stacy stated that the only way Cinderella got her needs met was through outside interventions (the Godmother) and by escaping from the step-family (marrying the Prince).

In summary, the three themes identified were: (1) negative emotions are unsafe; (2) make others happy so that you can remain safe; and (3) your own needs are not important.

When Stacy's responses to the questions about her family of origin were compared with the questions about her favorite fairy tale, some striking similarities became evident. Stacy's own mother had shifted back and forth between being Cinderella's loving biological mother and the wicked step-mother. At times, her mother was supportive, nurturing, and safe. At other times, without any apparent reason, she could shift into the role of the stepmother, becoming angry, harsh, and punitive. During these times, Stacy would either try to stay out of her mother's way, or do anything that she thought would help calm her down. During times of calm, Stacy focused her attention on keeping things running smoothly in her family. Just like Cinderella, Stacy worked hard at keeping the emotional climate in the family calm.

Thus, the goal of keeping the family's emotional climate calm (first theme) was achieved by making others, specifically Stacy's mother, happy (second theme). Stacy tried to placate her mother by anticipating her needs and fulfilling them. For example, if she thought her mother needed help with dinner, she would help without being asked. Her basic motivation was to avoid anything that would trigger an intense emotional reaction from her mother and jeopardize her own safety.

The third theme identified in Stacy's favorite fairy tale, "your own needs are not important," turned out to also be a significant theme in her family of origin. Stacy felt that she could not ask for her needs to be met because asking for something could "cause" an intense emotional reaction (first theme), and turn her mother into the wicked step-mother. Furthermore, asking for things did not fit with trying to please her mother (second theme). Therefore, a pattern developed that left Stacy's needs unmet. She recalled one instance in which she tried to keep her mother from getting upset by not asking for a new dress for her sixth grade graduation. Stacy knew it was coming up but she was afraid that her mother would become very angry if she asked for a dress. She vividly remembers walking up the church steps one Sunday morning while her mother yelled at her for not telling her about the graduation. Her mother told her that if she had known earlier, she would have taken her shopping for the dress. She was angry at her daughter for not giving her enough time to go shopping. Looking back on this experience, Stacy reported feeling "trapped with nowhere to turn." If she had asked for her needs to be met, she faced a possible intense negative reaction. Yet, when she didn't ask, she experienced that same negative reaction.

As has been demonstrated, Stacy's experiences in her family of origin were metaphorically represented in her choice of a favorite fairy tale. The next step was to examine how these themes were being played out in Stacy's therapeutic experiences with her clients.

In supervision, Stacy reported feeling stuck with one particular case. The family was comprised of a single-parent mother in her mid-forties and her two 15 year-old twins, one a boy and the other a girl. The mother originally brought in the boy, wanting Stacy to "fix him." The mother described her son as being "too shy" and "needing more self confidence." During the intake procedure, Stacy discovered that the twins had very little contact with their biological father. The mother stated that the father was "no good" and that he "did not really care about his two children." After a couple of sessions, the mother brought in the other twin wanting her to be "fixed" as well. The daughter was described as being sexually promiscuous and doing poorly in school.

Stacy, trying to be systemic, asked to see the entire family, including the biological father. She suspected that the children's "problems" were manifestations of problems in the family, especially between the parents. Both children reported a great deal of conflict between their mother and father. They described not being able to talk about their father in front of their mother. Making arrangements to visit their father was very difficult for them because they were afraid to tell their mother that they wanted to see him. The children expressed resentment, anger, and frustration at their parents for not getting along. Given this information, it was theorized that one significant factor that was contributing to the children's symptoms was the poor relationship between their parents.

When Stacy recommended involving the biological father in treatment, the mother refused. She told Stacy that she was obviously too naive and inexperienced to understand that it would be a waste of time to do family therapy. According to the mother, the children needed individual therapy and that was all. Stacy described this mother as becoming angry whenever Stacy tried to talk about the children's problems systemically (that is, as manifestations of problems in the family). Stacy was unable to effectively confront this mother and instead gave in by agreeing to see each twin separately. During supervision, her supervisor wanted to understand why Stacy had changed her plan for treatment when she thought that individual therapy might not be very useful. By looking back to the themes in Stacy's own family of origin, the supervisor was able to talk to her about her fear of intense emotional reactions (first theme).

Stacy realized that this mother reminded her a lot of her own mother and that she was reacting out of her own fear of making the mother angry. Stacy felt as if she was a "teenager" once again with this mother, fearing for her own safety. She was amazed at how strong her feelings of fear were with this woman and how unable she was to do anything but to retreat from any type of confrontation.

By realizing that this theme of fearing intense emotional reactions was being activated in therapy, Stacy was able to increase her tolerance for emotional intensity. She had to consciously differentiate her client from her own mother and remind herself that she was indeed safe with this mother. This client could get as angry as she wanted and Stacy could handle it by reminding herself that she was "an adult who could now protect herself."

However, Stacy continued to have difficulty working with this woman because the second theme of making others happy was also operating. Stacy felt incompetent whenever the mother challenged her treatment plan. She very much wanted to make this client happy and yet talking about the biological father's role in her children's difficulties clearly made this client resurrect unpleasant memories and feelings that she had repressed. So, even though Stacy was able to increase her tolerance for intense emotions, she still became derailed in therapy whenever she felt responsible for evoking clients' vulnerabilities and painful emotions.

Compounding Stacy's difficulty with this case was her pattern of not getting her own needs met (third theme). Stacy questioned whether it was her own need that motivated her to do family therapy with this case. Her own ambivalence made it difficult for her to insist that this be the course of treatment.

All three of these themes were being reenacted within this one particular case. Stacy repeatedly brought this case up for supervision, not understanding at first why she felt paralyzed in working with this family. By realizing how these themes were being re-enacted in her therapy, she became more aware of the sources of her own anxiety. By understanding her own fears, she was better able to understand the mother's fears of interacting with her ex-husband. As it turned out, this mother felt as unsafe with her ex-husband as Stacy had felt with her. In attempting to modify her in-therapy behavior, Stacy frequently reminded herself that she was "safe in the room," that she "did not have to please this mother," and that her plan for treatment was "worth fighting for and important."

Not surprisingly, in reflecting back, Stacy noted that this particular case had caused her the most problems in her training as a therapist. In our view, this was due to the fact that the dynamics of the case were intimately connected to the therapist's own central family of origin themes. By beginning with her favorite fairy tale, the supervisor was able to work with Stacy in identifying the important themes in her childhood. Once these themes were identified, it was then possible for Stacy to examine her own experiences in therapy and to determine how these themes were preventing her from being effective. By the end of supervision, Stacy had significantly improved her flexibility as a therapist. She was able to quickly sense when one of the themes was being activated in therapy. Instead of having her family of origin themes interfere in the therapeutic process, she was able to use this information to facilitate the process.

Conclusion

The family of origin is a storehouse of feelings, memories, and experiences, some based upon factual events and others upon reconstructions of actual events. These recollections play a key role in the development of one's personal mythology. It is our contention that the major themes that comprise one's personal mythology provide a sense of meaning and direction to our lives. When these themes are identified in our favorite stories, metaphors, redundant patterns of behavior, or recurring affective expressions, they can become powerful vehicles for interpersonal change. Whether the context is our own personal relationships, or the context is therapy or supervision, the central themes that comprise our personal mythology can become either obstructions to our growth and development, or a valuable tool for re-editing our personal scripts in a positive and adaptive way.

References

Anderson, S. A. (1992). Evaluation of an academic family therapy training program: Changes in trainees' relationship and intervention skills. *Journal of Marital and Family Therapy, 18,* 365–376.

Anderson, S. A., & Bagarozzi, D. A. (1983). The use of family myths as an aid to strategic therapy. *Journal of Family Therapy, 5,* 145–164.

Anderson, S. A., & Bagarozzi, D. A. (1989). *Family myths: Psychotherapy implications.* New York: Haworth Press.

Bagarozzi, D. A., & Anderson, S. A. (1982). The evolution of family mythological systems: Considerations for meaning, clinical assessment, and treatment. *Journal of Psychoanalytic Anthropology, 5,* 71–90.

Bagarozzi, D. A., & Anderson, S. A. (1989). *Personal, marital, and family myths: Theoretical formulations and clinical strategies.* New York: W. W. Norton.

Barton, C., & Alexander, J. F. (1977). Therapists' skills as determinants of effective systems-behavioral family therapy. *American Journal of Family Therapy, 5,* 11–19.

Boylin, W. M., Anderson, S. A., & Bartle, S. E. (1992). Symbolic-experiential supervision: A model for learning or a frame of mind. *Journal of Family Psychotherapy, 3,* 43–59.

Cleghorn, J., & Levin, S. (1973). Training family therapists by setting learning objectives. *American Journal of Orthopsychiatry, 43,* 439–446.

Connell, G. M. (1984). An approach to supervision of symbolic-experiential psychotherapy. *Journal of Marital and Family Therapy, 10,* 273–280.

Connell, G. M., Whitaker, C., Garfield, R., & Connell, L. (1990). The process of in-therapy consultation: A symbolic experiential perspective. *Journal of Strategic and Systemic Therapies, 9,* 32–38.

Dandeneau, M. L., & Johnson, S. M. (1994). Facilitating intimacy: Interventions and effects. *Journal of Marital and Family Therapy, 20,* 17–33.

Feinstein, A. D. (1979). Personal mythology as a paradigm for a holistic public psychology. *American Journal of Orthopsychiatry, 49,* 198–217.

Greenberg, L. S., & Johnson, S. M. (1986). Affect in marital therapy. *Journal of Marital and Family Therapy, 12,* 1–10.

Johnson, S. M., & Greenberg, L. S. (1988). Relating process to outcome in marital therapy. *Journal of Marital and Family Therapy, 14,* 175–184.

Kiser, D. J., Piercy, F. P., & Lipchik, E. (1993). The integration of emotion in solution-focused therapy. *Journal of Marital and Family Therapy, 19,* 233–242.

Kleckner, T., Frank, L., Bland, C., Amendt, J. H., & Bryant, R. D. (1992). The myth of the unfeeling strategic therapist. *Journal of Marital and Family Therapy, 18,* 41–51.

Myers Avis, J., & Sprenkle, D. H. (1990). Outcome research on family therapy training: A substantive and methodological review. *Journal of Marital and Family Therapy, 16,* 241–264.

Piercy, F. P., Laird, R. A., & Mohammed, Z. (1983). A family therapist rating scale. *Journal of Marital and Family Therapy, 9,* 45–59.

Pulleyblank, E., & Shapiro. R. J. (1986). Evaluation of family therapy trainees: Acquisition of cognitive and therapeutic behavior skills. *Family Process, 25,* 591–598.

Weingarten, K. (1991). The discourses of intimacy: Adding a social constructionist and feminist view. *Family Process, 30,* 285–305.

Weingarten, K. (1992). A consideration of intimate and non-intimate interactions in therapy. *Family Process, 31,* 45–59.

Whitaker, C. (1989). Thoughts about sex, love, and intimacy. In D. Kantor & B. F. Okun (Eds.), *Intimate environments: Sex, intimacy, and gender in families* (pp. 108–128). New York: Guilford Press.

Whitaker, C. A., & Keith, D. V. (1981). Symbolic-experiential family therapy. In A. S. Gurman, & D. P. Kniskern (Eds.), *Handbook of family therapy* (pp. 187–225). New York: Brunner/Mazel.

CHAPTER EIGHT

Stories from Your Mythic Depths

David Feinstein

Where do the ideas come from when you make up a story? Do they come from the same part of your psyche that creates your dreams? Do they come from the same area in your brain that enables you to look at a particular ink blot and describe what you see in it? Do they come from the same domain of your imagination that can envision your next vacation?

Take a moment right now to make up a story. Create a story about a storyteller. Have your story include a beginning, middle, end, and a lesson or moral. See if you can allow the story to unfold in your mind over the next minute or so. If it is easier for you, you may want to take a little more time and write the story as you are creating it. Go ahead now and invite your story about a storyteller to emerge.

What does your story tell you about yourself? It is not possible to make up a story that doesn't reveal something of your own inner life. Any story you might create is a reflection of how you see the world, of what you consider important, and of the ways you tend to cope with life. Ask yourself if there are similarities between the motivations of the storyteller you created for your story and your own motivations. Some people are primarily motivated toward achievement Others toward intimacy. Others toward power (McClelland, 1985). By examining the forces that motivate the characters in your story, you may get a glimpse into the workings of your own motivational scheme.

The following was created by a psychotherapy client in response to the assignment that he capture, in a story, a core dilemma with his wife, and that he map out for himself a new solution:

> Tom stretched out in the lawn and rolled about, luxuriating in the warmth of the July sun. There wasn't much a good stretch in the sun couldn't overcome, thought Tom, as he reached down to pull a burr from between his toes with his teeth. Yes, a little nap in the sun would soon put this old cat's world in order. Until this moment it hadn't been a good day.

Alley headed out in the early morning to do some mousing at a nearby farm and, after a good-bye kiss, things took a serious turn for the worse for Tom. While looking for the ideal spot for his morning constitutional, the neighborhood bully kid decided to grab him and give him a helicopter ride. This consisted of being swung by his tail above the kid's head until the centrifugal force nearly popped his eyes from their sockets and stretched his tail to twice its former length. Once he was dropped to the ground Tom tried to make a speedy exit only to stagger into a rose bush much to the amusement of the bully and his laughing cohorts. Well, there was still the business of some bulging bowels to tend to. There wasn't much time left to seek out the perfect pit stop so Tom dropped in at the old standby. The bark dust around the junipers at the neighbor's place. Just as he was committed to dropping his load — a terrible hissing surrounded Tom on all sides. It wasn't the attack by a pack of wild cats that Tom had imagined when he had leapt skyward in heart-reaming terror — it was the automatic sprinkler system doing its thing all over him — and his restroom. With no time to waste, Tom dove into the tall grass by the next house on the street. It provided good cover but all the neighborhood dogs had laid claim to it as their restroom and made a real mess of things. They didn't even try to bury those horrendous heaps they left behind. It was as if they were proud that they were able to empty their bowels or something. Well, dogs didn't have much to be proud of, figured Tom, as he proceeded to bury his handiwork. It was a far better example of fecal sculpture than any other on the premises and it was soon to be lost to the world of art. Except that the neighborhood dogs interrupted this ceremonial internment.

The next hour was spent in a tree as a bunch of howling, lapping, butt-sniffing dogs circled the base of the tree Tom had used for a not-so-quick getaway.

Then there was the shop-vac attack when he fell asleep in the car next door while the neighbor was waxing it. And when he retreated to the safety of the space beneath a shed he was greeted by the masked faces of a family of coons. It had truly been a bad day, but a little stretch and nap in the sun would melt away all those bad experiences.

The warmth and silence were pierced with the cold, harsh words as only Alley could deliver them: "Tom, is that all you've been doing while I've been out working my tail off trying to catch dinner? I wish I had it so easy. There are plenty of days I don't feel like going out trying to find a meal for us. Couldn't you for once bring something home for me so I wouldn't have to think about what to hunt and where and with whom?

I wish I felt comfortable whiling away the day in the sun without a care in the world but no-o-o-o, I have a conscience, I have ambition, and without my organizational skills your life would be a mess — not to mention the lives of those other cats I hunt with — you wouldn't believe how disorganized they are. They're space cadets. They think they have great leadership skills because they can get their tails to follow them. Today, I tried to organize a hunt with Tiger and the girls but Tiger jumps in and says, 'Maybe we could hunt longer if you didn't spend so much time talking, Alley, and trying to tell us how to do something we already know how to do.' Tom, can you believe that Tiger said that to me?"

Tom was quite irritated by this intrusion into his naptime and now he was being forced to answer a question that was probably put there just to make sure he was still listening. He thought seriously about saying, "No I don't believe Tiger would say such a thing — it's not possible to say that much in a conversation with you, Alley." Tom quickly reconsidered his reply when Alley said, "Well, can you, Tom?"

"No," Tom replied, "that was rude and totally tactless of Tiger to say that."

"Well, that's not half of it," blurted Alley.

"Oh God!" thought Tom. "There goes my nap in the sun, the moon'll be out before Alley's done yowling about her day. ... I'm doomed unless I can find some way to get Alley off track. ... I've got it," he thought confidently.

"I need cats to appreciate what I do for them," said Alley. "I do a lot for all the cats I know, and I'm pretty damn good with people, too, like owners for one."

"*Owners*," thought Tom. "If Alley thought being nice to 'owners' was an admirable trait, she needed serious help."

"Tom, what I need is ..."

"Alley, honey, what you need is a perfect end to a not-so-perfect day," interrupted Tom. "What do you say we head over to the house of that dustmop of a cat, Puffy, that always turns up his nose at that gourmet food that old lady gives him. I'll make his fur fly while you grab a bite to eat, and when I'm done fighting we can share a little romance together at the food dish.

"Oh, Tom, I don't know, ... "

"Well, Alley, I do know and what you need to do is relax and let your day and little spat with Tiger go. Now relax here in the sun and bathe yourself before we head out on the town. I'll get a few of those hard-to-get spots for you."

"Oh, okay, Tom, if you insist. But let me finish telling you about my day."

"No," said Tom, "I need to tell you about my idea for the rest of the evening. After dinner at Puffy's, we can strut on down towards the park — checking out the garbage cans as we go, of course. And after we catch the sunset in the park we can head back to where we first met that night. You know, where we romanced under the window until that fat guy yelled 'Get the fuck out of here you little noisy bastards.'"

"Oh, Tom I didn't think you still remembered that night," purred Alley. "It was magic — it was destined in the stars. It was sheer animal attraction."

Tom helped Alley wash up as they reminisced about the "good old days" or at least days better than this one. In the distance they both heard "Here kitty, kitty, kitty. Here, Puffy, come see what Momma has for you — a special treat."

With that Alley and Tom rose in unison and strolled side by side towards Puffy's and an evening of food, fun, and romance.

In this chapter, you will be introduced to an approach that draws upon your own natural ability to create stories. The approach uses storymaking as a tool for uncovering deeply personal myths. Each of us lives a personal mythology, an inner drama whose themes we instinctively live out in the world. This guiding mythology is the invisible hand that shapes what we think, what we feel, and what we do. It usually operates outside of our awareness, yet with uncanny accuracy, we choose the characters and create the scenes that correspond to our deepest visions. In some instances, our guiding myths serve us well; in others, they lead to self-defeating behaviors, destructive relationships, and unattainable desires. By uncovering your guiding myths through story, and using the power of story to project new visions, it is possible to not only identify where your mythology is obstructing or sabotaging you, but to transform it as well.

The Myth-Making Psyche

The anthropologist Eugene d'Aquili (1972) coined the term "cognitive imperative" to describe the human compulsion to order reality in a meaningful manner. According to d'Aquili this universal, biologically-rooted human drive to fashion unexplained external stimuli into a meaningful form is a critical element of humanity's evolutionary advantage over other creatures, and it was "the last development required for the emergence of culture" (p. 9).

The primary, although often unperceived, psychological mechanism by which the human psyche goes about this ordering of unexplained external stimuli is through mythmaking (Feinstein, 1979). For the human species, mythological thinking — the ability to symbolically address large questions — replaced genetic mutation as the primary vehicle by which individual consciousness and societal innovations were carried forward (Feinstein, 1990b).

Myths, in Mark Schorer's (1946) classic definition, are described as "large controlling images" that give significance to the rudimentary facts of ordinary life, organize these facts, and energize behavior according to those facts. Without such underlying mythic images, our experiences would seem chaotic and of little meaning, and our behavior would be disconnected from anything beyond the moment. Mythic images interpret the past, give purpose to the present, and provide direction for the future. They address the broad concerns of identity ("Who am I"), direction ("Where am I going?"), and purpose ("Why am I going there?"). They are experienced viscerally as well as cognitively (Feinstein, Krippner, & Granger, 1988).

According to Joseph Campbell (1986), myths are ultimately "motivated from a single psychophysiological source — namely, the human imagination moved by the conflicting urgencies of the organs" (p. 12). Over the course of human evolution, the epicenter of consciousness, and thus the locus of myth-making, has expanded from the life of the body to include the consensual reality of the group, and, in recent history, the vested concerns of the individual ego (Feinstein, 1990b). Thus, a distinguishing feature of the modern era in technologically-advanced Western cultures is that people have achieved greater autonomy than ever before in formulating the myths that guide their lives. No longer can a single storyteller sitting around a campfire convey a mythology that speaks to every member of the group. Mythology has become a personal affair.

The Personalizing of Mythology

Myths, in the sense we are using the term, are *not* falsehoods. They are, rather, the way that human beings code and organize their inner lives. The individual's mythology is, to an extent, the culture's mythology in microcosm. The great American psychologist Henry Murray (1960) thought of myths in this way: Myths serve to inspire, generate conviction, orient action, and unify the person or the group by "engendering passionate participation of all functions of the personality (*individual* myth), or all members of a society (*collective* myth)" (pp. 338–339). Myths in this broad sense are not properly understood as being true or false, right or wrong, but rather as ways of organizing experience that may ultimately be judged as more or less functional for the well-being and performance of an individual or of a group.

A personal myth is a constellation of ideas, images, and emotions. At its core is a central theme that serves as an inner model. Such a composite can be called a "personal myth" when that theme addresses one of the domains within which mythology traditionally functions. According to Joseph Campbell (1983), these include: (1) the need to comprehend the natural world in a meaningful way; (2) the search for a marked pathway through succeeding epochs of the human lifespan; (3) the desire to establish fulfilling personal and work relationships within a community; and (4) the longing to participate in the vast wonder and mystery of the cosmos. Thus, personal myths explain the world, guide individual development, provide social direction, and address spiritual longings in a manner analogous to the way that cultural myths carry out these functions for entire societies. Personal myths do for an individual what cultural myths do for a community. A *personal mythology* may be thought of as the system of complementary and contradictory *personal myths* that organize one's sense of reality and guide behavior.

Although usually at a level that is outside their awareness, all people take part in constructing the myths that shape their lives. Moreover, the historical record suggests that the capacity of individuals *to participate actively* in the construction of their guiding myths has been expanding as consciousness has evolved. Learning to consciously participate in the processes by which people shape their own myths has not only become feasible, it has become a requirement for successfully adjusting to a rapidly-changing world. The culture's evolving mythology is being hammered out on the anvil of individual lives. In a period in which the rate of social change antiquates the culture's guiding myths at a disorienting pace, it behooves us all to confront the mythology of our culture, to craft uniquely personal myths, and to bring our lives into greater harmony with the most wholesome guiding myths we can derive. To stretch your mythology beyond the limitations of your culture can be facilitated by a heightened awareness that courageously examines habitual patterns of thought and behavior, and that skillfully addresses the relationship of personal and cultural myths.

Because personal myths bring out some aspects of the personality and inhibit others, the mythologies people develop will, to a large extent, determine which of their multifaceted potentialities will be developed. The family is the primary institution involved in forming the individual's mythology. It is the crucible in which the imperatives of genetics and the mythology of a civilization are amalgamated into the unique mythic framework that shapes each person's development (Feinstein & Krippner, 1989). Personal myths are the individual's legacy from the past and a source of guidance and inspiration for the future. They are pregnant with the hopes and the disappointments of prior generations. Families actively select and adopt as their own "those cultural myths whose various components and symbols have meaning and importance for each family member" (Anderson & Bagarozzi 1982, p. 72). The family then has first claim on molding the development of the individual's guiding mythology, and it provides a microcosm as the person unfolds into the wider community.

Personal myths are, however, shaped by more than just the family. They are the product of four interacting sources (Feinstein & Krippner, 1997). The most obvious are: *biology* (the capacities for symbolism and narrative are rooted in the structure of the brain, information and attitudes are neurochemically-encoded, temperament and hormones influence belief systems, and so on), *culture* (the individual's mythology is, to an extent, the culture's mythology in microcosm), and *personal history* (every emotionally significant event leaves a mark on one's developing mythology). A fourth source is rooted in *transcendent experiences* — those episodes, insights, dreams, and visions that have a numinous quality, expand a person's perspective, and inspire behavior. Transcendent experiences vary in their strength and significance. Their most profound form is in the full blown mystical or religious experience. William James (1902/1961) reported that "mystical states of a well-pronounced and emphatic sort *are* usually authoritative over those who have them. ... Mystical experiences are as direct perceptions of fact for those who have them as any sensations ever were for us" (p. 332). For Philip Wheelwright (1942), "the very essence of myth" is "that haunting awareness of transcendental forces peering through the cracks of the visible universe" (p. 10).

The Mythic Structure of Psychological Development

The individual's mythology evolves according to lawful principles (Feinstein, 1990a). Personality development, in fact, unfolds around the tension between existing mythic structures and new structures that arise to challenge them. We oscillate between old constructions of reality and new ones, between prevailing myths and emerging myths. It is in the balance between the two that the challenges of psychological development are poised. The diametrically-opposed principles that permeate human growth are stability and change, and contrasting aspects of one's personal mythology support each. Daniel Levinson (1978) observed that, in stable periods, the major psychosocial tasks involved adapting to a "life structure" comprised of the way a person participates in a sociocultural environment and the aspects of the "self" the person is living out. In transitional periods, on the other hand, one is required to terminate the existing "life structure" to explore possibilities out of which new choices can be formed and to make the initial decisions that may provide the basis of a new structure.

In terms of the individual's guiding mythology during these transitional periods, prevailing myths begin to give way to new guiding myths. Myths that had been quietly supporting the old life structure may, for the first time, come into conscious awareness, and their recognition, paradoxically, often coincides with their repudiation. It is often not until we are ready to challenge a myth that we are first able to perceive and articulate it.

The prevailing myth is rooted in past experience, and although it may have become a dysfunctional or limiting structure, it is best understood in terms of the constructive purposes it once served in the individual's history. By examining the old myth for the creative role it played at an earlier time — perhaps when the child's legitimate emotional needs simply could not be accommodated — one becomes more able to appreciate the old myth for the heroic solutions it once attempted, to embrace the valid lessons it still holds, and to affirm strengths and abilities that may have been called into question by the consequences of the old myth's shortcomings. By understanding how the old myth developed, even while in the process of abandoning it, attention is also focused on the functions the myth that replaces it will have to fulfill.

Just as the psyche may produce inspiring dreams that point toward new directions for one's development, it also creates new mythic images whose guidance may be in direct conflict with more limiting prevailing myths. Latent qualities of the personality that are not supported by prevailing myths will naturally push toward expression. New mythic structures predictably emerge to challenge old, dysfunctional myths, and they often serve as a force toward expanding the individual's perceptions, self-concept, world-view, and awareness of options in the very areas the old myth was limiting them. We speak of such emerging mythic structures as "countermyths," because their premises run in counterpoint to the existing mythology. Countermyths are woven from the accumulation of life experiences, from a developmental readiness to accept more advanced myths of the culture, and from a reservoir of unconscious primal impulses and archetypal materials.

Countermyths are best understood as creative leaps in the psyche's problem-solving activities, but like dreams, they often play a wishfulfillment function that lacks real-world utility. They are untried in the court of experience and their guidance is fanciful and unreliable. Still, they serve as a force toward integrating unrecognized impulses and images into the personality and recapturing qualities that have been repressed under the constraints of the old myth. While the countermyth may remain outside of conscious awareness for a substantial period of time, additional experiences that are discordant with the prevailing myth may further its development until it breaks into consciousness, often in dream, fantasies, new ideas, or the emergence of a fledgling "subpersonality."

While the conflict that ensues between the prevailing myth and the counter-myth may be painful and disruptive, a natural, although often unconscious, mobilization toward a resolution will also be occurring, ultimately yielding a new mythic image. A dialectical process naturally unfolds in which a thesis (prevailing myth) is countered by an antithesis (countermyth), leading to a synthesis (new guiding myth) that incorporates the most functional qualities of each at a higher level of organization (Feinstein, 1997). The dialectic process may be viewed as a subterranean struggle between conflicting myths vying to structure the individual's perceptions, thoughts, feelings, and behavior. The dialectic occurs naturally and without attention or volition, but an optimum resolution of the conflict may be enhanced through techniques that attune your awareness to this deeper process. If you are able to bring the dialectic into consciousness, you have a greater chance of working out underlying mythic conflict as a drama in your inner life — rather than having to act it out on the rack of life.

Stories for Facilitating Mythic Change

Creating stories that address the three core elements of mythic change discussed above — the prevailing myth, the countermyth, and the synthesis emerging out of the dialectic that ensues between them — brings the process into focus and allows the conscious mind to participate in the evolution of a guiding mythology. Many cultural myths are expressed as stories from which moral or spiritual truths can be drawn, offering people guidance through imagery and metaphor. Sufi stories, Hassidic tales, Biblical parables, and other spiritual literatures are the bearers of great mythologies that may offer elevated insight into the human condition.

Today, with the intricacies of individual identity and the myriad role options allowed by complex societies, we need guidance that is highly personal to our unique circumstances. Discussing how modern men and women have developed the capacity to form identities separate from those prescribed by the tribe or nation, Anthea Francine observed that the "revelations of the Divine ... we once found revealed only in the form of myth and fairy tale, we must now seek also in the story of our own lives" (Francine, 1983, p. 77). Weaving your memories into a meaningful sequence of stories about your past, present, and future can deepen your relationship with your own mythology and place your self- understanding in a richer context.

An approach that exemplifies the power of story-telling in helping troubled children alter what we are speaking of as their personal myths was pioneered by the psychiatrist Richard Gardner (1971). Gardner asks the child to tell him a story that has a beginning, middle, end, and a moral. As Gardner listens for the psychological themes that run through the story, elements of unresolved conflict are revealed. Gardner, in turn, tells a story to the child that also has a beginning, middle, end, and a moral. His story is built around the psychological tensions that were portrayed in the child's story. In retelling the story, however, Gardner has the characters find better ways to handle the core conflicts. By speaking to the child at this mythic level, Gardner creates an opportunity for the child to adopt a new personal myth that may be more functional than the one that has been operating.

Gardner describes a story told by Martin, a withdrawn seven-year-old, with a bitter, self-indulgent mother who was sometimes warm and loving, but at other times openly expressed her dislike for her son. Martin's story was about a bear who was trying in vain to get honey from a beehive without being stung. In his response, Gardner's story also featured a bear who craved honey. Gardner's bear knew that bees were sometimes friendly and would give him a little bit of honey, and he also knew that at times they were unfriendly and would sting him. At these times, Gardner's bear would go to another part of the forest where he could obtain maple syrup from the maple trees. In this story, Gardner offered Martin a mythology for acquiring love from his mother without provoking her hostilities, and for discovering alternative sources of affection to compensate for his mother's deficiencies.

In our approach, people are instructed to create a three-chapter personal parable or fairy tale as they systematically work with their evolving mythologies. Each chapter of the fairy tale reflects one of the core elements of mythic change: prevailing myth, countermyth, synthesis. Viewing yourself as the hero or heroine in your own personal parable allows you, unlike Narcissus captivated with the reflection of his own surfaces, to peer more deeply into your nature and to more fully appreciate the wonder of the human drama as it manifests in your personal story. By drawing upon the power of your creative imagination, you are able both to gain some distance from conditions that are emotionally challenging and to place them into a mythic perspective. Creating the fairy tale is part of a larger approach with many other steps (Feinstein & Krippner, 1997), yet its three chapters serve as benchmarks that give definition to a very complex inner process. The remainder of this chapter examines one part of the three-part fairy tale, presenting its purpose, some of the techniques that lead to its creation, and a colorful example.

Stories That Reflect the Prevailing Myth

The first chapter of the personal fairy tale metaphorically represents the circumstances that led to the formulation of the prevailing myth. Several structured exercises, which we call "personal rituals," precede the creation of Chapter One of the fairy tale, uncovering the raw materials that will be woven into the story. These preliminary rituals excavate early memories; specify significant traumas, losses, and other emotional hardships from the past; identify visions, rules of conduct, and philosophies of life that were created for living with and overcoming these challenges; and evaluate the initial consequences of these attempted solutions. Chapter One of the fairy tale consolidates these findings into a dramatic vehicle for comprehending their place in an evolving life story, burrowing into their meaning, and beginning to sense their implications for deep change.

After the prepatory work, we offer instructions similar to the following for creating Chapter One:

The setting of your fairy tale can be an ancient kingdom, a futuristic city, a far-away galaxy, a land of elves and gnomes, a family of deer, chipmunks, chimpanzees, or sea otters, an ancient culture, a period of history, or any other context that might occur to you. Label a page of your journal "Fairy Tale — Chapter One." Compose Chapter One of your fairy tale using one of the following approaches: Find a comfortable setting and allow the story to emerge in your imagination; tell the story to another person as you are creating it; or speak it into a tape recorder. Record or summarize the story in your journal. Before you begin, take time to center yourself on the aims of Chapter One: to mythically portray an innocent and hopeful time from your childhood, its loss, and how you set out to make up for that loss.

Begin with the words "Once upon a time" and continue to talk or write, allowing the saga to unfold. It is not necessary to rehearse. Let your spontaneity take the story wherever it will go. Editing and interpretation can come later. At this point, do not judge what emerges. You may be surprised at unexpected twists in the plot or at new characters that may suddenly appear upon the scene.

I will illustrate the three-chapter fairy tale with one of the most colorful stories we have ever received, presented to us by Meg, a fifty-five-year-old professional writer. I will let her story speak for itself and refer you to our book, *The Mythic Path* (Feinstein & Krippner, 1997), for more details about her personal process. Here is Meg's Chapter One:

Once upon a time there was an island separated from a continent by a wild strait, impassable by boat or swimstroke. A little girl, Juanita Margaret, lived upon the island. She was busy from dawn to dark with her tasks. Two times a day she went to watch the tides change below the cliffs. She checked the quails' nests for eggs and new chicks. She monitored the polliwogs as they magically became frogs, and she gasped in wonder as the butterfly emerged from the cocoon and unfolded its wings. She spent time in gathering sour grass bouquets and driftwood dragons. She ate loquats and mulberries that grew on the trees, and she gathered seaweed and mussels from the rocks by the sea.

She kept an orphaned ground squirrel, a lame coyote, and a nest of swallows in her cave. The squirrel taught her about seeds, thrift, industry, foresight, and planting. The coyote showed her the value of patience, stealth, and suppleness. From the swallows she learned of delight, nesting, and freedom. At night she slept in a hollow she'd made in the notch of a cliff, facing the sunset, at the edge of the sea. The moon and the storms were her night-time companions.

Juanita Margaret did not know that she was in exile, a creature to be pitied, remarkable in an embarrassing way, to the people on the mainland. They were busy, too, in hurrying from this place to that place, talking about property and assets, arranging their clothes and their expressions, actively meeting one another in a continuing process of confrontation, seduction, deception, denial, torment, and illusion. Her wholesomeness offended them.

No one remembered exactly who had put Juanita Margaret on the island, but the truth was that they had been glad to get rid of her. They were uncomfortable when they saw that she would rather climb the Cyprus tree than try on a new dress. They became upset when they saw that she was loud, demanding, curious, and unhampered. They were annoyed with her coarse, naturalistic behavior. They kept sending her outside to play so that they could read their newspapers and magazines in peace. One morning she climbed into an old boat to play; a storm came up, carried her away, and she was washed ashore on the island. When she never came back, everyone seemed relieved.

One day, a man on the mainland took a telescope and looked at Juanita Margaret's island. He saw how many wonderful fruit trees grew on the island, and how clear the water was on the narrow beaches below the cliffs. He thought, "I could put a resort there and make a million dollars." Before long, engineers studied the strait between the mainland and the island. They put in a bridge and a highway. They took out the loquat and mulberry trees to build The Orchard Motel. They put a single loquat and a lonely mulberry tree into pots in the lobby. They cut stairs into the cliffs and made them as permanent as possible with cement and steel handrails. The trash cans overflowed.

Some men came and saw Juanita Margaret sitting behind the bushes in the parking lot, eating scrap food from bags thrown out of cars. She didn't go with them willingly at first, but they offered her warm socks and cinnamon rolls and, in the end, she agreed to return to the mainland.

Juanita Margaret went to school, leaving her squirrel, coyote, and swallow friends to save themselves if they could, because she didn't know what else to do. She was just a little girl. Inside, she was furious at the changes that had come into her life, and at the people bossing her around without asking her opinion. Now she had to sleep in a bed, wash in a tub rather than the ocean, speak softly, be respectful, make everyone proud, and live up to her potential. She was told that "some things aren't nice to talk about" and "your temper will be the death of you." The worst insult for a bungled job or sloppy workmanship was to call it "womanish." She was learning the ways of becoming a proper young lady.

Stories That Reflect the Countermyth

The countermyth, like a child guided by the pleasure principle, is based on the logic of wish-fullfillment. Its imaginative remedies to life's burdens are not bound by the "reality principle." Although its solutions may be impractical, they stimulate hope and inspiration while attuning us to actual possibilities. Chapter One of the fairy tale represented the storyteller's prevailing myth. In Chapter Two, the hero or heroine of Chapter One goes on a magical adventure that reveals the creative promise of the storyteller's underlying countermyth.

Free from the constraints of the reality principle, the storyteller is encouraged in Chapter Two to unleash the creative imagination in finding solutions to the dilemma in Chapter One. Chapter Two, like some dreams, is usually a blend of the real and the fantastic. It suggests new directions for approaching Chapter One. Its suggestions and solutions are often extravagant, and this is appropriate in Chapter Two. Its key ingredient, however, is not so much the revelation of new solutions to the dilemmas of Chapter One but the inner development required of the hero or heroine in order to be able to envision and effect those solutions.

Although Chapter One usually closely parallels events as they actually occurred in the storyteller's life, Chapter Two does not. Its emphasis is on inventive solutions and on the lessons needed to achieve them. One of the activities that serves as preparation for writing Chapter Two is an examination of Chapter One in terms of what the main character needs to learn — what perspectives or attitudes or understandings are necessary — to resolve the dilemmas depicted in Chapter One. Another prepatory activity is an age regression to a time at which events unfolded in such a manner that they might serve as a resource or prototype for envisioning a creative new direction, which I refer to as "Rewriting History through the Emotionally Corrective Daydream" (Feinstein, 1998).

The instructions for creating Chapter Two begin with contemplation on its purpose: to reveal to the hero or heroine of the fairy tale a vision of how to handle the dilemmas presented in Chapter One and to provide instruction on what personal changes are required if that vision is to be realized. Rather than extending Chapter One in a "life as usual" manner, the context is temporarily shifted for Chapter Two. The storyteller is instructed to invent a magical rite of passage that will bring the main character to the perspectives, attitudes, and understandings necessary for solving the difficulties presented in the opening chapter. This rite of passage takes the form of a story within the story. The main character may have a dream or vision, meet a sorcerer, be taken on a magical journey, see an enchanting play, encounter a wise master, speak with a power animal, or be captivated by any other imaginative literary device that leads to greater wisdom in relationship to the initial problem. Maximum poetic license is emphasized. But while Chapter Two may suggest new solutions, it never actually solves the initial problem as it must end exactly where it began (that is how it is a story within a story), except with the main character having grown wiser.

As in each of the fairy tale chapters, the storyteller is invited to choose among several approaches, ranging from telling the story to another person, speaking it into a tape recorder, or writing it in a journal. Here is Meg's Chapter Two:

> Juanita Margaret was sitting on the mainland beach one day, looking across the raging straits that separated her from her ruined island. She saw the harsh bridge, made of iron and asphalt, bristling with cars like busy ants on their hill. She was wearing a lovely pink ruffled dress, but she had soiled it by playing with puppies, and there were paw marks blemishing the ruffles. Imagine her surprise, when a porpoise swam up the shallow surf and called out to her, "Juanita Margaret! I've come to rescue you! Mount my back, and I will take you on a great journey."

> He was smiling at her and his voice was as vibrant as the ruby throat of a hummingbird. She went, of course, and climbed up on his grey-blue back, grasping his ribs with her legs and clinging to his dorsal fin for balance. He moved across the water in jubilant leaps, arching his back and singing joyously as he traveled. Juanita Margaret forgot that she was odd and foreign, riding a porpoise across the waters wearing her dainty pink dress.

> "You are learning a great lesson, Juanita Margaret, in the way you learn best by doing. Do not forget this lesson: Take time in your life to be spontaneous in nature, without agenda, without time constraints, and you will be wrested from your complaints. I am taking you now to visit some other teachers. Fear not that harm will come to you when I dive beneath the surface. You are equipped for survival and your faith will protect you even in an alien environment."

> So saying, the porpoise arched high into the air and dove beneath the surface, Juanita Margaret safe upon his back. The world beneath the sea was shimmering with green and golden light, the white sand lay in gentle mounds and a tall forest of kelp grew from black rocks. The porpoise swam into the forest of waving plants, each moving independently in the currents. "You see the flexibility of these stems and leaves, responsive to the moving waters? When mighty storms come through this part of the ocean, the kelp forest is whipped from side to side, scourged with driven

sand, tested to its limit. Only the weary, old, or poorly-rooted plants are torn loose to be cast on the shore. The plants that have gripped the stones with their roots, and that have put their growth into sturdy trunks, are secure and even invigorated by the storm. You see it is possible to be firm and still move with the currents, whether energetic or gentle." She thought she understood what he was talking about.

He took her to a submerged reef, and she saw that it was encrusted with abalone. The shells were as black as the reef, domed like oval cups and covered with volcano barnacles, hermit crabs, and sea-lettuce. If she hadn't seen them long ago, when she had her island to herself, she would have thought they were just bumps on the rock. The porpoise told her to speak to the largest abalone in the cluster. "Hello," she said, tentatively.

"Hello, yourself," answered the abalone in a slow and draggy voice. "What brings you here today?"

"I think you're supposed to teach me something."

"Do you have any idea what it is?" The abalone sounded puzzled and a little resentful.

"Maybe if you described yourself and your life I might get a clue. Right now I just think you're pretty much a dull and surly fellow." Juanita Margaret had the habit of saying what she thought without much consideration of how it might feel to the person she was talking to.

The abalone was silent and the bubbles coming from his vent holes nearly stopped. When at last he spoke, it was with a distant air, as if he didn't much want to have anything to do with her but felt obliged to answer. "I am, as you say, dull. I have been on this spot for many years. It is a good spot because the current sweeps a lot of plankton my way and I have flourished. It is true that I am not a scintillating personality, that I am politically isolated, that I am drab and lack a rapier wit. I have captured no prizes and have never been to war. My body is muscular, my personality is a yawn, and my attitude is tenacious. I fear only the marauding starfish who is both tenacious and mobile, able to pry me off the rock and eat me.

"I have a secret, though, Juanita Margaret. Under my drab and unprepossessing exterior, I am a great artist. I go nowhere, engage in no social activities, even family reunions, because I am at work on the most beautiful sculpture-painting-architecture imaginable. I am preparing the inside of my shell, hidden from sight, as a permanent memorial to God.

To learn from me you must be less concerned with your everyday outer shell and put your care into making the inside as beautiful as possible. With me, my secret beauty will be concealed until my death. With you, who knows?" With that the abalone let loose a long spout of bubbles and Juanita Margaret knew he had said what he had to say.

As if in a trance, Juanita Margaret pondered what she had learned from the porpoise, kelp, and abalone. She promised herself she would take time from her duties to find herself in Nature like the porpoise, to flex in the currents of life while maintaining her roots, like the kelp, and to be unbothered by the plainness of her exterior while privately, without fanfare, enriching her interior, like the abalone. The porpoise delivered her to shore, and she found she had a great deal to think about and even more to do.

If the fairy tale ended with Juanita Margaret and her porpoise sailing gleefully into the sunset, it might have had the ring of happily-ever-after, but it would do Meg a disservice, for there was still much for her to learn, as you will see her explore in Chapter Three of her fairy tale.

Stories That Promote an Integration of Conflicting Myths

Chapters One and Two of the fairy tale delineate the opposing mythic forces that are at play as the person's mythology evolves. One of our core assumptions is that the countermyth portrayed in Chapter Two has for some time been developing within the person's psyche and was challenging the prevailing myth long before the individual was able to consciously articulate it. Aspects of the countermyth may have been revealed in dreams, slips of the tongue, or may have broken through to consciousness via disturbing or seemingly foreign thoughts, fantasies, or impulses, but creating Chapter Two is often the first time the countermyth is given coherent expression.

The personal rituals presented as preparation for writing Chapter Three are designed to reflect the completed dialectic between the prevailing myth and the countermyth. As we have seen, the countermyth — unbound by the reality principle, lacking balance because its initial focus was on compensating for the shortcomings of the prevailing myth, and untested in the real world — has its own shortcomings. The prevailing myth, on the other hand, for however dysfunctional it may have become, is rich with the experiences accumulated during its reign. Each mythic structure has its own wisdom and its own failings. The dialectic promotes a synthesis that draws on the strengths of each. Among the personal rituals we use for furthering the dialectic are a dialogue between a character dramatizing the prevailing myth and another dramatizing the coun-termyth, the incubation of dreams and fantasies that promote integration between the opposing myths, and focusing on physical sensations that correspond with the mythic conflict, treating them as a "body metaphor" (Feinstein & Krippner, 1997).

Once a fresh vision — a new guiding myth that embodies a creative synthesis of the old myth's thesis and the countermyth's antithesis — has been formulated, creating Chapter Three of the fairytale becomes one of the first ways of testing this new vision. Chapter Three extends the journey of the main character beyond the trials of Chapter One and the magical adventures of Chapter Two. It leads to a plausible resolution of the dilemmas that the main character faced in Chapter One, attained through the lessons or inspiration of Chapter Two. Chapter Three begins where Chapter One left off. The problems confronting the hero or heroine at the close of Chapter One are met with the wisdom gained in Chapter Two. Chapter Three portrays actual solutions to the initial dilemma and closes with a motto, a brief phrase that summarizes the essential lesson of the fairy tale. Chapter Three of Meg's Fairy Tale reads:

> After the porpoise delivered Juanita Margaret to shore, the first thing she saw was a broken Annie Green Springs wine bottle bouncing in the surf. The second thing to happen was that her caretaker, Prudent, was appalled at the condition of her clothes and hair. The third thing was that her school teacher, Rational, heaped contempt upon her wild story that she had ridden a porpoise to the depths of the sea.

> Juanita Margaret decided that the first lesson she could practice was retreat to Nature, and this she did until her head and heart settled down and even ceased to ache. "Ah ha," she thought. "It works! When I am hassled, a retreat to a peaceful, timeless space is indeed healing. I will remember that."

> Being as flexible as the kelp had never been easy for her. She was undoubtedly a stubborn, even rigid child, in that she usually could see only one way to accomplish anything. That lesson came one day when she, a devoted health food nut, was offered a hot chocolate fudge sundae with whipped cream, three cherries, chopped pecans, and a little American flag on the summit. Her conflict was truly epic. "I want it! I want it! I want it!" cried her impulsive reckless part, with visions of sweet shudders passing through her mouth and limbs. "Oh no, never ever under any circumstances!" proclaimed her righteous, rigid self, snapping her mouth closed, tight as an abalone on the reef. Fortunately, at that moment, a vision of the flexible kelp came to Juanita Margaret. "I will stay rooted in my beliefs, but I do think I will eat this sundae. After all, it's only six weeks until my birthday!"

Being secret about her good works had never been Juanita Margaret's way. Keeping silent about her talents was not her strong suit. It is true that she often did genuinely good things for high motives. She had many skills and assets. But there is just no nice way to deny that she was a big mouth, often blowing her own horn in the town square. It wasn't so much that she was full of herself; it was more that she was actually rather empty inside, having been sent out to play so often. One day, while she was caroling her own virtues, she saw someone yawn. "Oh my," thought Juanita Margaret, "I am becoming the worst sort of a bore. Even I am bored. Boredom is a dreadful sign; it means I am sick of my own company. What to do?" She thought of the abalone with his boring exterior and palace of lights interior. She thought, "I believe I should pay attention. It seems to me that if I save some of my good stuff, my very best good stuff, and keep it inside, silently, it may serve me better. I will have to wait for someone to notice me to have the attention I love so much, but I can be occupied with adding lovely nacre designs to my interior canvas. I believe I will try this as a cure for boredom." It worked so well that no one ever yawned in her face again, and the people she invited in to see her mother-of-pearl and rainbow painting came to love her deeply.

Seeking a motto for her new myth, Meg described its essence as an understanding that "I am part of Creation. I, and all my relationships are, just like Creation, continually evolving and growing more interconnected through the forces of Love." The single guiding statement that summarized the new myth for her was "Serenity is gained through loving, thoughtful action."

Composing Chapter Three and a motto for the fairy tale allows the storyteller to experiment in the laboratory of imagination with a new guiding mythology. This mythic vision is often refined, and practical applications are further conceived, as Chapter Three is being written. Once Chapter Three has been completed, a series of personal rituals for further cultivating and applying the new myth include behavior rehearsals, monitoring "self-statements," and establishing contracts for behavioral changes that correspond with the new myth's guidance (Feinstein & Krippner, 1988). Through all of this and beyond, the fairy tale remains a dramatic portrayal of where the storyteller has been, is headed, and the reasons why. In the subsequent phases of the program — which work through, reinforce, and "anchor" the lessons of Chapter Three — the individual's new vision is affirmed and systematically woven into daily life.

References

Bagarozzi, D. A., & Anderson, S. A. (1982). The evolution of family mythological systems: Considerations for meaning, clinical assessment, and treatment. *Journal of Psychoanalytic Anthropology, 5,* 71–90.

Campbell, J. (1983). *Historical atlas of world mythology* (Vol. 1). San Francisco: Harper & Row.

Campbell, J. (1986). *The inner reaches of outer space: Metaphor as myth and as religion.* New York Alfred van der Marck.

d'Aquili, E. G. (1972). *The biopsychological determinants of culture.* Reading, PA: Addison-Wesley.

Feinstein, A. D. (1979). Personal mythology as a paradigm for a holistic public psychology. *American Journal of Orthopsychiatry, 49,* 198–217.

Feinstein, D. (1990a). Bringing a mythological perspective to clinical practice. *Psychotherapy Theory/Research/Practice/Training, 27,* 388–396.

Feinstein, D. (1990b). How mythology got personal. *Humanistic Psychologist, 18,* 162–175.

Feinstein, D. (1997). Myth-making in psychological and spiritual development. *American Journal of Orthopsychiatry, 67,* 508–521.

Feinstein, D. (1998). At play in the fields of the mind: Personal myths as fields of information. *Journal of Humanistic Psychology, 38*(3), 71–109.

Feinstein, D., & Krippner, S. (1989). Personal myths — In the family way. In S. A. Anderson & D. A. Bagarozzi (Eds.) *Family myths: Psychotherapy implications* (pp. 111–139). New York: Haworth Press.

Feinstein, D., & Krippner, S. (1997). *The mythic path.* New York: Tarcher/Putnam.

Feinstein, D., Krippner, S., & Granger, D. (1988). Myth-making and human development. *Journal of Humanistic Psychology, 28,* 23–50.

Francine, A. (1983). *Envisioning theology: An autobiographical account of personal symbolic journeying as a source of revelation.* Unpublished master's thesis, Pacific School of Religion, Berkeley.

Gardner, R. A. (1971). *Therapeutic communication with children: The mutual-storytelling technique.* New York: Science House.

James, W. (1961). *Varieties of religious experience: A study in human nature.* New York: Crowell-Collier. (Original work published in 1902.)

Levinson, D. J. (1978). *The seasons of a man's life.* New York: Knopf.

McClelland, D. C. (1985). *Human motivation.* Glenview, IL: Scott, Foresman.

Murray, H. A. (Ed.) (1960). *Myth and mythmaking.* New York: George Braziller.

Schorer, M. (1946). *William Blake: The politics of vision.* New York: Holt.

Wheelwright, P. (1942). Poetry, myth, and reality. In A. Tate (Ed.), *The language of poetry* (pp. 3–29). Princeton, NJ: Princeton University Press.

CHAPTER NINE

Mythic Discord: A Case Study

Stanley Krippner

Psychotherapy and counseling can be defined as processes that attempt to modify the behavioral patterns and lived experiences that clients and/or their social group deem to be dysfunctional, usually because they inhibit personal relationships, stifle competent performance, or block the actualization of one's talents and capacities (Krippner, 1990, p. 179). Psychotherapy, counseling, and similar procedures, by their nature, are conducted within the context of the culture's broader mythological framework, ideological struggles, and competing versions of reality. Not to understand the client's presenting problem within this mythological context is to miss important dimensions of his or her existential situation (Feinstein, 1990).

In the West, myths are looked upon as irrational, superstitious conjectures about the world. But some writers find it useful to take an anthropological perspective and describe myths as internalized constructs that express themselves in implicit or explicit stories, formal or informal statements, and/or social infrastructures that address existential human concerns and issues, and that impact behavior (Feinstein & Krippner, 1988). Myths can be cultural, institutional, familial, ethnic, or personal in nature. Hence, a personal myth can be conceptualized as a psychological unit composed of imagery and narrative that interprets sensations, constructs explanations, and directs behavior.

This case study demonstrates the clinical efficacy of helping a client identify those personal myths that underlie his or her dysfunctional performance and relationships, and of changing these myths to permit a fuller actualization of the client's potential.

Overview of the Case

Ethan F., an unmarried twenty-three-year-old junior high school teacher, was self-referred in 1990 for counseling with the specific request that hypnosis be utilized. He cited "a lack of joy in life" as the key reason he was seeking professional help. I used hypnosis during the second half of each session, working within the five-stage "personal mythology" process I had developed with David Feinstein (Feinstein & Krippner, 1988). At the end of eleven months and some two dozen counseling sessions, the client left for Peace Corps service in Asia. He remained in contact with me during over two years in the Peace Corps, and paid me a follow-up visit upon his return. During this visit, he expressed his satisfaction with the counseling sessions, citing specific ways in which "joy" had emerged in his work, his solitary activities, and his personal relationships.

Description of the Case

Ethan F. made an appointment in December, 1990. He had been recommended to me by a colleague when he requested counseling from someone who would use hypnosis. At the time of our first interview, Ethan was twenty-three years of age, a college graduate who was working as a junior high school teacher in a metropolitan area. Six feet tall, and swarthy in appearance, Ethan rarely smiled; a dour expression contorted his handsome face when in repose. He stated his presenting problem as "a lack of joy in life." He said that he carried "a suitcase in my stomach" and suffered from both digestive and sleeping problems. It was my impression that he was experiencing periodic episodes of subclinical depression.

An attractive young man, he had no problem obtaining dates with women, but took little pleasure in shared activities, in discussions about life events, or even in sexual intercourse, which he described as perfunctory and constrained. He felt that he was competent in his work as a teacher, and he received high ratings from the school administrators. But it was difficult for him to go beyond his task as an instructor and a disciplinarian. Ethan felt little satisfaction at work and suspected that he could do more to inspire his students were he not so inhibited.

When I explained that my approach began by assisting clients to identify and explore the underlying beliefs and attitudes that impacted their life, Ethan expressed considerable interest. Our discussion about belief systems, attitudinal habits, and worldviews struck a resonant chord, and he said that this seemed to be at the basis of his continual conflict with his parents, especially his mother. Because Ethan seemed highly motivated to experience hypnosis, we decided to proceed with a formal hypnotic induction. After his response to various arm levitation challenges convinced him that he was indeed "hypnotized," I suggested that he would re-experience emotional feelings associated with the recall of his early years at home. Within a few seconds, Ethan cited "guilt" as the overriding emotion. When I asked him to associate to this feeling, he almost immediately replied, "In the Roman Catholic church, the whole idea is personal salvation; I believed that if I led a life without pleasure, this would save me."

During subsequent hypnosis sessions, Ethan described several incidents from his early years in which his parents and church presented this belief and reinforced it. Upon termination of the first few hypnosis sessions, I established to my satisfaction that none of these events were "recovered memories" that had been previously "repressed," and that all of them would have been easily recalled without formal hypnosis (Sheehan, 1994). I explained to Ethan that his statement about "salvation" and "a life without pleasure" qualified as a "personal myth." It addressed an existential human concern and impacted his behavior. I gave him a copy of the workbook Feinstein and I had prepared, suggesting that he might consider working through some of its thirty-one "personal rituals" as homework assignments. By the time of our fourth session, he had begun this process and showed me a notebook in which the results were assiduously described.

In addition to whatever procedures the counselor or psychotherapist already employs, Feinstein and I have introduced a series of "personal rituals" to help clients work experientially with the inner symbols and metaphors his or her psyche continually generates. We believe that each individual can tap into a mythological underworld whose content is reminiscent of the great cultural mythologies. This rich foundation of waking life is revealed in the high drama and conspicuous creativity of the individual's dreams as they unfold and are appreciated. The five-stage process we have articulated (detailed in Feinstein & Krippner, 1997) will serve as a useful framework in which Ethan's personal and social growth can be described.

First Stage: Framing Personal Concerns and Difficulties in Terms of Deeper Mythological Conflict

Identifying areas of conflict in a client's underlying mythology is the starting point of our five-stage model. Repetitive dysfunctional behavioral patterns such as involvement in abusive relationships or chronic vocational failures, as well as such clinical symptoms as addictions or hypertension, may provide an entry into areas of the person's mythology that are ripe for attention. Dream symbols and other productions of the unconscious, such as drawings, sandplay, or free association, may also highlight such areas.

In his first counseling session, Ethan had identified an "outdated myth," a belief system that may or may not have once served the client well but which is now clearly inappropriate to his or her current life situation.

Second Stage: Bringing the Roots of Each Side of the Conflict into Focus

Examining this issue, Ethan traced the mythology that had been guiding him back to images of his parent's marriage: "My father's devotion to my mother was certainly unwavering, but it seemed to be a duty-bound love." Ethan had few early vivid memories of his father who "went to work, provided for his family, and attended Mass each Sunday."

Ethan's memories of his mother, especially those evoked during the hypnosis sessions, were more dramatic. Described by Ethan as a person of mercurial temperament, his mother reportedly tucked him tightly into his crib as a baby, and restrained him in his stroller as a toddler with a seat belt so firm that it was often painful. In retrospect, incidents of this nature initiated a confusion between pain (the tight seat belt) and pleasure (the comfort of security).

Ethan recalled that when he was about three years of age, his mother screamed at him for a childish misdemeanor and beat him repeatedly. As soon as possible, he jumped into his bed crying, pulling the blankets over his head. This provided a "blindfold" to the outside world, and was a maneuver he frequently put to use. Again, when a painful event (such as his mother's punishment) began to overwhelm him, he would counter it with pleasure (the comfort of his bed).

Ethan got along quite well with his older brother who was in elementary school at this time. Ethan recollected the times his brother would come home from school with licorice, and would invariably share this treat. Because his father's temperament was stolid and bland, and because his mother was volatile and unpredictable, the gift of licorice and other sweets from his brother was the only sustained pleasure he could recall in his early years. Ethan remarked, "Candy gave me a momentary feeling of life. Until my brother returned home from school, I felt that I was living in what the Bible calls the valley of the shadow of death." Ethan remembered that his mother kept their home dark, ostensibly to save electricity, but that his brother turned on the lights when he returned. Here again, his mother was associated with death and darkness, and his brother with life and light.

When he was four years of age, Ethan was sent to a parochial nursery school. He was pleased to leave his home for prolonged periods of time, but the school was a mixed blessing. He enjoyed interacting with the other children, but the nuns exerted strict control. Once again, he felt as he had when tucked tightly into his crib and restrained by his safety belt. When he expressed his curiosity concerning other rooms and events at school, he was physically punished and threatened with "hell and damnation" in the afterlife. On occasion, he was given treats at the nursery school, but only if he had been a "good child." Ethan began to wonder if the moments of pleasure he experienced at nursery school were worth the price he had to pay for them; it was difficult for him to stifle his inquisitiveness and to sit quietly when there were so many interesting boys and girls in the classroom.

Nevertheless, the compensatory psychological construct that Feinstein and I call a "counter-myth" began to emerge. Ethan did not recall any specific words by which this attitude could be described, but did recall recurring imagery in which he broke loose of the seat belt, jumped out of the stroller, and ran far, far away from home. In retrospect, he articulated this "counter-myth" as "I'd like to have some fun, even if I have to go to hell for it." He also recalled a recurrent childhood dream in which he was in a sweet shop eating licorice and other delicacies. A shadow appeared in the door. It was the devil, ready to take Ethan to hell to pay the penalty for his indulgences.

For Ethan, pleasure and pain continued to be intermixed during family interactions. When he was about five, his father took him on a trip to see an open top reservoir. Ethan stood in awe of this mammoth construction, but could not enjoy it because he imagined "falling off the deck into the water and drowning in a slow, painful death." Easter was a special occasion for the family. When Ethan was about six, the family went to Mass. Shortly afterwards, Ethan's brother played Easter Bunny and passed out baskets of candy to the three other members of the family. But Ethan could not fully enjoy this treat because his mother kept interrupting his enjoyment with such statements as "Don't eat so fast," "Candy always gives me a stomach ache," and "You'll probably get cavities from sucking on all this licorice."

During mental imagery sessions, Ethan frequently evoked metaphors and symbols, especially after it was pointed out that both are frequent concomitants of both cultural and personal mythology. During a hypnosis session, Ethan described his mother as "nurturant, loving, angry, and venomous." In his imagery, she took the form of a three-foot-tall coiled black snake, her head leaning toward him, intimidating him, and "ready to strike." He commented that this image was accurate because "my mother constantly threatened to harm me if I didn't do what she wanted me to do. And my mother's punishment was not the end of it; she vowed that God would send me to eternal damnation if I did not follow her orders. I did not have a choice so I just stayed out of her way as much as I could. And I had to look away from the snake; if I was afraid, she would know it and would move in for the kill."

During this hypnosis session, I proposed that Ethan confront the snake-mother in some way. Ethan responded by telling her that he no longer needed her nurturance and that he could now take care of himself. He stared her directly in the eyes — a task he described as extremely difficult because of her power. I encouraged him to claim his own authority, and to maintain the gaze until she backed down. After several tries, this gambit was successful.

Ethan shared his notebook with me. He had considered several names for the subpersonality dominated by his outdated but still prevailing myth — the "Vulnerable Man," the "Still Life" — but he settled on the "Little Torturer." This label acknowledged that the renouncing of pleasure was originally imposed by an outside oppressor, but now was maintained by an internal scourge. The part of Ethan that represented the "counter-myth," that is, "I'd like to have some fun, even if I go to hell for it," was designated the "Bouncing Ball." This moniker resulted from a hypnotic session in which he visualized himself turning into a "large, light, red bouncing ball that can travel far and have lots of fun." People enjoyed the "'Bouncing Ball because they would hold it, play with it, stick it between their legs, and sit on it." The ball enjoyed these interactions just as much as the people who played with it; it was always available, always nurturing, always playful. It could not be hurt unless it was "popped." Ethan recognized this outcome as "going to hell" as a consequence of his pleasure, but when I pointed out that holes can be patched, a smile crossed his face — an unusual event for his usually morose countenance.

Once a mythic conflict has been identified, the second stage involves excavating the foundations of the "prevailing myth" and of the "counter-myth" that is challenging it. Old, guiding myths become outmoded as the individual matures and as life circumstances change. The psyche is continually trying on alternative mythic images, that is, "counter-myths," that compensate for the old myth's limitations. Indeed, Carl Jung saw dreams as often "compensating," producing points of view in counterpoint to the stance of the conscious ego, reflecting his belief that the human psyche is a self-regulating system (Singer, 1972). "Counter-myths" highlight possibilities and reveal new ways of being, often supporting underdeveloped aspects of the personality. Their imagery is imaginative and inspiring, but like wish-fulfillment dreams, to which they are psychologically akin, they are typically framed in the logic of magical thinking and immediate gratification. Unlike the "prevailing myth," the "counter-myth" is untried in the real world.

The dilemma created when a "counter-myth" challenges an outmoded "prevailing myth" is that the person is caught between two worlds — no longer able to thrive under the guidance of what has been, but not yet having developed guiding images that give practical utility to the new direction that is being intuited. The task in this stage of the work is to bring these opposing internal forces into awareness, to honor each, and to trace their roots in the individual's culture and personal history.

Further exploring the sources of his "Little Torturer," Ethan produced ample material during the hypnosis sessions. When he was about six years of age, Ethan found a turtle in a nearby woods and brought it home, placed it on the dining room table, and implored his mother to let him keep it. While making his plea, the turtle urinated on the table. Ethan recalled that his mother "threw a fit, took the turtle outside, and immediately washed the table, berating me all the while." More than once she asked, "What will other people think?" and "What would the neighbors say if they smelled turtle piss all around the house?" Once again, Ethan's attempt to bring some pleasure into his home and some life into his house had curdled. Ethan, of course, blamed himself for the fiasco, never questioning whether his mother's behavior and statements might have been inappropriate.

Returning from school one day, Ethan let out an unaccustomed laugh. When his mother asked what had amused him, he recounted an incident at school during which a boy's loose pants accidentally fell down, "and we could all see his ass, even the girls." Ethan's mother exploded. She hauled him to the bathroom, washed his mouth out with soap, and told him never to use "dirty language" again or he would "go straight to hell." Once again, an attempt to lighten up the dark ambience at home had led to punishment and retribution.

Ethan's father did not threaten hellfire and damnation, but his faithful attendance at Roman Catholic church services gave tacit approval to his mother's admonitions, as did the nuns' threats and the priest's constant prattling about the necessity for salvation. When Ethan's brother spent time with him, the "Bouncing Ball" came to the surface. His brother skipped Mass as often as he could, spent a great deal of time away from home with his friends, but — according to Ethan — "knew how to charm my mother and say all the right things so that she never took it out on him like she did on me."

Third Stage: Conceiving a Unifying Mythic Vision

During a hypnosis session, I suggested that Ethan take the voice and the posture of the "Little Torturer." He slipped into this role-playing procedure easily. Ethan's face took on a maniacal grin, and he began to speak in an almost deranged cadence: "Yes, I really enjoy torturing Ethan because it is so easy. He is very vulnerable because he has bought into the crap that his mother has fed him for so many years. He actually believes that if he had some fun in life, he would go straight to hell. So every time he laughs or takes some pleasure in what he does, I lay on a dose of guilt. And, boy, does he suffer!"

I next suggested that Ethan become the "Bouncing Ball." Almost immediately, the lines of tension disappeared from his face and his body lost much of its characteristic rigidity. He sighed, "I stay away from the 'Little Torturer' as much as I can, but he's always just around the corner. I'm happiest with my brother because he cheers me up. I like being with my lady friends, but I wish I could feel as relaxed with them as I do with my brother. Someday I'm going to bounce away from all my troubles and have a really great time."

When Ethan attempted to bring the two subpersonalities into dialogue, the "Little Torturer" showed contempt for the "Bouncing Ball" while the latter entity displayed fear and wariness toward the former, as well as anger that he was so vulnerable. During almost every session, Ethan shared his notebook with me, and on this occasion he showed me a list of personal myths that supported the "Little Torturer": "Curiosity killed the cat," "The less I think about my own needs, the better off I will be," "A good baby sleeps a lot and stays in his crib," "If I stay out of peoples' way, I will avoid trouble," "I am still the baby of the family," "I am cursed, and will carry the curse for the rest of my life," "It is better to bear the pain than to experience pleasure because I know more about suffering than I know about bliss."

During several hypnosis sessions, Ethan evoked emotional feelings in his body and later described them, oftentimes in symbols and metaphors. Anger, for example, was "a pissed-off black cat." Affection was "travelling through space to pay attention to another person." Fear was "hiding from a snake that is out to bite and poison me." Sexual desire was "a combination of affect and fear; I want to give pleasure to my partner and to myself, but I am afraid that my penis is poisoned."

In discussing the latter image, Ethan reported a recurring dream: "I am in bed with a woman and we are having intercourse. It is delightful, but the woman begins to feel sick. I know it is my fault. My penis is poisoned. My semen is poisoned. I have been poisoned by my mother, and now I have passed the sickness on to someone else. I have disobeyed the church's teachings. Not only am I being punished, but my girlfriend is paying the price as well."

Ethan described in great detail how his sex life reflected both the "Bouncing Ball" and the "Little Torturer." Ethan's sexual experiences would begin by being enjoyable activities and an escape from his depression and torment. Before long, guilt and remorse would permeate the experience, often leading to premature ejaculation. A similar pattern characterized his conversations with women. Just as intimacies were being shared, he would hold back and change the subject knowing that if he continued to talk he would behave like the "pissed-off cat" and expose his anger toward his mother, the church, and his teachers. His mother's words echoed in his ears: "What will other people think?" What would his lady friends think if he revealed his animosity and resentment?

The symbol of the "poisoned penis" came up repeatedly, not only in dreams but in Ethan's mental imagery. I mentioned that poisons have antidotes and, during a hypnosis session, asked him to imagine an effective antidote for his infection. Ethan reported an image of his mother injecting him with the poison, an image that also imbued many of his dreams. But this time, he grabbed the hypodermic needle from his mother's hand, smashed it on the floor, and said, "You will never do this to me again." Reflecting on these images, Ethan remarked, "I know that I have the strength to heal myself if only I could stop getting those injections."

Christmas was only a few weeks away, and Ethan had planned to make his customary visit to his parents' home, several hundred miles away. He resolved to take some type of affirmative action that would "stop the injections." During the subsequent hypnosis sessions, we rehearsed several scenarios in which he would display the strength of his convictions and make himself invulnerable to his mother's berating and belittling. We tried to use the "Bouncing Ball" symbol to represent the buoyancy he would need for this encounter. It became apparent that buoyancy was not enough and Ethan, in a hypnosis session, evoked the image of a red hammer — something that was the same color as the ball but impervious to being punctured by his mother's hypodermic needle or her caustic remarks.

When our sessions resumed in January, Ethan entered my office smiling. He cited no fewer than seven instances when he had stood up to his mother, contradicting her statements. He defended his sex life, even though his mother felt that premarital intercourse was sinful. He admitted to such human frailties as feeling angry from time to time, and occasionally using rough language — but saw no need to change his behavior.

The most extraordinary event occurred near the end of his visit when his mother began to cry, exclaiming, "The way you talk, you make me feel like I was a failure as a mother. But I did the best I could. I only raised you the way that I had been raised." Ethan had known that his grandparents were extremely strict disciplinarians and very devout in their religious convictions. He could imagine a vulnerable little girl cowtowing before them, introjecting their myths and making them her own. He saw remnants of this little girl in his mother's face, walked toward her, and hugged her for the first time in years. All this while, Ethan's father maintained his usually passive role, but his brother tactfully encouraged him, eventually placing his long arms around both of the protagonists.

Once both sides of the mythological conflict have been differentiated, the third stage involves integrating the "prevailing myth" and the "counter-myth" into a higher order system. Promoting such resolution of psychological conflict is a natural function of the psyche, but actively participating in the process can facilitate better life choices at a time when the person is particularly vulnerable to act out unconscious conflict in self-destructive ways, a more rapid resolution of painful inner discord, a greater sense of personal mastery, and ultimately a resolution of the mythological conflict that is based on carefully examined beliefs and values as well as the person's deepest intuitive wisdom.

The counselor's task in this stage is to skillfully mediate and facilitate as the opposing myths push toward a natural synthesis. Having embraced both sides of the conflict, images of integration become more possible. The individual is taught to recognize that facing one's own inconsistencies without a retreat into the old or a flight into the emerging may be as difficult as it is desirable. The objective here is to foster a new mythic image that transcends the "prevailing myth" and the "counter-myth," while embodying the most functional aspects of each. This process represents the self-regulatory attempts of the deepest and most numinous part of the psyche, one that attempts to grow toward wholeness.

During a hypnosis session, Ethan again orchestrated a dialogue between the "Little Torturer" and the "Bouncing Ball." He physically assumed the posture of each as they carried out, at first a heated debate, and, after several sittings, a discussion of their differences.

> *Ball:* Look at how stiff and rigid you have become. I could give you new life. I'm soft and buoyant; you're hard and dry. But you don't trust me at all, do you?

> *Torturer:* Why should I trust you? You are so damn vulnerable that any little puncture could deflate you. If I didn't torture you, somebody else would. So why shouldn't I get the fun out of doing it?

> *Ball:* I am tired of being such a damn masochist. The only way I can have any fun is to bounce away from you. But the guilt catches up with me whether I am at work, with a woman, or simply out in nature.

> *Torturer:* At least my actions are deeply rooted in my religious faith. What sort of spiritual life does a bouncing ball have?

Ball: You bet your grounding is religious. What you do to me is straight out of the Spanish Inquisition! Whatever happened to the gentle Jesus and the loving God I read about but never experienced at home, in church, or in the parochial schools?

Torturer: But in pain there is power. The church is powerful. And I am powerful.

Ball: You are not powerful at all. You are just a "little" torturer. I am a big red bouncing ball. And I am about to turn into a big red hammer.

This statement indicated that the "counter-myth" had outlived its usefulness and saw the advantage of taking on some of the attributes of the "prevailing myth." The softness of the ball and the dryness of the torturer were rejected while the ball's buoyancy and the torturer's hardness were maintained. The "Bouncing Ball" realized that his vulnerability needed to be tempered by the resiliency of the "Little Torturer." He also admired the torturer's groundedness, although the religious convictions they represented were abhorrent. Ethan began to explore meditation, and I gave him some references both to books and to meditation classes in the area. In addition, I taught him the "relaxation response" which has been identified as the basis of many formal meditative systems (Benson, Beary, & Carol, 1974). Ethan's image of the "Red Hammer" occurred in dreams, in meditation, and in our hypnosis sessions. He spoke about it, drew it, and began to establish it as a viable visionary symbol.

Fourth Stage: Refining the Vision into a Commitment toward a Renewed Mythology

In the fourth stage, the client is called upon to examine the new mythic vision that has been synthesized and to refine it to the point at which a commitment to that vision may be maturely entered. Although it is necessary to allow the natural dialectic between the "prevailing myth" and the "counter-myth" to take its course, a time does come when deliberately identifying with a judiciously cultivated mythic image both shapes and hastens the resolution. As the old adage has it, "If you don't change your direction, you may wind up where you are headed." Challenging the person to formulate an explicit choice at this point exercises an active participation in the evolution of the guiding mythology and leads to an enhanced sense of mastery in that process.

Ethan felt that the "Red Hammer" represented a synthesis of what was most functional in both his "prevailing myth" and his "counter-myth." The "Red Hammer," Ethan's "new myth," could be put to immediate use; when appropriate, he could be angry and coarse. But a hammer is used to build, and Ethan felt he was constructing a new life for himself, a life based on a "new myth" he verbalized as "I take pleasure in my power, but it is a power that nurtures and builds." Ethan found that he was becoming more effective in his work. For the first time, he was able to express humor in the classroom. For the first time, students would come to him for one-on-one discussions, and Ethan felt that he was actually making a constructive difference in their lives.

Fifth Stage: Weaving the Renewed Mythology into Daily Life

Ethan was surprised at the changes that he associated with daily meditative practice. He slept better. He lost the feeling of having a "suitcase" in his stomach. His concentration improved. He was able to pay close attention to his students. His body awareness was enhanced to the point that his sex life bloomed. I taught him ways to control premature ejaculation (see, for example, Levine, 1992; McConaghy, 1993), pointing out that this was one of many techniques with which he could develop self-mastery and empowerment. Always an advocate and practitioner of "safe sex," Ethan wanted to learn about "sensate focusing," and I pointed out the similarities between this procedure and meditation. The "poisoned penis" was an artifact of the past, and we both noticed the obvious sexual symbolism of his "Red Hammer." At first, Ethan associated the color "red" with his acknowledgement of anger, but later he made a closer association with blood and the "life force," something that had been absent for the first quarter century of his life.

We continued to plan homework assignments at the end of each session, and Ethan would bring in reports at the beginning of his next session. When he returned to his parents' home for Easter, he did not resent attending the Easter Mass with the family. He told his parents that he had begun to explore Eastern religious systems and did not receive the condemnation he had expected. One reason was that his brother had chosen this occasion to tell his parents that he was homosexual, and was about to move into the home of his lover. This revelation surpassed in drama and confrontation anything that Ethan could have provoked. However, Ethan was supportive of his brother just as his brother had given him what sustenance he could over the years.

In the fifth stage, one's new mythology is tested in the world-at-large. The final stage of our model requires clients to become practical and vigilant monitors of their commitment to achieve a harmony between daily life and the "new myth" they have been formulating. The threads of this "new myth" need to be woven into everyday behaviors, thoughts, and actions. The essence of our five-stage model is conveyed in an old Hassidic saying that counsels: "We should each carefully observe what way our heart draws us and then choose that way with all our strength." The first four stages are a way of carefully observing what way the heart beckons. By advising that clients choose that way with all their strength, the proverb recognizes that old behavioral patterns, conditioning, and character armoring which were associated with the old myth will tend to persist. Choosing the way one's heart beckons with all one's strength is the fifth stage. Focused attention is required for anchoring even an inspiring new myth that has been wisely formulated. This stage particularly draws from cognitive therapy and behavior therapy — using techniques such as behavioral rehearsal, visualization, and autosuggestion — in assisting people to integrate the new mythology into their lives.

One of the most effective ongoing tools for Ethan was his daily ritual of morning meditation. Following his twenty-minute session, he would use the autosuggestion I taught him to program himself for the day. I emphasized the difference between meditation and hypnosis, urging him not to combine meditation (which, in essence, has no specific goal) with autosuggestion (which is goal-oriented). Both are forms of self-regulation and, as such, both are tools for empowerment.

Ethan joined a theatrical group in his neighborhood and found that his prior experience in enacting his mythic subpersonalities could be put to good use in this new venture. He was asked to be an assistant basketball coach at his junior highschool, and found this to be an enjoyable activity as well. For the first time, he was able to be forceful with colleagues at school, even arguing with them when the occasion demanded it. And he finally was able to make friends with other teachers and attend the social functions that he had once shunned.

From time to time, Ethan had discussed with me the possibility of joining the Peace Corps. Our early discussions had focused on whether or not this would be escapist behavior, just the type of maneuver the "Bouncing Ball" would use to distance himself from his mother, his church, and his daily problems. But the notion persisted, and Ethan filed his application. He had no problem being accepted and notified his school that he would not be returning for the fall semester.

The Ongoing Process

Ethan was assigned to teach English in a Southeast Asian country. This was a serendipitous choice because it gave him a chance to deepen his meditation practice and learn more about Taoism, the Eastern perspective of most interest to him. He lived in an area with a high incidence of AIDS, so maintained a relationship with only one woman during the twenty-seven months he was overseas. Because she was a single mother, the practical difficulties of bringing her to the United States were insurmountable. For Ethan, it was just as well because he felt no urgency to get married.

There was one incident that Ethan took great pleasure in relating. In his work as an English teacher, he had several opportunities to interact with the local Roman Catholic priest, an American. When the priest suggested that he should either marry his lady friend or abstain from intimate relations, Ethan flashed back to his upbringing. In as calm a manner as he could muster, he told the priest that he had been raised a Catholic, and had made considerable efforts to work his way through the guilt and torment that resulted from this early indoctrination. He also voiced the opinion that his relationship with the Asian woman was based upon mutual respect and enjoyment, as well as the knowledge that they might never see each other once he returned to the United States. They both accepted the Eastern adage that "nothing is permanent," including their relationship. Ethan felt positively about himself as a result of this confrontation, especially as the priest was left speechless at the end of their discussion and never raised the issue again.

Upon his return to the United States, Ethan arranged to see me for a two-hour consultation. He expressed gratitude for our work together, and had continued to use auto-suggestion, monitor his mythology, and to lead a more joyful life. He had brought renewed vigor and inspiration to his work as a junior high school teacher, and was dating one of the other teachers at this school. I last spoke with Ethan in early 1996 at which time he was continuing to do well personally and vocationally; Ethan made specific mention of his intense involvement in the homework assignments he had completed when we worked together on his personal myths.

Reflections

Ethan's story affected me very deeply on an emotional level, and I believe that my ability to express these feelings was a helpful model for him. I have known countless people who have been attracted to both mainstream religions and cults, only to suffer abuse, betrayal, and disillusionment. I could not sit by calmly and remain non-judgmental while listening to the threats heaped upon a young boy by his church and its representatives. Perhaps my emotional reaction would have been more subdued if I did not value spiritual experience so highly. But, for me, "spiritual" is not a synonym for "religious." I conceptualize a "religion" as an institutionalized body of believers who accept a common set of beliefs, practices, and rituals regarding spiritual concerns and issues. People who have internalized these beliefs and practices are generally "spiritual" but many people are "spiritual" without being "religious" in the sense of participating in organized religions. One can be "religious" without being "spiritual"; many members of religious institutions perform the necessary rituals and accept the creed (at least superficially), but their ethics, morals, and opportunities for day-by-day practice of their religion do not match their professed beliefs (Wulff, 2000, p. 430).

I use the word "spiritual" to describe those aspects of human behavior and experience that reflect an alleged transcendent intelligence or process. This transcendent entity inspires devotion and directs behavior. These spiritual aspects of life are evident among human beings whenever there is an awareness of a broader life meaning that goes beyond the immediacy of everyday expediency and material concerns (Krippner & Welch, 1992, pp. 5–6). I have known people who have been sexually abused by priests, physically abused by nuns, or emotionally abused by "devout" parents — and this abuse apparently crosses denominational lines.

Ethan's story reinforced my interest in those "postmodern" approaches to psychotherapy and counseling that admit their premises hardly qualify as a universally acceptable body of psychological knowledge, and that those principles they find most useful might need to be adapted or abandoned when dealing with women, people of color, and/or clients from economic and social groups with which the therapist lacks familiarity. Postmodern counselors realize that, like Ethan, their clients need to learn a variety of coping strategies to live in a world of increasingly multiple realities. The personal mythology approach is one of many "narrative psychotherapies" that discern a co-construction of the therapist and client that takes place in their interaction. "Modern" therapies, like "modern" science, technology, and philosophy hold that the proper application of reason and observation would produce universal "laws," "truths," and the comprehension of "reality." These "laws," in turn, would lead to the knowledge, prediction and control of human beings, and to social betterment.

An example of the modern stance in psychotherapy is the authoritarian psychoanalytic dream interpretation (in recent years, of course, many psychoanalysts have taken non-authoritarian positions). This holds that the analyst understands the dream's symbols (often assumed to be universally valid, irrespective of time and place) better than the client whose "defenses" are not only responsible for his or her unconscious use of obscure dream symbols but also for the client's resistance to the understanding of their meaning. In contrast, Ullman and Zimmerman's (1985) interpretive process takes the power away from the therapist or facilitator and places it in the hands of the dreamer. After the dreamer presents a dream (which can be conceived as a text) and answers clarifying questions, the other members of the group pretend that they have had the dream, separating the text from its author, and discussing it in a variety of ways that the dreamer may or may not find resonant (a "deconstruction" of the dream text which takes on a life of its own). Then the dreamer shares as little or as much of what he or she has learned thus far, giving a personal interpretation of the dream (similar to text "reconstruction").

Ullman and Zimmerman next provide for a discussion and conclusion, with the dreamer having the authority to stop the process at any time, and to supply the "last word." Needless to say, the Ullman-Zimmerman process is castigated by those psychoanalysts who see themselves as arbiters of the dream's "truth" and the valiant warriors who must smash through their clients' "defenses" and "resistances" to help them adjust to consensual "reality." This is precisely the technique that I used with Ethan in a one-on-one adaptation. Once Ethan knew what the dream would mean to me, he was stimulated to construct his own interpretation.

These, and other approaches that partake of the postmodern sensibility, do not reject the irrational, the metaphorical, and the undomesticated concepts of a client's psyche and behavior. But they do reject the notion of an absolute "truth" that works for everyone — preferring to help clients identify and articulate their life narratives and find ways in which these stories can be changed to more usefully facilitate the clients' life goals, whether they be happiness, wealth, love, creativity, excitement, or service to others. As DeBerry (1993) notes, postmodern diagnosis is teleological in nature, "focusing on a person/community narrative and theme that includes the future" (p. 177).

The postmodern psychotherapist or counselor might have a psychoanalytic, behavioral, existential, cognitive, humanistic, transpersonal, psychopharmacological, or eclectic orientation. But the therapist's intervention should proceed in a way that enhances a clients' sense of self-worth, makes no absolute claims about "truth" or "reality," and places no immutable value on "adjustment" as the most desired outcome. When using alterations of consciousness as therapeutic procedures, the postmodern therapist is careful not to reify them, but to adapt hypnosis, imagery, biofeedback, relaxation, and other procedures to the client's needs and expectations. The therapist's skepticism, flexibility, and humor need to be combined with common sense, curiosity, caring, and concern as well as an ethical code that respects human differences, condemns exploitation, and embarks on the quest for a just community — in whatever form he or she envisions that pursuit.

In summary, postmodern psychotherapists and counselors must bring considerable modesty to their therapeutic interactions, admitting that they have no certain "truths" or final "answers." However, they can assist their clients to narrate part or all of their life story, and to identify their options as to that story's next chapter. Postmodern therapists understand that they are engaged in a process of cooperative construction as their clients attempt to revise or change the meanings and values of their life narratives, and develop an ethical code consistent with this realization. Anderson (1990) observes that postmodern therapists do not operate from a standard dogma but join with their clients in "an exercise in ethics" (p. 138). This rejoinder prevents them from slipping into a naive relativism in which any decision a client makes should be encouraged.

The evoked symbols and metaphors (such as the snake-mother, the "Bouncing Ball," the "Little Torturer," the "Red Hammer") were pertinent to Ethan's existential life issues. They might have been as easily elicited had Ethan simply relaxed, breathed deeply, and closed his eyes. However, it is my reflection that working in the context of what Ethan considered to be "hypnosis" brought a conviction and an authority to the material that would have been otherwise absent. Furthermore, Ethan was a client who had been taught to distrust bodily feelings. Hypnosis gave Ethan tacit permission to get in touch with anger, fear, and pleasure, and to accept and own these expressions of his affect. It also initiated a course of self-regulation that led to a disciplined meditative practice, the use of autosuggestion, and the control of his premature ejaculation. These concepts originally were foreign to Ethan — but hypnosis was not. By starting with the known, we proceeded to learn about and to master the unknown.

References

Anderson, W. T. (1990). *Reality isn't what it used to be.* San Francisco: HarperSanFrancisco.

Benson, H., Beary, J. R., & Carol, M. P. (1974). The relaxation response. *Psychiatry, 37,* 37–46.

DeBerry, S. T. (1993). *Quantum psychology: Steps to a postmodern ecology of being.* Westport, CT: Praeger.

Feinstein, D. (1990). Bringing a mythological perspective to clinical practice. *Psychotherapy:Theory/Research/Practice/Training, 27,* 388–396.

Feinstein, D., & Krippner, S. (1988). *Personal mythology: The psychology of your evolving self.* Los Angeles: J. P. Tarcher.

Feinstein, D., & Krippner, S. (1997). *The mythic path: Discovering the guiding stories of your past.* New York: J. P. Tarcher/Putnam.

Krippner, S. (1990). Native healing. In J. K. Zeig & W. M. Munion (Eds.), *What is psychotherapy? Contemporary perspectives* (pp. 179–185). San Francisco: Jossey-Bass.

Krippner, S., & Welch, P. (1992). *Spiritual dimensions of healing.* New York: Irvington.

Levine, S. B. (1992). *Sexual life: A clinician's guide.* New York: Plenum Press.

McConaghy, N. (1993). *Sexual behavior: Problems and management.* New York: Plenum Press.

Sheehan, P. W. (1994, February). Memory and hypnosis. *The International Society of Hypnosis Newsletter,* 20–21.

Singer, J. (1972). *Boundaries of the soul: The practice of Jung's psychology.* Garden City, NY: Doubleday.

Ullman, M., & Zimmerman, N. (1985). *Working with dreams.* Los Angeles: J. P. Tarcher.

Wulff, D. M. (2000). Mystical experience. In E. Cardeña, S. J. Lynn, & S. Krippner (Eds.), *Varieties of anomalous experience: Examining the scientific evidence* (pp. 397–440). Washington, DC: American Psychological Association.

CHAPTER TEN

Story as a Personal Myth

G. Frank Lawlis

Whether we are aware of it or not, our self-concepts, the experiences we have in life, and even the actions we take in the world, are all determined by an inner mythology that has been forming within us, some say since the day of our conception. Within those mythologies are vast countries of the imagination, populated by men, women, children, and even animals and plants, with whom we closely identify. In a very real way, these mythologies provide us with models by which we measure our lives. We may turn to the heroines and heroes of inner mythologies as if they were real people who can counsel and guide us in the choices we make. They are role models for us, helping us to give meaning and purpose to our lives. Similarly, events that occur within these mythologies warn and inspire, frighten and comfort, furnish goals to which we may aspire and pitfalls we must avoid.

We may or may not be conscious of these mythologies and the characters who participate in them. But since the beginning of time, humans have shared stories of heroic deeds, villainy, love, and treachery that have inspired, frightened, and entertained. More than that, the best of these stories have lived on in the hearts of men and women, to be passed along to younger generations. Out of these stories have evolved today's spiritual and cultural mythology, embodying characters and actions that touch something very deep and essential within the human psyche. From the best of these have come universal archetypes — characterizations that for whatever reason have come to represent basic human drives that capture spiritual aspects of the human experience.

We need not look far for examples of how myths work in our daily lives. No doubt you know the fairy tale about Cinderella. When you were a child you may have deeply identified with how miserably she was treated by her sisters and how nobody acknowledged her true beauty. If you are a person who was moved by that story, it may continue to affect how you look at yourself and the world around you. Holding in your mind the injustices that Cinderella suffered, you might be particularly sensitive to any situation in which people are not given their due credit. In addition, you might have the perception that one day your "true Prince" will arrive, recognize your true beauty and sweep you off to his palace, where you will live "happily ever after." While the latter part of the myth is rosy, it also implies that if you just wait around long enough, somebody or something will fall in love with you and make all your dreams come true. You do not have to make any effort on your own, other than put up with the misery of your current existence.

Although few of us take these myths literally, they have a far greater impact on our lives than we might like to believe. Some years ago, an associate of mine interviewed twenty young women from the inner city, between the ages of fifteen and twenty-two. All grew up in lower income neighborhoods in the San Francisco Bay Area and were employed in Head Start Training programs. They were asked four questions: (1) "What is the story you best remember from your childhood?" (2) "What was that story about?" (3) "Do you ever think about that story when you are feeling depressed, blue, or troubled?" (4) "What, if anything, does the story tell you about life?"

Sixteen of the twenty interviewees revealed their favorite story was Cinderella. Most of them answered that it was about "people not treating you right." They said that sometimes they remembered it when they were depressed or blue, "because it shows how unfair the world really is." And finally to the forth question, three women answered that, "the only thing the story taught you was that there was not much hope of life getting better because Princes are just make-believe."

Although this was an informal study, it does point out how powerful we can be affected by the myths we learn when we are young. As we dig a little deeper, we can safely say that while the myths we hold within our minds can offer guidance and support, they can also limit the choices and decisions we make. Certainly that was true for at least the three women in the above informal study, who saw their lives as pretty hopeless because princes do not rescue damsels in distress anymore.

The myths we do not immediately remember can affect our lives. More than that, those myths we are least conscious of may be the ones that have the greatest impact on our lives. Becoming aware of these myths, the themes and models of behavior they insinuate on us, can be profoundly liberating for us.

Personal Mythologies and Health

For many years I have worked in a medical setting with people with injuries and catastrophic diseases that have incapacitated them to various degrees. Having interviewed literally thousands of men and women, I have seen, time and time again, how internal mythologies can become major impediments to recovery if not handled properly. This is easily illustrated in the people with whom I have worked who have intractable pain due to back injury. Many of them held within them the secrets of their continuing disability as well as their cure. When they explored their inner mythology, they found heroes who possessed great physical strengths. They had modeled their own lives after the lives of these mythic heroes. However, now that they themselves were no longer "strong people" who could carry the burdens of the world, their lives seemed to them useless and hopeless.

Although this is a relatively simplistic model, we can perhaps see from it that before their lives can be "healed," they must come to terms with their inner mythology. They must change the nature of the hero and redefine the meaning of "strength" before they can begin to value their own lives again. They must develop in their consciousness a mythology in which the "strong person" is not defined by merely physical brawn but by other visages of strength — the ability to use one's mind, to express one's emotions, to seek new avenues of self-respect and trust.

The principles have been constant with people recovering from accidents, chronic illness, and crushing emotional defeats. And in case after case, people's healings, that is, their abilities to get their lives working again, regardless of their prognosis, have been dependent on their ability to work with their own mythology. When they could go inside, find the stories that consciously or unconsciously guided their lives, and then literally change their minds by rewriting those stories, these people could recover, to live productive and happy lives.

Whether we are recovering from accident or injury, emotional trauma, or simply the normal stresses of daily living, our inner mythology shapes how we experience our lives and the events that come to us. And when we are able to get in touch with our inner mythology and then identify its impact on our lives, we suddenly move into the position of having a wider range of choices. We can expand the stories that make up our inner mythology, and we can change the characters of the leading players. In the process, we literally change how we perceive our place in the world.

For thousands of years, storytelling has been an integral part of every healthy society. Sharing stories that support or challenge a community's values has been an important tool for implementing growth and healing. Whether these stories are told to children as they go to bed at night, or are shared around a campfire high in the Andes, or are performed in a city theater or produced by a Hollywood film company, the themes, the particular interactions between the characters, the fate of hero and heroine, all these have an impact on how we view and experience life.

It is the belief of this author that storytelling is a necessary ingredient for growth, change, and health. There are times when, like the snake shedding its skin, we must slough off those personal myths that no longer serve us. That process used to be assigned to the shaman, whose healing rituals defined the old story for us, helped us abandon the parts of it that were no longer healthy, and then provided a new story to inspire and guide us, sometimes in song or verse or prose.

Since the beginning of time, storytelling has entertained us. We have used stories to pass the wisdom of one generation to the next, passing along those lessons gleaned from the experiences of living. The best of these stories entertain and inform us, and they do this because they capture themes and experiences that touch the human spirit. That is what archetypes and classic themes are about; that is why they endure from one generation to the next.

Themes such as those in Cinderella and Snow White, dealing with the experience of not being appreciated, supported, and loved, have captured the imaginations of children for the past hundred years. And these stories were derived from similar tales, from a variety of cultures, that can be traced back far longer than that. What is it in these themes that touches the human spirit, particularly the spirit of younger person? Perhaps it has something to do with being children, living amongst people much larger than themselves and feeling inferior or powerless. These stories express how it feels to be unappreciated for our true selves; they end with the magic prince who discovers who we really are and carries us off to the castle and the way of life we deserve. These stories capture the child's awe, bewilderment, sense of injustice — and their wondrous capacity to find a happy ending. But perhaps most interesting, they begin to feed the essential elements of our understandings of the spiritual realm — to believe in a fairy Godmother or to trust in the words of a spirit.

Storytelling always tells something of the storyteller as well. In psychology, the well-known inkblots of the Rorschach Test, and the Thematic Apperception Test (TAT) in which pictures of social interactions are interpreted, use our tremendous capacities to make up stories to reveal personal insights. Known as "projective" devices, the inkblots and TAT pictures have little real meaning until we give them meaning through our interpretation. Such devices further point out to us the fact that stories are one of the key ways we have for making sense of our life experiences. The stories we tell ourselves are created from the vast store-house of life experiences and symbols that we all hold within our minds. And then, consciously or unconsciously, those stories become models for living that we follow, sometimes blindly, sometimes in a very deliberate and purposeful way.

The goal of therapy is to explore how we make our inner myth-making a more conscious process in our lives. What are the stories we tell ourselves? How do these stories affect our decisions and our interactions with other people? How do these stories shape and color how we experience our lives? How do we rewrite those inner myths that limit us and cause us to have only a narrow view of the world? Most of all, how can we use the inner myth process to heal our lives?

In an effort to share the process with patients and students of life process, I offer guides for evaluating personal myths, to more clearly identify their themes and how they may be helping to shape the individual's decisions and perceptions of their lives. There are also lists of symbols and story plots that will help them both interpret what their present mythology is saying and develop stories to achieve new goals.

Webster (1972) defines "story" as the telling of a happening or connected series of happenings, whether true or fictitious, with the intention of entertaining or informing. In a therapeutic sense, this definition holds true; to entertain and distract attention, but more importantly to inform and educate. There are many forms of story; the fairy tale, the legend, the personal incident and the personal myth. Joseph Campbell (1972, 1976) has helped educate us about the power of myth in promotion of values, tradition and symbolic truths. Story can even be a reason for living. As Terrence Des Pres (1976) points out, many survivors of death camps find such strong motivation to survive to "tell the story," that he is convinced that this need is enough to persevere through inhuman conditions.

Story Telling and the Healing Process

Story has been deemed as an important feature of health care in that it addresses special needs and articulates an individual's unique understanding (Schoenhofer, 1991). The need to tell his or her story is important to honor one's experience and personal wisdom as well as to give relevant information (Akeret, & Klein, 1991). It is incumbent upon us as responsible caregivers to extend the space and time for our patients to engage in the valuable process of history taking. It is therapeutic in itself, and it provides valuable information relating to an individual's unique disease process. Even the most common topic can elicit critical information. For example, when childhood diseases are discussed, "Have you had mumps?" "Whooping cough?" and so on. I discover exciting and fruitful stories when I ask, "Tell me the stories when you were sick. Who took care of you? Were you frightened?" The response to the experience of being sick and vulnerable often repeats itself. It would be important to know these stories as possible repositories of state dependent learning mechanisms for coping with present illness, such as with fear, denial, resource-seeking, and so on.

However, this chapter is not about the skills and obvious wisdom of listening to our patients' stories. It is about telling stories as an integral part of the health care delivery process. Embedded in the skills of telling stories is the essence of health attitudes, education, and love. As a practitioner of behavioral medicine, I have been satisfied to observe the acceptance of behavioral approaches for many medical processes. For example, the behavioral research on pain (Achterberg & Lawlis, 1980), cardiac treatment (Ornish, 1990), and psychoneuroimmunology (Ader, Felten, & Cohen, 1991) have evolved into common protocols in many of the nation's hospitals. Much of this acceptance has to do with the bridges in communication among those interested in the links of the mind and body, and how to address them in appropriate terms for the health care practitioner.

However, in spite of all the advances in behavioral techniques, one of the most critical aspects of patient care appears to be missing much of the time, namely the ability of the patient to integrate these responses to life obstacles to ongoing situations in the absence of professional supervision. For example, I have personally met frustration in my efforts to help a person in coping with pain or anxiety regarding a medical process when he or she appears to lose even the concept of the technique the moment I leave the room. Although the patient might be inherently facile with relaxation and imagery, he or she may encounter difficulty generalizing from one treatment without the structure afforded by a professional. The obvious conclusion is that the individual has not integrated the alternative response into his or her personal myth. The role of "victim" may be so implanted in the person's personal story that all reactions are governed by that overall script.

Timmy was a six-year-old awaiting his spinal tap as part of the protocol for leukemia, this being his second time to undergo this procedure. He was obviously very nervous and fearful with tears welling up in his eyes as he stared at the door, expecting any moment for the nurse to come forth. I had been requested to work with him to help relieve his anxiety and decrease his pain behavior, although much of what I taught him about relaxation and imagery dissolved the instant he faced this procedure. His mother, who felt a sense of responsibility for Timmy's behavior, was as stressed as her son, and had no skills to deal with her own fears.

I asked if he would like to hear a story about a boy very much like himself. He appeared relieved to have some distraction and agreed to listen. As I began, "Once upon a time" his attention became totally focused upon my story about "Big T," who became a hero when he was called upon to show the others in the village how to deal with a disease that afflicted the city. He sought wisdom on his travels to the great teachers, who taught him the skills of breath control and focus of attention. He used these skills in his martial arts of defense as well as adversity. For example, "as Big T was trapped in the jungle, he became sick with a strange disease that could only be cured by drawing some blood from his body and mixing it with a powerful potion, then reentering it into the body. This would be a painful process, but Big T had been taught how to deal with pain. He would relax and breathe out his discomfort." (The conclusion of the story resulted in his achievement of the goal in serving as an example in using these arts. He was praised and honored.)

After the story, Timmy was quiet. After a short period of silence, he went to his mother and comforted her with soft words of confidence. I was gratified to witness his behavior during the spinal tap procedure as not only improved, but a source of personal pride in his ability to endure.

From my clinical experience, I have concluded that many of the concerns with our sophisticated behavioral techniques, although they may be deemed useful by the patients, are that they often are taught for a very specific event, unrelated to their underlying self stories. Moreover, they are usually administered in standardized and autocratic protocols. For example, the therapy of teaching breathing techniques is often conducted in an impersonal form, such as "take a slow breath in to the count of seven, now let in out to the count of seven." Relaxation therapy often regrettably consists of simply listening to a cassette tape. These forms are frequently perceived as components of a specific part of the immediate procedure which are not extrapolated from any other event in patients' lives. This is especially true in dealing with children, whose reality is more immediate than that of adults.

Telling a Therapeutic Story for Personal Myth Change

Implementing therapy skills and practices within the framework of the engaging plots and resolutions can yield a great deal of success in storytelling .

1. Partly by the way the story is told and partly by the resolution of the story, the listener's anxiety is lowered.

With regard to the process of the storytelling, the storyteller's level of relaxation and warmth is contagious to the listener (Lawlis, 1993). If the teller is consciously manifests referenced deep breathing and softening emotions for himself or herself, the content of the story can be presented in a much less threatening way to the listener. In the interest of pacing the listener, I think it is important to represent the hero as first manifesting the presenting affect and cognitions of the listener. If the hero is diagnosed with cancer, but is presented as confident and relaxed, the listener can also learn the attitude. Obviously, if the story has a positive ending, the anxieties about the future are relieved to some degree, because a path has been chosen. The use of positive expectancy and hope can be presented in realistic perspective within the total story theme. The role of hope in the success of medical care is unchallenged as the most critical of all psychological attributes of healing.

2. A hero can be presented who captures first the patient's reactive stance toward the illness, and then gradually adopts a proactive stance that fits within the patient's actual or potential skill set.

The patient can vicariously process that figure's reactions to the challenges of the presenting problem. Thus, the patient can learn from the hero's behavioral adjustment and coping with the issues at hand. For example, if the hero is suffering from pain, the coping strategies can incorporate deep breathing techniques, imagery, exercise, and so on, to deal with the situation. In this way, the symbolic person, the hero, can serve as a model.

Some questions have arisen as to the possibility that adults do not have heroes anymore, but in my experience everyone has at least one hero. It may be a grandfather or a TV character. Sometimes it is the process itself of discovering what a hero is for an individual that enables one to learn about the individualized value of empowerment.

3. Specifically, the story puts a coping technique in the generalized context of a person's experience, not in the situation-specific event.

As the hero deals with the pain of a medical procedure, or the aftermath of surgery pain,the patient can understand this generalization because it is in the scenario of his or her personal crisis instead of what others may perceive to be relevant or helpful. As the story unfolds, the "real" issue for the patient may not be the necessity of treatment that we as professionals and parents are concerned about, but rather the social significance of dealing with a disease. Social significance of a disease in this context is the value placed upon the disease and the response of the person to it by the family and community. If the person has a herniated disk in his lumbar spine, the family and community might have the judgment that that person's productive life is over. The consequence of that social significant value would be the role expected of the patient, whether to accept the role as an invalid, or as a warrior to combat the limitations. The social significance can also include the reinforcement of disease behavior, the exchange of receiving rewards for being sick or healthy. For example, diagnosis is frequently accompanied by the positive affect on the part of the patient resulting from heightened affection and attention from the family and friends. Many conflicts are resolved when one is sick. The hero's strategy would embrace these personal issues, and better individualize the protocol in a broader perspective.

4. Inasmuch as there is family participation, the members can be given roles to play in the coping and healing process that have power and prestige.

Social isolation of the patient can be pronounced in the relationship among family members in the face of disease. This discomfort is enhanced in the hospital house where family roles are immediately displaced by the authority of the medical system.

5. As the hero learns in the story of the importance of proper behavior, such as appropriate diet and exercise, the individual can understand the need for proper rehabilitation from the perspective of being a champion instead of a victim.

Resentment and frustration can occur when a person feels deprived of a lifestyle due to dietary or physical restrictions; however, if the change can be a part of a story of empowerment, compliance to a proper medical protocol is enhanced.

6. Probably most controversial but consistent with recent research is the enhancement of healing mechanisms, such as immunity systems, through imagery.

As demonstrated in many clinical research projects (Achterberg, 1985), through participation in a strong and believable image, one can manifest correlated physiological responses. This is a two-edged sword, because one would assume that negative imagery can cause destructive changes as well. Therefore, it behooves the medical team not only to direct mental processes toward constructive content but to direct them away from destructive content.

Features of Storytelling

In my research with storytelling, I wrote a story for patient education in the pilgrimage of cancer treatment called *The Cure* (Lawlis, 1993), a "Jonathan Livingston Seagull" type of setting. Basically the story is about a wolf who is diagnosed with cancer and goes through the forest, asking various animals, such as the bear, the snake, and so on, for answers. As I used the story I began to realize four basic features to it, or any story, that were critical to success: the way the storyteller told the story, the relaxation inherent in the concentration, the imagery of the obstacle or challenge to the hero, and the participation of the patient.

The Storyteller

One of the obvious requirements for a storyteller is to be able to create the setting for the story, similar to the creation of sacred space. The time and space should be respected for its own sake, being reserved for mystery and enchantment so that the breathing and intensity of the spoken words communicate the emotional tones to be conveyed. If the storyteller is too stressed or fearful, that emotion will become the emotional tone of the story.

The relaxation and voice quality of the storyteller are more critical than content and cannot be over-emphasized. I have produced total nonsense stories, but with appropriate affect and intonation, with good success. As the patient gets into the story, the emotionally-laden terms like "cancer" and "operation," even "death" itself, can be broached. An excellent time for patient education, the hero examines the problem from a distance, using the opportunity to judge the real crisis from the experience of another being.

A patient was listening to his wife reading the story of *The Cure* as he was coming out of anesthesia from an operation. He began to laugh about the frustrations of Alex, the main character. As the waves of consciousness would come and go, he would awake to request that the next chapter be read to him. For some reason, his wife offered a sense of humor in her storytelling, and the patient's recovery was remarkably interlaced with joy and happiness.

As Cameron, Snowdon, and Orr (1992) have demonstrated, parents of children with disabilities become patients themselves who have to deal with guilt and sadness in major dimensions. I have found that training the parent to be storytellers may have very constructive results for them as well as for the children. By helping them achieve a relaxing voice and focusing upon the story process, the storyteller can achieve a more positive attitude in interacting with the child, develop a closer role in dealing with the disease (as a coach), and learn what is going on with the child at a much more intimate level.

The Relaxation Skills

As stated above, skills in relaxation can be achieved vicariously through story. In fact, a form of desensitization often is consciously developed. By relaxing the patient through a series of implicit or explicit forms of stress reduction, tension producing words, such as "cancer" or "pain," or procedures, such as debridement or surgery, can be introduced in a form of a hierarchy of increased stress levels (Mills & Crowley, 1986). This is a classical approach to dealing with phobia responses. Similar to the process of hypnotically-oriented psychotherapy, the therapist uses metaphorical language and mental pictures to induce a trance, wherein selected topics can be incorporated in the story (Hilgard & LeBaron, 1984). As the topics are presented, therapeutic messages and skills can be suggested.

It is typical of my own practice to have the hero engage in some very terrifying situations, such as being diagnosed with a disease, sometimes resulting in a disability (such as an amputation). The hero becomes relaxed and uses the skills to overcome the enemy and utilizes the disability to an advantage. I remember Jan was a fourteen-year-old girl who was facing paraplegia as a result of a tumor on her spine. As her hero was facing a struggle with the enemy within her body, she became distracted from the story. I asked her what was the imagery for her in the story, and she replied that before she could see the hero win, she must first see what outfit she would be wearing. I asked her to describe the dress (or outfit) that would be empowering, and she detailed cowgirl apparel, much to my surprise. As we continued the story, she would use the articles from the clothing as cues for her relaxation.

Imagery

Whether or not one accepts the assumption that imagery can be a bridge in a person's physiological make-up, story imagery helps the patient understand the disease and the methods of management in a better and clearer perspective. Achterberg and her colleagues (Achterberg, Kenner, & Lawlis, 1988) utilized the story or metaphor of "skin embracing skin" in a study of severely burned children as a part of their skin graft operations. The story was broken into three parts in which the children had to participate both in their imagery and behavior.

The first phase was when the underlying tissues were preparing a "sticky" cement for the new skin. The imagery was visualized as hands painting some glue, and the children were told that they had to be very quiet and relaxed while this was going on; otherwise, the hands would stop moving.

The second step in the Achterberg et al. (1988) study was to image the white hands (not blood filled) reaching down to the red hands (blood filled) of the tissues, straining to touch. Breathing techniques were incorporated to help this process. Finally, the hands were joined (creating red flow) and celebration was given to success. The results of the story was evident from the evaluations, and successful grafts. It is important that imagery references be rich as possible in the visual, auditory, kinesthetic, olfactory, and gustatory realms.

Participation of the listener

As Krietemeyer and Heiney (1992) have articulated so well for children, the engagement of the listener is greatly heightened when he or she participates in the story line. There is also the great advantage of learning what some of the "real" issues are from the unfolding of the plot. I usually conduct the story by introducing the main character, and requesting that if the listener can "see" the hero, to complete the description by explaining dress, size, family and friends of the hero.

As I lead the hero into various challenges, especially the second or third time, I often ask the listener to help resolve the problem. Sometimes I am surprised and challenged myself. For example, I was telling Ron, a six-year-old patient with cancer, about our hero dealing with some scary situations that had some false intimidations. In the scene, the hero was in the dark and was hearing strange sounds. I had introduced the idea of relaxation earlier and explored "real" dangers as apart from those based only on fear. As the hero was facing this mysterious situation, I asked Ron to continue the story, expecting him to have the hero relax and find the sounds to be easily dealt with. Ron had the hero turn on the lights to find himself in a pool of sharks. Part of the strategy of storytelling is to maintain enough reality to generalize the fearful situation and equip the patient with successful skills, so having the hero whip out a lazer gun and kill the sharks would have lessened the power of the hero's personal abilities. I have also found that if the hero relies on some tool that is not available in reality there can be a sense of lingering vulnerability arising from the story, the principle being that if fanaticized weapons are not accessible, there is a induced lack of power or protection without them.

As we approached the sharks, I was engaged in suggestions of how the hero was going to get out of the situation. We took a break from the story and discussed the "script" and tried various scenarios. We agreed to have the hero make friends with the sharks and train them to help his white blood cells eat up the cancer cells. He stamped a big "H" on them for "Helpers."

By having Ron participate in the story, I was engaged in his story. I have always been amazed at the creativity that comes from patients as they interact at this level. The outcomes are as mysterious and marvelous as stories always are. I never know what is going to happen exactly, except that we are going to learn something.

Special Aspects of Storytelling

As part of the research with imagery scripts and evolving story themes, three parts of story appear to be critical in its use for health-related issues: the symbol or challenge presented to the hero; the internal sources (skills, wisdom, and so on) of the hero in dealing with the disease or challenge; and the external sources of support (family, community, and medicine, for example). These three aspects are addressed as therapeutic elements and have been documented as significant factors in the prediction of disease, such as cancer and intractable back pain (Achterberg & Lawlis, 1984).

The disease or challenger

In order to become proactive, one has to "look the foe in the eye." If one is always running from shadows, there is greater strength to the foe than in reality. As part of the story, the hero must size up the opponent and the situation for what it is. Perhaps there is a time or two in which the hero becomes disheartened or discouraged, but part of the plot is to overcome the fear or burden within oneself. Sometimes this "weakness" is part of a broader family story. If everyone in the family history has had alcoholism or heart disease, then it may be a sense of honor to bow to life's limitations.

If disease is a metaphor for a greater lesson to be learned by the individual, there might be justification in personifying the disease or challenge, giving it voice or character in order to hear the message. One example comes quickly to mind of a eighteen-year-old girl who was facing a long term rehabilitation as a result of an automobile accident. As she was participating in a story of a young hero facing a terrific mountain climb, she asked the mountain why she had to undergo all of the strife and pain in the challenge. The mountain replied that she must learn true wisdom through her body if she was to know true beauty, because she always had physical beauty before the accident. This was very important to her because it brought meaningfulness to the process and struggle, making it a true hero's journey.

The projection of personality and motivation to disease should be handled with some caution. Whenever any element receives any symbolic meaning, there is the investment of strength. I usually recommend divesting the disease and challenging any power other than its existence.

The Internal Source

Whether the story has a personification hero or a mythical one, the real source of power should be the internal sources. Usually I have found skills and wisdom to be most accessible, but I have also found personality traits to be helpful. For example, if the person has a history of being intelligent or clever, the foe can be tricked. What needs to be constantly a part of the education is that the hero (and the patient) has tremendous reserves in the form of systems of protection and decision-making for use in response to adversity and threat.

Personal sources include the many physical powers, the psychological abilities and the underlying spiritual features within a person. It is not unusual for a patient to reveal a power animal, spirit guide, a fairy godparent, or a religious figure who enters into the story as a personal source of encouragement.

The External Sources

These are the allies and friends that help promote our well-being. These can also include food (such as spinach for Popeye), vitamins, medicine, and so on. Mothers and fathers get a lot of credit for support but they also can play the "audience." As part of a larger community, parents can be part of the story by observing and approving the action of the hero and being available for celebration. The audience is no small part of the story and often serves as a major participant in ordinary reality when the patient is successful in dealing with challenges. It is typical for the child to expect applause when he or she has concluded the story or the medical procedure.

Story and Culture

Story is one of the oldest forms of teaching about health. It was used in all forms of religious teachings and values. Certainly the entertainment industry has utilized this form of messenger. During the wars, the nation has required story to understand the meaningfulness of the effort, but more importantly, to recognize its role and behavior in response to them. The movie enterprises certainly portrayed different role responses to the Vietnam War than to World War II.

On November 22, 1994, I was listening to Public Radio and I heard the story of a fifteen-year-old girl who had run off from home to escape chemotherapy. Her family was from Laos and either did not understand the concept of cancer, or had another name for her disease. They did not approve of her treatment, and were confronted by county police, and charged with "medical neglect." After the loss of her hair (which the family has kept as part of their tradition), the girl was not to be found.

The fear and confusion of mixed-cultural myths of disease is not new to this country, especially as the Western Science explanatory model clashes with those of more personal dynamics of taboos and community structure. Yet what application could story introduce itself in order to melt the myths into a more meaningful process? In fact, that is the purpose of story, to place the patient as an active participant in the healing process and to develop personal myths of strength and honor.

As our personal universes are placed in turmoil with such unexplainable events as disease, accidents, and violence, we search for meaningfulness, and for appropriate roles to play. Without story, we are faced with too many unknowns and can only remain reactive to the environment. This process reinforces passivity and victim consciousness. In this context, the real hero is the storyteller, whether it be the patient or the shaman, or both.

Storytelling is an art and science. It requires the storyteller to model the affect and skills portrayed of the hero as well as the sensitivity to the listener's more immediate needs. There are well documented implications for patient education, imagery and hypnotic approaches integrated within story to affect and improve health care and management. Strategic use of the theme and hero skills can provide a model for effective management issues involving anxiety and pain, especially when there are medical interventions. However, the central ingredient in storytelling is the empowerment of the patient and the facilitation of the hero's personal path through the morass of illness.

References

Achterberg, J. (1985). *Imagery in healing*. Boston: Shambhala.

Achterberg, J., Kenner, C., & Lawlis, G. F. (1988). Severe burn injury: A comparison of relaxation, imagery and biofeedback for pain management. *Journal of Mental Imagery, 12*, 71–87.

Achterberg, J., & Lawlis, G. F. (1980). *Bridges of the body-mind*. Champaign, IL: Institute for Personality and Ability Testing.

Achterberg, J., & Lawlis, G. F. (1984). *Imagery and disease: Image-CA, Image-SP, Image-DB, diagnositic tool*. Champaign, IL: Institute for Personality and Ability Testing.

Ader, R., Felten, D. L., & Cohen, N. (Eds.) (1991). *Psychoneuroimmunology* (2nd ed.). New York: Academic Press.

Akeret, R. U., & Klein, D. M. (1991). *Family tales, family wisdom:: How to gather the stories of a lifetime and share them with your family*. New York: Morrow.

Brady, J. (1977). *The craft of interviewing*. New York: Random House

Cameron, S. J., Snowdon, A., & Orr, R. R. (1992). Emotions experienced by mothers of children with developmental disabilities. *Children's Health Care, 21*, 96–102.

Campbell, J. (1972). *Myths to live by*. New York: Viking Press.

Campbell, J. (1976). *The masks of God: Creative mythology*. New York: Penguin.

Des Pres, T. (1976). *The survivor: An anatomy of life in the death camps*. New York: Oxford.

Hilgard, J. R., & LeBaron, S. (1984). *Hypnotherapy of pain in children with cancer.* Los Altos, CA: Kaufman.

Krietemeyer, B. C., & Heiney, S. P. (1992). Storytelling as a therapeutic technique in a group for school-aged oncology patients, *Children's Health Care, 21,* 14–20.

Lawlis, G. F. (1993). *The cure: The hero's journey with cancer.* San Jose, CA: Resource Publications.

Lawlis, G. F. (1993). *Manual for storytelling.* San Jose: Resource Publications.

Mills, J. C., & Crowley, R. J. in collaboration with Ryan, M. O. (1986). *Therapeutic metaphors for children and the child within.* New York: Brunner/Mazel.

Ornish, D. (1990). *Dr. Dean Ornish's program for reversing heart disease: The only system scientifically proven to reverse heart disease without drugs or surgery.* New York: Random House.

Schoenhofer, A. (1991). Story as link between nursing practice, ontology, epistemology. *Image, 23,* 245–248.

CHAPTER ELEVEN

Style

Rachel Naomi Remen

Although an impulse toward wholeness is natural and exists in everyone, each of us heals in our own way.

Some people heal because they have work to do. Others heal because they have been released from their work and pressures and expectations that others place on them. Some people need music, others need silence, some need people around them, others heal alone. Many different things can activate and strengthen the life force in us. For each of us there are conditions of healing that are as unique as fingerprints. Sometimes people ask me what I do in my sessions with patients. Often I just remind people of the possibility of healing and study their own way of healing with them.

Some time ago a young man was referred to me by an imagery-training program for people with cancer. Despite a diagnosis of malignant melanoma, he had been so poorly motivated that only a month after completing the intensive training, he could not remember to do his daily imagery meditation. The referral had been clear: perhaps I could turn around his self-destructive tendencies and encourage him to fight for his life.

Jim was an air traffic controller at a major airport. He was a reserved and quiet man who might have been thought shy until you noticed the steadiness in his eyes. He told me with embarrassment that he was the only one in the imagery class who couldn't stick to the program. He didn't understand why. We talked for a while about his plans for his life and his reaction to his diagnosis. He certainly cared a great deal about getting well. He enjoyed his work, loved his family, looked forward to raising his little boy. Not much self-destruction there. So I asked him to tell me about this imagery.

By way of an answer he unfolded a drawing of a shark. The shark's mouth was huge and open and filled with sharp, pointed teeth. For fifteen minutes three times a day he was to imagine thousands of tiny sharks hunting through his body, savagely attacking and destroying any cancer cells they found. It was a fairly traditional pattern of immune system imagery, recommended by many self-help books and used by countless people. I asked him what seemed to prevent him from doing the meditation. With a sigh, he said he had found it boring.

The training had gone badly for him from the start. On the first day, the class had been asked to find an image for the immune system. In the subsequent discussion, he had discovered that he had not gotten the "right" sort of image. The whole class and the psychologist/leader had worked until he came up with the shark. I looked at the drawing on his lap. The contrast between it and the reserved man was striking. Curious, I asked what his first image had been. Looking away, he mumbled, "Not vicious enough." It had been a catfish. I was intrigued. I know nothing about catfish, had never even seen one, and no one had ever talked about them in this healing role before. With growing enthusiasm he described what catfish do in an aquarium. Unlike other more aggressive and competitive fish, they are bottom feeders, sifting the sand through their gills, evaluating constantly, sorting waste from what is not waste, eating what no longer supports the life of the aquarium. They never sleep. As an air traffic controller, he admired their ability to do this. I asked him to describe catfish for me in a few words. He came up with such words as "discerning, vigilant, impeccable, thorough, steadfast." And "trustworthy." "Not bad," I thought.

We talked for awhile about the immune system. He had not known that the DNA of each of our billions of cells carries a highly individual signature, a sort of personal designer logo. Our immune cells can recognize our own DNA logo and will consume any cell that does not carry it. The immune system is the defender of our identity on the cellular level, patrolling the Self/Not Self boundary constantly, discerning what is self from what is other, never sleeping. Cancer cells have lost their DNA logo. The healthy immune system attacks them and destroys them. In fact, his unconscious mind had offered him a particularly accurate image for the immune system.

As a medical student I had been involved in a study in which a micrograft, a tiny group of skin cells, was taken from one person and grafted onto the skin of a second person, and I told him of these experiments. In seventy-two hours, the second person's immune system, searching through the billions of cells that carries his own DNA signature, would find this tiny group of cells which carried the wrong DNA signature and destroy them. I described many ingenious things we did to hide or conceal the cimrograft. Try as we might, we could not outwit the immune system. It found those cells and destroyed them every time.

He still seemed doubtful. The teacher and the class had talked of the importance of an aggressive "fighting spirit" and of the killer motivation" of effective cancer-fighting imagery. He flushed again. "Is there something else?" I asked him. Nodding, he told me that catfish grew big where he had been raised, and at certain times of the year they would "walk" across the roads. When he was a child this had struck him as a sort of miracle and he never tired of watching them. He had kept several as pets. "Jim," I said, "what is a pet?" He looked surprised. "Why, a pet is something that loves you, no matter what," He replied.

So I asked him to summarize his own imagery. Closing his eyes, he spoke of millions of catfish that never slept, moving through his body, vigilant, untiring, dedicated, and discriminating, patiently examining every cell, passing by the ones that were healthy, eating the one that were cancerous, motivated by a pet's unconditional love and devotion. They cared whether he lived or died. He was as special and unique to them as he was to his dog. He opened his eyes. "This may sound silly but I feel sort of grateful to them for their care," he said.

This imagery touched him deeply and it was not hard for him to remember it. Nor was it boring. He did his meditation daily for a year. Years later, after a full recovery, he continues this practice a few times a week. He says it reminds him that, on a deepest level, his body is on his side.

People can learn to study their life force in the same way that a master gardener studies a rosebush. No gardener ever made a rose. When its needs are met a rosebush will make roses. Gardeners collaborate and provide conditions which favor this outcome. And as anyone who has ever pruned a rosebush knows, life flows through every rosebush in a slightly different way.

CHAPTER TWELVE

Vietnam Combat Experiences and Rites of Passage: Healing through Telling One's Story

Daryl S. Paulson

One of the biggest problems Vietnam combat veterans faced after returning from Vietnam was finding positive meaning from the experience. Let me provide an example from my own life.

Upon high school graduation in the late 1960s, I joined the Marine Corps. Shortly after basic training, I was sent to Vietnam to serve in an infantry unit, an experience that nearly killed me physically and psychologically. I was not prepared to deal with the violent deaths I witnessed on a daily basis, routinely killing fellow human beings, and losing all my moral concerns except for personal survival. When I returned home, I was a devastated and broken twenty-one-year-old. My life quickly became one of suffering and drinking, suffering and drinking, as protesting peers pounded guilt into my already guilt-ridden self. One night, I found my way out. I looked at my loaded .38 caliber revolver. My suffering would be over in a flash and I would have the last laugh. One 158-grain hollow-point in my brain and it would be all over. But as I looked at my gun, I thought about the biblical Job's suffering and how it had been for a purpose. Then I thought about my comrades who had been killed and the despair they would feel with no one to tell their stories. I started to cry and then decided to find a psychotherapist who could help me.

During the psychotherapeutic process, I learned the value of personal stories. I needed to tell my story to others over and over until I knew they understood my experience. But even when I knew they did understand my experience, I did not. I then needed to retell my story over and over until I understood it.

Much later in time, I would come to understand this process, but not until I studied the depth psychology of Carl Jung (1964), the mythical processes presented by Joseph Campbell (1968, 1972, 1988), and led rap sessions with fellow Vietnam combat veterans.

I believe I have discovered an effective way of assisting veterans to find positive meaning from the Vietnam war. It is a process of viewing the Vietnam war as a male initiation rite. Because the bulk of the Vietnam war was fought by men, I will restrict this work to a male rite of initiation. However, future work in this area will undoubtedly include women as they too become "front line" combatants.

The manner in which I use "initiation rite" is not a staged ritual as seen in movies about the old Roman Empire. Rather, it is a physical, emotional, and mental process of leaving a previous stage of life in order to enter a new stage. It serves as a bridge between the new and the old (Bridges, 1980; Metzner, 1986).

In ancient times, initiatory experiences were used as entry vehicles into the new life stages (Jung, 1964). The unique individual experiences were interwoven into a larger mythical story. As the individual initiatory experiences were interpreted in terms of the mythic story, the myth served as a reference point for the initiate (Whitmont, 1969). It provided a point of reference as to who he or she was, where he or she was going, and how he or she would get there. In short, it provided meaning (Feinstein, 1979; Feinstein & Krippner, 1988; Frankl, 1956; May, 1991).

As previously stated, an effective way to help the Vietnam veteran is to help him to reframe his combat experiences into the context of an initiation rite.

Let us begin, then, with the experience of combat. Physical combat has been with humanity since the beginning. Even with the technological advancements in warfare, it is still the common infantryman or "grunt" who fights the bulk of the war. It is the infantryman who must experience the physical, emotional, and mental anguish of war: being sick, being wounded, facing the tension and anxiety of impending death, and dealing with the deaths of others on a daily basis. For the modern infantryman, like his predecessors, life will never again be the same. No longer can he dismiss death as an event far in the future. Even if he survived the war, he knows that death is but an instant away. No matter where he is, no matter what job or position he holds, no matter who he marries, no matter how financially secure he is, he will always know that life on this earth holds no permanence for him (Paulson, 1994).

For the most part, his worldview is contrary to the worldview of his peers who did not experience combat. For the noncombatant, death is deniable; for combat veterans, it is an overshadowing truth. While the non-combatant's worldview is generally very predictable — graduation from high school, entering college, marrying, raising a family, working, and ultimately enjoying life in retirement — the combatant's worldview is usually one of living in an unpredictable world which is undergoing constant, threatening change. He has seen so much death, so much suffering, and has been forced to live with so much insecurity that he can no longer feel secure (Lifton, 1973). Often the veteran's life has no meaning, no purpose, and no direction, once he has experienced war.

Additionally, the majority of Vietnam combat veterans were unprepared to experience this psychic trauma. The lack of psychological support they received from their government while serving in Vietnam was painful and traumatic, but being attacked, put down, and protested against by their peers for their involvement in Vietnam upon their return was excruciating (Lifton, 1973; Paulson, 1994).

For our purpose, myths are constellations of images, feelings, and ideas that provide meaning to our past, a purpose to our present, and a positive direction for our future (Feinstein & Krippner, 1988). We will begin our journey, using mythical stories as the basis for our work. According to Campbell (1968), three recurrent themes are present in both myths and rites of passage: (1) the call to adventure; (2) the initiation; and (3) the return.

The call to adventure — the separation phase — consists of leaving the known behind and entering the adventure, or new dimension in life. The initiation proper is the actual series of events that one must experience before passing into the new dimension of life. The return is experienced only after a successful initiatory passage into the new developmental stage of life. The experiences and knowledge gained from this journey are integrated into one's own life as well as passed on to others in order to aid them.

The combat veteran also experienced the call, initiation and, perhaps, the return. And, as we will see, the personal narratives of each combatant will fit into one of these areas. But that is not all. Veterans who have made a successful passage will have gone through all three stages in the process. Let us begin with the call to the adventure, the separation from one's known life.

Call to Adventure

It is a mystery as to why the mythological hero was called for a specific adventure but it most assuredly happened. The same was true for the Vietnam veteran/hero.

The country was split. On one side were the protestors, the hippies, and other members of the counter-culture, who were not only against the war but were at the very heart of American society's peace movement. On the other side were mainstream Americans, often referred to as the "silent majority." A young man growing up during this period was in a no-win situation. If he left the country to avoid the draft, he would have to abandon his nation and be labeled a traitor; if he went to serve in Vietnam, he risked death.

During a rap session, one of the men who chose to go to Canada during this period told us his story. Jeff graduated from high school in the spring of 1966 and entered college that fall. He was interested in pursuing a business administration career and he was deeply in love with a classmate he was planning to marry. Jeff never seriously considered having to join the military; that was for the others — the poor or the dumb ones. But, as fate would have it, one-and-a-half years into Jeff's college career, his father unexpectedly died of a heart attack, ending his financial support. Because so many young men were in college at that time, using college deferments to avoid the draft, Jeff could find no student aid. As a last resort, he got a part-time job to support himself but flunked out of college. Within three months, he was drafted.

Jeff could not envision himself killing anyone or, worse yet, being killed in a war fought on the other side of the earth for reasons unknown to him. His brother and mother encouraged him to join the Coast Guard to avoid combat; he tried, but they were no longer accepting enlistments. Jeff's girlfriend wanted to get married and have children but her father, a World War II veteran, urged Jeff to "serve his country." He said it was Jeff's duty. But Jeff just could *not* fight this war. It was against his convictions. He left his mother, his brother, and his girlfriend and went to Canada. Jeff had "refused the call for the military adventure," but heeded the call for his own adventure. He paid dearly for what made sense to him, encountering another initiatory experience, which was certainly no easier. Jeff's story, however, is not our real focus; ours is that of the combat veteran's separation.

I shall begin with my own story. During my senior year in high school in 1966, I was deeply infatuated with a girl who did not care about me. I was discouraged over my lack of success with her, bored with school, and could see no reason to go to college. I was unskilled in any kind of trade, such as carpentry or auto mechanics. I felt a sense of "power" when I told people I was thinking of joining the Marine Corps after graduation.

Art, also a Marine Corps veteran, had a different story. He had been in and out of trouble with the local police and, finally, with the federal government. He and a friend had spray-painted a federal hydroelectric dam with twenty-five obscene words. Because Art had repeatedly been in trouble with the law, the judge gave him a choice: join the military or go to jail. He chose the Marine Corps.

Most of us who joined or were drafted into the military had a vague sense of apprehension but the military experience was still weeks or — at least — days away. There was still time to party and adopt the facade of a tough role with our friends.

In my enlistment group, I doubt that any of us realized just what was in store for us but, as we got closer and closer to the Marine Recruit Depot, I noticed our joking and laughing became less and less frequent and intense. That we were now in the United States military was becoming a reality. It was no longer an abstract concept. Right now, we were owned by the government, by the Marine Corps; it could do with us what it chose for our entire enlistment. For us, this realization was very sobering. Our lives, as we knew them, were over. What would be next? What would military life be like?

As I looked out of the 727 Delta airliner during our landing approach to San Diego, I made a commitment to myself that, although I was unsure of what lay ahead, I would not screw up. Then we landed. As soon as we got off the plane, we were loaded into buses and driven to the Marine Corps Recruit Depot (MCRD), where we reported for duty. So far, things were not so bad, and since it was about 2:30 a.m., we were directed to a temporary staging area where we could sleep until morning.

That morning, I woke up to the peaceful whine of a small propeller-driven aircraft cruising through the air overhead. I was in a state between sleep and wakefulness and, because I grew up near an airport, I felt as though I was at home listening to an airplane. Abruptly, I was brought back to reality when a drill instructor marched into the squad bay yelling, "Get the hell out of the racks, you pukes! You goddamn maggots!" He started yanking recruits of their bunks, yelling, "This ain't no picnic, girls! Get the fuck up!"

We were dumbfounded. What was he talking about? What were we supposed to do? Two more drill instructors came into the squad bay, also yelling and screaming about what miserable-looking pukes we were and that we were now lower than whale shit which lies on the bottom of the ocean.

A hippie-ish recruit next to me had grown a scraggly beard, with which a drill instructor became obsessed. He walked over to the recruit, pulled his beard and told him if he did not have it cut off in fifteen minutes, he would set it on fire with his cigarette lighter. Then he dragged him out of the room to the barber shop. He screamed for the rest of us "scuzzy looking pukes" to follow him down the stairs into the courtyard to get our haircuts. One at a time we sat in the barber chair and had all of our hair shaved off, a process which took about nine seconds. Then we were commanded to line up and take a shower in the receiving barracks next door. There, the eighty-seven of us were instructed to remove everything we were not born with and place it in the plastic sacks provided. We were then each issued a small bar of soap and marched naked to a communal shower. All eighty-seven of us were crammed into a shower stall which would normally have held about twelve men. But the drill instructors kept yelling and screaming, "Shower up, maggots! Assholes to belly buttons, girls, get your asses in there and get cleaned up'"

After showering, we were commanded to line up in four rows — naked, humiliated and terrified. We wondered what would be next. We were issued underwear, socks, tennis shoes, a sweat shirt, utility trousers, and a utility cap. We could barely recognize each other. From now on, we had no individuality, no sense of identity, and no contact with the outside world. We were totally separated from our communities, parents, friends, wives, and girlfriends. Looking at each other without ever talking, our eyes asked: *What have we gotten into?*

Over the next several weeks, our spirits were further broken. We were constantly humiliated and harassed, humiliated and harassed, and humiliated and harassed. It was not long before we lost our ability to care. We were dead to our past lives; they were from a different world and time. We had no hopes or aspirations beyond just getting through the moment.

However, after about three weeks of living in dread and despair, we began to identify with the Marine Corps. It seemed as if we had had no other life, as if we had always been in boot camp. We noticed that the drill instructors also began to change their attitude toward us. We were now called "men" and "Marines" instead of "girls," "pukes," or "scum," and we began to live up to it. We learned to march; we learned to fight; and we learned to work together. We were preparing for our own initiation experience, that of combat as a unit, as a professional military machine.

Initiation

The initiation is the actual experience of the rite of passage. Once we completed our infantry training, we were destined for South Vietnam. Although we had not actually experienced combat, we had a pretty good idea of what we were getting into. We had viewed report after report on the nightly news and we had seen a lot of combat footage in movies shown in boot camp. We were committed to the adventure and there was no turning back. This was a time when we thought about leaving our parents and loved ones and about going to a foreign country to "lay down our lives for America."

Over and over, I wondered how it would be to really experience combat. Was there a lot of shooting or just a little? What was it like to be mortared? Rocketed? Was it non-stop, twenty-four-hour fighting? Could I kill another human being? If I could not, would I be hung as a traitor? If I was killed, would my body be lost? Would it be mutilated? Would anyone remember me?

We did not have much time to dwell on how combat might be, for we were flown to Vietnam very quickly. After a four-day layover in Okinawa, we were flown to Da Nang Air Base where we were immediately assigned to our in-country units. We certainly had doubts about our performance in combat, but our morale was high, fueled by our indoctrination in boot camp. We felt that we had some control over our combat destiny — whether we lived or died. Our thoughts were based on our boot camp indoctrination: if we did everything we were told to do and did not "fuck up," we would live; if not, we "would be shipped home in a body bag, dead. Yet we were scared to death.

In my first two weeks of combat, our radio man was shot through the head just in front of me, while on patrol. He had moved into the path of a bullet while talking to another unit and then it was over. He was gone. Just like that. He was simply "tagged" and "bagged," that is, he was identified by his unit and put in a body bag to be sent home. Just like that. I saw seventeen of my comrades who were coming in on a helicopter for a ground assault killed by a direct hit of a 121 mm rocket, all killed. Just like that! At the end of those two weeks, I watched six seasoned veterans destroyed by an incoming mortar round as they ate their C-rations. Just like that, they were gone. They were tagged and bagged. Combat was far too ruthless, random, and absolute for me to be able to predict or prevent my death.

In classical mythology, this portion of the initiation is often referred to as the "Road of Trials" (Campbell, 1968). It was during this period that the hero was severely tested. I, too, was tested during the combat ordeal, by continually witnessing young friend after young friend brutally killed, and by killing Viet Cong and North Vietnamese Army (NVA) members as if they mattered no more than rats, gleefully enjoying their suffering and pain. I was becoming progressively numb to my humanness by living this life. Soon there was no boundary between the war and myself. Now we were enmeshed, the war and I — united in this senseless butchering. My proud motto became, "Kill all the gooks, let God sort the fuckers out!" I had become a true killing machine.

Still, during times alone, I wondered just what I had gotten myself into. I knew I was in a situation way over my head. What I was doing and how I was doing it somehow did not seem right. I was terrified that I would never again see a friendly face, a face of one who would care about me and not try to kill me. I knew I was deeply, emotionally wounded but I was determined to survive at all costs or, at least, kill as many NVA as I could before I was killed.

Because I was new to combat and ignorant of the actual ways of combat, I knew that I would not survive long. I prepared to accept my death as well as I could. I no longer had any hope of living. I clearly saw that it did not matter how proficient I was; a random rocket or mortar hit could end my life in an instant. This was not an abstract threat of tomorrow or next week; it was thirteen months of "now" — thirteen months of wondering if I would be alive to eat the next meal, to see the next sunrise or the next sunset. I began hoping that because I would surely die, I would like to get it over soon, rather than prolonging my suffering. This, I found later, was a prominent attitude among infantrymen.

In mythological motifs, the hero often experiences an encounter with the "father" figure (Campbell, 1968). The father figure is often discussed and described by veterans because he was the force who fiercely guided them through the trying times of the initiation. After having proven our worth (still alive after a number of battles), we were "taken in" by a more experienced combat veteran, "the father." This person acted as our guide and took an active role in teaching us to survive combat.

A leathery old Marine took an interest in me and taught me how to survive. He taught me the laws of combat; I learned the sound differences of incoming and outgoing mortars and rockets, and I mastered the art of "walking point" without being killed or, worse, getting the entire squad killed. In Vietnam, walking the point was dangerous. It meant one walked twenty-five to fifty meters in front of the rest of the patrol. It meant the point man was the first to get shot, step on a booby trap, or set off a mine.

In addition — like the heroes in mythology — after suffering and enduring and surrendering to apparent utter failure, we sometimes felt that we were assisted by supernatural forces. For me, this assistance came in the form of "intuition." I actually began to feel warnings about dangerous situations before they occurred. I was truly amazed at how these extra "survival senses" seemed to develop as I needed them.

For example, during the 1969 TET offensive, I was with my unit at the An Hoa Combat Base, awaiting helicopter transportation to a very hot, bloody battle taking place in an area called Elephant Valley. Elephant Valley was a treacherous place and we dreaded going there. I was very preoccupied with what kind of shit (combat) was going on there, but the weather was bad and we could not go that night. I had a very strong feeling of impending danger while lying in my tent. I could not sleep, my heart raced, my anxiety escalated, and a voice inside me said "Leave the tent, now!" I gathered my flack jacket, helmet, ammunition, and poncho and walked to the perimeter trenches, where I tried to sleep. About two hours later, our compound was overrun by NVA. During this attack, our camp was pounded with hundreds of high explosive rockets and mortar rounds. The ground shook from the impact of these rounds exploding; a series of violent fire explosions engulfed the entire northern side of the compound. We thought we would never survive the night, as we repelled wave after wave of NVA attackers. Finally, by morning, they retreated.

I was tired and sore as I limped back to my tent to get some sleep. But when I got there, I was shocked to discover a huge hole in the tent, directly in line with the spot where my head usually rested on my cot. A boulder, approximately three feet across, lay on top of what was left of my cot. That boulder would have killed me had I stayed in the tent. From that time on, I depended on personal intuition to keep me alive (Campbell, 1968). Time and time again, intuition assisted me in surviving the initiation of war.

At some point in the initiation process, we began to realize that you are not killed until "it's your time." Our motto became, "When your number is up, you're wasted — but not a second before." This brought us some comfort. There was reason and purpose to the apparent random killings. We felt a part of a larger system and would die only when it was our time. How could such a drastic perceptual change have occurred in us? One would think mere chance was the arbitrator of life or death. The more shit (combat) you saw, the worse were your chances of surviving. This was how we first perceived it; but as we survived situations that were "unsurvivable," our perceptions changed. Let me explain this with some examples.

Larry, an army artilleryman, was in his tent with eight other men. Suddenly, his camp took five 121 mm rocket hits. His tent took a direct hit, killing everyone in it but Larry. He was not hit by any shrapnel. He was burned and had both eardrums ruptured, but that was it. The 121 mm rocket, a very lethal weapon, is considered to have an absolute kill range of fifty meters. Larry had been about eight meters from the rocket center. His number was not up.

Jeremy drove a large tow truck which accompanied convoys in case any of the vehicles got stuck in the muddy, backroad trails. On one trip, his truck hit a mine, which was reported to be one of our 500-pound unexploded bombs The impact blew the entire engine and cab off the hoist unit. He was blown into the air and landed about twenty meters away, in the soft, cushiony area of a rice paddy. Urinating in his pants, he suffered no wounds except to his pride. His number was not up either.

These experiences were very powerful and brought us to a more peaceful, fatalistic stage. When your number is up, it's up. There is no death before that time.

Once the hero entered this stage, the actual initiation was nearing completion He had survived everything the war could present him and he had not crumbled. It was during this period that the combatant felt most comfortable being an infantryman. He was no longer an initiate; he was a full-fledged combat veteran.

Pseudo-Return

For those of us who survived the "Nam," our day to leave the country finally came. We were going back to the "World" — a name we gave the United States — home to round-eyed, friendly, warm, and affectionate women. Home to a world where the streets were asphalt-paved and there were flush toilets, hot and cold running water, food other than C-rations, and plenty of cold beer.

Unlike the mythological hero going through the initiatory ordeal to find the Pot of Gold, the Golden Fleece, or the Holy Grail, and who brought back his trophy to share with everyone, the Vietnam veteran brought back no treasure. That is, he attained no positive knowledge (treasure) which he could share with others in his community.

When our 707 jet landed at El Toro Marine Air Station, I was secretly preparing for a hero's welcome. I think all of us reasoned that we would get a doubly strong welcome because we had fought in spite of the absence of any explicit government plan to win the war. For example, Congress and/or the President would decide to bomb North Vietnam one week, but stop bombing the next. This on-again, off-again strategy was terrible for our morale. We would often wonder, "Why the hell are we here if our leaders cannot make up their minds whether to fight the war or bail out?" Given these unusually hard conditions, now we thought we would be rewarded.

We landed and walked out of the plane to our homecoming reception. I saw *three* people waiting for us. That was it! They were Marine wives who had volunteered to serve cookies and Kool-Aid to us. Where were the beautiful young women to welcome us home? They should be here, I thought.

Other veterans had similar experiences. Joey, for example, found that he was no longer wanted. His fraternity brothers no longer wished to associate with him. He was "flawed." He was a Vietnam veteran. He could not deal with that, so he ended it by shooting himself in the head.

Art, a Marine Corps veteran, came back to the states and went to college. He suppressed his entire Vietnam experience, never speaking a word about it to his non-military friends. But he was guilt-ridden. To compensate for this, he tried to be all things to all people. He tried to be the best, most caring friend to the women he knew, and he tried to be the best, most caring friend to the men he knew. In the process, however, he denied his own needs. On the outside, he put on a good show, but his inner conflict was betrayed by his ever present need for a drink, a Canadian whiskey on the rocks.

As he continued to avoid himself and his inner needs, Art's guilt and inner conflict worsened. He compensated by being even nicer to the people he knew. Finally, under this self-imposed pressure, school became too much of a burden for him. He dropped out of school, left the country, and went to live in Cozumel, Mexico.

It was during his stay in Mexico that he began to question his involvement in Vietnam. Had he screwed up? What if he really had not gone to defend the country? What if he had been wrong? He assuaged his doubt and guilt with even more alcohol.

Art was not alone in this introspection. I think most of us who were veterans shared a sense of condemnation. We felt a kind of deep guilt which sent terror to the very core of our being. If we had been wrong about the war, were we not similar to Nazi war criminals? Was there really a reason to keep on living? How could we live with ourselves, having seen and experienced all the brutalities of war and survived them, only to realize that our involvement served no positive purpose?

Then one day, it happened. I had an anxiety attack. I was sitting in an accounting class when I suddenly felt as though I was dying. My heart began to pound; I was dizzy and my eyes would not focus. I began to gasp for breath and sweat profusely as I "freaked out." I walked out of class, pretending everything was fine, and went immediately to the student health service. There, the doctor who examined me could find nothing wrong. To me, this meant that something very serious was wrong. I began to relive feelings of being near death, as I had in Vietnam. This totally confused me.

I tried to go on picnics and relax with my friends but I became too anxious, even with the tranquilizers, to enjoy the picnics. I kept feeling that someone — the enemy — hidden in the trees, was stalking me. At times, I became so tense and anxious on the picnics that I would have to belt down whiskey just to get through the ordeal.

Other veterans have reported similar experiences. They have reported panic attacks when a fire alarm is set off, when a helicopter flies over them, and when hearing loud noises. This period is pure hell for the veteran. We expected to have gained some positive feelings from our Vietnam experiences but instead we found that the quality of our lives was eroding quickly, especially as we began to experience panic during benign events.

In mythological stories, after the hero had successfully completed his initiatory experience, he returned to the world to share his newly-acquired knowledge with the common people, in order to be of service to them (Campbell, 1968). But for the returning Vietnam combat veteran, there was nothing of value which he could share. There was only pain, frustration, and anguish. And instead of being treated as a hero, he was avoided by his friends for being a veteran; he was shunned by the World War II and Korean veterans for losing the war, by the hippies for being a "warmonger," and by himself for allowing himself to be duped by his country into fighting in the war. Vietnam was not a war to save the enslaved Vietnamese people; it was not fought to protect America. It was a cruel joke and a cruel turn of fate for the veterans who fought it. It seemed just one more thing that he had screwed up in his life.

Unlike the mythological hero, the Vietnam hero's return was not his physical return from the war (Paulson, 1994). When he returned physically, he had one more obstacle with which to contend in the initiation process. This is a critical point. The vast majority of people, veterans included, think that the physical return from Vietnam was equivalent to the "return" of the mythological hero. Hence, the majority of veterans were caught in a sort of limbo. They were caught in a hellish state, trapped between a war that was over and a society that did not care about their pain even though they needed society's help to be reintegrated into its cultural and social fabric. The real return for most of us — if we had one — began only after we dealt with what we had done in Vietnam. That usually took place in the therapist's office.

Actual Return

After being back in the United States for some time, many Vietnam veterans realized that they could no longer escape their emotional agony through denial. They were no longer in Vietnam, nor had they "returned" from the war. They were stuck in a wasteland of a pseudo-return. As their pain affected more and more areas of their lives negatively, they had to admit to themselves that they were in deep trouble and it was getting worse.

Many Vietnam veterans were caught in a dilemma. How could they be brave, strong men if they could be victims of emotional pain and suffering? To be a victim of pain and suffering and to admit it was the equivalent of being a wimp.

Chris, an army combat veteran, finally came to the end of his emotional tether after struggling for eighteen years. He could endure no more. The nightmares, the drinking, the drugs, and his divorce drove him to seek help at the Veteran's Administration Center. There he was given a pep talk by a Veteran's Administration physician. He was told to stop feeling sorry for himself and to be thankful he was not *really* wounded. To have been actually hurt, according to this doctor, meant to be physically wounded. Chris went home in total despair, feeling weak and worthless. He sat down on the porch, drank a beer, went to the woodshed and ended it all by shooting himself in the heart with a .45 caliber handgun.

Mike, an Army infantryman, was also traumatized by his painful experiences. He came back to the United States and was rejected by his friends and his country. In an attempt to do something positive with his life, he enrolled in college, but he had so much guilt, he could not concentrate enough to study. After flunking out his second quarter, he moved to Detroit to work on an automobile assembly line, installing bumpers. Mike quit after only five weeks, because the air-powered ratchets sounded too much like machine gun fire and the sound made him too jumpy. He then hitchhiked around the country, trying to find himself. During this search, he met a lot of people who had experienced varying degrees of personal catastrophes. He found that for many of these people, their catastrophes were merely temporary setbacks. Out of their setbacks, they arose with renewed strength and greater wisdom than they had before. Mike realized that, even though his life was a psychological mess right now, it did not have to be so forever. He began to accept his life as it was; he was a Vietnam veteran and he could do nothing about the past, but he could determine, to a large degree, the life he now lived. Mike began to heal.

A number of veterans reported that they started to get better when they began studying and applying psychology in their lives. The psychologies reported to be of most interest to these veterans were Transactional Analysis, Gestalt, existential psychology, and psychosynthesis. Although the precise therapeutic modality seemed not to be important, the most critical aspect was that the veteran began to examine his life *authentically* and to tell stories about it to other people.

During rap sessions discussing choice, responsibility, and self-control with one another, veterans often find they share a common pattern. Prior to examining their lives, they professed to be in charge of their lives but they clearly were not. They were running their lives on automatic pilot, the automatic pilot of their conditioned behaviors. These automatic behaviors were based on previous stages of life, from their interactions with their parents, role models, and various other significant figures in their lives. They thought these behaviors were their own choices, but they were the ideals of those with whom they identified. They were living their lives based on the insights of others. For most of them, even when they clearly saw this through psychotherapy, they hesitated to let go and choose for themselves authentically. Being aware of and taking full responsibility for one's choices and actions is very, very frightening when one is not used to doing it.

Often in mythological stories, upon finishing the initiatory experience, the initiate "returned," sharing his wisdom and knowledge — his treasure — with others. But, many Vietnam veterans became stuck in a "pseudo-return," where they could not find positive meaning in their experiences and hence were unable to return with the ability to aid other veterans.

Art, a Marine veteran described previously, is one of these persons. He had gone to Vietnam as an infantryman and, of course, experienced brutal combat. He had also volunteered for many dangerous special missions, to spare married men in his unit from being killed. When Art returned to the United States, he found that he was totally out of synchronization with his society. He was psychologically in Vietnam but physically in the United States. To reduce his psychic tension, he began to drink heavily. By the time he was twenty-seven, he was an alcoholic. When he dropped out of American society and went to Mexico to escape, he continued to drink and drink and drink. The last time I saw Art, five years ago, he had just returned from Mexico and was being hospitalized for alcoholism at the local Veteran's Administration hospital. He was forty-two but looked as though he was seventy. Art had not been able to return to society.

Another veteran, Scott, who had been an Army infantryman, also could not return to society. After his physical return from Vietnam, he drifted from job to job and from relationship to relationship He just could not find his niche, his place in life. Finally, he left New Jersey and retreated to Wyoming, where he continues to live alone near the Grand Teton Park. He has retreated from society and chosen not to "return."

However, not all veterans have refused to "return." A minority of combat veterans have made the return passage and integrated themselves back into society. They have something of positive value to offer society. This is the critical point. From an outer perspective, the combat veteran brought nothing of benefit back to society, but after a successful passage of psychotherapy —or sorting out the experiences and sharing them through storytelling — the veteran did bring back an assortment of treasures to share with society. What he brought back was his ability to go on in spite of hardships, his ability to put a cause he believed in ahead of his own interests, his ability to handle pain — emotional and physical — yet to continue to function. Finally, he has the treasure of "walking the talk." He stood up and acted on something he believed in instead of just talking about it. He moved from narrative to action.

Cohn, a former Army infantryman who served in the Mekong Delta, spent years trying to bury the war and become a "normal human being living a normal life." Finally, he decided to enter counseling and, shortly after, began telling his story. He stated that he had fooled himself into thinking his pain would go away if he ignored it but the "ghost of Vietnam" continually shadowed him. Every time he thought his pain could get no worse, it got worse. But as he told his story over and over and later reframed his combat experiences in terms of a male rite of passage, his pain subsided.

As he stated in a letter to me: "Telling my story in the frame work of a male rite of passage has made more sense and has given my life more meaning than anything else … "

Mike, a former Army Ranger, drifted from one job to another, from town to town, over a twenty-year period, doing everything he could to forget his Vietnam experiences. One day, he decided to use his Vietnam service as a way to get disability from the government, something he felt he deserved. Part of the process in establishing a service-connected disability was to participate in group or "rap" sessions. It was here he began telling his story to fellow veterans. Slowly, over time, his storytelling changed from personal confessions to an adventure of near "mythical" proportions. He realized for the first time that he was only eighteen years old when he was forced to kill and to witness his comrades killed over and over again. He clearly saw he was not some weak, fragile person but a person who stood up for what he believed.

During this period, he also viewed the television series, "The Power of Myth." In this series, Bill Moyers interviewed Joseph Campbell concerning his study of mythical structures. Mike identified with many of the mythic processes and clearly realized that what he experienced in Vietnam was a male rite of passage. From this realization, his life began to acquire new meaning. His participation in Vietnam was a very important life passage: a true rite of initiation.

These traumatic experiences are common to veterans. Individual positive meaning from them is not. Hence, it is up to the veteran to realize that his combat experience was a rite of passage which needs to be told and honored.

Conclusion

The importance of telling one's story, and then retelling and processing it is necessary so as to see the stories as describing a mythic male initiatory rite of passage. This provides a grounding of the stories into a larger process. The meaning of the rite of passage is unique to each person. Once found, however, it is the "Holy Grail" or treasure for the veteran. And, once found, each veteran will have discovered the tremendous inner value obtained from that which seemed so senseless: the Vietnam war.

References

Bridges, W. (1980). *Transitions: Making sense of life's changes.* Reading, MA: Addison-Wesley.

Campbell, J. (1968). *The hero with a thousand faces.* (2nd ed.) Princeton: Princeton University Press.

Campbell, J. (1972). *Myths to live by.* New York: Viking.

Campbell, J., Moyers, B., & Flowers, B. S. (1988). *The power of myth.* New York: Doubleday.

Feinstein, D. (1979). Personal mythology as a paradigm for holistic public psychology. *American Journal of Orthopsychiatry, 49,* 198–217.

Feinstein, D., & Krippner, S. (1988). *Personal mythology: The psychology of your evolving self: Using ritual, dreams and imagination to discover your inner story.* Los Angeles: Tarcher.

Frankl, V. (1956). *Man's search for meaning.* Boston: Beacon Press.

Jung, C. G. (1964). *Man and his symbols.* Garden City, NY: Doubleday.

Lifton, R. J. (1973). *Home from the war: Vietnam veterans: Neither victims or executioners.* New York: Simon & Schuster.

May, R. (1991). *The cry for myth.* New York: Norton.

Metzner, R. (1986). *Opening to inner light: The transformation of human nature and consciousness.* Los Angeles: Tarcher.

Paulson, D. S. (1994). *Walking the point: Male initiation and the Vietnam experience.* Plantation, FL: Distinctive Publishing.

Whitmont, E. C. (1969). *The symbolic quest: Basic concepts of analytical psychology.* New York: G. P. Putnam's Sons.

Section III.

Narrative and Creative Arts in Therapy

CHAPTER THIRTEEN

Dream Drama:
Social Healing Through
Group Dreamsharing

Harold R. Ellis

Preface

Two mysteries have puzzled humans throughout history. One: *Which came first, the chicken or the egg?* Another: *What are dreams and dreaming?* If, as many suspect, the answer to the first may yield to the fantastic new advances of genetic research, that in turn may let us approach the presently inconceivable answer to the second. For the present, however, I'm sorry to say, we have to admit: Most dreams are crazy.

That is to say, dreams are unmistakably not quite normal, to put it mildly. By definition, you would be crazy to give up your familiar everyday life and live as you dream. We are not referring to waking fantasies; we're speaking of night-time "REM" dreams. Can it be that the suspicion of being thought cuckoo if we reveal our "crazy" dreams is why many of us don't like to admit, or remember, or think about, or certainly tell others our dreams? There is a hint of support of that possibility in the December 14th, 1999 statement of the U. S. Surgeon General, Dr. David Satcher (1999).

Yet, by forfeit of our dreams we throw away what for most of us might possibly be the most creative part of our lives. From observation of our own dreams and hearing those of others, we increasingly suspect that a great many breakthrough ideas, inventions and inspiration can be traced back to REM dreams. Obviously scientists can't prove this — yet. But it could make an interesting thesis.

We're fond of saying that dreams are all feelings, presented to us as metaphors. In working with dreams, we rely upon that precept. We look at every element in a dream, be it visual object, sound, tactile, kinesthesis, odor, person, animal, vague impression, movement, internal bodily feeling, atmospheric condition, weird mood, identifiable emotion, however you name it, as metaphors. The personal meaning of these metaphors for the dreamer are there, but difficult to recognize. Very young people, eagerly seeking meaning in their brand new world, and old people with their world of experience to draw from, are good at sensing the metaphors. In between, are introspective people, and those who are creative in any sense of the word. Especially those who keep dream diaries, review them, free associate to them, and discuss their dreams with others.

Yes, dreams are all feelings. And, we agree with Carl Jung, we are everything in our dreams. But astoundingly, within these dream stories, we can also find objective solutions to scientific puzzles, intricate mechanisms, elusive theories, ingenious music, art, business opportunities, and every kind of intuition. Some dreamers, at times, discover they have had precognitive experiences without any possibility of direct knowledge or communication. During our REM dream sleep, no less! While dead to the world! Maybe genetic research will soon explain this. Meanwhile, don't worry about it: Use it! Become learned of your dreams. As you record more, remember more, share more, understand more, you will become more at peace with your world — that is, with your mind. And with the people in your life.

For in sharing our dreams, it soon dawns on us that others and we, deep down, are very much alike. Your dream could very well have been my dream! No need to feel self-conscious, hidden, or constrained. Based on this we cannot help but develop tolerance, notice the qualities we had previously rejected, and then we may gradually feel more liking, and possibly even love.

Which brings us to a most distributing problem facing Americans today — a pervasive lingering alienation and intolerance among our people that has lately made frightening headlines. We've always known that for some people power corrupts morals, but we have the example of the Surgeon General of the United States, Dr. David Satcher, who reports that "Twenty-two percent of the population has a diagnosable mental disorder" (Satcher, 1999, p. A1). Not a week goes by but that the newspapers we read do not report one or more murders. Not just the same old story, not just by criminals, mobsters, or motivated by money, political or military intrigue, or alleged adult passions gone out of control. Now nice kids are murdering. More and more. Monkey sees, monkey does. Sort of competitive fun. That giggling child finds Daddy's gun and shoots up the works, just like on TV, like being a hero, like Big Daddy. And when brought down from the clouds, with little or no comprehension of the crime. Living a dream. Real crazy.

School? Oh, don't be a nerd. Sports? Build those pecs, slam hard, win against the other guys — or gals. Let's talk scores, heroes, TV games, computer games, website games, stock market games. Have you read those new, proliferating message boards on the internet? Try to find a sincere, meaningful, "heart to heart talk" as we say. Good luck. And the pity is, that in comparison, those children are the ones who could most easily be weaned from the incipient mental aberrations, at negligible cost according to Dr. Satcher's report.

People are frustrated, confused, angry. Who is to blame? That other person, right? They're different, not like us. Yes? No. You want to know something?

You couldn't tell apart their dreams from yours. Underneath, we're very much alike, emotionally, creatively, intelligently, physically. Where we differ is in the stuff that's been laid on us, our outsides. The prejudices and intolerances, about our looks, the way we talk, work, sing, eat, dance, relax, associate; where and how we live, follow a leader. Our choices, good or bad, of parents, of authorities, family, funds. All the surface stuff laid on us. How do we break out of the mold? How can we get to know each other if we're too afraid to meet, to talk from real feelings? It's really quite simple, needing no high-priced university-trained specialists to show the way to our self-help.

We just tell stories — our dreams. Telling each other our dreams remembered from sleep is humanity's most ancient, original way of overcoming that reticent barrier. Even the ancient ruler of his world Gilgamesh did it, perhaps 5,000 years ago, as described by the Assyrian King Assurbanipal (Ellis, 1986). Like fairy tales, our dreams are obviously unreal, not to be taken literally. We know we cannot judge each other by our dreams, because we realize that then we would be judging ourselves. If in our most secret, deep self, we are as alike as brothers and sisters, how can we fail to feel affinity, empathy, to develop cohesion? Therein lies the truest value of small group dreamsharing.

Membership in such a group should be free, open to anyone the group wants to include, although keeping in mind that the group needs consensus about the good will of any invitee. Dream Drama tolerates, in fact encourages, strong expression in enacting metaphors, because this often helps the dreamer to connect with the underlying, latent meaning. But it should not countenance abusiveness generated from latent ill-will or from projection of the actor's own problems. And remember that the group is a free voluntary association, free to leave one location and meet in another, notifying only people they want to keep in the group, and that these are mutual growth groups, for the facilitators equally with the members. In this short chapter I can simply say "try it, you'll like it." If you want to do it, you may quickly learn how to start one in your own home or a free facility, or perhaps locate an existing free dreamsharing group near where you live, through the Dream Switchboard of the Community Dreamsharing Network, or the other organizations named below.

A disclaimer: The Dream Drama I will describe pursues social and societal healing, not psychotherapy. Although not discussed here, there are other types and applications for the basic Dream Drama principles. It has been used in business environments to ameliorate stress among staff, elicit creative inventions, products and programs. History is replete with evidences of dreams used for art inspirations. And, under professional guidance, it provides an effective psycho-therapeutic method.

There are very experienced dreamsharing group facilitators and training consultants willing to demonstrate a dreamsharing method, such as the one explained below, or many variations of other humanistic dreamsharing approaches. I suggest your group try getting the benefit of several. The group should take some time to discuss and evaluate the effects of the procedures they try, while avoiding any individual's domination. New dreamsharing groups will find their own preferred style. I strongly urge that attendance be nominally free, and if funds are needed, to allow any member to contribute voluntarily, as the individual desires, without comment. This should be, at least, one activity that anyone can afford.

Some teaching facilitators or training consultants may ask a modest fee of the group, for one or more sessions. There are many who will contribute their services without charge, provided they know that other equally qualified consultants are likewise doing it. The Center for Dream Drama and the Community Dreamsharing Network will be more than happy to provide such references. Or ask for referrals from such organizations as the National and Regional Self-Help Clearinghouses or the International Association for the Study of Dreams.

Dreamsharing groups were probably active for many years and in many places, before the New York/Northern New Jersey Dreamsharing Community was formed to provide an effective organizing center and a newsletter. From that source the Dreamsharing Grassroots Network drew support and was initiated in uptown Manhattan in 1968, and then transitioned into the Community Dreamsharing Network located in Levittown, New York in the mid-1980s. The results of doctoral dissertation research prompted the transition into Dream Drama around 1985. Dream Drama is of the same genre as Psychodrama, which, however, rarely if ever works with dreams (Moreno, 1946, 1969; Moreno & Moreno, 1959) and has several additional roots such as the Stanislavski Method (Stanislavski, 1936, p. 48), group dynamics, movement therapy, and the precepts of Sigmund Freud's student Harry Stack Sullivan (1953). A more complete derivation with extensive references is available in my book *Dream Drama: Small Group Enactment of Dreams* (Ellis, 1990).

In Dream Drama, group members focus on enacting, rather than discussing, their narrated dreams. Every element of the dream is role-played. Every member takes a role as a dream figure or as part of the chorus. The group designates a director for each Dream Drama, deferring to the dreamer's preference.

The dreamer narrates the dream in all possible detail from memory and/or from notes while the group attends to how the words are expressed. Observing the dreamer's posture, movements, and facial expressions, members seek cues to underlying kinesthesias and other sensations the dreamer is re-experiencing or recalling from the dream — visual, acoustic, haptic, thermal, olfactory, gustatory, and so on. Then, by emphatically "living" the dream, each person in the group attempts to "own" it as if it were one's own dream.

Each dream enacted has dramatic elements representing focal concerns in the dreamer's life, even if not consciously present and accounted for in waking. These elements are amplified in several ways: by repetition; by synergistic group involvement; by the spontaneous "what ifs" that members probe by their actions;

and by the evocative use of sounds, rhythm, colors, props and physical stimulation.

Rationale

To the dreamer, the "unworked" dream is like an unopened letter. The information in the sealed envelope parallels the mystery behind the surface dream image. The narrating of a remembered dream, even one described as a nightmare, may seem to the dreamer a pale ghost of the experience itself. Simply to narrate a dream, or even to run through it with motions as if reading the lines of a play, will not accomplish enough. When creating Dream Drama, the task we set ourselves was to help retrieve for the dreamer the experience in its bodily and sensory dimensions, unblocking and uniting the semantic, episodic and presentational memories represented in the dream.

We are helped by at least two phenomena. One is the resistance-dissipating group dynamic, particularly Sullivan's "risky shift," in which one person's self-disclosure encourages others' while the second is the cathartic effect of the thaumaturge of drama, known to Plato, Aristotle, Goethe, Stanislavski, and Moreno, which strongly affects the participants and audiences.

This drama experienced every night in our dreams may transcend most emotional passions to which we are accustomed when awake. Its spell might stir an ecstatic fever that might approach an agony if fully aroused in waking life. But we want dreamers to reapproach this engrossing dream open to its message — the healing story it has for us. The ability to evoke it may be defined as our dramatic sense. We are born with the ability to remember our dreams, and although we may choose to disregard them, the ability remains and can be redeveloped.

The group is available to be used instrumentally, to open the dream by re-experiencing or amending it. By modeling each element represented in the dream, and answering requests for details and information, the dreamer often already begins to understand some of the dream's messages, and has the leeway to express these thoughts.

As actors we each bring our own unique intuitions, feelings, and understanding which can be of great value to the dreamer. Each actor's subtle projection on the portrayed dream element helps cut through the inscrutable facade of the image the dreamer has described without understanding.

It may seem a contradiction — to enact faithfully another person's product, yet in our own unique way. But performing artists do exactly that. It is only a matter of finesse, to insert our intuitive feeling, yet the dreamer is reassured that we are guided by his or her personal image. We do not explain in advance to the dreamer what we intend to do.

As is obvious from the above, the Dream Drama method is a royal road to dissipating resistance. Unlike psychoanalytic approaches, it does not deal with transferences. A psychology credential is not required. A consultant leaves the group after training it. A director is chosen by the dreamer and group, and changes with each dream. Of course, affections and attachments easily form, as in any warmly-supportive intimate group, but they are probably realistically based.

Working Assumptions

Dream Drama's special contribution to dreamsharing is based upon four assumptions:

(1) The dreamer's physically-expressive telling and symbolic enacting of the dream involves verbal, sensory, and bodily channels, thus encouraging, liberating, and rebalancing multiple forms of memory and associations: semantic, episodic, and presentational.

(2) The physical enactment actualizes the thoughts which are presented by the dream largely in visual metaphors; it creates a bridge of awareness between verbal and nonverbal areas of the brain, thus giving the dream "meaning." This may be an evolutionary function of the peculiarly *human* mode of dreaming: to unify the faculties of the mind and body.

(3) Dramatic interaction generates its own momentum; it is difficult to avoid, in mid-action, revealing feelings and thoughts entering awareness. A great deal of previously non-conscious mentation and personal information is revealed to both dreamer and group by the latter's close mirroring of the dreamer's facial expressions and bodily cues.

(4) By the dream externalizing proprioceptive awareness embedded in its imagery, the dreamer can more readily reflect on the proprioception from dissonant perspectives, external (objective) and internal (subjective). This opens up a dialectic which may then be resolved creatively by the dreamer and/or helpers.

After the drama, this information is validated by the dreamer via the "feelback" (discussed below); in most cases a satisfying resolution is attained.

Confidentiality
In so personal a process, members need a high degree of mutual trust and explicit confidentiality. Therefore Dream Drama is best added to the skills of a dreamsharing group after the members have come to trust and to know each other fairly intimately.

Previous experience

Prior exposure to dreamsharing is desirable. Nevertheless, permanent Dream Drama groups have formed after ten weeks of an experiential dream course, in which people with no dreamsharing background had enrolled.

Setting

A meeting place which inspires a dramatizing attitude is helpful. Ideally, if indoors, the space should be carpeted and free of excessive furnishings, with colored lighting of variable intensity. If outdoors, for example, a secluded lawn with a spectacular mountain view has been effective. Privacy is needed; a stage or an audience that is not encouraged to participate is contraindicated.

Effective props include pillows and cloths varied in size and color; a bongo or drum and a flute are useful. Cloths become "costumes." Raggedy Ann dolls are very useful. A small one can represent a baby; a large one can stand-in for a partner in an explicit sex dream. Groups quickly acquire a collection of improvised multiply-applicable props. Optimal seating is in a circle, on large multi-colored and patterned throw pillows which may readily be moved out of the way, stacked to represent a staircase, or a wall, laid end-to-end as in a bridge, a river or an aisle, and so on.

Method of work

Dream Drama has been taught to ongoing groups in their customary meeting places (usually members' homes), in five or ten three-hour sessions or several weekends by a consultant from The Center for Dream Drama. Membership should be free, as befits a social group. The goal of the training consultant is to teach the skills of directing Dream Drama, so that finally a paid consultant becomes unnecessary.

Meltdown

First, the group does a *mind-body preparation* of about twenty minutes, to enter a dream-receptive and physically-loose expressive state. For example:

(1) Pairs of two people stand face to face; while one slowly improvises movements, the other mirrors them; they take turns.

(2) Every person imagines a non-human organism, and all interact, simultaneously acting out their choice, making appropriate nonverbal sounds.

(3) Members form two facing lines. Each person in turn steps forward and nonverbally strongly expresses a feeling directed toward a person in the opposite line who does not react, accepting the expressor as the sole

owner of the feeling, and remaining aware that this is only a risk-taking training exercise.

Unfinished business

After the meltdown, members sit in a circle, and residual feelings that any member has, perhaps left over from the previous session, are expressed.

Members' dreamsharing pitch-in

The director (or the consultant) first narrates a dream from memory (not notes), with expressive motion. He or she models the desired attention to details of dream kinesis (visually "observed" movements of dream elements) and kines-thesias (the dreamer's bodily feelings and sensory perceptions) while speaking in the first person, present tense. The group listens without comment. Then, in similar style, everyone in random order "pays dues" by narrating part or all of a dream. If a recent dream is not remembered, the group urges that an older dream may be used, or repeated, or a vague feeling upon awakening may be described and symbolized. Notes may be taken by group members.

Selecting the dream

The group plans session time to work on two or more dreams, and by consensus determines which dream to work on first. Selection criteria include: (1) the dreamer's eagerness to work on the dream; (2) the recency of the dream's occurrence; and (3) special qualities (such as a "dramatic" dream; or a short, "easy" dream). An experienced group requires from only a few minutes to seventy-five minutes or more to work with a dream.

Pre-work title and context

The selected dreamer announces a title for the dream without suggestions from the group, and slowly, expressively, retells the dream in detail. Before or after the telling, he or she gives the waking context, and then is gently invited to reveal feelings, associations and "meanings" of which she or he already is aware.

Clarification

Actors owe it to the dreamer, as to any playwright, to enact the dreamscript's *given circumstances*. To do so, they must clearly understand their roles. The dreamer explains and *models*. Group members now ask "factual" questions of the dreamer, to help them *get into* the dream. For example, "Is that dream character John a person you know?" "Does that room exist?" "What color is the car?" "What do you see in the background?" "Do you think something may be missing?" "How do you feel when you awaken?"

The listeners try to put themselves into the dream: "What part of me resonates to that image? What role would I like to play in this drama?" If an actor evidences too much trouble "getting it," the director replaces him or her, if possible *before* the scene begins or for a subsequent run-through. Changing actors in the midst of a scene may be disruptive.

Speculations remain unvoiced

Everyone's normal waking thoughts are heavily populated with personal metaphors. One person's beautiful scenery may be another person's frightening wilderness. Consequently, people could readily project purely personal meanings on to others' "typical" dream symbols. As previously stated, *subtly coloring our acted images is good,* but we ask that these not be voiced, because such direct and extraneous associations may divert the dreamer's attention from some deeper metaphorical message which could occur only to the dreamer.

Nevertheless, privately-held speculations may properly influence the actors' *nonverbal* role-playing, which, more than obtrusive leading questions or authoritative statements, may stimulate recall of dreamed thoughts, actions, and feelings.

Casting

Every group member undertakes one of the following roles.

Director

This person suggests who will play which role (except that of dreamer), but the dreamer has the final power of choice. The dreamer's feelings about suitability for a role are significant, may reveal a non-obvious dream message, and is to be respected.

The director monitors the acting, watching for ignored sequences or details, too-far-fetched portrayals or amendments (discussed below). If necessary the director reminds the group of details of the dream narration, from memory or notes. During enactment the dreamer may not be director.

Dreamer

The dreamer chooses between two role options which may alternate during dreamwork: (1) If he or she had experienced actively participating within a dream scene, to play that role (the subjective position); and (2) If she or he felt like an observer in a dream scene, to appoint someone to *stand in* the role of the dreamer, then stand aside to watch (the objective position). Ideally, the dreamer oscillates between positions. A useful approach is for the dreamer to show the stand-in how to act the part, then, after the scene is acted, to correct or refine the latter's portrayal.

The dreamer indicates spatial arrangement, colors, intensity of lighting, and requests props. The dreamer may halt the action at any time with or without explanation, or may interrupt the process to declare an association which may have suddenly come to mind.

Actors and Animate Characters

Prop-box clothing, large drapes, and sometimes suitable masks or makeup, are used by actors in dressing to represent human dream characters as accurately as possible. This helps them feel their roles. Babies are often represented by Raggedy Ann dolls. Animate non-human characters have the same standing as human ones, as all represent aspects of the dreamer.

Inanimate Elements

Inanimate objects, and even concepts such as atmospheric conditions, spiritual entities, and missing features are concretized and enacted. Actors have the especially difficult task of turning an "indifferent" dream stimulus into the salient memory-laden symbol that it may well be, and must be alert to noting and evaluating significant resistance from the dreamer.

With inanimate elements, movement, light and shade, color, sound, texture, weight and outstanding objects (for example, high tension electrical lines), unusual positions or changes in velocity or direction, are key contents. In accepting and preparing to undertake the role, the actor might ask the dreamer for a feeling associated with the inanimate element.

An actor may sense that the "character" of the inanimate dream element should be further developed, and may tentatively do so, carefully observing the dreamer's reaction to guide possible further development. Enactors of inanimate objects never improvise language, which would be too raw a projection, but may make sounds, especially in concert with movements, and may use props. The director pays careful attention, ready to signal moderation when necessary.

Chorus

Those not "in the scene" stand well out on the periphery as a chorus, but remain vigilant observers, especially of the dreamer's bodily expressions. Like players in an orchestra, the chorus is guided nonverbally by the director.

With experience, the chorus learns to provide synergistic *background support* for actors' portrayals, without competing or attempting to alter them. They never "double" in the Psychodrama sense, by substituting for the dreamer. Members of the chorus may use the drum or a musical instrument as background effects to inject mystery, excitement, inevitability, or other feelings.

The Actions

Life Context action

After the original telling of the dream, the dreamer again narrates the dream slowly, pausing while the actors do *faithful* portrayals in a slow run-through.

They empathically experience the dream, sensing the dreamer's expressed emotions, and transforming themselves into the images. Everyone is getting in touch with his or her own feelings and forming *private* hypotheses of meanings.

The physical realization inevitably prompts questions the simple verbal rendition did not engender. The dreamer answers verbally, deriving more awareness of feelings from this "show and tell" rehearsal. For example, a male dreamer described a "nightmare":

> I am with my brother on top of a mountain, too high even to attempt to help my father who is floundering in the river far below. I am agonized because he is a non-swimmer. I yell to him, but he doesn't hear me, because the wind is blowing in my face. Then to my relief he stands up in the water; it's only waist deep. He has caught a big fish with his hands.

Roles of father, brother, fish, and director are assigned. The chorus fans up a wind. Father kneels down, partly covered by a large aquamarine cloth for the river. The dreamer balances atop a high pile of large pillows. As we go slowly through the action, more clarification is wanted.

Choruser: Where's the big wind coming from?

Dreamer: It's high up. My head's in the clouds.

Fish: How shall I behave? How do I feel?

Dreamer: Like a fish out of water.

Father: What am I like?

Dreamer: He's in business; works too hard. My brother and I want him to retire.

Father: Do I really not hear you?

Dreamer: Maybe he's ignoring me.

At the end of the run-through the director requested an impromptu feelback. The dreamer spoke first:

> I begin to know what this is all about. My brother and I have been pressuring dad into retiring. Maybe we were thinking of our own feelings more than his. He'd be like a fish out of water. I'll phone my brother.

Often, as in the above instance, the insight gained from the life context action suffices for the dreamer. Further enactment of such an "easy" dream would have been superfluous.

In many cases it is appropriate to postpone further feelback and to continue to the *amendment action*. Once everyone has a fair idea of his or her role, the dream may be re-enacted *unfaithfully*. The director announces that the group will *play* with the dream, and reminds the group to be careful not to arouse resistance by getting too far out of the dream script.

Intuition and spontaneity take over. We do what the dream asks of us, at least symbolically, not only enacting dream scenes that would be bizarre in waking life, but *amplifying* them. In effect we *nonverbally challenge* the dreamer to break out of his or her usual social lock, extend his or her horizon, and "achieve the impossible dream." Here is where Stanislavski's famous "what if" is used.

Guided by an acquired intuitive understanding of dream language and of the dreamer's life context gained through prior dreamsharing, the enactors subtly and nonverbally amend the image portrayals in order that the dreamer consider unacknowledged aspects of the feelings and thoughts represented in the remembered dream. The following example may best clarify the approach.

In a dreamsharing group formed expressly for introducing Dream Drama, most participants were experienced dreamsharers. Several shared the same career field, three of whom knew each other in that field, namely Hedda, Dina, and Beth. At a recent camp reunion Beth, now in her thirties, had seen her girlhood best friend, Emily, who remains aloof and distant. Her attitude reactivated Beth's still strong but frustrated youthful wish to remain close friends as adults. Her dream was of Emily (condensed version):

> First I am at a tennis match, sitting in left field. Then I am in a rug store, where I see Emily looking for small items. I go over and do it too, but we don't communicate. I'm with a group of people; I think they were past friends from college days. Only one of them, Jennie, at whose house I left my jacket, is a current friend. We are shopping for a large rug.
>
> None of the rugs I see and touch has exactly the right color and texture combination. One is strange, and I rather like it, but I feel leery. We're told if we pick one as a group, we will have to pay more. I wonder, who will keep it after we split up? Then they all disappear, including Jennie. I hear music: "Sooner or Later We All Sleep Alone."

Roles

Emily and a store saleswoman enacted by dreamgroup members; members of the past-friends group within the dream, who at times drape themselves to become rugs; Beth plays herself.

Life Context Action

As we enact the dream, it becomes clear to Beth that the rugs represent men she knows, none of whom quite please her. Apparently "everybody is out of step but Beth." She's determined to march to her own beat, but we experience no movement. Hedda, who knows Beth and is an experienced verbally-oriented dreamworker, becomes impatient and attempts to lead Beth into associating to specific dream images. She desists when Beth expresses resentment.

Dina, likewise experienced, suggests we try an *amendment*; Beth agrees to take the objective position. Dina role-plays Emily; at times Beth and Dina exchange roles. Dina begins with "Emily looking for small items," but going beyond the dream narrative physically and verbally, Dina expresses friendship, warmth, and the desire to recover their old relationship. Beth "throws the book" at Dina, but the latter persists. Beth cannot completely stifle her tears. During the *Feelback* (explained below) she says she'll consider contacting Emily.

In a telephone follow-up interview a year later, Beth says that in role-playing with Dina the feelings represented by Emily was "a big moment." Giving her the chance to work through her feelings by taking emotional risks through role-playing enabled Beth to recognize an underlying issue; Emily herself is no longer important. She has transformed the vague "rug store" group into a reality group of new good friends. She feels secure with them, and in better control of her own life. The Dream Drama process also helped her to gain the courage to get to know the man who was represented by the strange rug.

Beth evaluates the Dream Drama process as having been therapeutic. She was very influenced by the dream-group dynamics, encouraging her to go beyond her comfort level to reach new learning. She is about to embark on the next voyage in her academic career.

The actors' *presence* and imaginative, uninhibited style of acting is crucial. In the amendment we cast off customary reserve by caricaturing the images, and dwell on scenes that have dramatic value. But we do not permit abrasive overly-discrepant intimations. Because the animate dream characters may be persons important in the dreamer's waking life, an actor's voice (unlike a physical portrayal) might cause undesirably strong reactions in the dreamer.

The *nonverbal* mode is less obtrusive than the verbal, and interventions will generally go unnoticed or be forgotten by the dreamer when they fail to elicit a responsive association. This permits each actor to try various approaches, casting his or her nonverbal "lines" with varying baits, until the fish bites.

Nevertheless, an experienced enactor of animate dream characters is allowed some minimal liberty to give words to the character's feelings, but only when quite sure of what those are, especially from words that were literally part of the dream report, or from the dreamer's explanation, or by obvious implication. Most often this is done by innuendo, the *way* something is said, rather than *what* is said, and always cautiously. The method requires awareness and sensitivity, not a deliberate display of emotion for effect.

Director

The director may enliven the entire process. This does not mean having the enactment move quickly; on the contrary, the director often slows down the group. Enlivening may involve having the cast and/or chorus use dance or movement to reinforce a dream image; or bringing out appropriate masks for some actors; or drumming to accent the rhythm, pace or potential importance of a dream image. There have been times when we even uncorked a bottle of champagne to accent a dream motif. All of this develops the dramatic sense and skills of the participants.

Some dreamers respond fully and openly, while others, including supporting actors, hold back. If the Dream Drama seems to be getting nowhere (generally due to the dreamer's resistance) the director calls a *freeze* and asks for group consensus about continuing. The dreamer is always free to interrupt.

The Feelback

The whole group now sits in a circle, and the dreamer is encouraged to report his or her present feelings. Although not discouraged from giving contextual information, no attempt to persuade or badger the dreamer to reveal personal matters or "meaning" is tolerated by the director.

Then the actors try to state, simply and briefly, at least one *feeling* (not interpretation) they experienced in playing their roles. Next, chorus members do the same. The group may initiate a second feelback go-around, at this time feeding back to the dreamer any unintentional nonverbal communication they observed.

If the dreamer has been through an intense experience in the Dream Drama, it is reassuring to him or her for members to talk about their own real life experiences of similar situations or feelings. The feelback process in Dream Drama does not envision *anyone*, other than the dreamer, giving a definitive analysis or summary of the dream's meaning. However, the dreamer is encouraged to re-title the dream. No one other than the dreamer may suggest a title. The new title often contrasts notably with the original title, summing up succinctly and often very memorably what the dreamer has learned from sharing the dream with the group.

Although the feelback is generally a good ending, the dreamer may feel too moved to listen. He or she may want some private time. If so, the feelback will be offered at the start of the next session, but only in the dreamer's presence.

Structural Safeguards

Because the amendment has therapeutic implications, it is mandatory that the Dream Drama consultant teach the group to have the dreamer in control of the process at all times. By the time all members have experienced being the dreamer and the director they will be attuned to preventing the extremely rare case of attempted bullying by an inexperienced visitor.

Outcomes

We have differing needs at different times in our lives. As important and entertaining Dream Drama may be for us at one time, we may feel the urge to apply our new-found strength and understanding beyond the group's province. At the Network, we have found it deeply satisfying to receive feedback from our former fellow group members, letting us know how much the Dream Drama experience has meant for them. Let the Network hear from you. And won't you join the dance?

References

Ellis, H. R. (1986). *Dreamsharing from 5000 B. F. (Before Freud).* Unpublished paper.

Ellis, H. (1990). *Dream drama: Small group enactment of dreams.* Ann Arbor, MI: University Microfilms International.

Moreno, J. L. (1946). *Psychodrama.* Beacon, NY: Beacon House.

Moreno, J. L., & Moreno, Z. T. (1959). *Psychodrama, Volume II: Foundations of psychotherapy.* Beacon, NY: Beacon House.

Moreno, J. L. (1969). *Psychodrama, Volume III: Action therapy and principles of practice.* Beacon, NY: Beacon House.

Satcher, D. (1999). [Statement.] *New York Times,* December 13th, A1, A30.

Stanislavski, C. (1936). *An actor prepares* (E. R. Hapgood, Transl.). New York: Theatre Arts Books.

Sullivan, H. S. (1953). *The interpersonal theory of psychiatry* (H. S. Perry & M. L. Gawal, Eds.). New York: Norton.

CHAPTER FOURTEEN

The Fundamental Things Apply: Parallels Between the Structures of Drama and Psychotherapy

Frederick J. Heide

You must remember this
A kiss is just a kiss
A sigh is just a sigh
The fundamental things apply
As time goes by.

Herman Hupfield (1931)
As Time Goes By

There is an old theater story about the time that Molière's company was preparing to stage a new play by Corneille. One of the actors could not fathom the meaning of a particular section, and when Molière said that he didn't know what the lines meant, the actor went to the great Corneille himself. The playwright read the lines several times and then admitted that even he no longer knew what they were supposed to mean. "What am I to do?" asked the actor. "Nothing," replied Corneille. "Just say the lines as written. There will be some in the audience who won't understand them yet will deeply admire them."

This joking anecdote actually makes a small but important point about the nature of theater, that is, that the essential element of a play is not the words per se, no matter how beautiful, but rather the way in which they contribute to the development of the action. If we were to translate the point into the world of psychotherapeutic constructs, it would probably be something like, "It matters not how eloquent the interpretation, but rather whether the client gets its meaning." It thus serves as one very small illustration of the more general point to be made in this chapter: that psychotherapy, theatrical plays and films share structural similarities, the understanding of which can elucidate principles that unite diverse forms of psychotherapy. It will be my thesis that psychotherapy succeeds to the extent that it effectively embraces these dramatic principles.

This chapter will argue that psychotherapy is inherently dramatic, that is, that it follows rules that have informed the writing of plays and films since the time of the Greeks. Several of these rules are not unique to drama (see Bruner, 1990; Burke, 1945; Schechner, 1990; Turner, 1990), and may show up in such diverse human activities as tribal rites of passage, Caribbean carnivals, Icelandic sagas, and Mexican insurrections (Geertz, 1980). However, drama does seem to be a particularly fruitful arena for examining them (MacCormack, 1997), for no other reason than its familiarity and accessibility.

The theatrical or drama metaphor has a distinguished history in our field. From Greek theater Freud borrowed the concept of catharsis and the characters of Oedipus, Electra and Psyche. Perls, Kelly, Moreno and Wolpe made heavy use of dramatic enactment in their therapeutic methods. Concepts such as "acting out," "role-playing" and "behavior rehearsal" all have been prominent in the thinking of clinicians. The present chapter does not provide an in-depth review of the application of the theatrical metaphor to therapy. (For an excellent summary, see MacCormack, 1997). Rather, it will explore a handful of structural similarities between the worlds of psychotherapy and drama.

The American film classic, *Casablanca*, will serve to illustrate the similarities between drama and psychotherapy. The choice is fairly arbitrary, and based primarily on my own long-standing fascination with the film. Although the screenplay to *Casablanca* is generally considered one of the finest ever written (and won an Academy Award in 1942), the same principles it exemplifies occur in virtually every play or film ever created, whether it is *King Lear* or *King Kong*, *A Midsummer Night's Dream* or *Nightmare on Elm Street*. Certain modern dramatic works deliberately violate several of these principles (such as the theatrical pieces of Ionesco or the performance artists), but such works are arguably not plays in the classical sense. Thus, this chapter will confine itself to classical theatrical/film forms (sometimes referred to as narrative forms because of their storytelling focus) in its search for parallels to therapy process. Incidentally, it should be noted that there are some compositional differences between plays and films such as their relative reliance on the spoken word versus action to advance the story. However, these differences are not relevant to the particular themes being discussed here, and for our purposes the two arenas can be considered interchangeable.

For those unfamiliar with it, *Casablanca* is set in the Moroccan city of its title during 1941. The protagonist, Rick (played by Humphrey Bogart), owns the most popular saloon in town. Rick is a cynic; we gradually discover that his hard exterior is the result of a major disappointment in love. While living in Paris, he had been passionately involved with a mysterious woman named Ilsa (played by Ingrid Bergman) with whom he was supposed to leave immediately before the German army arrived. However, Ilsa never came to the railroad station to meet him, and in the years since he has become demoralized and bitter. This brief synopsis of exposition will hopefully make clearer the meaning of incidents recounted later, as we show how *Casablanca* embodies long-standing principles of play construction.

Artistic Metaphors for Psychotherapy

By emphasizing the dramatic aspects of psychotherapy, this chapter joins a growing body of work employing the arts as a lens through which to examine the therapeutic enterprise. Much early thinking about therapy utilized metaphors from the sciences, such as the mechanistic and physiologically-based metaphors of psychoanalysis and behavior therapy (Sarbin, 1990) or the cybernetic metaphors of family theorists (see, for example, Keeney, 1983). The Newtonian atomistic metaphor has been postulated (Capra, 1982) to have influenced therapists to think of separable internal entities (e.g., ego, maladaptive thoughts) interacting by means of psychic forces (libido, conditioning, etc.) in spatial relationships ("deep" unconscious processes, "underlying" assumptions). Medical science and practice have provided many of "clinical" psychology's most enduring metaphors, including those of "psychopathology," "diagnosis," and "symptomatology" (Szasz, 1974). Several of the cognitive therapies invoke the metaphor of science itself as the vehicle for cure (Neimeyer & Mahoney, 1995).

An alternative approach, whose origins can be traced at least as far back as the early work of Otto Rank (Lieberman, 1985), has conceptualized therapy as an art form not readily reducible to the objective methods of natural science (Bugental, 1987; Frank, 1987; Robbins, 1998; Zukowski, 1995). This school of thought has pointed to the many parallels between the task of the therapist and the work of the artist, including shared interests in putting ideas into fresh relationships, intensifying experience, dealing with situations in their individuality, connecting conscious and unconscious orders of experience, and creating worlds where new ways of being can be born (Heide, Rosenbaum, Horowitz, & May, 1989; MacCormack, 1997; McNiff, 1987).

The application of artistic metaphors to psychotherapy appears to have accelerated recently with the rise of postmodern and constructivist perspectives in psychology (Hoyt, 1996; Neimeyer & Mahoney, 1995). The erosion of faith in an objectively knowable universe and increasing acknowledgment of the socially-constituted nature of knowledge have led a number of scholars to entertain analogies for therapy drawn from the humanities and interpretive traditions. The arts have seemed particularly relevant to a realm like therapy that traffics not in absolute truths but in "explanatory fictions" (Efran, Lukens, & Lukens, 1990). Among the art forms which have been mined recently as metaphors for psychotherapy are novel writing and storytelling (Howard, 1991; Polster, 1987; White & Epston, 1990), dance (Gergen, 1988), music (Rosenbaum, 1990), and theater (Keeney & Ray, 1996; MacCormack, 1997; Weiner, 1997).

Which metaphors will ultimately prove most useful to understanding psychotherapy is not yet obvious. What *is* obvious is that our choice of metaphors will profoundly affect psychotherapy's conduct and development. Recent scholarship reveals that the metaphor lies at the heart of human cognition, guiding our thought and action (Lakoff & Johnson, 1980). Rather than merely describing scientific theory and practice, metaphor has been shown to help constitute it (Leary, 1990). Indeed, Thomas Kuhn (1987) has argued that the most consequential characteristic of scientific revolutions is a central change of metaphor. With this in mind, there may be considerable value in entertaining fresh psychotherapeutic metaphors that can liberate us from traditional explanatory frameworks.

Before proceeding to identify principles of drama and how they relate to psychotherapy, a major problem needs to be touched upon, namely the lack of agreement on terms, rules, or defining characteristics in either the realms of psychotherapy or drama. Those interested in psychotherapy integration who have been despairing that the field has been unable to develop a common language in the last decade or two may be relieved to discover that playwrights have yet to arrive at such a language in twenty-five centuries. Such basic terms as "crisis," "climax," "proposition," "exposition," and even "tragedy" have been subject to multiple, frequently contradictory, definitions.

Disagreement extends beyond the definitional arena into more fundamental questions such as whether underlying principles which might guide play construction can even be identified. The field appears to encompass a spectrum of opinion on the subject roughly equivalent to the differences in the psychotherapeutic world between the behaviorists and humanists, that is, between those who seek to identify universal laws of skilled conduct versus those who believe that the nature of the topic defies (or even rightfully abhors) lawful analysis. The afore-mentioned French playwright Corneille reduced these contradictory positions to one postulate when he declared that "it is certain that there are laws of the drama, since it is an art, but it is not certain what these laws are" (cited in MacGowan, 1951, p. 24). In *How to Write a Play*, Robert Finch (1948) inverted this sentiment by arguing that "the mastery of drama is further complicated by the fact that, being an art, it simply is not governed by a set of laws." Maxwell Anderson, a leading American playwright of the 1930s, whose wonderful historic plays (*Elizabeth the Queen, Valley Forge, Anne of a Thousand Days*) unfortunately are rarely revived, weighed in on the "humanistic" end of the spectrum when he suggested that "so far as I could make out, every new play was a new problem, and the old rules were inapplicable" (Cited in MacGowan, 1951, p. 35). This skepticism about the value of rules has hardly prevented their widespread multiplication; the literature on playwrighting in the twentieth century is replete with dozens of volumes detailing the author's idiosyncratic opinions on this age-old question. For the purposes of the present chapter, we will suspend judgment on whether ironclad rules of play construction can or should be found, and embrace the commonsensical stance of William Archer (1912), a highly respected theoretician of play structure, whose observation on this subject might apply equally to training in the skills of psychotherapy:

> There are no rules for writing a play. It is easy, indeed, to lay down negative recommendations — to instruct the beginner how *not* to do it. But most of these "don'ts" are rather obvious, and those which are not obvious are questionable. ... As no two people probably ever did, or ever will, pursue the same routine in playmaking, it is manifestly impossible to lay down any general rules on the subject. There are one or two considerations, however, which may not be wholly superfluous to suggest to beginners. (pp. 3, 35)

Here, then, are five general "considerations" that seem to structurally unite psychotherapy and play/film structure.

Conflict and Problem

The first striking parallel between the structure of the play and of psychotherapy is that both are commonly agreed to aim at the resolution of a conflict or problem. On the simplest level, this is what brings an audience to the theater in the first place (or client to the clinic), what motivates an audience to return to their seats after intermission (or a client to continue to pay sometimes exorbitant bills), and what keeps the attention and investment of an audience late into the night until the final curtain (or of a client until the final session): both want a resolution of some conflictual or problematic situation. In the anthropological literature (Turner, 1990), this situation has sometimes been called the "breach" and "crisis" stages of a process; in the narrative tradition it has been termed simply "trouble" (Burke, 1945; Polster, 1987).

Virtually all writers on playwrighting agree that the suspense generated by the unresolved conflict/problem is the key to a successful play (See, for example, Archer, 1912; Freitag, 1894; Gallaway, 1950; Howard & Mabley, 1993; Seger, 1987). "A play lives by suspense," observed MacGowan (1951, p. 36). "We come to the theater to worry. Whether we see a tragedy, a serious drama, or a comedy, we enjoy it fully only if we are made to worry about the outcome of individual scenes and of the play as a whole." A good playwright deliberately generates suspense by keeping that outcome in question as long as possible, knowing full well that as soon as resolution is achieved, the play will be over (or so the audience hopes!). Thus the play is energized by the tension created through a suspension of resolution. As Archer (1912) pointed out, "to engender, maintain, suspend, heighten, and resolve a state of tension, that is the main object of the dramatist's craft" (p. 125).

Although there is general agreement that this tension is needed, significant disagreement exists over whether a conflict between opposing forces is necessary to generate it, or whether some other means of maintaining tension is possible. This debate can be seen as parallel to the one in the psychotherapy literature on the same topic, that is, whether therapy should focus on the understanding and working through of internal conflicts (as psychodynamic theorists would insist) or whether therapy simply aims to help clients resolve problems, complications, or crises in living (as argued by the cognitive-behaviorists and systems theorists). The majority position in the playwrighting literature has been to emphasize conflict, ever since this view was first articulated by the French theorist Ferdinand Brunetiere in the late nineteenth century:

> The theater in general is nothing but the place for the development of the human will, attacking the obstacles opposed to it by destiny, fortune, or circumstances. ... Drama is a representation of the will of man in conflict with the mysterious powers or natural forces that belittle us; it is one of us thrown living upon the stage, there to struggle against fatality, against social law, against one of his fellow mortals, against himself if need be. (In Archer, 1912, p. 19)

Many writers have endorsed this view of conflict as the essence of drama (among them, Freitag, 1894; Griffiths, 1982; Lawson, 1936) and some have detailed particular categories of conflict which occur with frequency in many plays and films. For example, Hollywood script consultant Linda Seger (1987) has identified five common types of conflicts in movie scripts: inner conflicts (such as Dustin Hoffman's character displaying his insecurities about his physical appearance as a woman in the film *Tootsie*), relational conflicts (such as the battle between Rose and Allnut about torpedoing the German ship in the *African Queen* or between Buzz Lightyear and Woody in *Toy Story*), societal conflict (such as the lovers defying social convention in *Shakespeare in Love* or *Titanic*, or Luke Skywalker and Princess Leia against the evil Galactic Empire in *Star Wars*), situational conflict (for example, people versus natural disaster or accident in such movies as *Apollo 13* or *Armageddon*), and even cosmic conflict (for example, Salieri declaring war on God for favoring the brilliant Mozart in *Amadeus*). Seger, like many others, argues that the best films have one main conflict at their core (which in the world of brief dynamic therapy might be referred to as the *focal conflict*), but that many smaller conflicts will occur in individual scenes to add extra "punch" to the scene (which may form a parallel to the focal issues dealt with in the course of one therapy session).

Although the view that conflict defines drama is probably endorsed by the majority of playwrights and screenwriters, a number of other theorists have questioned this stance. Perhaps the first person to forcefully challenge this model was William Archer (1912), who argued that although it is "the plain truth that conflict seems to be one of the most dramatic elements in life," it is nevertheless "clearly an error to make conflict indispensable to drama" (p. 31). In support of his position he cited several prominent plays that appear to lack any overall conflict, such as *Oedipus Rex* (whose title character "does not struggle at all ... [but] simply writhes under one revelation after another of bygone error and unwritten crime"), and Othello (in which, Archer argued, "There is no struggle, no conflict, between him and Iago. It is Iago alone who exerts any will; neither Othello nor Desdemona makes the smallest fight"). Like Archer, Kenneth MacGowan (1951) observed that many well-constructed plays seem to work admirably without an overall pattern of conflict, as evidenced by such modern classics as *Ah Wilderness!* and *Our Town*. Such plays may embody conflict within individual scenes, but an underlying conflict appears to be absent.

Those who argue against conflict as necessary to play structure nevertheless insist that something is required to maintain suspense and to carry the action of the play forward. What this "something" is varies between authors; for Archer it is the crisis (about which more will be said later in this chapter), for MacGowan (1951, p. 31) it is the complication ("a fact or a character, already planted in the play, which is brought forward to spur the plot into mounting suspense"). Both authors would propose that a play can work without an overarching conflict as long as it maintains suspense in discrete scenes, an idea that seems highly analogous to the view of behaviorist or strategic therapists that therapy may consist of separable problems that are treatable without attention to any unifying dynamic. A similar note is struck by the Pulitzer-winning playwright David Mamet (author of *Glengarry Glen Ross* and *Speed-the-Plow* as well as such films as *The Untouchables* and *The Verdict*) who has defined a play as "a quest for a solution" (Mamet, 1986, p. 8).[1]

Joseph Niggli (1967, p. 39) has viewed a play as "one giant crisis," which he in turn defines as "a choice between two possible solutions." This adds an existential tone to the understanding of what drives a play forward: a conflict from another perspective can be considered a choice posed to the protagonist about how to act (such as the classic example of Hamlet choosing, not only between being and nonbeing, but also between violent action and paralyzed inactivity).[2]

---

1. Mamet has made an intriguing analogy between plays and dreams, suggesting that plays seek to solve problems in the nation's consciousness much as dreams seek to resolve problems for individuals.

2. This idea of the play as "quest for solution" also bears remarkable similarity to the concept of therapy being developed by the solution-focused movement (e.g., DeJong & Berg, 1998), wherein therapists may de-emphasize problem or conflict in favor of an imagined "miracle" where the problem has vanished.

Although there is disagreement as to the source of the suspense that energizes a good play, there would likely be general assent that all plays worthy of the name succeed at posing some problem or question to which the audience fervently desires an answer. This question may or may not be based on a conflict, but must at least be engaging and clear. All plays which hold to a classical form appear to embody such questions. Will Hamlet kill the king? Will Macbeth manage to hang onto power? This is as true in comedy as in tragedy. Will the twins be reunited in *Twelfth Night?* Will the lovers get together in *There's Something About Mary?* This approach appears to encompass problematic cases for the conflict model such as *Oedipus* and *Othello*, because both plays generate audience interest in the question of the fate of their respective protagonists.

More recent variants on classical form also appear to retain our interest by posing such questions (for example, will Emily manage to find joy or understanding by returning to the land of the living in *Our Town?*). We can disagree over whether there is a conflict posed in *Waiting for Godot*, but presumably would agree that the audience, like the protagonists, is engaged in the question of whether or not the mysterious Godot will ever make an appearance. Those dramatic forms that lack such a structure based on an unresolved question would probably not be considered "plays" in the traditional sense of the word. They may be entertaining revues, or performance art, or deconstructionist theater, but a play demands the suspense of an unresolved question, just as does good psychotherapy.

Our case example, the film *Casablanca*, clearly is built around at least two central questions: (1) How will Rick resolve his relationship with Ilsa?; and (2) Will Rick recover from what Jerome Frank (Frank & Frank, 1991) would term his "demoralization" and find purpose in his life again? As in many of the best films, these two questions have been interlocked by the screenwriters such that the resolution of the first will impact the resolution of the second, a feature which dramatists refer to as "unity of theme." This concept is at least as old as Aristotle and has held appeal for psychotherapists as well, especially those of the psychodynamic school.

The first question posed by *Casablanca* is presented initially in a scene in which Ilsa, seeking Rick in his Moroccan nightclub, comes across Rick's piano player Sam and persuades him to play *As Time Goes By*. Rick arrives, tells Sam angrily, "I thought I told you never to play that," sees Ilsa, and halts, paralyzed. Although this initial on-screen meeting is interrupted immediately by the arrival of chief of Police Renault and Ilsa's heroic husband Victor Lazlo, the audience has already seen enough to realize that Rick and Ilsa have some sort of fascinating history together and we as an audience begin to suspect that in it may be buried clues which will help account for Rick's cynicism. Understanding and working through this relationship will become a central focus of the film; as such, it represents the dramatic equivalent of a focal conflict in psychotherapy.

Empathy

The second and third similarities between play structure and psychotherapy structure are closely related. The second similarity is that both plays and psychotherapy require *empathy* toward the protagonist; the third similarity is that both require a strongly *motivated* protagonist. As we will see in a moment, these overlap because empathy is created in plays largely by means of motivation; hence the strongly motivated protagonist typically becomes one with whom we empathize.

The idea that empathy is essential in good psychotherapy is so obvious that it is virtually a platitude. All forms of psychotherapy have embraced the utility of empathy; even those forms that downplayed the role of the therapeutic relationship early in their history (such as behavior therapy) have recently placed more emphasis on empathy's value (Safran & Segal, 1990).

Although empathy's role in therapy is presumably clear to all, its role in the world of the play is probably less obvious to those outside that world. Thus, it may not be apparent to the casual observer that one of the precepts of good playwrighting is to create a central character (or protagonist) who invokes an empathic response from the audience. As Seger (1987) puts it, the protagonist "is the person we are expected to follow, to root for, to empathize with, to care about" (p. 161). Many writers on playwrighting have underscored the necessity of a central character with whom the audience can empathize (see, for example, Freitag, 1894; Gallaway, 1950; Howard & Mabley, 1993), and many a critic has taken a play or film to task because there was no one on stage or screen to whom the audience could warm up.[3] Agnes Platt (1920) stated this principle boldly when she declared, "Let us have people about us whom we can like, people who inspire our sense of comfort and goodwill. It is just as unpleasant to meet tiresome people on stage as it is to meet them in real life" (pp. 48–49).

---

3. It is easy to find examples of movie critics disliking a film because they found a central character unappealing. For example, *San Francisco Chronicle* critic Mick La Salle (1995) blasted the film *Miami Rhapsody* for having a protagonist he found repellent: "Once you realize Gwynn (Sarah Jessica Parker) is a caustic, opportunistic cynic, much of the fun goes out of *Miami Rhapsody*. ... She is without taste, faith or unique aspiration. Why are we watching her?" (p. E1). Or consider his lacerating critique of Oliver Stone's *The Doors*: "If Jim Morrison really was the way he is portrayed in Oliver Stone's *The Doors*, it's hard to see how he rates a movie. What you get is the story of a slobbering drunk who wrote embarrassingly bad poetry, abused and disappointed everyone he knew, and dropped dead in a bathtub. ... It's hard to get worked up about someone who isn't really there, and if he doesn't care enough to stay awake for his life, why should we?" (La Salle, 1991, p. E1)

To the uninitiated, it might seem that the means by which an audience is made to empathize with a character is good acting on the part of the performer, and this certainly can be useful. For example, an actor of the stature of Anthony Hopkins can imbue an evil antagonist like Hannibal Lecter or an ambiguous protagonist like Richard Nixon with such complexity that members of the audience may root for him against their better judgment. However, the main means by which empathy is invoked in most plays is not personal, but structural: The playwright writes the part of the character in such a way that he or she is innately attractive (Gallaway, 1950). This is done in a variety of ways, but two methods that have particular relevance to psychotherapy are: (1) behavioral: the protagonist is shown engaging in laudatory activity; and (2) motivational: the protagonist is given an attractive objective.

The behavioral establishment of empathy is a particularly useful method in a world like playwrighting where action is so central. Ever since Aristotle, plays have been thought to convey meaning primarily through action, and even the word "drama" is Greek for "a thing done." Thus, much of what a playwright seeks to portray about a character is apt to be revealed behaviorally, and characters whom the playwright wishes us to see in a positive light need to be shown behaving in ways that we are apt to find admirable. One frequent method used by playwrights to accomplish this goal is to use "plants" to establish a character's place on the scale of likability early in the play. Marion Gallaway (1950), a noted teacher of playwrighting who counts Tennessee Williams among her more successful pupils, defined a plant as "a form of preparation designed to increase the credibility and the emotional effect of material that is to be used later" (pp. 258–259). Early in the play, a character will be established as a "good guy" or "bad guy" (or occasionally both) through the valence of the actions he performs; in other words, his goodness or badness will be "planted" for us.

In *Casablanca*, we are intended primarily to take a positive view toward Rick and empathize with him. Thus he is shown behaving in a number of admirable ways early on: we see him send a drunken woman home rather than allowing her to continue drinking; we see him refusing to allow a brash German banker into his casino, which establishes his antipathy to the Nazis; we see him give help to a young couple who need to win at his gambling table in order to buy a visa and escape to America. All of these actions win our empathy for him, and countermand the natural antipathy which would be generated by several other actions he engages in (for example, his insistence that "I stick my neck out for no one" as the police take Ugarte to his doom).

The operation of this behavioral principle of empathy is obvious in the psychotherapeutic arena: Most of us are more likely to empathize naturally with the victim of abuse rather than the abuser, for example. In those cases in which a person's behavior would instinctively invoke a rejecting attitude on our part, many psychotherapists have learned to employ the second principle of empathy used by playwrights, that is, ascribing to the protagonist some laudatory motivation. Gallaway (1950) has pointed out the utility of this method to playwrights, and the same point holds for psychotherapists:

> If the protagonist is to seem attractive, as he must if the audience is to care what happens to him, one simple means of making him so is to provide him with an attractive objective. ... Nothing will so easily give the protagonist the quality of attractiveness ... as an objective which the audience recognizes as praiseworthy and desirable. (pp. 81–82)

The great plays of the world are full of examples of this principle. Hamlet is given the laudatory motivation of trying to avenge his father's murder, Oedipus is motivated by the desire to rid Athens of the plague, Romeo and Juliet are driven by purest love, and so on.

In *Casablanca*, Rick is revealed to have at least two attractive goals: (1) He wants Ilsa, or love (which could probably be considered the world's oldest goal, or at least its second oldest, and probably the most frequent goal of comedic plays); and (2) He wants, or at least has wanted in the past, to defeat Fascism, as evidenced by his history of gunrunning in the Spanish Civil War. We begin to forgive him for his seemingly heartless, cold exterior and his apparent apathy in the face of the Nazis as we come to appreciate how these traits emerged as a defense following his loss of the beautiful Ilsa. If all we were shown of Rick was his defensive shell, we would probably find him repulsive. Instead, the screenwriters have carefully planted indications of his romantic and heroic motivations to win our approval, a process which culminates in the depiction of his extraordinarily self-denying behavior at the close of the film wherein he chooses the social good over personal need. By this time, our reaction to him has gone from ambivalent fascination to glowing admiration, all of which have been accomplished by writing his character such that his positive motivations are behaviorally expressed.

Of course, the ascription of motivation is somewhat clearer in the movies in which screenwriters can stack the deck in a two-hour presentation to get us to like or dislike a protagonist, than it is in the realm of psychotherapy in which the therapist's own theoretical framework plays a considerably larger role in the interpretation of ambiguous human behavior. Therapists hear a confusing variety of client statements and then have the daunting task of attempting to attribute underlying motivations to the client, often with few touchstones available to determine whether one interpretation is more accurate than another (Watzlawick, Weakland, & Fisch, 1974).[4] In this misty realm, the therapist's theoretical orientation may have substantial impact on whether the motivational

---

4.   Strategic therapists have taken advantage of this inherent ambiguity to design "reframes"

attribution selected will be positive or negative. Unfortunately, the field of psychotherapy appears to be overloaded with, and perhaps even dominated by, motivational attributions that are actively counterproductive of empathy rather than facilitative of it.

In a provocative paper, Daniel Wile (1984) has argued that many of our standard conceptualizations of clients, and hence our assumptions about what motivates them, are inherently perjorative. A short list of such pathological motivational attributions would include viewing clients as "dependent, manipulative, narcissistic, hostile, symbiotic, controlling, masochistic, regressed, resistant, dishonest, irresponsible, pathologically jealous or competitive, engaged in game playing, or refusing to give up their infantile gratifications and grow up" (Wile, 1984, p. 357). Such perjorative conceptualizations are not confined to psychodynamic therapy; for example, cognitive therapists have their own set of negatively tinged conceptualizations, seeing clients as irrational, immature, misconstruing reality, and so on (Heide, 1989), and the systems literature is filled with descriptions of family members sabotaging therapists' efforts through deceit and manipulation (Wile, 1992). Wile points out that psychotherapeutic interpretations derived from such conceptualizations are likely to be perceived by many clients as accusatory:

> A woman may already feel self-critical about her tendency at times to whine. She is likely to feel even more discouraged and hopeless if her therapist were to interpret her whining as an attempt to manipulate or control, an expression of masochism, an indication that she is basically very angry, a reluctance to take responsibility for her own needs and feelings, a result of her failure to achieve separation-individuation, or a consequence of unresolved feelings toward her parents. (Wile, 1984, p. 357)

It follows that such negativistic attributions also serve to undermine empathy. Wile's alternative to viewing clients as suffering from an underlying pathology is to see them as having an "underlying normality"; rather than being resistant and regressively gratified, they are considered to be motivated by a sense of

which reconceptualize the client's problem in terms that frequently attribute more positive motivations to the client than other observers normally would. For example, the harshly punitive parent who shrieks at his children when they don't mind their mother may be told that his desire to get his children to display respect for adults is absolutely proper, but that by intervening he is keeping his wife from learning how to demand respect herself (see, for example, Chubb, 1982). Thus he is explicitly given a positive motivation by the therapist which presumably makes him feel validated and thereby more receptive to the intervention that follows.

unentitlement to their feelings, which is normal in view of their life experience. Seeing clients as "deprived and stuck" rather than "resistant and gratified" is an approach that will much more naturally draw out from the therapist feelings of empathetic understanding. In other words, the principle of "positive motivation as the root of empathy" applies equally well to psychotherapy as to the world of the playwright. Just as playwrights choose motivation for their characters, therapists choose to attribute motivations to their clients and in both cases the degree of empathy generated will presumably be roughly proportional to the attractiveness of the motivation chosen.

Motivation

The third similarity between psychotherapy and drama concerns the necessity of a strongly-motivated protagonist in both realms. If characters need *positive* motivation in order for us to empathize with them, they must have *strong* motivation in order to create drama (or therapeutic change).

The necessity of absolute commitment on the actor's part to his or her goal has been a truism in the teaching of acting at least since the days of Stanislavsky. Broadway casting director Michael Shurtleff (1980) put it succinctly when he said, "The actor must find the strongest, most positive goal possible. Nothing less will do" (pp. 42–43). What fascinates us about the theater is to a substantial extent this very process of watching someone want something so very badly. This is life shorn of its stretches of tepid interchange and humdrum activity; on stage, everything matters intensely. David Mamet (1986) described the necessity of the actor embracing this principle without reservation:

> [The actor] must have the courage to say to his fellow actors on stage (and so to the audience): "I am not concerned with influencing or *manipulating* you, I am not concerned with *nicety*. I am here on a mission and I *demand* you give me what I want." (p. 127, italics in original)

What holds true for actors applies every bit as strongly to playwrights who must give their protagonists objectives that will be sought with passion and commitment. As Gallaway (1950) put it, "A conflict of views is not drama unless the arguments threaten the well-being of the protagonist. … Drama does not occur because a character thinks something right or wrong; it occurs because he wants something intolerably" (pp. 93–95). The influential writer John Howard Lawson (1936) made much the same point when he argued that strength of will was the *sine qua non* of playwrighting, for "drama cannot deal with people whose wills are atrophied, who are unable to make decisions which have even temporary meaning, who make no effort to control their environment" (p. 168). Indeed, most of the great protagonists in the world's dramatic literature exemplify the exact opposite of atrophied will; they pursue what they want with all their might and whatever the cost. Thus, Oedipus so desires to lift the curse on Athens that he will face a truth so horrifying that its knowledge will drive him to gouge out his very eyes. So, too, Macbeth will persevere in his scheme although it leads to his wife's suicide and his own death by the sword; Othello will be driven by jealous rage to break the neck of his own beloved; Thomas More in *A Man For All Seasons* will face the ax of the executioner rather than renounce his belief, and so on. Even Hamlet, whose indecision is notorious, manages to kill Laertes and Claudius once his mind has been made up. And on a more mundane level, Rick in *Casablanca* ends up demonstrating extraordinary willpower as well; once he discovers Ilsa still loves him, he is able not only to willingly give her up to the man who needs her but even to gun down a Nazi officer to insure her escape.

It should be obvious that motivation is as necessary in the psychotherapeutic arena as in the dramatic. To paraphrase Gallaway (1950), we might say that therapeutic change does not occur because a client thinks something is right or wrong; it occurs because she/he wants something intolerably. Although motivation has been remarkably difficult to operationalize as a construct, numerous studies suggest its relationship to therapeutic outcome (see, for example, Garfield, 1980; Weiner, 1975) and motivation has been used as a selection criterion in virtually all the brief dynamic therapies (Strupp & Binder, 1984). Interestingly enough, a standard psychodynamic means of assessing motivation attempts to ascertain the same information that Gallaway (1950) considers central in discussing dramatic motivation, that is, the extent to which the problems "threaten the well-being of the protagonist" (p. 93). The degree of a client's motivation for therapy is considered roughly proportional to the extent of the distress and anxiety generated by the presenting complaints (Weiner, 1975, p. 62). In both the dramatic and psychotherapeutic cases, greater threat to well-being leads to more provocative results.

It should be clarified that neither playwrights nor psychotherapists assume that strong motivation is necessarily in place at the beginning of a drama or therapy. Indeed, it may be the role of the dramatic or therapeutic process to strip away obstacles to the emergence of motivation. Our example of *Casablanca* illustrates this well: Rick's demoralization is gradually undone over the course of the film until by the end he has forcefully contradicted his earlier declaration that he is concerned solely with self-preservation. Whether or not it is there initially, however, motivation needs to emerge to shift the balance of forces and create change — the process that occurs in what playwrights refer to as the crisis.

Change Through Crisis

There may be no word in the psychotherapeutic literature that corresponds precisely to what playwrights call "crisis," but perhaps there should be, for it refers to the fundamental building block of the change process that lies at the heart of both therapy and theater.

The centrality of this construct in playwrighting is illustrated by Archer's (1912) labeling it "the essence of drama" and by Niggli's (1967) declaration that "any good play is one giant crisis" (p. 40). Although terminology is slippery in the field of playwrighting and definitions vary, crises are typically thought of as moments when something new happens, "straining points in the conflict that cause a realignment of focus or some change in the character" (Blacker, 1986, p. 17). The hallmarks of crises are instability and uncertainty; an old pattern of relationship breaks up and a new one is instituted (Gallaway, 1950; Lawson, 1936). The use of the term in playwrighting is thus not equivalent to its use in the mental health professions, where it is apt to refer to a temporary flare-up in problem intensity which needs to be resolved quickly in order to return the client to his or her previous level of adjustment (Garfield, 1980). The playwright is likely to see the crisis as the birthplace of new ways of acting, thinking, and relating. As such, it represents the core of drama, and the playwright deliberately induces it in as many scenes as possible, frequently constructing each scene as a crisis or series of crises. Because of the centrality of the construct of change in both drama and therapy, it may be instructive for therapists to consider the rules that have been generated to guide these moments' development and efficacy in play construction.

The first characteristic of a good crisis applies to most other aspects of a good play as well: it needs to be prepared for adequately (Gallaway, 1950; Griffiths, 1982). Another way of stating this is to say that it must be credible to the audience. Events must be arranged such that the crisis will appear to grow naturally out of what we know about the characters and their relationships. The playwright accomplishes this through careful preparation, planting clues about characters that lead us to believe they are capable of whatever they are eventually drawn to do.[5]

Thus we believe Rick (Humphrey Bogart) is capable of shooting a Nazi because we have been told that he was a gunrunner before the war; we accept his severe cynicism because we see how much he loved Ilsa in Paris; we even believe it when we see him give up Ilsa at the airport because we have seen his immense respect for the work of her husband Victor Laszlo on several occasions.

---

5.   Lack of credibility in a script frequently calls forth attacks from critics. Consider Mick LaSalle's (1992) assault on the Sean Connery film *Medicine Man*: "*Medicine Man* suffers from a script that aims for cuteness over truth or substance, so you get mind-boggling moments such as the one in which Campbell (Sean Connery) tells Rae (Lorraine Bracco) that he's found a serum that can cure cancer overnight, and she's too annoyed with him to be impressed. Imagine that. A scientist whom you know is no flake, a man at the top of his field, tells you he's just *cured* cancer, and you don't want to hear it. You're in a bad mood that day. Moments like this undermine the audience's belief in and respect for the Rae character early on" (p. D1).

This belief is only possible because of preparation, the art of which (as Platt clearly stated) is "to make us ready to receive as probable the intelligence that the author later in the play wishes to put before us as a surprise" (Platt, 1920, p. 64).

The necessity of developing credibility in this way in plays has apparently been recognized at least since Aristotle, whom Archer (1912) quotes as having said, "The probable impossible is to be preferred to the improbable possible" (p. 180). In other words, plausibility is more important than reality as far as the stage is concerned, an idea that has been echoed twenty-four centuries later by systems theorists (such as Watzlawick et al., 1974) in regard to the world of therapy. In fact, the heavy emphasis on credibility and preparation in the playwrighting literature bears considerable resemblance to the stress given to these topics lately by psychotherapy writers.

For example, Jerome Frank (1987), long known for his view of psychotherapy as a persuasive process, has recently drawn explicit parallels between psychotherapy and the ancient art of rhetoric, arguing that therapists might do well to adopt the devices of rhetoricians to "focus the patient's attention on ideas central to the therapeutic message and make the therapist's ideas *more believable*" (p. 296, italics added). Similarly, Sue and Zane (1987) have given credibility a central role in their reformulation of the problems raised by therapy with cross-cultural pairs, suggesting that making therapists and their interventions believable to individual clients is more powerful than indiscriminately applying presumably culture-specific therapeutic techniques to all clients of a particular ethnic group. The notion of credibility is also the basis for what Pentony (1981) has referred to as the contextual therapies, those approaches (such as Milton Erickson's) that attempt to alter the context in which a problem is perceived as a way of empowering a client to change that problem. Such approaches, which typically emphasize brevity, must embed their interventions within a client's pre-existing values and beliefs in order to avoid the resistance generated when clients find their world views being challenged. A major feature of brief strategic therapy is its injunction to therapists to avoid taking a premature position that might violate client values, and instead to maintain maneuverability and credibility by asking questions to elicit the client's position first (Fisch, Weakland, & Segal, 1982). Credibility is as critical for the success of a brief therapeutic intervention as it is for the success of a dramatic development, and in both cases is accomplished by careful preparation.

In addition to needing to be prepared for adequately, crises in plays and films are characterized by a number of other features which also typify psychotherapy interventions. One way of appreciating the nature of good crises is to look at errors that beginners make when attempting to set them up. Gallaway (1950) has listed five such beginner's errors, all of which are shared by beginning therapists as they present their interventions. The first error has already been mentioned, that is, failing to prepare the audience (client) for the crisis. The others are: allowing the crisis to come too quickly to a solution; avoiding the crisis entirely; dissipating the tension in talk; and substituting for the real crisis little scenes of inactivity that have no bearing on the stakes of the scene.

Clinical illustration of each of these errors abound in the daily experience of those who supervise beginning psychology graduate students. An example of insufficient preparation for an intervention occurred for me when observing a student role-play a therapist in a classroom demonstration with a client whose presenting problem was the desire to stop shoplifting. In an attempt to get the client to view the shoplifting behavior in a more neutral manner and to lessen self-criticism around it, the student therapist suggested that shoplifting was "an addiction like alcoholism," assuming that the client would see addictions as controllable. Unfortunately, the therapist had not taken the time first to discover the client's own view of alcoholism, which as it turned out was considered to be an intractable disease largely outside of control. Thus, by taking a premature position and not adequately preparing for the intervention, the therapist worsened rather than ameliorated the client's self-view. In this particular class the student was learning about cognitive therapy, which uses "Socratic dialogue" or directed questioning by the therapist to try to avoid this very pitfall. Skillful cognitive therapy instead prepares for interventions by first gathering evidence from the client's own experience that will lead the client to adopt a more positive view of self and world.

Examples of other beginners' errors in creating crises can be readily cited. DeJong and Berg (1998) provided an instance of the second error, "allowing a crisis to come too quickly to a solution," among therapists who seek to identify exceptions to clients' problematic patterns:

> In exception exploration, as in goal formulation, practitioners new to solution-focused work tend to push for closure too quickly. As soon as a client mentions an exception, they want to turn this difference into a solution. For example, a couple seeking help to reduce the conflict in their relationship may say, "We fight less when we go out for dinner." The novice at this point will often be tempted to say, "Well, do you think it would help if you started going out to dinner more often, say once a week?" For most clients, such a move for closure will be premature. (p. 105)

An example of the fifth error, "substituting for the real crisis activities that have no bearing on the stakes of the scene," occurred for me while supervising a student therapist who was treating a suicidal client. Instead of asking about the client's suicidal ideation, planned method, availability of lethal means, and so on, the therapist immediately focused on the client's relationship with her parents — a potentially interesting topic at a later date, but not relevant to either the immediate danger or to the motivation for suicide, which had to do with the client's relationship with her boyfriend.

When all of these errors are avoided, a crisis will emerge that is believable, sufficiently developed, and instigative of change. Such is the case in *Casablanca*, which is full of one finely honed crisis after another, each built upon the momentum of those preceding it. The central crisis of the film, in my opinion, is the scene wherein Ilsa comes to Rick's darkened apartment to obtain the letters of transit that will allow her and her husband Victor Lazlo to escape Casablanca. I consider it central because it is the scene that has greatest bearing on the two main questions posed earlier: how Rick and Ilsa will resolve their relationship; and whether Rick will recover from demoralization. It has been exquisitely prepared for; we know of their previous romance in Paris, of Rick's cynicism resulting from Ilsa never showing up at the train station to leave Paris with him, of his possession of the letters of transit and of her urgent need to get them. The scene is given sufficient development: Ilsa must try everything she can think of to obtain the letters from Rick, including threatening his life with a gun. No tension is dissipated in talk; instead, tension builds through the characters talking about the heart of the matter. And it qualifies as a crisis because it will fundamentally alter the pattern of their relationship from formality and distance to a rekindling of torrid passion.

This crisis hasn't resolved the first main question of *Casablanca*; that will come later in the famous airport scene. But it has shifted the momentum fundamentally, and allowed Rick to recover sufficiently from his apathy to enable him to instigate a new course of action. It should be emphasized that *Casablanca*, like a good course of therapy, consists not merely of this one crisis but of perhaps two dozen, each interlocked to build the audience's emotions in a particular direction. Each crisis, like each session of therapy, adds further to the understanding of the focal problem, introduces some means of grappling with it, and builds on the preceding crises (or sessions) to lead to the resolution which the audience (and client) awaits.

Resolution

The final shared feature of plays and psychotherapy to be discussed here is that both are successfully concluded only through a resolution — either characterological or situational — of the original focal problem.

In a debate that again bears eerie similarity to the fight between theoretical orientations in the psychotherapy field, writers on play structure have argued about whether a good play requires an actual change in the protagonist's character or whether merely resolving the focal problem is sufficient. The predominant view, in keeping with the generally "dynamic" cast of authors' thinking about these topics discussed earlier in this chapter, is that characters must change or grow. Thus Linda Seger (1987, p. 147) argues that "in the best of films, at least one of the characters will be transformed in the process of living out the story"; Irwin Blacker (1986, p. 24) insists that "*the conflict and its resolutions must change the character*" (author's italics); and Lajos Egri (1960, p. 60) claims that "there is only one realm in which the characters defy natural laws and remain the same — the realm of bad writing." As in therapy this character change is frequently attributed to a process of insight or self-discovery. Playwright Maxwell Anderson described this notion with his usual clarity:

> The mainstream in the mechanism of a modern play is almost invariably a discovery by the hero of some element in his environment or in his own soul of which he had not been aware — or which he has not taken sufficiently into account. ... A play should lead up to and away from a central crisis, and this crisis should consist in a discovery by the leading character which has an indelible effect on his thought and emotion and completely alters his course of action. (Cited in MacGowan, 1951, p. 35)

It is easy to think of plays and films in which a major character undergoes such a personal transformation through self-discovery. Nora in Ibsen's *A Doll's House* is perhaps the sterling modern example; others range from August Wilson's stunning *Joe Turner's Come and Gone* to such films as *Pulp Fiction*, *Unforgiven*, *Toy Story*, *The Shawshank Redemption*, and even *Star Wars* and *The Wizard of Oz*. Such transformation is not always positive as the ancient example of *Oedipus Rex* attests, and indeed the stuff of tragedy is frequently this unfolding personal realization of limitation as the hero engages in a "doomed struggle with necessity" (Corrigan, 1979, p. 94).

Although many of our finest and most uplifting films and plays involve some kind of personal transformation (and *Casablanca* again fits perfectly, with the resurrection of Rick from demoralized cynic to moral agent), there is no shortage of movies and plays available to serve as counterexamples. This has prompted writers like Kenneth MacGowan (1951) to proclaim that "there are many strange and foolish dogmas about important characters. One is that they must change and develop" (p. 77). MacGowan points out that there are many great plays in which no true character growth or development takes place: "Hedda [Gabler] and Hamlet are the same people at the end as they are in the beginning, except that they have suffered and died" (p. 78).

There are also many not-so-great plays and films that lack any character development, and in fact whole genres exist (for example, the murder mystery or the cop buddy movie) in which the outcome steers clear of personal change almost completely. Thus the resolution of movies like the *Lethal Weapon* series or the James Bond extravaganzas depends primarily on the death of the villain. To the extent that the protagonists change at all, they might show some small grudging acceptance of a partner who previously was considered excessively conservative, eccentric, and so on, or (in the case of James Bond) the hero may finally act on sexual impulses held in check for the preceding two hours. This hardly qualifies as character change, and suggests that dramatic structure can operate in the absence of significant personal transformation, a point echoed by nondynamic therapists (Pentony, 1981).[6]

Interestingly enough, it has been suggested by some authors that character change as we usually think of it cannot easily occur in the course of the typical play if for no other reason than the time scale of the average drama is not long enough for a character to undergo significant alterations in mental habits or character structure. Many a play occurs over the course of a day or perhaps a week, which is too brief for many protagonists to undergo lasting personality transformation. Of course, a playwright may artificially contract a normally longer-lasting change process for the purposes of dramatic effect. The stage, after all, is the realm of heightened intensity; as Bernard Grebanier (1961, p. 14) puts it, "Because art is selective, it is more vivid than life." Thus, Ibsen's Nora (in *A Doll's House*) is transformed much more rapidly on stage than she ever would have been in reality, undergoing in a week an evolution which would have taken months in the real world (Archer, 1912). This probably is fairly typical of the kinds of personal transformation we see on stage, because the playwright has purposefully selected the most intense and intimate moments to engage our interest. If plays are considered a metaphor for therapy, then we might think of the personal transformation play as being similar to the atypical form of brief psychotherapy developed by Habib Davanloo (1980), in which intense confrontations of the part of the therapist are said to lead to personality change in a much more rapid fashion than is claimed by other forms of brief therapy (Strupp & Binder, 1984).

In some plays, then, character change seems to occur, whereas in others (especially comedies, mysteries, and action adventures) simple problem resolution is sufficient. Regardless of which of these are seen as the outcome, as I have argued earlier in this chapter, it is important to recognize that virtually all plays or films worthy of the name do succeed in resolving the central questions posed at their outset. Thus, the questions of whether Hamlet will kill the king and whether Luke Skywalker will destroy the threatening Death Star are resolved in the affirmative, as is the question of whether Woody and Buzz Lightyear will

---

6.   The belief in this possibility has been described as "the crux of the disagreement between solution-oriented therapists and long-term therapists of other orientations" by Bill O'Hanlon and Michelle Weiner-Davis (1989): "As change-oriented therapists, we want to focus our attention on the changing and changeable aspects of our clients' experiences. We do not, therefore, focus on entities or aspects of the client's situation that are not amenable to change. ... To cure a borderline personality is beyond our ken, but to help a person get a job or make friends or have a satisfying sexual relationship or refrain from cutting herself is well within our abilities" (pp. 49–50).

settle their differences in *Toy Story*. We wish, as an audience, to know whether or not the protagonist gets what he or she wants. Note that there are plenty of cases in which the protagonist achieves the objective but doesn't get to enjoy it. Hamlet kills Claudius but dies trying; Romeo and Juliet achieve an everlasting bond, but unfortunately only in the next world, and so on. Enjoyment of the objective is not important (at least from the standpoint of play structure) but resolution of the objective is almost always desirable.

Those instances in which the objective is not resolved tend to be unsatisfying in plays (and the same point might be made about psychotherapy). A good example of lack of resolution is the film *Ironweed*, based on the Pulitzer-Prize-winning novel by William Kennedy and starring Jack Nicholson and Meryl Streep. Nicholson's character is an alcoholic who has long ago abandoned his family. In the course of the film he returns to his former home, begins a reconciliation process with his wife and children, and then abruptly leaves them again. In the final scene he has just caught a train out of town, when he stands up and throws a bottle of booze against the wall of the boxcar. Then we see a scene of a chair surrounded by mystical light. What are we to make of this? Do we assume that his pitching the bottle into the wall is a sign that he is giving up drinking or merely an indication of frustration? What is the mystical chair supposed to mean? We may well share the protagonist's frustration as we leave the theater, our reaction strongly influenced by this indecipherable ending.

Equally unsatisfying are those endings which resolve the principal conflict but introduce a new one in its stead. Sometimes this is done deliberately to keep the audience hanging in suspense for a sequel, as in *Back to the Future II*. Here the protagonist Marty manages to reclaim the sporting almanac which has been used by the evil Biff to alter the future, and thus resolves his major objective; however, the time machine is almost simultaneously sent by a jolt of lightning into the nineteenth century, setting up the intense need for all of us to see *Back to the Future III* to find out how this new problem will be resolved. Occasionally this substitution of conflicts is used in the absence of a planned sequel, as exemplified by Sam Shepard's *A Lie of the Mind* which frees the protagonist from his bonds only to have him replaced by his brother, now in an equally dire situation. This might be thought of as the dramatic equivalent of symptom substitution, and tends to be emotionally jarring, presumably the effect intended by the playwright.

A related case are those plays that never resolve the main conflict at all. Probably the most celebrated example is Beckett's impactful *Waiting for Godot*, which wreaks havoc on the audience's tradition-sanctioned expectation of a resolution by deliberately suspending it. Rollo May (Personal communication, April 19, 1989) has argued that *Godot* might be a better metaphorical example than *Casablanca* in understanding psychotherapy structure from a dramatic standpoint, based on the view that true psychotherapy does not ever succeed in actually solving personal problems but instead deepens clients' understanding of them. I would still argue that therapists want to aim for the resolution level of a *Casablanca*, which it will be remembered does not eliminate Rick's struggles at the end (he is last seen walking off into the fog with Renault to continue the fight against the Nazis that he had earlier abandoned) but merely resolves enough of the central conflict to permit Rick to engage in new behavior and to embark on fresh, yet-to-be-resolved, conflicts. (The same point can be made about other noted films that end with partial resolutions such as *Gone with the Wind* or *Dances with Wolves*). We would feel that we let our clients down if every case ended with the hopeless indeterminacy of *Waiting for Godot*. It is more appropriate to attempt to deal sufficiently with the client's main problem that something that *feels* like resolution occurs even though we (like the playwright) must acknowledge that ultimate resolution will not be achieved until the grave. Elizabeth Hunt (1924) has made this point in regard to playwrighting and, with a paraphrase of major terms, it applies equally to the realm of therapy:

> The world continues to move. If it is possible to do so the author/therapist must allow his audience/client to depart realizing that even though mistaken identities are cleared up, virtues rewarded, etc., the characters/clients are after all neither more nor less than human beings who, if they are to remain in this vale of friction, will probably find other joys and sorrows in store for them. (pp. 56–57)

Conclusion

The preceding view of features uniting the structures of plays/films and psychotherapy has been intended merely as a prelude (or, to use a more pertinent metaphor, an opening scene) to the rich possibilities inherent in the cross-fertilization of these two disparate fields. Many other points of similarity between these realms might have been developed, including the following: both plays and psychotherapy frequently involve realignment of a primary relationship, often by means of more authentic encounter; both frequently create change through emotional arousal; both investigate similar themes as the root of the change process, and so on. All of these ideas and others yet unspecified deserve further development, as do the fascinating parallels between the function and process of plays and therapy.

The overarching point that has been made here is that psychotherapy is inherently dramatic. It operates according to principles remarkably similar to those that playwrights have been developing at least since the time of Aeschylus. It succeeds or fails depending to a significant degree on how well it employs rules that playwrights have articulated almost as well as psychotherapists. Throughout my research in this area, I have been stunned to find statements by dramatic theorists that, with a change of the sentence's subject, could have been drawn

Table 1
Therapeutic Themes Explored in Drama

Family Conflict (Systems)

King Lear	*A Long Day's Journey Into Night*
True West	*A Doll's House*
A Lie of the Mind	*The Seagull*

Existential Themes (Humanistic)

Responsibility:	*King Lear, Les Miserables, All My Sons*
Mortality:	*Riders to the Sea, Spoon River Anthology*
Choicefulness:	*Hamlet*
Meaning and Meaninglessness:	*Macbeth, Our Town, Waiting for Godot, Hedda Gabler*

Lifting Repression (Psychodynamic)

Twelfth Night
Midsummer Night's Dream
The Rainmaker

Self-Efficacy (Cognitive-Behavioral)

A Doll's House
Joe Turner's Come and Gone
A Few Good Men
The Iceman Cometh

from a psychotherapy textbook. Consider this definition by Gallaway (1950) of what constitutes the fundamental action of plays:

> The pursuit of a *strongly desirable objective* by a *protagonist* who has *chances* to succeed against a *powerful antagonist* and whose course of action is made somewhat devious by a number of *complications*. (pp. 314–315, italics in original)

Now compare this statement to the following description of the fundamental conditions necessary to avoid resistance in therapy by noted Gestalt therapist John Enright (n.d.):

> When we are working with a *client* on a problem that he *wants to work on* and *actually experiences as a problem* or barrier in his life, yet *feels is solvable*, and if the client feels trust in us and our way of working and has *no values competing against success*, then there is likely to be no resistance. (pp. 1–2, italics added)

The presence of these parallels is not recounted here in order to suggest that we should have playwrights doing therapy or that we should have our graduate students study, say, Beckett instead of Beck. Rather, the intention is to suggest that attempting to understand therapy by focusing on therapy alone may blind us to universal processes which become evident only when a more inclusive viewpoint is adopted. Identification of these broader themes may also have implications for the conduct of therapy. For example, if therapy is indeed a dramatic process, then its failures can be understood in part as misapplications of dramatic technique, and its quality can be enhanced in ways similar to those a playwright uses to tone up a script. Before this can happen, however, it will be necessary to further explicate these fundamental parallels between the realms. For now, we can only encourage a greater rapport between psychotherapy and dramatics, and hope, in the words of Rick at the conclusion of *Casablanca*, that "this is the beginning of a beautiful friendship."

References

Archer, W. (1912). *Playmaking: A manual of craftsmanship.* Boston: Small, Maynard.

Blacker, I. R. (1986). *The elements of screenwriting: A guide for film and television writers.* New York: Macmillan.

Bruner, J. (1990). *Acts of meaning.* Cambridge, MA: Harvard University Press.

Bugental, J. F. T. (1987). *The art of the psychotherapist.* New York: Norton.

Burke, K. (1945). *A grammar of motives.* New York: Prentice-Hall.

Capra, F. (1982). *The turning point: Science, society and the rising culture.* New York: Simon & Schuster.

Chubb, H. (1982). Strategic brief therapy in a clinic setting. *Psychotherapy, 19,* 160–165.

Corrigan, R. W. (1979). *The world of the theater.* Glenview, IL: Scott Foresman.

Davanloo, H. (Ed.) (1980). *Short-term dynamic psychotherapy.* New York: Jason Aronson.

DeJong, P., & Berg, I. K. (1998). *Interviewing for solutions.* Pacific Grove, CA: Brooks/Cole.

Efran, J. S., Lukens, M. D., & Lukens, R. J. (1990). *Language, structure, and change.* New York: Norton.

Egri, L. (1960). *The art of dramatic writing.* New York: Simon and Schuster.

Enright, J. (n.d.). *Therapy without resistance.* Unpublished manuscript.

Finch, R. U. (1948). *How to write a play.* New York: Greenberg.

Fisch, R., Weakland, J. H., & Segal, L. (1982). *The tactics of change: Doing therapy briefly.* San Francisco: Jossey-Bass.

Frank, J. D. (1987). Psychotherapy, rhetoric, and hermeneutics: Implications for practice and research. *Psychotherapy, 24,* 293–302.

Frank, J. D., & Frank, J. B. (1991). *Persuasion and healing: A comparative study of psychotherapy* (3rd ed.). Baltimore: Johns Hopkins University Press.

Freitag, G. (1894). *The technique of the drama.* Chicago: Scott Foresman.

Gallaway, M. (1950). *Constructing a play.* New York: Prentice-Hall.

Garfield, S. L. (1980). *Psychotherapy: An eclectic approach.* New York: John Wiley and Sons.

Geertz, C. (1980). Blurred genres: The refiguration of social thought. *American Scholar* (Spring), 165–179.

Gergen, K. J. (1988). If persons are texts. In S. B. Messer, L. A. Sass, & R. L. Woolfolk (Eds.), *Hermeneutics and psychological theory: Interpretive perspectives on personality, psychotherapy and psychopathology* (pp. 28–51). New Brunswick, NJ: Rutgers University Press.

Grebanier, B. D. N. (1961). *Playwriting.* New York: Harper and Row.

Griffiths, S. (1982). *How plays are made: The fundamental elements of play construction.* Englewood Cliffs, NJ: Prentice-Hall.

Heide, F. J. (1989, April). *Failures in cognitive therapy.* Paper presented at the Fifth National Convention of the Society for Exploration of Psychotherapy Integration, Berkeley, CA.

Heide, F. J., Rosenbaum, R., Horowitz, M., & May, R. (1989, April). *Symphony, scene and synthesis: The lively arts as metaphors for psychotherapy integration.* Paper presented at the meeting of the Society for Exploration of Psychotherapy Integration, Oakland, CA.

Howard, G. S. (1991). Culture tales: A narrative approach to thinking, cross-cultural psychology, and psychotherapy. *American Psychologist, 46,* 187–197.

Howard, D., & Mabley, E. (1993). *The tools of screenwriting: A writer's guide to the craft and elements of a screenplay.* New York: St. Martins.

Hoyt, M. (Ed.) (1996). *Constructive therapies 2.* New York: Guilford.

Hunt, E. R. (1924). *The play of today: Studies in structure.* New York: G. P. Putnam & Sons.

Keeney, B. P. (1983). *Aesthetics of change.* New York: Guilford.

Keeney, B. P., & Ray, W. A. (1996). Resource-focused psychotherapy. In M. F. Hoyt (Ed.), *Constructive therapies 2* (pp. 334–346). New York: Guilford.

Kuhn, T. S. (1987). What are scientific revolutions? In L. Kruger, L. J. Daston, & M. Heidelberger (Eds.), *The probabilistic revolution* (vol. 1) (pp. 7–22). Cambridge, MA: MIT Press.

Lakoff, G., & Johnson, M. (1980). *Metaphors we live by.* Chicago: University of Chicago Press.

La Salle, M. (1991, March 1). *The Doors* raises the dead. *San Francisco Chronicle,* E1.

La Salle, M. (1992, February 7). Connery lost in the jungle. *San Francisco Chronicle,* D1.

La Salle, M. (1995, February 3). *Rhapsody* without rapture. *San Francisco Chronicle,* E1.

Lawson, J. H. (1936). *Theory and technique of playwrighting.* New York: G. P. Putnam's Sons.

Leary, D. E. (Ed.) (1990). *Metaphors in the history of psychology.* New York: Cambridge University Press.

Lieberman, E. J. (1985). *Acts of will: The life and work of Otto Rank.* New York: The Free Press.

MacCormack, T. (1997). Believing in make-believe: Looking at theatre as a metaphor for psychotherapy. *Family Process, 36,* 151–169.

MacGowan, K. (1951). *A primer of playwriting.* New York: Random House.

Mamet, D. (1986). *Writing in restaurants.* New York: Viking.

McNiff, S. (1987). Pantheon of creative arts therapies: An integrative perspective. *Journal of Integrative and Eclectic Psychotherapy, 6,* 259–281.

Neimeyer, R. A. & Mahoney, M. J. (Eds.) (1995). *Constructivism in psychotherapy.* Washington, D.C.: American Psychological Association.

Niggli, J. (1967). *New pointers on playwriting.* Boston: The Writer.

O'Hanlon, W. H., & Weiner-Davis, M. (1989). *In search of solutions: A new direction in psychotherapy.* New York: W. W. Norton.

Pentony, P. (1981). *Models of influence in psychotherapy.* New York: Free Press.

Platt, A. (1920). *Practical hints on playwriting.* New York: Dodd, Mead.

Polster, E. (1987). *Every person's life is worth a novel.* New York: Norton.

Robbins, A. (Ed.) (1998). *Therapeutic presence: Bridging expression and form.* London: Jessica Kingsley.

Rosenbaum, R. (1990). *Music of the mind: The analysis of patterns and processes in time as pathways to psychotherapy integration.* Unpublished manuscript.

Safran, J. D., & Segal, Z. V. (1990). *Interpersonal process in cognitive therapy.* New York: Basic Books.

Sarbin, T. R. (1990). Metaphors of unwanted conduct: A historical sketch. In D. E. Leary (Ed.), *Metaphors in the history of psychology* (pp. 300–330). Cambridge: Cambridge University Press.

Schechner, R. (1990). Magnitudes of performance. In R. Schechner & W. Appel (Eds.), *By means of performance: Intercultural studies of theatre and ritual* (pp. 19–49). Cambridge: Cambridge University Press.

Seger, L. (1987). *Making a good script great.* New York: Dodd, Mead.

Shurtleff, M. (1980). *Audition: Everything an actor needs to know to get the part.* New York: Bantam Books.

Strupp, H. H., & Binder, J. L. (1984). *Psychotherapy in a new key: A guide to time-limited dynamic psychotherapy.* New York: Basic Books.

Sue, S., & Zane, N. (1987). The role of culture and cultural techniques in psychotherapy: A critique and reformulation. *American Psychologist, 42,* 37–45.

Szasz, T. (1974). *The myth of mental illness.* (Rev. Ed.) New York: Harper & Row.

Turner, V. (1990). Are there universals in performance in myth, ritual and drama? In R. Schechner & W. Appel (Eds.), *By means of performance: Intercultural studies of theatre and ritual* (pp. 8–18). Cambridge: Cambridge University Press.

Watzlawick, P., Weakland, J. H., & Fisch, R. (1974). *Change: Principles of problem formation and problem resolution.* New York: W. W. Norton.

Weiner, I. B., (1975). *Principles of psychotherapy.* New York: John Wiley and Sons.

Weiner, S. (1997). The actor-director and patient-therapist relationships: A process comparison. *American Journal of Psychotherapy, 51,* 77–85.

White, M., & Epston, D. (1990). *Narrative means to therapeutic ends.* New York: W. W. Norton.

Wile, D. B. (1984). Kohut, Kernberg, and accusatory interpretations. *Psychotherapy, 21,* 353–364.

Wile, D. B. (1992). *Couples therapy: A non-traditional approach.* New York: Wiley.

Zukowski, E. M. (1995). The aesthetic experience of the client in psychotherapy. *Journal of Humanistic Psychology, 35,* 42–56.

CHAPTER FIFTEEN

Hearing the Body's Story

Stephen R. Koepfer

Durinda, a woman with a chronic frozen shoulder lies down on my massage table for her regular session. After some time she mentions and draws an image which had appeared in her mind. It was a representation of her painfully immobilized shoulder seized within the jaws of a wolf. This metaphorical portrait was the first installment of a personal story which would gradually unfold with each session, mirroring and recording her progress in therapy. The exploration, illustration, and telling of this story was integral to the successful rehabilitation of her shoulder.

Introduction

Why are art therapy and storytelling viable adjuncts to massage therapy? How can these modalities be used to address the psychological needs of persons with physical disabilities or injuries? What role does imagery and emotion play in the rehabilitation process? Can the combined effects of these modalities help bridge the gap between psychological and physical medicine?

I am not a researcher in the strict sense of the word and the work presented in this chapter is not the result of formal scientific method. Quite the opposite, I am a practitioner. As such, rather than establishing norms, my objective has been to fluctuate with and meet the individual needs of each client. I do believe however, that the clinical experiences presented here are the antecedents for future study.

Individually, art therapy, massage therapy, and storytelling have been subject to much theorizing and research in the past. My decision to incorporate these three modalities was based on many observations I had made over a period of time, both as a massage therapist and art therapist. I believed that there were aspects of art therapy and storytelling which could benefit my massage clients.

The idea that art therapy and storytelling could benefit massage clients was born while I was still a student massage therapist. Oftentimes instructors would tell stories of clients who occasionally had spontaneous emotional reactions while receiving massage. Stories of outbursts of crying or seeing imagery were often used as examples. As my education continued, I too experienced imagery while being massaged, some of which has been quite amazing. Unfortunately however, when questioned about how to handle such situations, most instructors replied with something akin "to use your intuition." Furthermore, my massage therapy education did not consist of any psychology curriculum which would begin to explain why these events occurred. Fortunately, I had prior education and experience as an art therapist and was familiar with working with people on a psychotherapeutic level.

Do not misunderstand my intention here. I have a strong belief in trusting one's intuition, and depend on mine quite often. In fact, I feel that the ability to listen to one's intuition is a quality needed by any good therapist. However, intuition can not always carry the burden of making treatment decisions. A combination of education and intuition provides a stronger base from which to determine therapeutic directions.

Working as a massage therapist, especially in a medical situation, is challenging for many reasons. In addition to the client's physical needs, one must also account for his or her psychological needs.

Although massage therapy has many similarities with other physical therapies, its uniqueness lies in the resulting state of relaxation that often occurs. Not unlike meditation, this relaxation may facilitate an altered state of consciousness (Lusebrink, 1990). According to Tart (1992), an altered state of consciousness is defined as "a radical alteration of overall patterning of consciousness (compared to ... our usual waking state) such that the experiencer ... can tell that different laws are functioning, that a new, overall pattern is superimposed on his [or her] experience" (p. 14). This definition is quite congruent with the dreamlike experiences described by many of my massage clients. It is during these times when many such interesting events as imagery and spontaneous emotional reactions occur. It is also these events which lend for the inclusion of visual expression and/or storytelling in the massage therapy session.

In order to understand how these three modalities can unite, a basic knowledge of each modality and its corresponding functions is required. Therefore, I will begin this chapter with a brief explanation of a psychology of disability and rehabilitation followed by individual descriptions and theoretical foundations of massage therapy, art therapy, and storytelling. Finally, I will present a brief methodology and some clinical experiences.

I am not advocating the use of art therapy, storytelling, or any other psychotherapeutic technique by massage therapists who are not educated or qualified to do so. Nor would I suggest that any psychotherapist begin using massage therapy without proper education and credentialing. My desire is that, through my experiences, other practitioners will be inspired to further explore and research wholistic and creative approaches to rehabilitation. It is also my hope that by reading these stories, any therapist who works with people in physical rehabilitation will have a greater understanding and respect for the oldest storyteller: the human body.

A Psychology of Injury, Disability, and Rehabilitation

Integral to treating any physical injury or disability is a willingness to address the emotional needs of the injured. In doing so it is important to realize that although there are general psychological reactions which can be anticipated from people who sustain injuries or disabilities, individual variations do occur and no single approach can satisfy every persons needs (Falvo, 1995; Garner, 1996; Stein, 1988). Additionally, people are not generally aware of the impact that their feelings and emotions can have on the rehabilitation and healing process. Therefore, the therapist must be careful not to place blame with the client when exploring psychological contributions (Viney, 1993). Keeping these concerns in mind, let's examine some psychological perspectives.

When a person suffers an injury or acquires a disability, a series of normal emotional stages can be expected (Falvo, 1995; Lask & Fosson, 1989). Initially, a brief period of shock and denial is experienced. Although one may remain in denial indefinitely, once the severity of the injury is realized, sadness and anger usually follow as the persistent emotions. During this time the therapist must be watchful for the onset of depression.

Aside from depression, emotional and behavioral regression are also possible during the anger or sadness stage. Being mindful that it is normal for someone who is injured to want to be taken care of, the therapist must weed out the client's realistic from their unrealistic desires for assistance. If the therapist prematurely assumes the role of caretaker or provides too much assistance, regression can be reinforced and rehabilitation or adjustment can be delayed (Erskine, 1994; Lask & Fosson, 1989). It is during these stages that the therapist's patience and empathy are fundamental. To this end, visual expression and storytelling can assist the therapist by providing a safe container in which to support and escort the client through these painful and often long periods of time.

There are no specific time parameters for these stages which can fluctuate during the course of the injury or rehabilitation (Falvo, 1995; Lask & Fosson, 1989). A client may revert back to denial from the anger stage if there is a positive response to treatment and a return of previous functioning. Likewise, newly-attained self-esteem can be corrupted by sadness during times of physical deterioration. There is a positive correlation, however, between the intensity of the emotional response and the severity of the injury (Lask & Fosson, 1989).

Regardless of the severity and longevity of the injury or disability, the final phase is adjustment. This is the stage at which the person accepts and adapts to life with an injury or disability. Adjustment is contingent upon recognition, expression, and processing emotions during the preceding stages (Falvo,1995; Lask & Fosson, 1989; Viney; 1993; Zalidis, 1994).

People who sustain an injury or disability will attempt to find meaning and make sense of what they are experiencing (Achterberg, 1985; Viney, 1993). Oftentimes this is difficult due to the onslaught of unfamiliar medical terminology which practitioners use to describe medical conditions. In my practice, clients often come to therapy with an innate visceral understanding of what is happening in their body, yet they are often confused by the diagnosis and explanations presented by their physicians. Furthermore, Achterberg (1985) suggests that "people who find themselves requiring medical care are primarily concerned about what their own personal experience is likely to be, and only secondarily interested in the technical details of their care" (p. 92).

In one's attempt to find meaning in a recently-acquired injury, outlooks may be either self-defeating or self-empowering. It is believed by many that the success of rehabilitation is actually dictated by the client's anxiety and beliefs about the injury or outcome of therapy rather than their reactions to physical symptoms (Achterberg, 1985; Lask & Fosson, 1989; Lusebrink, 1990; Viney, 1993; Zalidis, 1994). In fact, the client's beliefs about disability may have been present long before the onset of their personal injuries. Consequently, it should be a responsibility of any medical practitioner to be mindful of their client's psychological as well as physical needs. With appropriate education, the combination of visual expression and storytelling can provide one avenue by which to do this.

Massage Therapy

Historically, in clients and practitioners alike, the mainstream health care community has held the belief that illness can be categorized as either mental or physical. This duality, while still common, is slowly changing and the division between the psyche and soma is disappearing (Achterberg, 1985; Erskine, 1994; Lask & Fosson, 1989). As a massage therapist I have often witnessed the intimate relationship between mind and body.

Massage therapy is traditionally defined as the systematic application of various manual soft tissue manipulations which may positively affect the health of a client. These manipulations can influence numerous bodily systems including the musculoskeletal, circulatory, respiratory, lymphatic, nervous, endocrine, digestive, urinary, integumentary, immune, and limbic systems (Gerwitz, 1993; Koepfer, 1995; Zerinsky, 1987). Accordingly, there are countless indications for massage including, but not limited to, bone fracture, AIDS, heart disease, and Parkinson's disease (Gerwitz, 1993; Hungerford, 1992; Koepfer, 1995). However, there are additional functions of massage therapy which actively involve the client's psyche.

Although massage therapy is commonly recognized as a modality for treating somatic issues and reducing stress through relaxation, it has been successfully applied to address psychological disorders and concerns as well. Depression, recovery from substance and sexual abuse, and adjustment disorders have all benefited from regular massage therapy treatments (Baily, 1992; Fire, 1993; Koepfer, 1995). Even when treating physical concerns, the client's state of relaxation can facilitate the arousal of conscious and unconscious feelings concerning the injury. Often experienced as spontaneous emotional reactions or imagery, these events can serve to bridge the gap between emotional and bodily processes (Achterberg, 1985; Knaster, 1993; Koepfer, 1993; Loo, 1993; Lusebrink, 1990).

Imagery and emotional reactions may be welcome or intrusive events for clients and are, in my experience, usually relevant to the treatment issue at hand. For example, a particular stretch might remind a client of an instance when he or she was abused. If left unaddressed, a recollection such as this could sabotage rehabilitation by setting up a frightening transference in which the client places the therapist in the role of abuser. Conversely, the same stretch on a different client may facilitate an image of playing sports, an indication that the client may be mentally rehearsing for the day when rehabilitation is complete. Clients may also experience images which are based in memory or are metaphorical in nature, such as the wolf example cited earlier.

Images can often be used to address changing body image, provide motivation, and tap into the client's desire to heal (Landgarten, 1981; Koepfer, 1993). Exploration of these episodes can be a significant factor in developing a trusting therapeutic relationship and successful rehabilitation. Unfortunately, many of these experiences go undisclosed by clients and unaddressed by massage therapists who do not have the appropriate education to process them, nor resources to whom to refer clients. With proper training and education, the addition of art therapy and storytelling into a massage therapy treatment plan can provide opportunities to process imagery and emotional reactions thus attending to the person's psychological and physical needs (Koepfer, 1993; Loo, 1993).

Art Therapy

Art therapy is "a method of treatment in which the unique blending of art and therapeutic practice is used as a vehicle for exploring individual problems and potentials" (Farber, 1995, p. 74). Through the use of visual expression the client can begin to address his or her need to find meaning in their personal experiences while combating self-defeating attitudes and promoting self-empowerment. Art therapy can also facilitate the client's psychological adjustment by providing a safe container in which to work through the preceding emotional stages of denial, anger, and sadness (Landgarten, 1981).

Unlike verbal therapy, art therapy helps to elaborate the relationship between conscious, unconscious, and bodily processes by exploring emotions and imagery in the visual context in which they are originally experienced (Lusebrink, 1990; Wadeson, 1980). However, examining a client's emotional needs, particularly during a massage therapy session, must be done gradually and with sensitivity. Projection can bring forth emotional material quickly without cognitive censorship due to most clients' unfamiliarity with artistic communication (Hammer, 1980; Wadeson, 1980).

As a result, the therapist may see emotional indicators in the art before the client is aware of having projected them. When this occurs, it is important to keep in mind that therapists can also project and therefore, can not determine objectively what meaning is depicted in a drawing (Golomb, 1992; Moore, 1994). Of equal importance is that massage clients generally have lowered defenses and increased vulnerability due to the disrobing, touching, and relaxation which take place during a session. Therefore, it is imperative that the therapist view the interpretation of drawings as a conjoint process and allows the client to dictate the pace of exploration.

Wadeson (1980) states that creating art does provide a measure of safety for clients through objectification. The externalization of emotions in an art object allows the client to identify feelings while maintaining control over the distance he or she keeps from them (Wadeson, 1980). Clients often feel they can't reasonably verbalize what they have experienced thus, illustrating spontaneous imagery and emotions allows a client to explore feelings without the burden of translating the experiences into words. This can be especially beneficial for clients with speech difficulties. Furthermore, confusion and fear which often result from attempting to understand unclear diagnoses and difficult medical terminology can be defused through the creation of art. Visual expression allows for metaphorical exploration and understanding of the person's individual experiences with disability or injury (Koepfer, 1993).

Another benefit of art therapy is mental rehearsal. Creating an art piece can concretize imagery in which the client prepares for future events and improved health. Drawing future behaviors and activities can provide a motivational source as well as an opportunity for the client to rehearse risks and challenges which will be faced at later dates. Along with mental rehearsal, creating art requires active participation and allows the client to experience a sense of accomplishment and assume greater responsibility in their rehabilitation (Landgarten, 1981; Lusebrink, 1990). This will aid in confronting emotional and behavioral regression.

Visual expression can transcend mental rehearsal and address the physical needs of a client through actual behavior. Producing art is a means of engaging the body and providing mastery experiences (Landgarten, 1981; Robbins & Goffia-Girasek, 1987). For example, Durinda, the woman who visualized a wolf biting her shoulder, initiated the use of mural paper over the usual letter-size paper we had been previously using. This was significant in that it suggested she was unconsciously ready to risk increased movement in her shoulder by drawing on a larger scale. Her motivation was not consciously directed by a need to increase her mobility. Rather, she stated that she felt confined by the small paper.

Drawing on such a large scale provided her with a safe, controllable opportunity to test her improved range of motion.

Unique to art therapy is the idea of permanence. Through the creation of art objects the client has a means to record and track his or her progress and experiences in therapy (Landgarten, 1981; Wadeson, 1980). During the rehabilitation process, people often have difficulty seeing their progress in retrospect. Especially during times of relapse or setback. These artistic records can be viewed at future points in therapy as a means of validating the past progress. When storytelling is used to integrate the client's visual expressions with the overall rehabilitation experience, greater opportunities become available to the therapist and client.

Storytelling

Art therapy and storytelling have many similar advantages (Eldredge & Carrigan, 1992) which can compound to help the client find meaning in the injury experience and facilitate psychological adjustment. Telling personal stories during the rehabilitation process can assist in identifying characteristics of the specific injury while illuminating the client's beliefs about the injury and the outcome of rehabilitation (Viney, 1993). These stories can be self-empowering or self-defeating corresponding to the client's beliefs about disability and rehabilitation. However, comparable to mental rehearsal, the client's creation of a desirable ending to a story can provide motivation, instill hope, and facilitate self-empowering attitudes (Viney, 1993). These factors in conjunction with the active participation needed to create and tell stories can address emotional and behavioral regression.

Storytelling, like art therapy, relies on the therapeutic use of metaphor and projection which aid in the expression of conscious and unconscious processes (Eldredge & Carrigan, 1992; Kalt, 1986; Miller & Boe, 1990). Akin to artistic objectification is the degree of safety which comes with self expression through storytelling. The act of creating and verbalizing a personal story, fictitious or reality-based, provides an opportunity for sheltered expression of emotions (Crabbs, 1979; Eldredge & Carrigan, 1992; Miller & Boe, 1990). There are also added advantages to storytelling which are not present in visual expression.

Unlike to art therapy, storytelling allows the client to process and express their experiences in a familiar verbal forum. Furthermore, while an image and a story may both contain a specific message, a story is unique in that it has a beginning, a middle, and an end. A single drawn image may be considered a snapshot of moment in time while a story is not limited by constraints of time (Crabbs, 1979) and can encompass long or short periods of the persons rehabilitation. This is significant for two reasons. Storytelling can serve to integrate a timeline of multiple drawn images under the umbrella of the client's overall experience in therapy. Secondly, because of its lack of time limits, a single story can meet the emotional needs of a client by fluctuating with the journey towards adjustment.

Integral to the combination of art therapy and storytelling is that the visual expression occurs before verbal expression. If done in this sequence the benefits of storytelling can be greatly magnified (Eldredge & Carrigan, 1992). Wadeson (1980) states that the process of creating art often stimulates new images, thoughts, and ideas. If storytelling is used subsequent to art therapy, these new thoughts and their preceding visual expressions can both be processed in the familiar verbal medium. Furthermore, Foulkes (1977) suggests that once internal experiences are expressed non-verbally they are subsequently easier to express verbally (Eldredge & Carrigan, 1992). How then do we bring together art therapy, storytelling, and massage therapy?

Methodology

As we have seen, art therapy and storytelling are two methods which can be used to address the psychological needs of a person in rehabilitation as well as process imaginal and emotional reactions which often occur during massage therapy sessions. The challenge is to arrange a meaningful merger between the three modalities. The key principle in this endeavor is flexibility. Images and emotional reactions can surface at any point during a massage or not appear at all. Therefore, the therapist needs to be open to using art and storytelling at various points during treatment in accordance with the client's needs.

I generally begin each session with a brief autosuggestion relaxation exercise. This period of relaxation serves a few purposes. Through relaxation the client maintains an active role and can prepare for the sometimes painful physical manipulations which will be preformed during the massage (Koepfer, 1993). As the client becomes increasingly familiar with the relaxation and massage process it will become ritualized and increasingly easier to enter into states of relaxation quickly. Secondly, as Lusebrink (1990) maintains, "A relaxed state in turn is associated with an altered state of consciousness, which enhances the link between imagery, emotions, and bodily functions" (p. 218). Lastly, clients are oftentimes more aware of what they are feeling in their body while in a state of relaxation.

During the relaxation period clients may begin to have imagery or emotional reactions. If this is the case, art therapy can be used after the relaxation exercise to process any images or emotions which occurred. Once again, flexibility is the key. The client may or may not feet ready to process the experience or, if processed, the therapist may have to adjust the upcoming massage based on what is disclosed. For example, if any images were extremely emotional the therapist may opt to change from a deeper medical massage to a more soothing, supportive, non-invasive massage.

Whatever the case may be, a massage therapy session needs to be based on communication between the client and therapist. The therapist should always ask the client if the massage feels safe and comfortable. After the relaxation segment is complete and any reactions are processed the massage treatment begins. During this time the client has an opportunity to reflect on the previously drawn images. Additional images and emotional reactions may also occur during the massage which can be processed as well.

Storytelling is the unique aspect of this process in that it is not restricted to any single part of the session. Although one can't draw during a massage, ability to speak is not restricted. However, telling stories becomes integral for the processing and integration of the drawn images with the person's experience in rehabilitation. Oftentimes, life stories are told which will explain certain images. A story can mirror the events of a single session or build from week to week. Plots can change or they can be cliffhangers which do not reveal the endings until future points in therapy. There may be more than one story told throughout the rehabilitation process. Storytelling in this context can be as happy, sad, frightening, and fluid as the rehabilitation process itself.

In the following case material, in order to maintain consistency with this text, I will limit my discussion to how art therapy and storytelling were able to assist each client with addressing the emotional aspects of their rehabilitation experience. Although each client did receive regular medical massage therapy treatments, the specific massage methods are not relevant here. The reader should be aware however, that the following experiences did not occur independent of massage and that massage therapy did play a significant role in the subsequent improved health of these people.

Durinda: The Big Good Wolf?

By this point you are somewhat familiar with Durinda's story. She is a forty-seven-year-old, divorced white female. At the time of our meeting she was the aerobics director at a health club, actively engaged in strength training, and had a successful competition history as a body builder. Prior to her fitness career she was a choreographer and ballet dancer. Years before our meeting, Durinda had suffered a right rotator cuff tear which required surgery to repair. Subsequently, her range of motion (ROM) never reached full capacity. During our initial meeting, shoulder movement was extremely painful and she had poor ROM. Specifically with abduction and flexion, I suspect that over time, neglect and heavy weight training aggravated her already poor ROM.

Durinda and I had met for a few sessions prior to incorporating art and storytelling into her treatments. At one point I had asked her if she had ever experienced imagery during past sessions. She had. We decided to begin illustrating the images on a weekly basis. As it turned out, Durinda had tremendous artistic skill. The first image drawn was the one of the wolf cited

Figure 1

earlier in this chapter (Figure 1). One might suspect from viewing this image that in metaphorical terms the wolf was the cause of the frozen shoulder. On the contrary, however, the wolf was identified as an ally with an important message to give. This is very similar to the Native American shamanic belief in spirit allies who are couriers of knowledge and often appear to their human counterparts in the form of animals (Achterberg, 1985).

While processing the wolf image, which had appeared during the initial relaxation period, Durinda revealed that, unlike its appearance, she felt that the wolf had not really bitten her. Rather, she felt as though she had placed her shoulder in the wolf's mouth in order to muffle any unpleasant news it may have had to tell her. Unable to determine the wolf's message, we proceeded with the massage session.

After the completion of the massage Durinda disclosed and drew a new image which had appeared. The second image (Figure 2) was of Durinda floating in an oasis with the wolf watching protectively over her. Durinda stated that the wolf image was very strong and stayed with her throughout the entire massage. She also mentioned that once her shoulder was free from it's mouth it told her that she should not be afraid to take risks and begin moving

Figure 2

her shoulder. Durinda never drew the wolf again. However, she claimed that she often felt as though it were around to support her, much like a guardian angel.

It is important to note here that the symbolic interpretation of the wolf, nor of any other images for that matter, was not of great interest to Durinda and, therefore, not a primary goal. The wolf may have represented her need for the

Figure 3

therapist's support, her own desire to mobilize her shoulder, a spiritual ally, or all of the above. Likewise, other aspects of the drawing may have had numerous symbolic meanings. However, what or who the wolf represented, although certainly interesting, was not as important as the message and motivation it brought. Regardless of the specific symbolic interpretations, the images and story of a guardian wolf provided Durinda with a metaphoric realm in which to consider her personal experience in rehabilitation: Specifically the issue of taking the sometimes painful physical risks involved in re-mobilizing her shoulder. Drawing the images also allowed her to record the day's experience in therapy.

Figure 4

During the remaining months of her treatment many new images were drawn. Some were metaphorical descriptions of the pain she felt (Figure 3). Others were memories accompanied by life stories which also reflected her fear of taking risks. One week Durinda viewed an image of herself fearfully standing on a mountain top (Figure 4). The image was an early childhood memory of a time when her father took her hiking. As it turns out Durinda's father was an avid mountaineer and would often take her on hikes and climbs. Unfortunately however, when spots on the trail seemed too difficult for her and she did not wish to continue, her father would hike ahead leaving her alone with the message that she would find a way to keep going. Durinda had many memories of being left alone, fearful of moving forward or back, and crying on dangerous mountain trails.

It was no coincidence that this image manifested at a time when Durinda needed to take significant physical risks in order to move forward in therapy. The image and story provided a means for us to discuss the idea of risktaking and how important it is

Figure 5

for the rehabilitation of her shoulder. Importantly, it afforded me with the opportunity to understand how Durinda viewed risktaking and let her know that unlike her childhood experiences, she would be supported through the entire rehabilitation process.

Durinda used art for the purposes of mental rehearsal as well. In one instance she drew an image of what she would like to do when her shoulder was completely mobilized (Figure 5). The following week, as mentioned earlier, Durinda passed beyond mental rehearsal to actual behavior when she began drawing on a larger scale (Figure 6).

During Durinda's final session, at which point she had full ROM, we viewed all of her work which chronicled the story of her rehabilitation process. It showed her progression from immobilization (Figure 1) to movement (Figure 6). Viewing the separate images as a whole story allowed her to integrate her weekly experiences in rehabilitation with the improved ROM she was now experiencing, thus celebrating her success and reinforcing her decision to take risks.

Figure 6

Thomas: There Once Was a Man Who Swallowed a Spider

Thomas is a middle-aged single white male who began receiving massage therapy upon the recommendation of his physician. He was diagnosed with cervical radiculitis and occipital neuritis. Simply put, he had inflammation of the cervical nerve roots which resulted in consistent pain and stiffness in his neck and shoulders. According to Thomas, his pain was aggravated by stress and neither medication nor any other form of medical treatment had been able to help. He identified the precipitating injury as an incident a number of years ago when he strained his neck while chopping wood. Thomas also had occasional pain in his groin which doctors found to be idiopathic. Interestingly, Thomas had faked having an inguinal hernia in order to avoid going to Vietnam.

During our initial consultation I learned that Thomas was currently in his tenth year of sobriety. He worked for a resume preparation business and attended graduate school at night for his Masters Degree in English literature. Thomas appeared to have low self-esteem which was exacerbated by the facts that he had waited until middle-age to begin graduate school, and that he had not been able to publish any of his written work. After some time in treatment it was also disclosed that, as a child, he had been regularly sexually abused by a male adult member of his community. Additionally, his father, who committed suicide, had also been an alcoholic.

For Thomas, storytelling and art therapy played an extremely significant role in his rehabilitation. He had a positive reaction to my proposal that we explore possible emotional contributions to his physical health. The suggestion alone was validating because he had felt that stress was a primary cause of his pain and until that moment, nobody had ever suggested exploring emotional connections. Using art and storytelling in conjunction with massage therapy also stirred his creative interests. Being a writer, Thomas was very comfortable expressing himself metaphorically. In fact, he built a very intricate story around his experiences in therapy.

His story evolved from week to week, much like a soap opera. Unlike Durinda, who allowed the images to manifest spontaneously on their own, Thomas often initiated his own imagery based on how he was feeling that day or where the previous week's story left off. The inspirations for his story came from images he experienced during relaxation and massage as well as his own life experiences. Thomas actively used metaphor to explore and understand how his feelings about his body, sobriety, his father's suicide, and his childhood sexual abuse all played a role in his current state of physical health.

Thomas' story began during a relaxation period early in therapy. He had initially observed an image of a spider living in his neck. Much like Durinda's wolf, the spider eventually became an ally and protector. The spider image was present for a number of weeks and in his story, Thomas labeled it as the cause of his pain (Figure 7). The spider would migrate throughout Thomas' neck, shoulders, and groin causing pain wherever it ventured (Figure 8). During one session, Thomas described his relationship with the spider in writing and in doing so began to disclose his deeper feelings about his painful condition:

Figure 7

> The spider said "Ha, ha, even though I've wasted my time in your body, I've been successful in nearly destroying you !" I said, "You've had your way with me long enough. Now it's time for you to go." The spider clung on for dear life and didn't want to let go, leaving me to believe that he had really chosen me, and it wasn't a mistake that he had spent so much time in my body. The spider felt he had really chosen a worthy subject. Had I not been worthy, he would not have spent so much time terrorizing me.

Figure 8

In his imagery, Thomas attempted to evict the spider by placing it in a box and throwing it away (Figures 9–10). From Thomas' story, I suspected that on some level he believed that he deserved the pain he was receiving from the spider. Although the spider did not reappear in Thomas' imagery until some months later, the issue of punishment would soon solidify as the theme of his story.

For a few weeks after the eviction of the spider, Thomas claimed that his neck pain had almost disappeared and his groin pain had stopped altogether. However, the pain returned during the upcoming months in which Thomas faced both his father's birthday and his own anniversary of sobriety. During these months it was difficult for Thomas to do art therapy or explore his imagery as he felt to vulnerable. Therefore, many sessions were restricted to only massage therapy and storytelling. During these sessions he told many life stories which further explained why he believed that he deserved the pain he was experiencing.

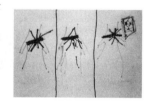

Figure 9

Figure 10

Thomas held tremendous shame regarding his own alcoholism and childhood sexual abuse. He believed that he was a terrible son and responsible for his father's alcoholism and suicide. As an adolescent, Thomas was bounced out of numerous high schools for poor behavior. He had been arrested for driving while intoxi-

Figure 11

Figure 12

Figure 13

Figure 14

cated and felt as if he were a failure. His father was a successful lawyer who had very high expectations and Thomas felt as though he let him down. The apex of Thomas' shame and self-blame came when he was twenty-five years old and had to identify the body after his father committed suicide. Thomas admitted that he wanted to change his outlook, however he believed that the physical pain he was now experiencing was punishment for his past behaviors.

A few weeks before his anniversary date, Thomas was again experiencing intense pain in his neck and wanted to explore some imagery he had during the relaxation portion of the session. He had again sighted the spider. This time however, the spider was hanging from a web in a cave which Thomas identified as a metaphor for his own mind (Figure 11). In this image he could not see inside the cave but was very curious about it's contents. During the subsequent weeks Thomas recalled the image, but was afraid to walk past the spider and explore the contents of the cave. However, his final attempt at entering the cave yielded different results.

The week of his anniversary Thomas said that as he viewed the cave in his imagery (Figure 12), there were now two spiders who seemed to be cleaning the cave. They had a much different manner about them and contrary to the previous spider's role of punisher, seemed to be guardians or keepers of the cave. Thomas was still afraid to enter the cave so he decided to create an image of himself with a miner's helmet on and a rope tied around his waist. In his imagery he tied the other end of the rope to a tree and entered the cave (Figure 13). Upon entering Thomas saw an image of various angry parts of his personality "throwing out" the "bad" self-blaming part of himself (Figure 14). While we were processing these images, Thomas verbalized that he would no longer punish himself and that he did not deserve the pain he was feeling.

It is interesting to note that on his tenth anniversary, there were ten figures in the image. Additionally, these recent drawings reflected Thomas' growing courage and self-esteem. They were much more confident and colorful than his previous work indicating more emotional involvement (Hammer, 1980; Robbins & Goffia-Girasek, 1987; Wadeson, 1980). Demonstrating his willingness to take risks, Thomas chose to use oil pastels, which had always been available to him rather than pencils and markers he had previously used. Unlike pencils and markers which are safe, controllable media, oil pastels are more difficult to control and often intimidating to persons unfamiliar with them (Hammer, 1980; Robbins & Goffia-Girasek, 1987; Wadeson, 1980). Thomas never again used pencils or markers.

Over the next few months Thomas' health continued to improve and the pain in his neck and groin significantly decreased. During this time he wanted to focus primarily on the massage treatments and dispense with the art therapy and storytelling unless he saw any images he considered to be significant. During his final weeks in therapy, Thomas saw two very significant images which validated his decision to stop punishing himself, provided closure to our time together, and created a positive ending to his story.

The first image which Thomas observed was one which he had while receiving massage to his neck. The image was of an ant farm (Figure 15). After the massage Thomas drew the ant farm and we processed it for any possible symbolic meanings. Thomas was confused and not sure what an ant farm had to do with his neck pain which, at this point, was very mild. We proceeded to discuss the concept of an ant farm when he realized that an art farm can't exist unless someone feeds the ants. In other words, the ant farm was a metaphor for his pain, and if he stopped feeding the pain, like the ants, it would cease to exist.

The absence of pain had lasted for some time. Thomas felt that he had achieved his goal and regular massage therapy was no longer needed. I supported his decision and we decided upon a date for termination. A few weeks later, on his last day, Thomas came to therapy with a dream he had the previous night. He wished to imagine it during the relaxation period and process it afterward. As it turns out, the dream provided a wonderful ending to Thomas' rehabilitation experience and was the

Figure 15

conclusion to his story. It served beautifully to integrate his previous experiences and indicate his movement towards a healthier future.

The dream was depicted in an drawing (Figure 16) which illustrated Thomas leaving a church where he had just been to confession. He had disclosed to a priest the shame and self-blame he had been carrying for so long. Thomas believed that leaving the church through the graveyard indicated that he was finally putting his father's death behind him. Symbolizing the primary goal of his therapy, Thomas left his old pain-ridden head and neck sitting on a tree stump in the graveyard. He took with him a new pain-free head. In the dream

Figure 16

he left the graveyard with an unidentified Asian man. He did not know who the man was, however he believed him to be a supportive figure.

We explored the possibility that the figure might represent myself. The fact that he left the church with a supportive person may reflect the support he felt from me during his therapeutic journey. Although I am not Asian, Thomas was aware that I am very active in the Asian martial arts. Additionally, at that time, my office had been decorated with Asian art. The figure may have had many other symbolic meanings. Regardless of the figure's symbolism however, it allowed us to process, and bring closure to, our time spent together.

Prior to writing this chapter, I followed up on Thomas' progress. It has been two years since our last session. He is actively maintaining sobriety and has had no relapses of his radiculitis or neuritis. Having completed his master's degree he now teaches English at a local college and has published some of his writing as well.

Barbara: The Weight of the What On My Shoulders?

Barbara is a thiry-two-year-old single white female who makes her living as a disk jockey at various local night clubs. As a result of carrying heavy music equipment and consistently listening to her headphones through one ear (by holding them between her ear and shoulder), Barbara developed severe back and neck pain.

Barbara's rehabilitation consisted primarily of medical massage therapy although she did, on occasion, experience imagery which we processed through art therapy and storytelling. Unlike the two previous cases, Barbara's stories never encompassed more than the single session in which they were created. However, they did provide some valuable opportunities for Barbara to get an idea of how her emotions could contribute to her physical health.

On more than one occasion Barbara and I had processed imagery together. One particular session stands out as a powerful example of how emotions can perpetuate physical suffering and processing imagery can bridge the gap between the two realms. Barbara came to this particular session, which was the day before Mother's Day, feeling extremely tense with abnormally severe pain in her neck and shoulders. She could not think of any preceding physical activity which may have intensified her pain. We proceeded with the relaxation portion of our session.

During the relaxation, Barbara viewed an image of herself lying nude inside a cage (Figure 17). She described the cage as a safe comfortable place made of white wood, almost like a womb. There were no locks on the cage, and she had the impression that she could get out if she tried. Nevertheless, she couldn't figure out how. In the drawing of her image she omitted the arms and legs of the figure, focusing primarily on a bloated abdominal area.

Figure 17

After briefly drawing and describing the image to me, we proceeded with her massage during which she saw additional images. After the massage, which focused primarily on her neck and shoulders, she drew the additional imagery she had experienced. During the subsequent imagery she decided to have a conversation with the cage (during an earlier session I had suggested that she might use this technique if she experienced any imagery). She said that the cage turned out to be her mother who had died years ago of abdominal cancer. This would explain the womb-like feeling of the cage and the bloated stomach of the figure.

The new image which she had observed was that of her mother hugging her (Figure 18). This image was drawn in a warm pink and like the previous figure, accentuated the abdominal area and omitted the arms and legs. Barbara felt as though this was the first time she had a positive experience while thinking about her mother since she died. She claimed that she never really felt that her mother's death "was okay" and that she usually dreaded Mother's Day.

During the imagery experience, Barbara had a conversation in which her mother told her that her death was "okay" and that everything was fine. Barbara described the conversation as "weird" because not a single word was actually spoken. In place of words, images appeared such as a heart and a flower

Figure 18

which let her know what her mother was saying. Barbara left the session that day feeling relaxed, pain-free, and thankful for having had the opportunity to change the ending of what had been a very long painful story in her life.

As with Durinda, Barbara was not interested in interpreting the images. In this case it was important to accept the images at face value, provide support, and allow Barbara to hear the message that was unfolding in the story. After listening to this story and seeing these images it was plain to see that Barbara's anxiety about Mother's Day was expressed somatically through her increased neck and shoulder pain. If these images had not been processed, Barbara may not have the opportunity to fully address the cause of her increased neck pain.

Conclusion

As Lask and Fosson (1989) posit, wellness might better be described as a continuum in which there is no division between mental and physical health.

Rather, health concerns could be viewed as falling somewhere on this continuum with psychic and somatic contributions playing joint roles. As demonstrated by the previous case studies, emotions can contribute to the story of one's physical health.

Through art therapy and storytelling, therapists and clients can begin to explore ways of bridging the gap between psychological and physical medicine. The desegregation of emotional and bodily processes can provide many benefits for people with injuries or disabilities. This is especially true in the case of massage therapy. The state of relaxation which occurs during massage treatments may facilitate an altered state of consciousness in which spontaneous images and emotional reactions can occur. These experiences open a door for the exploration of psychological contributions to the perceptions and perpetuating factors of the injury or disability at hand. Through the use of symbols and metaphor, storytelling and art therapy both provide a container in which the client can safely progress through the psychological stages of adjustment and begin to gain an increased understanding of his or her own experiences with injury and rehabilitation.

References

Achterberg, J. (1985). *Imagery in healing: Shamanism and modern medicine.* Boston: New Science Library/Shambhala.

Baily, K. (1992). Therapeutic massage with survivors of abuse. *Massage Therapy Journal, 31,* 79–85, 116–120.

Crabbs, M. A. (1979). Fantasy in career development. *Personnel and Guidance Journal, 57,* 292–295.

Eldredge, N., & Carrigan, J. (1992). Where do my kindred dwell? Using art and storytelling to understand the transition of young Indian men who are deaf. *Arts in Psychotherapy, 19,* 29–38.

Erskine, A. (1994). The initial contact: Assessment for counseling in the medical context. In A. Erskine, & D. Judd (Eds.), *The imaginative body* (pp. 43–59). Northvale, NJ: Jason Aronson.

Falvo, D. R. (1995). Psychological adjustment. In A. E. D. Orto, & R. P. Marinelli (Eds.), *Encyclopedia of disability and rehabilitation* (pp. 599–605). New York: Macmillan Library Reference USA.

Farber, D. (1995). Art therapy. In A. E. D. Orto, & R. P. Marinelli (Eds.), *Encyclopedia of disability and rehabilitation* (pp. 74–76). New York: Macmillan Library Reference USA.

Fire, M. (1993). Providing massage therapy in a psychiatric hospital. *Massage Therapy Journal, 32,* 76–77.

Foulkes, W. E. (1977). *The principles of art psychotherapy.* Unpublished manuscript.

Garner, R. L. (1996). The NAT model: Factors in neuropsychological art therapy. *American Journal of Art Therapy, 34,* 107–111.

Gerwitz, D. (Ed.). (1993). *Touchpoints: Touch research abstracts* (Vol. 1). Miami: Touch Research Institute, University of Miami School of Medicine.

Golomb, C. (1992). *The child's creation of a pictorial world.* Berkeley: University of California Press.

Hammer, E. F. (1980). *The clinical application of projective drawings* (6th ed.). Springfield, IL: Charles C Thomas.

Hungerford, M. (1992). A patient's notes: Massage therapy after open heart surgery. *Massage Therapy Journal, 31,* 71–72.

Kalt, H. W. (1986). The construction of therapeutic allegories. *American Journal of Psychoanalysis, 46,* 33–44.

Knaster, M. (1993, March/April). Massaging out bad memories. *Natural Health,* pp. 42–43.

Koepfer, S. R. (1993, July). Enhancing massage therapy through use of the image. *New York State Society of Medical Massage Therapists, Inc.,* pp. 14–17.

Koepfer, S. R. (1995). Massage therapy. In A. E. D. Orto, & R. P. Marinelli (Eds.), *Encyclopedia of disability and rehabilitation* (pp. 454–456). New York: Macmillan Library Reference USA.

Landgarten, H. B. (1981). *Clinical art therapy: A comprehensive guide.* New York: Brunner/Mazel.

Lask, B., & Fosson, A. (1989). *Childhood illness: The psychosomatic approach. Children talking with their bodies.* New York: John Wiley & Sons.

Loo, N. (Producer/Reporter). (1993, May 10). *New York living health report.* New York: New York 1 News.

Lusebrink, V. B. (1990). *Imagery and visual expression in therapy.* New York: Plenum Press.

Miller, C., & Boe, J. (1990). Tears into diamonds: Transformations of child psychic trauma through sandplay and storytelling. *Arts in Psychotherapy, 17,* 247–257.

Moore, M. S. (1994). Reflections of self: The use of drawings in evaluating and treating physically ill children. In A. Erskine, & D. Judd (Eds.), *The imaginative body* (pp. 113–144). Northvale, NJ: Jason Aronson.

Robbins, A., & Goffia-Girasek, D. (1987). Materials as an extension of the holding environment. In A. Robbins (Ed.), *The Artist as Therapist* (pp. 104–115). New York: Human Sciences Press.

Stein, D. G. (1988). In pursuit of new strategies for understanding recovery from brain damage: Problems and perspective. In T. Bolls, & B. K. Bryant (Eds.), *Clinical neuropsychology and brain function: Research, measurement and practice* (pp. 9–55). Washington, DC: American Psychological Association.

Tart, C. T. (Ed.). (1992). *Transpersonal psychologies: Perspectives on the mind from seven great spiritual traditions* (3rd ed.). San Francisco: HarperSanFrancisco

Viney, L. L. (1993). *Life stories: Personal construct therapy with the elderly.* West Sussex, England: John Wiley & Sons.

Wadeson, H. (1980). *Art psychotherapy.* New York: John Wiley & Sons.

Zalidis, S. (1994). The value of emotional awareness in general practice. In A. Erskine, & D. Judd (Eds.), *The imaginative body: Psychodynamic therapy in health care* (pp. 180–199). Northvale, NJ: Jason Aronson.

Zerinsky, S. S. (1987). *Introduction to pathology for the massage therapist.* New York: Swedish Institute for Massage Therapy and Allied Health Sciences.

CHAPTER SIXTEEN

Finding Wholeness:
A Tale of Writing and Sharing

Patricia Perrine

My mother used to tell me I always do things the hard way. I'm afraid that's true, because I find it very hard to take on faith other people's instructions. For me, experience is a sometimes difficult, but always effective teacher. A lot of what I know about stories that heal comes from being there; hearing the stories and telling them myself. So I'll start out by telling you a story.

I didn't know what to do. It was August, in my third year of graduate school, and my brain had become a stranger. Classes would begin again at the end of September, and now I couldn't follow a logical argument if my life depended on it. Granted, my intuition and emotional understanding had never been better, but that wasn't so helpful when you had to construct a coherent discussion about states of consciousness!

I kept reminding myself that it was because of the medication. I was being treated, post-surgically, with Lupron Depot, a powerful drug that induced a temporary menopause. What I hadn't known when I chose this treatment was how it would turn my understanding of myself upside down. This was graduate education on the experiential level, and it was a very effective teacher.

In retrospect, going through three months of menopause at age thirty-five was a real gift. It was a rite of passage into a much deeper knowledge of my abilities and gifts as a woman. It sharpened my understanding that my life's work was to work with and learn from women. It was in my healing process that I began to see how important storytelling would be to that work.

Storytelling to Heal

Healing is defined as "a making whole" (Skeat, 1911, p. 235). It took my body about a year to fully recover from the trauma of my six hours in the operating room. My experience of recovery, from the surgery and the subsequent drug treatment, could not be simply focused on my body. Healing the emotional and psychic trauma was essential for me, and this took much longer. Although my doctor had prescribed a regime of medicines for my body, I found that telling the story of my illness and surgery led to the far more important healing — knowing more deeply who I was.

It might be because I spent so much time alone as a youngster that stories became so important to me. The *Oxford English Dictionary* reminds us that the word "story" is derived from "history" and tells us that it means "a recital of events that have or are alleged to have happened" (1971, p. 1041). But from the time I learned to read, I knew the truth of what Ursula LeGuin (1989, p. 40) asserts — that a story needn't be factual to be "true." In the world of books, I could learn about places and ways of living very different from what I knew. Joanna Spyri's (1952) Heidi took me to the Alps, and showed me her life there. I could also see that behavior could follow other models than what my family had shown me. Pippi Longstocking was a cheerful and energetic nonconformist who always managed to land on her feet (Lindgren, 1950). Learning diversity is a very important part of stories. However, simply reading stories or even listening to them does not have the same effect as telling them.

What Value is There in *Telling* Stories?

In the book *Women's Ways of Knowing*, the collective comprised of Mary Belenky, Blythe Clinchy, Nancy Goldberger and Jill Tarula (1986) wrote "all women grow up having to deal with historically- and culturally-engrained definitions of femininity and womanhood — one common theme being that women, like children, should be seen and not heard" (p. 5). It is this silencing that underscores the importance to women (and to men as well) of being able to tell stories to others. Telling a story and being listened to validates that we and our words are worthy. By telling a story, I assert that what I am saying is worthy of speech. This means that I take my experience seriously enough to share it. The fact that you are listening to me means that you agree (at least enough to listen). These factors enhance our self-confidence and self-esteem, important at every developmental stage.

There are tasks of logic and judgment involved as well. Before I can even begin to tell you my story, I must at least have the confidence that I can narrate a sequence of events which you will be able to understand. I must also have judged in some way that this story is appropriate or important for me to tell you.

The story I tell makes a connection between the past (the event about which the story is told) and the present (me telling the story and you listening to it). As we tell stories from the past, we remember that time. As we speak, we notice how our listeners are responding, which at times can shift our attention to what we are saying: their presence seems to give us a new pair of eyes. We can now listen to our own stories with a little bit of distance. This gives us a different perspective on what we have experienced. Before telling the story, we were just in it. Now, we are both in it and looking at it. Creating a distance between ourselves and our stories allows us to take on the ability to witness our own actions.

As I told my friends about my illness, I could no longer make light of it or ignore that something important had happened to me. I had to readjust my image of myself from someone who was always healthy, to someone who had been sick enough to need surgery. In seeing their responses I drew back enough to look at myself in a new way. As we tell stories of our past, sometimes it takes this distance in order to apply newly gathered wisdom and experience. For example, in telling a story of our childhood as an adult, we can understand parts of the experience that we could not understand as children. In turn, this allows us to learn more about the event we are narrating.

Telling the stories of endometriosis led to talking about its symptoms, which include severe menstrual cramps. Now, from the perspective of someone who had been diagnosed with, and treated for, an illness, my perception had shifted enough that I could reevaluate symptoms I had been having since I was sixteen. In a flash, I went from someone who had suffered a capricious fate to someone who had a long undiagnosed condition. The story had shifted both my image and my understanding of what happened in the past, like one domino hitting another. Learning had taken place.

I've been discussing stories that we tell about ourselves, but similar events occur when we tell stories about our families and family members. One of the tragedies of dysfunctional families is that there are stories about the family that are kept secret. Frequently, in these situations, telling any kind of family story runs the risk of revealing "too much" and so all personal stories become forbidden. This is a great loss, because it cuts us off from the knowledge of how we were shaped, and who we are. Not only do those family members learn not to tell the stories of pain and abuse, but even the stories of joy and triumph are forbidden. Adrienne Rich (1977) reminds us "where language and naming are power, silence is oppression, is violence" (pp. xiv–xxiv). We have seen in the last twenty years how alcoholism has gradually been changed from an unspeakable weakness to a condition that is amenable to control. For example, through participation in the twelve-step group Alcoholics Anonymous, alcoholics share the stories of their lives and condition, and in hearing and telling stories come to find they are not alone. Perhaps because of AA's successes, other "unspeakable" tales — of child abuse, spouse abuse, and sexual harassment — are now being told.

The old saw goes that "he who does not know history is doomed to repeat it" and this can be true in these families. Just as telling stories can reinforce self-esteem, not telling stories can contribute to a loss in self-esteem, and certainly, to an increase in feelings of alienation, despair, and pain. These are often the very traits that can lead people into using forms of anesthetization (drugs, alcohol, food, sex) that can spiral into further dysfunction. The interaction of storytelling, and the validation of the storyteller's tale by listeners is crucial in ending the psychic distress that people suffer because they feel alienated and alone.

A very important contribution of twelve-step self-help groups of all kinds is that they provide time and space in which people have permission and encouragement to tell their stories: good and bad, painful and hopeful — all kinds of stories are allowed. My own participation in a twelve-step program taught me a great deal about how healing telling stories can be. Week after week, I sat with about twenty-five other people in the kitchen of a local church hall. We would listen to one another telling the stories that made up our lives — stories of the pain we had endured and of the pain we had inflicted as well as stories of the triumphs of overcoming destructive behavior patterns. Taking responsibility for our actions (and making amends when necessary) is a big part of the work in a twelve-step program. The first part of that is in coming to see ourselves clearly: when we have been victims and when we have lashed out to become victimizers. Hearing and telling many stories allowed us bit by bit, to see how our attitudes affected our behavior. We came to see that changing the attitude changed the behavior.

Over the course of several months of seeing the same faces, I became aware that the patterns of various individuals' stories (myself included) were changing. It seemed that telling these stories gave us the distance from them that we needed to truly see ourselves. Only then could we make changes: to how we understood our stories, and changes to the attitudes and behaviors and changes to new stories. In learning to tell our stories to others, we were taking the authority to alter those stories to alter our lives.

Writing the Stories

Telling stories has a particular kind of power but, as Westerners, we belong to a literate society. We have lost the ability of oral cultures to weave deeply complex tales solely in the oral medium. For us, as William Zinsser (1988) says, "writing is thinking on paper" (p. 11). Writing is a form of storytelling which can allow us to take our stories to greater depth, to more fully reveal the complexity in human endeavor.

In the summer of 1988 I was thirty. The previous two years had been filled with changes as I took the time and energy to look at my life, telling my stories to my therapist and in my weekly twelve-step meetings. I had regained interests long submerged and now had the willingness and resources to pursue them. One of these was an interest in holistic living, which drew me to the Omega Institute, in Rhinebeck, New York. I was registered for two of their workshops that summer. One was a spiritual retreat, which I hoped would give me clear direction on what my spiritual path should be. The other was a writing workshop I was taking "just for fun." With the frequent irony of such events, it was the writing workshop which opened up pathways that to this day I am still following.

The group I was in was about half men and half women. Each writing session followed a specific ritual procedure: we sat quietly and composed ourselves, and then lit a candle. At this point, the workshop leader would hit the play button on the tape player, and quiet music would begin. It had been explained that the music had a particular rhythm, sixty beats per minute, which would help us to relax. We had been instructed in a form of "free writing: putting our pens or pencils to paper and writing continuously for the period — no editing, just the flow of thoughts being put down on paper.

After each writing session we took turns reading our work aloud. We were carefully coached on positive feedback styles, which soon took the form of people reflecting back to the writer the effects their words had on the listener. Often this took the form of validation: "Oh, something like that happened to me when ..." "Yes, I know exactly what you mean ..." Sometimes the room would catch the giggles, and sometimes there was the deep silence of sadness and pain, as the account being read reminded the listeners of their own times of darkness. It was a remarkable experience, listening to each voice so recently heard only in the writers' head. Each round of writing and reading aloud increased the feeling of trust in the room. I recall listening to Alex reading his painful confession of his need to compete with the other men in the room, lamenting that he could not simply accept the pain in the other men's writing, but feeling compelled to display his own pain as if to say "I'm in more pain than you." And in the next writing session, I heard the responses of other men, both agreeing and taking issue with Alex's statements. Their voices expanded on the pressure and hurt caused by the constant need to prove themselves, even to compete in not competing! It was powerfully moving, this revelation of men's often hidden pain.

As the days passed, the pieces I wrote gradually went deeper. The trust that was building in the environment of the writing group was reinforced by the natural beauty that surrounded us. Omega is located in the gentle mountains north of New York City, and is surrounded by gracious old forests. Being in the midst of this beauty began to remind me of something special that seemed obscured, as though veiled by the morning mist over the pond near my campsite. On the fourth day, as we wrote I entered an almost dreamlike state, and my pencil flew over the paper. That writing period seemed both infinitely long and as short as a breath.

This writing was different from the other pieces I had written that week. It was poetic, more impressionistic. As I read it to the group, unexpectedly my voice began to quaver, and tears came to my eyes. I had not known how deeply ran my bereavement over moving away from our farm when I was seven. When I finished reading, there was a silence, the kind in which people who are far away are gradually brought back to their bodies. It felt to me as if I had cast a spell with my words, had invoked memories of place for each person there. As my fellow writers found their voices they shared their recollections of their own very special places, some often revisited, and others lost forever. Their responses confirmed my tremulous belief that what I had written had true power.

Over the next few years, I worked on that piece, and finally titled it "My Heart's Home." It would be eight years after its writing, before I would learn whose voice was speaking through that spontaneous writing.

Someone once told me "be careful what you ask for, because you will get it." I had gone to Omega looking for my "way." What I found out was that, like Dorothy in *The Wizard of Oz*, I didn't really need to go anywhere to get home — I was already there. I knew that telling stories had healing power. What I learned in that workshop was a form I hadn't known: the process of writing and sharing. By continuing to work with this, I came to learn its rewards, not only for myself but for others as well.

The Varieties of Writing Experience

I have long been puzzling out what makes the combination of writing and sharing such a powerful one. In itself, that question is too big to easily yield its secrets. So, it means looking at each component separately. I've already discussed some of the important aspects of storytelling, especially about the importance of the interaction of the teller and the listener; how telling a story can engender a "witness" state in the teller; and how we can learn new things about an event by telling about it.

Those elements can be present in written accounts as well, but it depends on what kind of writing we are talking about. In the Omega workshop, I learned that writing could be an effective form of storytelling for healing. However, we had been engaged in a particular kind of writing. William Zinsser (1988) describes two different kinds of writing — explanatory and exploratory. Andre Virly (Personal communication, November 3rd, 1995) adds a third: evocative. The three types of writing range over a continuum from logical and rational to emotional and intuitive.

According to Zinsser (1988), explanatory writing is "writing that transmits existing information or ideas. ... [It] is what most people need to get through the day, both as writers and as readers. Its sole purpose is to inform; it has no deeper content that the writer will discover in the act of writing" (p. 56). Exploratory writing on the other hand, is "writing that enables us to discover what we want to say. ... [It is a] voyage of discovery into the self. Only by going into uncharted territory can a writer find his potential and his voice and his meaning. Meaning, in fact, doesn't exist until a writer goes looking for it" (pp. 56–57). Although Zinsser makes some useful distinctions here, I would note that there is certainly overlap. The kind of explanatory writing that appears in this article for example, has certainly led me to discovery of deeper content.

Virly's (1995) category of evocative writing incorporates self-discovery and information. In that respect, it may be seen as a hybrid of Zinsser's categories.

As a writer begins to write, she may be engaged in explanatory writing (how I came to be a writer) or exploratory (what kind of a person am I?). In either of these kinds of writing, the writer may tap into imagination, memories, imaginal realms, and sometimes into unconscious and archetypal material. Successful evocative writing is distinguished from exploratory and explanatory writing by an emotional component that moves the writer (and the reader) beyond a solely rational or intellectual response to the material. This is the language of poetry, drama, mythology, and ritual. It is helpful here to note that "evoke" means "to call forth" (Skeat, 1911, p. 173) and is related to "invoke: to call upon" (p. 267) and "vocal: uttering sound" (p. 595); these are etymological clues to how writing and reading aloud may be connected.

Both fiction and non-fiction can employ evocative writing. Examples of this kind of non-fiction writing can be found in the work of naturalists Barry Lopez (1989) and Annie Dillard (1974). Not only do these keen observers teach us about aspects of the environment, but in an almost hypnotic writing style they evoke a moving experience in the reader. Ursula LeGuin is a master of this form in her works of speculative fiction, taking us to times and places far removed from our daily reality.

How Does Writing Promote Healing?

Each type of writing described above has its own kind of healing power. Explanatory writing allows us to gather together what we see as the "facts" of a situation into an understandable context. We connect the unfamiliar with the familiar, and in so doing, learn how they are related to one another. Putting the facts in a row, so to speak, can help us understand the relationship of cause and effect. For example, "I am interested in storytelling because as a child stories were an important source of information and a form of escape."

There is a quality of certainty in explanatory writing that is comforting: knowing how things work and where we fit in protects us from the fear of the inexplicable. This is a kind of conceptual map-building which allows us to place ourselves in our world — writing which makes sense of our world. It is this quality of certainty which is at the edge of healing. On one hand it provides a useful stability for us — after all, a house cannot stand without a foundation. However, especially at times of crisis, the explanatory maps that we have developed for ourselves may prove inadequate. If we cling too tightly to any one story, it will take extreme measures for us to revise our views.

My husband went through much of his early life believing that his intelligence would be sufficient to bring him satisfaction in his work and in his relationships. But in his mid-thirties, this belief began to break down as he witnessed the death of his intelligent but angry and embittered father, saw how his own relationships mirrored those of his father, and how in both cases, intelligence had not been enough to secure happiness. As with many men confronting mid-life, my husband had to go through a period of extreme turmoil as the old maps, the old certainties were torn away. Gradually, he found a new understanding of himself based on a broader range of values and a new stability emerged.

When the old maps no longer work, when we feel the foundations begin to shift, but we don't know why, exploratory writing can help. Either explicitly or implicitly, exploratory writing has as its basis a question that the writer is asking of herself. This is especially healing when the writer needs to be able to distinguish what she thinks as opposed to what others think.

Suzannah, one of the participants in my workshops captures this well: "So much of the time not being able to say what I see, accustoming myself to not speaking from the truth. Here is a way, a place to become accustomed to that manner of speaking. To remember to grow the rooms in my life, the world to create that, hollows under large rooted trees for people to gather, go in and find a true voice. Why does writing do that for some of us, because it is quiet? Because we are not stopped mid-sentence, because the brain connects to the hand, because at some point the outer voice became disconnected, severed, the inner voice became unavailable to the mechanism of speaking. ... My brain-hand connection working better than my brain-mouth connection (or is it heart-mouth, heart hand?), is it like that for a lot of women?"

The style of writing that Suzannah uses begins in an exploratory mode but moves quickly into the evocative mode. Her language is poetic, impressionistic, with a rhythm and sense of repetition that is almost hypnotic. Her profound image of "hollows under large rooted trees for people to gather" prefigures a later statement: "This workshop affirmed that writing can be a way to connect with self and others ..." Early in the piece she writes of the disconnection of an inner voice and an outer voice. Later, this disconnection comes full circle into connection as she links gathering with going in to find a true voice. These are fertile images that over time can connect with other experiences, other images, to weave a very meaningful story from a very deep place within, beyond the awareness of usual waking consciousness.

As the study of dreams has taught us, symbolic images are powerful in that they mean so much more than simply "this equals that." Their power lies in their multiplicity of meaning. In one workshop, the image of the spider appeared in one woman's writing. In the next round, another woman picked up the image, applying it to her own life and to all the participants in the workshop: "Suspended in time — like a spider hanging on her thread, waiting for the breeze that will take her to a point of contact, my pen waits above the paper. Suspended in time, I breathe, and allow the words to form lines, and sentences, to lead me on, to lead me back, sometimes to lead me astray. Like elements in suspension, the thoughts slowly or quickly settle, becoming words, ideas, points of contact, connecting points in a web, our writings relate and interrelate, there is a flow to the revelations where each one's contribution adds, amplifies, and clarifies the rest. Weaving one big story, herstory, we become womankind listening to herself, dreaming." By the end of the workshop, all of the participants became aware that we had been woven together in a creative community web. As we returned to our daily lives, each of us had a different sense of ourselves, as writers and as weavers.

Giving Voice to the Written Word

The power of each type of writing is reinforced by reading aloud what has been written. Storytelling ranges along a continuum from the private to the public. At first you think about the story, then perhaps you write it down. Even though you may be thinking of a reader as you write, and your writing is shaped by what you assume the response to be, the story is still private to you. If you tell the story to one other person, it becomes a little more public, and you get the immediate interaction of a listener. When you read the story to a group of people, you are stepping still further out into the public eye. Now you have a variety of responses that range from the body language of your listeners as you read, to comments they may make about your story. You have clear evidence that you are not alone.

As my Omega group wrote and shared repeatedly over the course of the week, what became evident was how similar our hopes and fears were. We all worried about being somehow unacceptable to those around us. We had all suffered loss. We all hoped to find fulfilling relationships. We had even overcome assumptions about the opposite gender. In themselves, these are not earth-shaking revelations. But in the atmosphere of vulnerability and trust we had developed, hearing the particularity of each individual's stories led to a very powerful and immediate recognition of our mutual humanness.

This became startlingly clear in an unusual way. One of the participants was a woman who had been born and raised in France. She had written and read several of her pieces to the group, translating them from French to English as she read. What she wrote about was interesting enough, but there was no strong impact there. However, in one session the workshop leader suggested she read her writing as it had been written in French. Few of us in the room understood French, but even fewer did not understand the emotional impact of Elise's story as she read it. Her voice as she read in French had a whole range of nuances we did not hear when she read in English, and her body language communicated forcibly her pain of being so far away from the land of her youth. I felt a visceral resonance with her as she spoke, and in looking around the room at the faces of the others, some in tears, I knew I wasn't alone in feeling this connection.

Somehow, the act of reading aloud made connections for the writer and the listeners that writing alone just did not have. It seems like a kind of magic, a mysterious force that arises from the alchemy of breath and voice. In my continuing quest to understand just what goes on in this writing/sharing process, I sent questionnaires to women who had participated in workshops that used this format. I asked them what it meant in their lives to participate in such a workshop with other women. The answers I received were moving, and reiterated the theme of mutuality. Helen Beth answered: "Writing is a revelation for me. Sharing it with other women is a validation that I am not alone." Elena said: "Through writing in the company of women, I have discovered my own womanhood, and even more, my humanity at a level before hidden." Alena added: "Sharing, and writing with the purpose of sharing, has opened new doors, given me insight into other women's lives and thoughts. It has brought me new friends, new ideas, a new outlook on life and our mutual experiences. It has brought comfort; a feeling of connectedness. I'm not alone!" And Lily Storm emphasized: "Although the act of writing is a solitary process, it is only through sharing our words with others that we can truly validate them."

One of the most powerful stories that emerged from my collection of questionnaires came from Del Emerson, a woman of seventy-four, living on a limited income in an apartment with two younger women. Near the beginning of her response to me she mused, "At this time, I was contemplating writing down some of my life stories — which I'd refused to do before — as my life had been 'too unhappy.' ... I've always looked for people to read or listen to what I've written — and the fact that very few were truly interested had not bolstered my confidence in my writing." In reflecting upon what being part of a writing and sharing group has meant to her, she writes that the group response has "increased my confidence and trust in my own writing." And: "This ongoing pleasure and inspiration, the awareness that I have a writing group in my life, has simply made my life more enjoyable and has added focus, confidence and purpose to it." She illustrated by sharing that she had put together two books of writing in the past year, and has planned and launched a writing group for women over sixty. In three short pages, which represent a course of just a few years, she reveals a movement from being a woman who could not write about unhappy events, to one who is a leader of other writers.

The two activities, writing and then sharing aloud what was written becomes a powerful synergy. By cycling repeatedly through them, the members of a group can build up trust in the process and in one another. Suzannah did not reach the depths of that hollow beneath the tree in the first writing cycle. It took several cycles for her to permit herself to go inside so deeply and to the level of trust to read it aloud. Many of the women who responded to my questionnaire remarked about the importance to them of being able to communicate at this level with the other members of their groups. It seems that intimate communication has become so scarce that when it is found it is doubly precious.

Writing is an active process, creating a static document. Sharing is an active process, contributing to ongoing relationship and growing understanding. The relationship of static and dynamic is very important: there is a constant conversation going on between what is static (the stories written) and what is changing (relationships, mental and emotional states, and our understanding of these).

These polarities, of the static and the dynamic, can be very generative. By "freezing" the movement of experience in a written account, we can provide ourselves with a perspective that can enhance our ability to understand our stories in new ways and to discover new meanings.

New Perspectives: Writes of Passage

Going through three months of menopause at age thirty-five became a doorway to a deeper understanding of my abilities and gifts as a woman. A rite of passage is the transition from one state or condition to another. In other words, it is an event or marker that we are shifting from one kind of self to another. Traditionally, anthropologists have considered such experiences as a girl's initiation into womanhood, as in the Navaho Kinaalda ceremony, or a couple's initiation into marriage with a wedding as a rite of passage. These are public ceremonies, whereby the community knows that the individuals involved were girls and are now women, were single and are now married. In Western culture, the number of those meaningful public ceremonies dwindles in number and complexity in comparison to "small scale, relatively stable, and cyclical societies, where change is bound up with biological and meteorological rhythms and recurrences rather than technological innovations" as Victor Turner (1987, p. 4) classifies them.

In our postmodern world, the events that mark our shifts in self-understanding are often not as obvious as in times past; and they may be very local or idiosyncratic events. In my case, surgery became a key transition. Getting a promotion, or going on a trip might have similar effects for other people. Life-changing events are often not acknowledged, either publicly or in our private circles. It is then easy to overlook them, and ignore the influences they have on us, until one day we realize we no longer know who we are. This was the situation my husband found himself in after the death of his father. The realization that his life (so similar to how his father had lived) was not working fell onto him like an avalanche. He went into crisis. He had to painstakingly examine how his attitudes and behaviors were linked. By understanding that his attitudes were based on values he now found empty, he had to rebuild his identity and attitudes on a more profound set of values. This follows Arnold Van Gennep's (1960) model that rites of passage go through three stages: separating from the past, going through a transitional phase, and reincorporating into life in a changed form.

Twelve-step groups can serve as containers for certain kinds of transitions: active alcoholic to recovering alcoholic, active gambler to recovering gambler, and so on. The storytelling format serves to document the steps taken from admitting the problem, to building a new identity without the addiction. But what about other kinds of changes? These changes may be purely our own, or they may be shared more widely. For example, my "menopause experience" and the way I came to understand it was my own in that its unfolding and its meanings for me were not widely shared. But of course, any women who lives to be old enough goes through menopause, and could approach that change as a positive rite of passage. The process of writing and sharing can retrospectively recognize, honor, and validate those changes.

An example of an event that served as a marker of change for girls in my generation (born in the late 1950s) was getting our ears pierced. This was the topic of group consideration in a study I conducted in 1993. Using a combination of writing and sharing those writings, a small group of women came to understand that earlier experience as a true rite of passage.

Carol wrote: "We had just moved from the house behind the church to our very own house. I was twelve, and it was fall. I was starting junior high. Everything was new. Except everything was old. I came in from school, and my sister and her friend were in the kitchen. That was exciting to me. They were in there talking. I wanted to go be with them. I went into the kitchen. My sister showed me what they had been doing. Jan had pierced her ears and she had pierced Jan's. I couldn't believe it. I'd never thought of it. Pierced ears! Like fashion models, or fancy rich women, or beatniks."

Talia remembered: "We decided that it was time, our periods were woefully late in coming on, our chests painfully flat, but there were some aspects of this growing-up stuff we could get a handle on: the wearing of jewelry. We wanted to pierce our ears and take over our mother's role (not to mention her juicy costume stuff.) All the cute ones were pierced. Remember?"

And with her written invocation which she read aloud, we did remember and delighted in telling one another so! In hearing each written tale, together we were transported back in time, to that not-so-comfortable, in-between stage of the beginnings of as Talia puts it "the makeup and nylons and shaving of legs, having begged my mother to allow it. Remember the smell of Nair?" Maybe reading this brings you back to those days in your own past. I'd never go back to that time. But by remembering it through writing and sharing with Talia and Carol, we were able to celebrate that we had survived it, reasonably intact.

In hearing each others' stories, we were able to revisit that uneasy time that Victor Turner (1967) so eloquently terms "betwixt and between" adolescence and adulthood. Our stories reflected how we saw ourselves before "the big event" and our separation from those self-images.

Talia wrote "I wanted to live with animals and be a philosopher, delving into truths with whomever would brave the forest out that far to see me. But the world pushed in. Afraid even of the building of the Junior High school — the summer before seventh grade I'd ride by on my bike and curse it, challenging its very bricks to crumble, before September please." And Carol caught the poignancy of that in-between time in her phrase "Everything was new. Except everything was old. It was the old time of year, autumn, November. The house was old, Aunt Carol was old, my sister and her friend were old, five years older than me." And from my account: "I was twelve. At that time I was minimally interested in the paraphernalia of womanliness. As far as clothes and makeup, I wasn't particularly interested, I was more into books. But getting my ears pierced was symbolic that I was moving into my mother's world. There was something about the elegance I aspired to. I was looking for ways to be less clunky than I felt. It was a movement from some prosaic animal to a gazelle — it seemed to be a mystery of beauty." With these words, the three of us stepped through the veil of memory to a time when things were changing for us — we were moving into womanhood, which meant leaving the old behind.

As I learned in that difficult style I call my own, betwixt and between can also be the interval separating being ill, and finally, being well again. It can be any "between time." Recently Anne, a workshop participant, introduced herself by saying: "I'm going through a lot of changes right now. I know when I get through them I'll be a different person, but right now it's really hard, because I can't see where I'm going; I'm just really confused." And during a similar stage in my life, when asked by friends how I was, I would growl irascibly "I'm growing" to a frequent response of the laughter of recognition.

Being betwixt and between is tough. But not having the structure of knowing you are going through a rite of passage makes it even tougher. That's why it is so important for us to tell those stories of passage. In telling them and hearing those of others, we begin to get the sense that, even though the particulars are different, the process is the same. "You're just going through a stage" my mother would counsel. As an awkward adolescent that was scant consolation. But as an adult, it seems greatly reassuring. This too shall pass. In the voice of workshop participant Chris Miller: "It strikes me that I have changed, and I am glad. Although we are always changing and I am always changing, I rarely take advantage of a chance such as this to take stock of where I've been and where I am now. ... Our sameness reassured me and our differences inspired me." Trisha writes: "I suppose I should know enough about perspective now to recognize you see what you look for, but there has again been the understanding that knowing in the brain and knowing at the intersection of hand, pen and paper are two different things. In looking at my passages I have acknowledged that I have changed, grown. That is important. And somehow that recognition contributes to a sense of strength now."

In traditional rites of passage, participants go through an experience which is acknowledged and witnessed by the community. Both experience and public acknowledgment are essential in confirming an individual's new status. Twelve-step groups provide a structure for those whose former identity was tied to an unhealthy addiction. For those whose changes have been of a different kind, the process of writing can provide a container to acknowledge personal recognition of life changes. Reading those stories aloud to others provides a forum for validation and public recognition. Having written and read; gone through the experience and been witnessed, the passage is complete and a new understanding of self has emerged.

When Words Don't Work

In his autobiography, *Memories, Dreams, Reflections,* Carl Jung (1961) discusses his life-long work with fantasies and the contents of the unconscious. Finally he gets to a point in his work where he says: "Words and paper, however, did not seem real enough to me; something more was needed. I had to achieve a kind of representation in stone of my innermost thoughts and of the knowledge I had acquired" (p. 223). This is a quandary eons of mystics and explorers of land and soul have faced. How can we capture in words experiences that are so much bigger than words? And how can we shape a story of our experience when it is sharply different than anything our past has prepared us for, when what has happened to us does not fall into any category that we know? For example, deep bodily knowledge does not always lend itself well to expression in words; sometimes the translation is too far a stretch. Sometimes the story calls for a different medium.

Under the influence of the hormones I was taking for my treatment, my ways of knowing had shifted significantly from very rational to strongly intuitional and symbolic. My understanding was not yet sufficiently formed for me to be able to shape it into writing or telling stories. Following a hunch, I decided to experiment with mask-making, a physical, non-verbal process, that I hoped would spark some insight about this different way of knowing.

For me, the creation of artwork is a very intuitive process. I may "hear" gentle suggestions, or my hands may "feel" that something needs to be added. As I worked with paints and other materials I gradually came to know what was needed to change the pallid white plaster cast of my face into a finished mask. What emerged from my hands gradually became a specific personality. Her face was mottled green, a representation of how the summer light sparkles on the leaves of a weeping willow. She gained a wreath of braided willow branches. Draped from her eyes like tears was a cascade of audio-tape, a recording of a talk I had given on my life as the child of an alcoholic. Her home became an old hat-box that had once belonged to my grandmother now lined in willow green fabric to swaddle this mask. During the painting of the mask, I had come to know her as "Willow Shines the Light." She represented the girl I once was, living among the growing things on our farm in New Jersey. It was her voice that spoke to me as I wrote, years ago, at the Omega workshop. "My Heart's Home" was her story.

As I had worked on this mask I had gradually come to understand that she was to be one of three masks, each representing what in ancient Greek mythology was seen as the triple goddess; girl, woman and crone. And so I went about the process twice more.

Telling The Tales of The Masks

The non-verbal creativity of the arts such as crafting, dancing, and making music, may provide us with personally significant symbols. The three masks took on for me the force and complexity of symbols — not a direct correlation of my face at that time and place, but a numinous image of an internal aspect of my soul — mysterious and not readily understood. Even so, with self examination and research, we may be able to learn from these unfamiliar communications. We can use the symbol as a mirror of our internal processes or of attributes we may not recognize in ourselves. We need to learn our own particular symbolic language, just as anyone who wishes to work with their dreams needs to learn the way those dreams communicate — their "dream language." This requires a process of interpretation. In order for me to move to the next level of under-standing, I would have to interpret the physical symbolism of the masks into my more accessible symbolism of words.

Like others before me, I sought understanding from more ancient sources. The story of Persephone, Demeter, and Hecate came to mind, representing the three ages of women. The story of Demeter and Persephone can be seen as a rite of passage in which Demeter's descent with Hades to the underworld moves her from being an adolescent "mother's daughter" to being a woman in her own right — Queen of the Underworld. Her descent into and emergence from the underworld allows her to take full command of her own power, and can be read as a parable of a woman's powerful transition into self.

I had made a translation from the images of the mask into an allegorical story of initiation. In considering these personae, I noted that Skeat (1911) adds that the Latin *personare* means "to sound through" (p. 385). It seemed appropriate then, that the story of the masks needed to be sounded, or told. Now, finally, it seemed like it was time to share this story.

At that time I was a part of a small group of women who had been studying women's artistic processes. Telling my story to them would permit me to express what had been brewing inside. I set up the storytelling as a ritual performance. In many traditional cultures, such as the Salish, Hopi, and Balinese, masks are gods, goddesses, and powerful spirits. When you put on such a mask, you are that spirit; the mask provides the transformative catalyst.

What I did not know as I prepared, was how deeply this story would be felt by the women in the group. As I told my tale, they laughed, and cried, and allowed themselves to be moved deeply into the story. Their responses as they listened allowed me to know things in my tale that I had not before understood. As I finished, there was a momentary silence, as if they were surfacing from far below the surface of a woodland pool. And then, they began to speak. Several of them picked specific parts of the story and related stories of their own, of their own experiences. Mona told the group how her menopause had shifted her understanding of what was crucial in her life: silence and solitude. She told us about her cabin an hour from her home and her husband, where she now spent several days a week painting, writing, reading, and just being alone. Betsy quietly related her painful realization that her early menopause meant it would be impossible for her to have a child. For those who had not gone through this passage, there rang the familiar sound of other life transitions. Lisa, a younger woman, reflected upon her struggles with her mother as she went through a tumultuous adolescence. She wondered to us if some of those difficulties arose from her mother's unacknowledged transit into menopause. In sharing their own experiences, each woman in the room somehow validated my experience.

Although this storytelling was far more elaborate than what I wrote and shared at Omega, the effect of intimate revelation and evocation was similar. The use of costumes and props in ritual storytelling allowed me to become each persona as she spoke through the story, providing a kind of induction into another reality. When teller and listeners share this other world, an atmosphere of mutual trust is created. In this almost-familiar other world the alchemy of transformation can take place.

Summary

It has been more than a decade since I began learning through my own experience about the process of telling stories that heal. Beginning with telling stories to a therapist, and then in a twelve-step group, I found relief in knowing that I was not alone in my difficulties. Hearing other's stories over time let me see that we were changing — perhaps due to telling stories?

The training in writing and sharing that I received at Omega Institute provided me with a powerful tool for working with stories, one that I continue to use and research. And it was in this workshop where I began to delve into evocative writing — that strongly imaginative and emotional writing that gives entry into the symbolic and mythic depths of the psyche. Finding the voice of the young girl who had lived on the farm allowed me to recognize a long hidden grief over the loss of an idyllic green paradise — and to begin to acknowledge my need for a pastoral environment.

With the trauma and disruption brought by illness and surgery to my rational life as a graduate student, it became clear that a new path of understanding would have to be found. In adapting the creative processes of writing to the non-verbal form of mask-making, I was able to explore very different modes of intelligence. Learning the language of emotions, intuitions, and body sensations now allowed me access to a symbolically- and metaphorically-rich form of story — allegory. Within the theatrical setting of ritual storytelling, the force of "telling my story" again appeared, as it had in the writing and sharing format at Omega.

Over and over, the combination of creating and sharing, writing and sharing, proved to be a potent force in contributing to my understanding myself more fully. If healing means to make whole, this combination has been a major part of my healing.

Were it only my experience, this tale that you have been reading might be only a mildly amusing diversion. But in many ways, I have seen that this synergistic form has contributed to a more meaningful life for others as well. The tumultuous changes that my husband went through were written and shared in a variety of ways, from poetry to the more prosaic form of a Master's thesis. The women who participated in writing and sharing groups echo this feeling of significance in their moving comments about how important this form is to them. And participants in a workshop on grief have found in themselves an unrecognized profundity as they shared their written musings on the meaning of death.

There are many books appearing yearly on writing instruction, and yet how many of those who purchase these books will publish even one word? There must be something about writing that holds out some promise of reward. The process of writing and sharing may help to feed some of that hunger for the expression of life's meaning and for the longing to share it with others. I believe in this process as a way for people to begin to recognize their own worth and their place in humanity. I believe that stories can heal.

References

Belenky, M., Clinchy, B., Goldberger, N., & Tarule, J. (1986). *Women's ways of knowing: The development of self, voice, and mind.* New York: Basic Books.

Dillard, A. (1974). *Pilgrim at Tinker Creek.* New York: Bantam.

Jung, C. G. (1961). *Memories, dreams, reflections.* New York: Vintage Books.

Lopez, B. (1989). *Crossing open ground.* New York: Vintage Books.

LeGuin, U. K. (1989). *The language of the night: Essays on fantasy and science fiction.* New York: HarperCollins.

Lindgren, A. (1950). *Pippi Longstocking.* New York: Viking Press.

Oxford English Dictionary. (1971). New York: Oxford University Press.

Rich, A. (1977). Conditions for work: The common world of women. In S. Ruddick & P. Daniels (Eds.), *Working it out.* New York: Pantheon.

Skeat, W. W. (1911). *A concise etymological dictionary of the English language.* New York: Clarendon Press.

Spyri, J. (1952) *Heidi.* New York: Dutton.

Turner, V. (1987). Betwixt and between: The liminal period in rites of passage. In C. L. Mahdi, S. Foster & M. Little, (Eds.), *Betwixt and between: Patterns of masculine and feminine initiation* (pp. 1–19). LaSalle, Il: Open Court Press. (Original work published 1967)

Van Gennep, A. (1960). *Rites of passage.* (M. B. Vizedom & G. L. Caffee, Transl.) Chicago: University of Chicago Press.

Zinsser, W. (1988). *Writing to learn.* New York: Harper and Row.

CHAPTER SEVENTEEN

Psychotherapy:
The Art of Experience

Robert Rosenbaum & Arthur C. Bohart

There has been considerable recent interest in treating psychotherapy and personal history from a narrative perspective (Omer, 1993; Russell & Van den Broek, 1992; Schafer, 1981; Spence, 1982; White & Epston, 1990). Rather than see therapy as a task of uncovering information to reveal an accurate picture of a client's past, this perspective insists there are many ways of telling the clients' stories, each equally "true." Therapy works by developing a story with a client which organizes his or her experience in a way that offers wider possibilities for the future (Omer & Strenger, 1992; Omer & Alon, 1997).

Because narrative schemas are constructed rather than revealed, they offer more room for creativity than treatments which seek to uncover purportedly objective historical truths. Once we let go of the myth of historical accuracy, though, how can we evaluate the truthfulness of a narrative? We would suggest that the truth of a narrative resides in *aesthetic* factors: in its beauty and meaningfulness. At this point, psychotherapy begins to converge on the realm of art, and psychotherapeutic narratives can be viewed, in part, as literature. Literature relies on style and form as much as on content to attain its expressive power. Psychotherapy has been perhaps overly focused on content, and can learn a good deal by exploring the stylistic principles of literature in particular and art in general.

Art and psychotherapy have long held a mutual attraction for each other. We are not interested in saying that therapists should be more artistic, or that artistic techniques should be added to existing psychotherapies. Rather, we assert that aesthetic qualities are always an inextricable aspect of *all* therapies, being embodied in the formal and stylistic organization of the therapeutic process. Art takes experience and re-presents it to us in a created form that lets us know it in a different way. Psychotherapy does the same thing: the therapist offers an open and receptive reading to a client's story, and as the therapist resonates empathically to the client's experience, the client can appreciate his or her experience in a new form.

We contend that form is crucial in psychotherapy just as it is in art. Form is always present, but we may not be aware of it. We can listen to the finale of a Beethoven symphony and be moved by it, without realizing that it derives its power not just from the sound of its main theme, but also from having extended the length of the coda in a sonata-allegro form. It is helpful, though, if you wish to recreate that kind of experience, to learn the forms through which it is accomplished. We will therefore attempt to use art to illuminate psychotherapy by treating the *formal* aspects of psychotherapy from an artistic perspective, in a manner similar to that advocated by Rothenberg (1992) and Keeney (1982, 1983; Keeney & Spreckle, 1982). As an example, let us see how formal considerations affect beginnings in psychotherapy.

Formal Beginnings

The opening of a psychotherapy or a piece of art establishes a context, sets the stage, and defines the "rules of the game" for what will follow. This happens rather rapidly. In a musical performance, as soon as the music starts — even a little before — we know whether the piece will be an orchestra work or a chamber piece, simply by looking at the cast of characters. No program notes are necessary. If a husband and wife enter the therapist's office, a different context is established than if an individual comes in and sits down. Within a few measures, it will often be clear if this will be a tonal or an atonal piece; whether it will have the short phrases of a classical work or the long lines of a romantic composition. Often the first five minutes of the first therapy interview will establish whether the client is effusive or shy; quick-witted or slow; frightened or eager.

All of these are formal elements, having little to do with the content of the material. Independent of the whether the musical theme plays the notes "C E G C" or "D F# A D, " whether the couple is talking about the death of a child or the death of a grandparent, the form of an opening gesture offers a great deal of very specific information about what will follow and how it will govern future processes. In both music and in therapy, we will get a sense from the first few minutes whether discordant or concordant harmonies predominate; whether the mode of expression will be blunt or elegant, terse or elongated; whether the tempo will be fast or slow; whether the rhythmic flow will be regular or choppy. The beginnings of a pattern emerge not just in their content, but equally in their form: indeed, formal features serve to generate content (Rothenberg, 1992).

Although a client's first words are always important, if we listen only to the content of the client's chief complaint, we may be surprised when the client seems less than eager to directly change what they assert has been the problem. If we listen to the *form* of their first gesture — not just what they say, but how they say it, how the different ideas and feelings are connected to one another — then we may have a better sense of how the therapy will proceed. In discussing aesthetics of form, we are not simply talking about paying attention to nonverbal and contextual cues, but rather how the material is organized, and how its organization affects its "feel."

Here literature is a good guide. The author's craft involves writing and re-writing until the phrase's form carries its feeling. Consider the famous opening of Dickens' *A Tale of Two Cities*:

> It was the best of times, it was the worst of times, it was the age of wisdom, it was the age of foolishness; it was the epoch of belief, it was the epoch of incredulity, it was the season of Light, it was the season of Darkness, it was the spring of hope, it was the winter of despair ... In short, the period was so far like the present period, that some of its noisiest authorities insisted on its being received, for good or for evil, in the superlative degree of comparison only.

The pairing of opposites creates a formal need for their reconciliation. When we read this we begin to anticipate, without being fully aware of it, that the rest of the novel will alternate successively between the two sites, but that gradually events will overlap and intermingle until they reach a resolution. In this opening paragraph, the "resolution" occurs in the last sentence, where finally the opposites appear conjoined in a larger comparison of that time to the present time.

Contrast this to the following:

> In England, it was the best of times: an age of wisdom and an epoch of belief. It was the season of Light, and the spring of hope. In France, it was the worst of times: the age of foolishness and the epoch of incredulity. It was the season of Darkness and the winter of despair. In short, the period was so far like the present period, that some of its noisiest authorities insisted on its being received, for good or for evil, in the superlative degree of comparison only.

Although there is still a contrast between two alternatives, it is much weaker. The two foci could proceed in parallel. By not pairing them point by point, the need for intermingling (and consequent resolution) is lessened. Notice how the last sentence has less impact due to the change in the formal structure.

These kinds of formal characteristics can be heard in the opening statements of clients in psychotherapy:

> Client No. 1: When I turned fifty, a few months ago, I moved in with this woman; *before then, I'd been living alone most of my life.* She's wonderful, *but sometimes she's a pain;* she makes me feel things I've never felt before, *though I don't know, it kind of feels like we don't connect.* When I'm with her I feel tremendously alive, *but I really can't have the kind of discussions I want with her, like about books I'm excited about.* She believes in the power of positive thinking. *I'm very analytical.* She has a strong

faith. *I'm skeptical.* She's clear about what she wants and decisive. *I like to think things over.* She aims high; *I have a tendency to settle for things.* She's ready to move ahead and get married. *I think I want to, and think I don't.*

I want to be of one mind.

Client No. 2: When I turned fifty a few months ago, I moved in with this woman. She's wonderful, and makes me feel things I've never felt before. When I'm with her I feel tremendously alive. She believes in the power of positive thinking, and has a strong faith; she's clear about what she wants and decisive. She aims high, and is ready to move ahead and get married, and I'd like that.

Sometimes, though, I feel like we don't connect. I really can't have the kind of discussions I want with her, like about books I'm excited about. I'm analytical, and skeptical; I hesitate and think things over, and I tend to settle for things. Sometimes I just feel full of doubts about the relationship.

I want to be of one mind.

The first client is unable to entertain a positive thought without immediately negating it with its opposite. Consequently, when we hear the first client, we start thinking of an obsessional organization, in which there is constant vacillation between opposing alternatives. With the second client, though, we are less likely to think of obsessional traits: this client may be someone who is faced with a major life decision, and needs to review the pluses and minuses: he may be undecided, but in a different way than the first client. When Client No. 2 says "I want to be of one mind," we feel that perhaps he has been of one mind on other matters, whereas for Client No. 1 such unity of purpose may have been a much rarer experience. The therapist may need to interdict the first client's "switching" between states (Horowitz, Marmar, Krupnick, Wilner, Kaltreider, & Wallerstein, 1984) and help him learn how to stay on one "side" of the two opposing ideas and feelings for a longer period of time, before reviewing the underlying reasons for the ambivalence; the second client may be able to work immediately toward resolving the main issue. Even though the content is largely the same in both clients, different strategies may be called for, based on how the form of the content is organized.

Just as the form of clients' opening statements gives crucial information to the therapist, so the form of therapists' opening statements gives crucial information to the client. The therapist who starts off by saying "Why don't we get started by your letting me know what brings you here?" is using passive constructions ("get started"; "brings you") and is sending a message that we are lived by our experience; the therapist who starts off by saying "Please tell me what you want to accomplish today." is using active constructions ("tell me," "want to accomplish") which send a message that the therapist expects people need to consciously work at creating new experiences.

Neither opening is "better" than the other. However, it is important to suit the opening to the work that the therapist is best able to do. We have heard trainees who temperamentally lean to a "passive listening" style try to learn gestalt therapy; they usually start the session with the first opening statement, thus creating a very mixed message for the client. Such therapies frequently founder. (We also have seen the opposite, where "let's do it" types try hard to be their image of "Rogerian," but keep speaking in a very action-oriented prescriptive manner, with similar negative results). Style is not separable from substance; *how* the therapist does an intervention *is* the intervention.

In order to understand how this can be so, we must understand how experience depends on formal and stylistic qualities as much, or even more, than it does on content.

Form, Content, and Experience

Psychotherapy, treated as an art, takes as its subject matter the client's experience. It is important, then, that we acquire a clearer understanding of the nature of experience. John Dewey (1934/1987), writing on *Art as Experience*, has helped illuminate this territory:

> An experience has a unity ... constituted by a single *quality* that pervades the entire experience in spite of the variation of its constituent parts. This unity is neither emotional, practical, nor intellectual, for these terms name distinctions that reflection can make within it. In discourse *about* an experience, we must make use of these adjectives of interpretation. (p. 208)

As many therapists have repeatedly emphasized, talking about an experience is not the same as the experience; the map is not the territory. Experiencing is the ground of Being, and psychotherapy seeks to grapple with experience itself. However, because psychotherapy stands at least partly outside the client's experience, it must rely on "distinctions that reflection can make" about that experience. One of us (Bohart, 1993) has recently attempted to widen the concept of experiencing beyond its current usage in psychotherapy. While depth of experiencing is often used to investigate the process and outcome of psychotherapy (Gendlin, 1991), experiencing is often seen as access to deep, congruent emotion. As cognitive psychologists have taught us over the past few decades, though, there is no emotion without cognition. Yet experience cannot be identified exclusively with either emotion, or cognition, nor even their sum. Experiencing is much broader than this: it not only includes all aspects of a person's life, in a more profound sense, experiencing *is* the person's life.

> Experience occurs continuously, because the interaction of live creature and environing conditions is involved in the very process of living. ... Oftentimes, however, the experience had is inchoate. Things are experienced but not in such a way that they are composed in *an* experience (Dewey, 1934/1987, p. 207).

Experience is continuous and inchoate; in order to point to or describe experience, it must be structured in a particular kind of encoding. The various arts, as well as the different psychotherapies, represent various kinds of encodings. The imposition of structure is inherent in any mode of encoding, whether it be linguistic, iconic, or enactive; such structure always highlights some aspect of the whole of experience, while leaving out other aspects. Similarly, all psychotherapy, as it attempts to encode and communicate some of the flow of experience, involves punctuation (Bateson, 1972, 1979; Keeney, 1983; Watzlawick, Beavin [Bavelas], & Jackson, 1967). A line must be drawn; a difference must be distinguished and pointed out, so that clients and therapists have something with which to work. *How* one punctuates the flow of experience, so that it becomes *an* experience amenable to being analyzed, reworked or changed, is crucial, because the mode of punctuation is in itself an experience, and gets reinserted into a feedback loop that alters and is altered by the experience it is punctuating.

The first act in painting a scene is to put boundaries around what is to be painted; the painter decides what will be included and what will be excluded from the painting simply by facing the easel toward this and not that. As soon as the scene is "framed," though, it looks different, as anyone who has ever looked at a landscape through the viewfinder of a camera can testify. The form of the frame influences what is framed. It is not just what experiences are included or excluded from a story which defines the story: a narrative of an experience will appear differently if its frame is a short story, a novel, or a poem. Similarly, the formal qualities of the boundaries of a psychotherapy help determine the quality of the experience which the therapy then contains. Langs (1976b) has written extensively from a psychoanalytic standpoint on how the frame influences the therapeutic relationship; we would contend that frame issues affect all therapies, regardless of school, in a wide variety of areas not necessarily confined to transference and alliance issues. Certainly the establishment of a focus — crucial for all short-term psychotherapies and also for the stages of long-term treatments — constitutes an important kind of framing.

The same story can be told in a short story or a novel, and both can have a similar sense of resolution; the writing technique involved, though, is very different for the two forms. A short story is not the same as a chapter in a novel, though both may be of the same length; the short-story is self-contained. The same is true of short-term and long-term psychotherapies. Long-term and short-term treatments affect the nature of the therapy not only because the former has more meetings and more time than the latter, but because the nature of the frame determines the treatment of the material within it. This can be seen more clearly if we compare two psychotherapeutic forms of equal length.

Take, for example, the difference between agreeing to meet "for a maximum of twelve sessions" as opposed to meeting "exactly twelve times." If a client's presenting symptoms have largely improved by the fourth session and he is thinking about terminating treatment, both therapist and client will experience the possibility of termination differently in the two frames. Even when the level of symptom reduction is the same in both cases, in the context of meeting "For a maximum of twelve visits" stopping therapy may feel quite solidly appropriate; whereas in the context of meeting "for exactly twelve sessions" ending treatment may feel premature, simply because the frame implied more would be forthcoming. The latter case would be rather like buying a thick novel, reading a good story, and finding it comes to a conclusion in half the number of pages expected, so that the remaining pages of the book are blank. No matter how satisfactory the story, it would feel incomplete. The sense of completeness depends not only on the content of what is covered, but on the formal aspects of the frame.

Experiencing always involves an inherent balance between form and content, between *what* we experience and *how* we experience. The formal aspects of how we structure and organize our experience are more readily modifiable than the content aspects, because they are reflexive: the self presenting its experience to itself becomes one more experience to present to itself. When an experience is presented in a different way, the nature of the experience changes. A movie of a Shakespeare play presented in an eighteenth-century Tuscan setting "plays" differently than when it appears on a stage set in Elizabethan England. A traumatic memory will feel different if it presents itself as a five-second flashback in the middle of a business meeting than if it is being intentionally reviewed, projected on an imaginary television set, in a self-hypnotic trance.

This is the level at which psychotherapy operates: the formal organization of how a client presents her experience to herself. When we punctuate, we frame our experience; we offer this framing not only to others, but also back to ourselves. We live in a world of immediate experience, but as the self presents its experience back to itself in a self-referential manner, all "representation" becomes "re-presentation" and transforms the *representor*. As Dewey (1934/1987) says, in "representation … the work of art tells something to those who enjoy it about the nature of their own experience of the world: … it presents the world in a new experience *which they undergo*" (p. 211, italics added). When a human subject takes himself as his own subject, when created and creator meet, then experience folds in on itself, and life experience becomes a work of art.

An important mode of how experience is re-presented involves the balance of activity and passivity: the marble sculpts the sculptor, but the sculptor brings forth something new from the marble. It is sometimes difficult to keep a good balance here. It is easy to err on one side or the other of doing and receiving; an excess of the former may lead to anxiety, and an excess of the latter to depression. The role a person plays in shaping their life raises issues of free will versus determinism, "philosophical" questions that make many therapists uneasy. Questions of this sort, though, are critical. Clients come to us not when they are having anxiety or depression — both of which are normal — but when they feel out of control in their experience of anxiety or depression. At such times, clients may feel they are being tossed about by the whims of life, or they may feel the depletion of over-exertion. They are out of balance; they no longer know whether they have "will" or are fated to suffer in misery. Then "abstract" aesthetic questions about proportion and balance take on a very real presence.

In such cases, the task of the psychotherapist, of course, is not to engage the client in a philosophical discussion, but to intervene effectively. It is not, however, sufficient to decrease anxiety or depression or increase calm and pleasure; the question is always, decrease or increase relative to what? Health involves a balance and a sense of proportion: the previously depressed client who leaves therapy *always* smiling may have a very brittle adjustment (Keeney, 1982). The task of the therapist, then, is to provide a forum for experience which addresses the imbalances or disconnections in a client's life; judgments of balance and propor-tion, though, are always aesthetic ones.

In all art, and in all experience, form is what distinguishes coherent versus inchoate experience. All art deals with the *form* of expression, and these formal attributes are crucial to the identity of the work of art. In a similar fashion, the task of psychotherapy is to grapple with and re-organize experience so that its form better suits the client's function.

> Form ... marks a way of envisaging, of feeling, and of presenting experienced matter so that it most readily and effectively becomes mate-rial for the construction of adequate experience. ... The work itself *is* matter formed into esthetic substance. ... the act itself is exactly *what* it is because of *how* it is done. In the act there is no distinction, but perfect integration of manner and content, form and substance. (Dewey, 1934/1987)

Psychotherapists are concerned with that "integration of manner and content, form and substance" which defines a client's personal identity. The character of a work of art, a life, or a psychotherapy emerges not just from the content of an experience, but also from how the experience is organized; a person is *who* they are because of *how*, as well as *what*, they live. Many psychotherapists, and many clients, assume that their identity as a person is a sum of the content of their experience. This may be troubling for clients whose lives have been filled with trauma, violence, and grief. Yet is the essence of Velasquez's "Las Meninas" identical with dwarfs? Intuitively, we would say no. Psychotherapy, however, to the extent that it has concentrated on client experience, has tended to focus on content. We can be more effective psychotherapists if we analyze not just the content of a client's experience, but also its form. A good way of beginning to do this is through paying attention to *style*.

The Substance of Style

Susan Sontag (1966) has pointed out that an overemphasis on the idea of content leads, in art, to an overemphasis on interpretation. When this occurs, the work of art is treated as if it is not "really" what it appears to be; interpretation is necessary to show us what it "really" means. Much of psychotherapy shares this endeavor. This is obvious in the psychodynamic approaches, but any therapy which asserts that a client distorts, suppresses, or misinterprets experience — and virtually all psychotherapies assert this to one degree or another — in effect abrogates to the therapist the role of describing the "true" meaning of a client's experience. The net effect of this, as Sontag points out, is an impoverishment and depletion of the world as it exists:

> It is the same with our own lives. If we see them from the outside, as the influence and popular dissemination of the social sciences and psychiatry has persuaded more and more people to do, we view ourselves as instances of generalities, and in so doing become profoundly and painfully alienated from our own experience and our humanity. (p. 29)

When this occurs, a person separates himself from his immediate experience, in favor of treating himself as a member of a class. Many clients will present by identifying themselves as "adult children of alcoholics," as "survivors of sexual abuse," and so forth. Paradoxically, this distances the client from the very experience they are trying to reclaim; overemphasizing the content of *what* happened avoids the qualitative aspects of *how* it was experienced, the way it contributes to the overall organization of the person's life. This is why when two individuals experience the same traumatic event, one may develop symptoms while the other may not. Emphasizing content leads to interpreting people as exemplars of a general type, and minimizes the individual aspects of experience.

Much of what we call psychopathology arises from the tendency to look for meaning outside of the realm of immediate experience, by instead interpreting (and thus, standing apart from) the content of experience. While some meaning relies on external referents — signboards and symbols must point to something outside of themselves — still:

> ... there are other meanings that present themselves directly. ... Here there is no need for a code or convention of interpretation; the meaning is as inherent in immediate experience as is that of a flower garden." (Dewey, 1934/1987, p. 211)

Art honors immediate experience through expressing or embodying it in a new form. This is different from attempting to *interpret* experience, which Sontag (1966) argues vitiates the experience by paying overmuch attention to content:

> Interpretation takes the sensory experience. ... for granted, and proceeds from there. This cannot be taken for granted, now.
>
> What is important now is to recover our senses. We must learn to *see* more, to *hear* more, to *feel* more. ... our task is not to ... squeeze more content out of the work than is already there. Our task is to cut back content so that we can see the thing at all. ...
>
> The function of criticism [we would say, of psychotherapy] should be to show *how* it is what it is, even *that* it is what it is, rather than to show what it *means*. In place of a hermeneutics we need an erotics of art. (pp. 13–14)
>
> An approach which considers works of art as living, autonomous models of consciousness will seem objectionable only so long as we refuse to surrender the shallow distinction of form and content. For the sense in which a work of art has no content is no different from the sense in which the world has no content. Both are. Both need no justification; nor could they possibly have any. (p. 27)

Sontag's definition of art as a "living, autonomous model of consciousness" connects it intimately to psychology; the existence of a personal self could take the same definition. In this view, all people's lives are works of art which need no justification. The client is in a more difficult role than an artist, in that they are, themselves, their own artistic medium; their experience is the stuff with which they have to work. Clients, however, often have difficulty accepting their experience, in part because they mistakenly equate experience with its content and make negative interpretations about what that experience "must" mean for their self-identity.

Acceptance of what is, as opposed to what one wants, is a necessary first step to any subsequent creative work, therapeutic or artistic. Any creative work must start with the materials that are given and face those materials directly, recognizing them for what they are. It does not help an artist painting a sunset to wish for the sun to stand still (things will continue to change); it does not help a sculptor to wish his block of marble would never crack (all materials have some flaw or limitation). How one organizes the material — the interplay of form and content — becomes the creative task. Michelangelo's sculpture of David is the "solution" to how to carve a piece of flawed marble. Clients who have undergone difficult events in their youth may feel flawed; clients who experience difficult recent events in the present may wish to turn back the clock. These feelings arise from a mistaken view that we are what we experience, rather than how we experience it.

One of us (RR) was seeing a forty-five-year-old obese woman who had come in originally for anxiety secondary to the failure of her husband's business and the resulting bankruptcy. One session she came in extremely upset because her teenage son had gotten his girlfriend pregnant. This revived intense traumatic memories, previously inaccessible, of how she had been sexually-abused when a child. The memories were accompanied by waves of intrusive feeling. Although she was angry at the perpetrator, the predominant affect was that she felt besmirched; she felt dirty, flawed, soiled. During the session she recalled memory after memory, each of which served to heighten her self-disgust, accompanied by intense de-pression, anxiety, and nausea. Supportive, cognitive, and interpretive interventions failed to have an effect; her self-disgust and panic feelings continued to spiral. It felt like she was sinking deeper and deeper into her memories; the therapist experienced a spontaneous image of a series of mirrors, where each mirrored the other's image until it seemed the image had infinite depth, so it was impossible to break free.

Finally, the therapist commented that it seemed she thought that since these things happened to her, they *were* her, or somehow in her, as if she had become the event. The therapist reminded her that if you place dung in front of a mirror, the mirror will reflect the dung, but the mirror remains unblemished. The therapist pointed out that as she recalled the sexual abuse, she was treating herself as if she were the dung; in fact, she was the mirror, and however much dung you place in front of a mirror, and however many reflections of dung the mirror holds, the mirror itself remains unblemished.

This intervention resulted in a dramatic change in the patient's pres-entation. Her cascade of intrusive memories stopped. She looked stunned, then heaved a big sigh. "You mean, I'm not what happened to me?" she said. She paused, took this in, and visibly relaxed, experiencing tremendous relief. This made it possible to continue therapeutic work productively.

This intervention appeared to have substantial effect, perhaps because it was directed toward the "how" rather than the "what" of the client's experiencing and in so doing was more able to "resonate" with the client's experience.

Art's aim is not to elucidate or inform, but by its very existence to *resonate* to existence. Art, like therapy, is thus a form of empathy. When Sontag states that "a work of art is an experience, not a statement or an answer to a question," the therapist would do well to apply the dictum to clients' lives. Too many therapists will regard an intake interview as a task requiring an answer to a diagnostic question, leading to a tendency to regard the client as posing an exemplar of a psychopathological type. When, instead, psychotherapy aims at resonating to existence, it clarifies rather than classifies it; if a client is met with an openness to experience, frequently psychotherapy can make a substantial difference even in a single session (Bloom, 1981; DeShazer, 1985; Hoyt, Rosenbaum, & Talmon, 1992; Malan, Heath, Bacal, & Balfour, 1975; Rosenbaum, Hoyt, & Talmon, 1990; Talmon, 1990). The key here is to take an aesthetic approach in which "the knowledge we gain through art [therapy] is an experience of the *form* or *style* of knowing, rather than a knowledge *of* some *thing* (Sontag, 1966; italics added).

Unfortunately, the reifying tendency to fall back to content from process, to view the *what* as somehow separable from the *how*, is a perennial problem in psychotherapy. As far back as 1925, Freud bemoaned that prior to his *Interpretation of Dreams,* people mistook the manifest content of the dream for the dream itself, but that after the publication of his book, people made a similar error by mistaking the latent content for the dream itself. Freud insisted on identifying the dream with the *dreamwork* — an essentially processive approach which focuses on the formal characteristics of expression (Freud, 1900/1963).

Thus Sontag (1966), in attempting to rescue and re-legitimize the immediacy of experience, is led to the importance of formal qualities in art, which she sees as a matter of *style*.

> Practically all metaphors for style amount to placing matter on the inside, style on the outside. It would be more to the point to reverse the metaphor. The matter, the subject, is on the outside; the style is on the inside. As Cocteau writes: "Decorative style has never existed. Style is the soul. ..." Even if one were to define style as the manner of our appearing, this by no means necessarily entails an opposition between a style that one assumes and one's "true" being. ... In almost every case, our manner of appearing *is* our manner of being.
>
> Style is the principle of decision in a work of art, the signature of the artist's will ... "style" consists of the set of rules by which [the] game is played. In other words, what is inevitable in a work of art is the style. ...
> (pp. 17, 32–35)

When we approach style in this fashion, we can see that much of the essence of both a work of art and of personal psychological identity is a matter of style (Rosenbaum, 1988; 1990). It is common to talk of a therapist developing a distinctive style (Keeney, 1990; Mahoney & Norcross, 1993; Rosenbaum, 1988), but where we may treat the style of an artist with considerable respect, acknowledging its centrality to the definition of the artists' identity (Rosen, 1972), when we talk about style in therapy it is often treated as a minor appendage somehow distinct from the substance of the therapy.

Style, though, is precisely that which provides an essential aspect to its constituent elements; it brands them with a distinctive set of characteristics which identifies them, pointing to a historical context and often a specific creator. A person knowledgeable about musical styles, hearing just a few measures of an unfamiliar piece, will be able to recognize the composer, or at least the approximate historical epoch when the piece was written purely from the stylistic aspects of the piece. The same holds true for prominent therapists; it takes just a minute or so of audiotape to recognize you are listening to Albert Ellis and not Carl Rogers!

Style is sometimes unfairly regarded as merely a set of tricks: a preference for using one combination of musical instruments more often than another; for making interpretations more often than staying silent; for wearing one's hair in a certain fashion. Yet it is the totality of these small gestures within a defined sphere which form the "handwriting" by which we can recognize the identity of the composer, writer, therapist, or individual personality. Style tends to stamp itself indelibly, distinguishing and classifying whoever or whatever manifests the style. Style is the set of differences which make a difference; style allows us to apprehend the distinctive qualities which set something or someone apart. Because style, by providing recognizable distinguishing characteristics, is clearly intertwined with the concept of identity, it is possible to view individual (or family) "personality" as essentially expressions of distinctive *styles* of functioning (Kantor & Lehr, 1975; Shapiro, 1965; Horowitz et al., 1984).

Many will object to the idea that psychological (and artistic) identities are mostly a matter of style, arguing that distinctiveness and identity are provided by substantive internal characteristics. They argue that if we wish to discover what it is that lends distinctiveness to forms and processes, we cannot turn to style, which seems to be comprised of minor "surface" phenomena; that some substance, some content exists independent of its expression. We often seem to desire that the distinguishing characteristics of a work of art will lie deep "within" it; we wish to assert that something defines Stravinsky besides the use of doubled leading tones, ostinatos, and simultaneous minor and major thirds. We want to assert that it is something in Rembrandt's "soul" that distinguishes his paintings, rather than his use of browns and suffused light. In the same way, we often want to assert that our basic personal identity resides in some "inner person" rather than in the cut of our clothes, the cadence of our speech, or the mannerisms of our walk which allow people to identify us even from a distance.

The fact is, though, that we live in a world of appearances, and identity must be manifested through appearance. As Hannah Arendt points out (Arendt,

1978) it is the outside, surface features of living organisms which lend them individualized appearances; inside, we all look like. There are millions of discernible variations of facial features; kidneys, however, are fairly uniform. We can be identified not by our hearts, but by our fingerprints. Inside we are all more human than otherwise (Sullivan, 1954); even our inner wishes and fears are relatively monotonous and uniform. The "surface" style by which we manifest and display these fears and wishes, though, distinguishes us one from the other.

> Since we live in an *appearing* world, is it not much more plausible that the relevant and the meaningful in this world of ours should be located precisely on the surface? ... Our common conviction that what is inside ourselves, our "inner life," is more relevant to what we "are" than what appears on the outside, is an illusion. (Arendt, 1978, pp. 19–30, italics in the original)

Style provides a sense of identity to a piece of music, a psychotherapeutic school, or a personality. Style is more than a catalogue of idiosyncratic gestures and the relative frequency with which they are employed. If style were a static list of mannerisms, then we would be able to generate new pieces of music which would be indistinguishable from, say, Beethoven's originals merely by copying those mannerisms; similarly, we would be able to clone effective therapists from carbon copies of master clinicians. In fact, though, when this is attempted, the results are far from satisfactory, and are always recognizable as imitations rather than originals. It is possible to analyze the rules by which Bach wrote chorales, and then write a chorale following those rules. Whether it is unfortunate or fortunate we cannot say, but the fact remains that when you write such a chorale, it never sounds as good as one of Bach's.

In fact, when Bach wrote his chorales, he was not following the rules; he was simply writing music. Bach frequently did not follow his own rules: those "rules" we associate with Bach are merely things we can point to that he did frequently, abstractions we formulate, after Bach has finished writing, to help us understand the formal process which governs the experience of his music. Thus when we write a chorale following Bach's style it sounds like a stereotyped approximation rather than a work of beauty, precisely because in following the rules over-closely, we miss the deviations which lend it life.

The same holds true for therapeutic styles; although it can be useful to study the master therapists, it is hopeless to imitate them. Even though an appreciation of psychotherapy as a process of artistic creation may give us new insights into the pragmatics of technique, we must be careful not to apply our knowledge blindly, in a cookbook fashion. Because psychotherapy rests in the *modification* of experience, it will always be expressed stylistically, and style is not merely an accumulation of preferred gestures or techniques, nor is imitation the same as creation. Minuchin and Fishman (1981) have — like many artists — cautioned against seeking technique as an end in itself. Technique is necessary but not sufficient; one must learn technique, one must learn the formal structures, in order to then be able to develop a style for oneself. Otherwise, psychotherapy is "bad art," imitative and sterile. In the art of experience which constitutes psychotherapy, therapist and client can modify, but cannot escape, the necessity of creating and constantly reinventing their own styles.

Temporal Form in Psychotherapy

But where does this leave us? What use is the aesthetic perspective, if it doesn't tell us what to do differently? If we approach psychotherapy from the aesthetic perspective, must we rely on wild improvisation, with no guidelines? Does approaching therapy as an art mean there are no rules, no guidelines to tell us what to do? Must we forego all analysis and research, trusting instead to intuition and spontaneity?

Not at all. Quite the opposite, in fact. The romantic view that the creation of a work of art is essentially a process of inspiration is about as accurate as the lay view that psychotherapy consists largely of saying "uh-huh" and looking sympathetic. It is true that if we treat psychotherapy as an art, the therapist is condemned to be creative. Creativity, though, is always expressed through technique and form. Every modality of art is subject to an aesthetic analysis which reveals a large body of techniques which tell us how employing specific formal or stylistic elements conveys particular qualities of experience; approaching psychotherapy from an aesthetic perspective can help reveal formal elements which contribute to how therapy works. Space constrains us from a full exposition, but let us give some examples involving the structuring of time in psychotherapy.

Psychotherapy takes place in time; it examines patterns of current client experience in relation to past patterns, with a view to altering experience in the future. To do this, psychotherapy takes client experiences and subjects them to a temporal structure; the most common of these is the fifty-minute hour, occurring at the same time every week. Of course psychotherapies differ in this regard to varying degrees, but all psychotherapies ask a client to call forth experience within the closed time frame of the therapeutic session.

If we wish to see how the formal aspects of temporal organization affect psychotherapy, we can learn much from music. Music is the aesthetic ordering of patterns of sound which repeat and change over time; it is therefore isomorphic to psychotherapy in particular and to human experience in general. Music tells a variety of stories in patterns which develop rhythmically while speaking powerfully to our emotions; because these "stories" are devoid of linguistic content, music is particularly instructive for learning how altering form and process over time influences emotion and meaning.

As an example, take the scheduling of therapy sessions across a treatment. Therapies acquire a certain rhythm depending on how frequently and how regularly one meets with a client. If you are seeing a client every week on Mondays at 3:00 pm, and you go on vacation or become ill, it will not be surprising if on Monday at 3:00 pm on the week of your absence the client will sense "something is missing." This may occur regardless of the content of the previous session. This sense of something missing need not indicate the client has unusual dependency needs or transference issues: in music, such interruptions create similar emotions as a function of disrupted expectations; the expectations arise, though, from the formal process rather than from any instinctual "need." Similarly, a client's feelings about a missed session can be a response to a gap, an interruption or a delay in a well-ordered pattern. In other words, client responses can be at least partially due to purely formal considerations.

Interruption and delay within regular structures creates uncertainty and frustration; however, a client who experiences these feelings which arise in response to formal processes — that is, to a therapist missing a session — may then need to *explain* the feelings to himself. Focusing on content rather than process, the client (or therapist) might well ask what the feelings *mean*, and treat them as saying something significant about the client's personality. This can be a red herring, if the affective response is mostly a function of the therapy's formal structure. It is quite likely that if the client were being seen once a week, but sometimes on Mondays at 3:00 pm, and sometimes on Wednesdays at 10:00 am, and sometimes on Thursdays at 3:00 pm, that missing a Monday 3:00 pm meeting will not occasion the same feelings in the client. One of us (RR) worked in a setting where he had the opportunity to compare clients seen weekly at a regular time with clients seen weekly at varying times; missed sessions did tend to result in "transference" issues with the former, but not the latter, clients. This is an instance of how the aesthetics of musical rhythm can have a substantial influence on therapeutic technique.

Why should the scheduling of sessions create an affective "feel" in the absence of substantive content? We can gain some answers to this question by examining how music can cause deep emotions in the absence of any obvious semantic content. Generally in music a pattern is set up; it is then repeated, to further identify the pattern by establishing its starting and stopping points. Once a pattern has been established, on subsequent appearances, if a listener hears part of the known pattern, she expects the rest of the pattern (or highly related material) to follow. Meyer (1956; 1973) relates this basic musical assumption — that listeners expect patterns to be continued in accordance with the way they initially appeared in such a way that they appear "complete" — to the Gestalt law of good continuation (Pragnänz). A more modern cognitive approach to this phenomenon would be couched in terms of expectations. The repetition of patterns in time invokes memory. Simply stated, on one level, we expect things to stay the same, to continue on as they always have.

Because of the tendency to good continuation, if there are gaps or interruptions, we fill in the missing pieces and continue what has been delayed. If we hear the famous rhythm of Beethoven's *Fifth Symphony* — da-da-da-DAH — repeated a few times, then subsequently if we hear "da-da-da-" we'll feel something is incomplete unless the "DAH" follows. If a client comes to us who in the past had a relationship with an authority figure in which, whenever the client accomplished something, the authority figure would find a way to punish or demean them, we are not surprised if, when the client accomplishes something now, they wait for the negative consequences they expect to complete the established pattern.

So far this tells us little beyond conventional knowledge regarding the role of expectations. Music teaches us, however, that our expectations are not based only on mere repetition, but also on the inherent *structure* of a pattern. Because of this structure, patterns will still sound like "themselves" when they are altered in certain ways, but not others. Thus, for example, the "Ode to Joy" theme in Beethoven's Ninth Symphony sounds fine played in a minor key, but we would not expect to hear it played backwards; although some musical themes (such as fugal subjects) are often played in retrogression, the particular structure of the Ode makes such retrogression a highly unlikely event. Similarly, in our client whose accomplishments have been followed by disparagement, there are a number of more or less probable modes in which the client may expect to be demeaned: perhaps he will anticipate, to various degrees, being ignored, or sneered at, or punished. The client may even expect or hope to be rewarded, as a low-probability event; he will not, however, expect that if he tells his superior of an accomplishment, the superior will respond by standing on his head and reciting "You are old, Father William." Certain sequences and progressions are expected, allowed, "regular"; others are not.

Once we establish expectations, deviating from these expectations generates a sense of tension and anticipation; it is only through creating tension that we are able to achieve a satisfying sense of eventual resolution. Music must have enough regularity to constitute recognizable patterns but not so much as to be boringly repetitive; it must have enough variation to be interesting but not so much as to seem chaotic. A therapist must match a client's patterns with sufficient regular acceptance that they meet the client at his view of the world and establish an alliance, but not be so accepting that the therapist gets caught in the client's world-view and, therefore, is unable to alter it. The therapist must introduce sufficient unexpected consequences to the client to promote change, but not so much that is unexpected that it will overwhelm the client or lead to the dissolution of therapy (Rosenbaum, 1990).

Just as the composer must come up with specific methods to work out the implications of a pattern and resolve them, so clients and therapists need to take specific actions to move treatment forward. Music teaches that the degree and kind of resolution of a structural "problem" — be it a pattern with inherent conflict or a pattern with inherent incompleteness — depends in large part on the ways in which the expected process of working out implications is (purposefully) disturbed. There are many ways in which the unfolding of the expected consequences to a pattern may be frustrated or interrupted; music gives us a means of classifying the kinds of disturbances and their effects. The interested reader can find a discussion of the psychotherapeutic applications of musical techniques such as delays, interruptions, anticipations, saturations, and processive switching in Rosenbaum (1989).

A Musical Model of Termination in Psychotherapy

Having started this paper commenting on the structure of beginnings, it makes a nice symmetrical form if we end by examining the influence of structure on psychotherapeutic endings. Given that clinical lore often makes much of the process of termination, it is surprising that comparatively little is written regarding how to terminate therapy. Even within therapeutic schools, there is considerable controversy regarding termination. For example, within the fairly circumscribed camp of psychodynamic brief therapy, Mann (1973; Mann & Goldman, 1982) sees termination as crucial; Sifneos (1987) and Davanloo (1978) see it as a relatively minor manner. This is usually explained in terms of *content:* Sifneos and Davanloo focus on Oedipal issues, while Mann focuses on separation-individuation.

When termination focuses on the level of content rather than on pattern, termination is treated as a time to review what is stopping: what issues have been worked out, what remains undiscussed, and how one deals with the losses and disappointments inherent in any finite relationship. Such issues are certainly germane; every ending of a relationship, a therapy, or a piece of music will, by the very fact of ending, invoke to some extent the human struggle with finitude and mortality. However, dealing with termination only from this "content" perspective ignores the formal and processive aspects of therapy. Without knowledge of the formal aspects of therapeutic structure, we will find it difficult to determine whether, in the context of a particular therapy, the "content" issues of cessation and finitude are or are not important.

For example, it is our experience that treatment contracts which, from the outset, are time-limited and overtly establish a fixed number of sessions, tend to result in termination becoming a "hot topic" for clients; when we have left the treatment contract open-ended, even within a brief therapy frame, termination has been much less of an issue (Hoyt, Rosenbaum, & Talmon, 1992). Something similar seems to occur at the level of single sessions. In a research project which attempted to maximize the work clients could accomplish in their first treatment session (Rosenbaum, Hoyt, & Talmon, 1990), when the form of the treatment was altered by making the length of the session flexible — clients were told they and the therapist could take "as much time as we need, up to two hours" — clients often felt they had completed more work than usual. What is interesting about this was that usually the actual duration of the session did not surpass fifty minutes, the length of an "ordinary" session. Simply altering the form — open-ended rather than closed-ended — appeared to affect the way clients (and therapists) worked.

The way a therapy is organized and configured interacts with how it proceeds, and this will affect the sense of completion at the end of a treatment. Meyer (1956; 1973) has argued that what creates a sense of closure in music is how formal structure interacts with the processive working-through of thematic implications. In both music and therapy, the *process* by which patterns' implications are worked out may or may not be congruent with the *formal* articulation.

For example, a process may end before its formal structure is completed. In music, a phrase may be shorter than its meter; in this situation, the composer usually employs echoes and extensions of the phrase so that the meter and the working-out of the phrase will coincide. The same thing occurs in psychotherapy. A client may be dealing with certain issues and reach some conclusion in a session before the "standard" fifty minutes are up; if the formal structure of the therapy demands sessions of equal length, what do client and therapist then do with the extra time? Simply continuing talking may feel forced. Another frequent example of processive completion anticipating formal endings is in time-limited therapies with a fixed number of sessions. Frequently, the penultimate session completes most of the emotional processing. The very last session may be anticlimactic, a mere echo or extension of the previous process; it fills out the formal structure of a fixed number of sessions, but the emotional processing has ended previously.

Conversely, processes may continue beyond their formal structures. Audiences often leave a concert with the music still reverberating in their minds; even when the concert is "over" it may continue to influence how audience members react to music they hear later on. In a similar fashion, when a therapist says at the end of a session "It will be interesting to see what you (dream, think, feel, notice differently, experience) over the coming week," the same prolongation of process past form occurs. Psychotherapies often continue even after they are formally "finished" (that is, after clients and therapist are no longer meeting); the client will continue to "metabolize" the emotional significance of the treatment for months after it has formally ended and may think about the therapist in critical life situations (see, for example, Shectman, 1986; Mann & Goldman, 1982; Hoyt, 1990; Rosenbaum, Hoyt & Talmon, 1990).

The alignment of form and process is important because music and therapy tend to move forward when these parameters are noncongruent, and slow down or stop when these converge. Closure depends on both: we must first have a sense of divergence, of noncongruence, so that when noncongruence is resolved, we can have a sense of something completed. Within the formal temporal organization, closure is determined by departures and returns; within the processive aspect, closure is determined by how the various possible pathways implied by the structure of a pattern are worked out.

Let us deal with formal temporal organization first. In music and psychotherapy, one establishes the boundaries of a pattern by repeating it. This marks where it begins and where it ends; by establishing where the stopping point of a pattern is, the pattern becomes distinct. This creates the possibility not only for the pattern to be repeated, but also for the pattern to *return*. When other intervening events occur before a pattern is repeated, then the repetition becomes transformed into a return. Such repetition and return is frequently used to lend rhythm to lines of poetry or episodes of stories. Returns, as opposed to repetitions, come after a departure from the original material; hence returns can signal a re-arrival. *Returns,* but not repetitions, enhance closure.

To obtain closure, one must digress from the original pattern. When the earlier pattern reappears, it will seem different on its return because of what has happened during the intervening time period. Even if the pattern appears in its "original" manifest appearance, note for note and point for point, its context and its history have changed, and thus its meaning has changed forever. The old saying goes "one cannot step into the same stream twice," but it would be more accurate to say that one cannot step into the same stream twice *once having stepped out of it* ; as long as you are immersed in the stream, you may step through it again and again, repetitively. Stepping out of the stream, though, means any re-immersion in its waters will be a return rather than a repetition. In a way, each psychotherapy session offers an opportunity for clients to step out of the stream of patterns they are currently immersed in; if this occurs, then any subsequent recurrence of a problematic pattern begins to take on the quality of a return rather than a repetition. In the process, the pattern is changed forever.

Although clients may come to therapy with some hope that they will be able to banish a problem immediately and forever, and may even become discouraged if a problem reappears during the course of treatment, therapists realize that a working-through process is often necessary. This requires revisiting the problem, but this is not the same as *repeating* it; as long as there has been some divergence from the original problem in the interim, this will alter the context through which the problematical pattern is viewed on its return.

This is particularly important toward the end of a piece of music or a psychotherapy. Just as a piece of symphonic music may return, in its finale section, to themes articulated in the beginning, so too psychotherapies often recapitulate, in miniature, the original presenting patterns as the end of a therapy approaches. Although clients may become alarmed, many therapists have learned not to be surprised if a symptom returns near the termination of treatment. The recurrence of a symptom in this fashion does not necessarily indicate a regression. Rather, the reappearance of a symptom during termination can satisfy an aesthetic necessity by providing a return which enhances closure. When new patterns have emerged since the last appearance of the symptom, the return of the symptom can represent a way of attaching new meanings to an old pattern and reinforcing these new meanings within a larger structure of change; the return offers an opportunity for a last goodbye, a movement toward making an end which both creates the possibility for, and is created by, an openness to new experience. In this way, new beginnings are achieved through endings.

Endings activate memory through returns: reminders of what has gone before. The sequencing of *what* was repeated and remembered *when* constitutes the *formal* organization of events which influences the experience of closure during termination. Because the original material has been departed from, returns punctuate the fact that certain implications of a pattern have been realized and worked through, while others have not. An additional contribution to the experience of closure thus comes from the working-through of patterns' implications: this constitutes the *processive* aspect of termination.

From their first appearance the structures of patterns inherently generate expectations regarding their future development. Patterns imply not a single goal, but a number of alternative goals, and in any musical or therapeutic process, some implications will be realized while others will not. The processive aspect of closure revolves around the number of alternative goals which have been considered, the degree to which each has been explored, and the extent to which the actualized implications were originally seen as highly probable or as unlikely to occur. If we hear a brisk musical theme introduced by a trumpet, on some level we expect to hear it treated subsequently as a martial air; the composer, however, may or may not oblige. The martial theme may not be introduced at all, or it may appear as a passing episode, or as a major part of the movement. All of this will affect our sense of how complete the music will sound.

In psychotherapy, if a client tells us one parent was alcoholic, we may expect we will subsequently hear themes about abuse or neglect. It is possible these themes may come to be major issues for the therapy; or perhaps treatment will focus on other matters and devote little or no time to themes related to these concerns. Sometimes clients and/or therapists may collude, in a misalliance, to avoid exploring important implications of a pattern (Langs, 1976a, 1976b); at other times it will be necessary to eliminate the wheat from the chaff and ignore certain implications in order to establish a coherent therapeutic focus (see, for example, Hatcher, Huebner, & Zakin, 1986; Strupp & Binder, 1984). An important part of treatment involves *not* enacting certain implications; when the client is expecting or "testing" (Sampson, 1976) whether the therapist will respond in a way consistent with maladaptive interactions in the past, it is, of course, important that the therapist not respond in this fashion.

Each treatment will differ in the extent to which it attempts to exhaustively explore the implications of relevant patterns or leaves some implications unresolved, and this will affect the sense of closure. However, our understanding of an event always includes not just what occurred — the realized implications — but also what *might* have happened. Because of the availability of multiple implications from patterns, *beginnings cannot be understood until the end*. Implications must be comprehended largely in retrospect; endings give meaning to events by illuminating the consequences of the initial event, by finalizing what route was actually traveled and what routes will never be surveyed, now that the journey is over. It is not until the therapy has ended that the client knows for certain which implications will and will not be realized: up until the final session, there is the possibility that other feared or hoped for implications will emerge. Ultimately, we don't know the full consequences of any of our actions until we die; similarly, we cannot know the implications of a psychotherapy until it is completed.

Because closure depends on the structure of departures and returns, and on the degree of realization of implications, there are multiple methods to handle termination. Composers, therapists, and clients have choices about when and how to make an ending. Rosenbaum (1989) explored musical finales and was able to identify several methods composers use to end pieces of music (Table 1). Each of these musical terminations can be a useful way of ending a treatment session or a complete psychotherapy. The full details of these, and of how to choose a modality of termination, are beyond the scope of this chapter. By way of illustration, though, let us examine two of the techniques listed in the table — transformation and restatement — by considering the differences between termination in variation form and in sonata-allegro form.

Forms in Termination: Variations and Sonatas

Musical forms vary in both the degree and kinds of change the original material undergoes over the course of the form. Variation form in music consists of transformations of a single rather well-formed theme — often a hummable "tune" — in which the essential nature of the theme is gradually revealed through successive elaborations or condensations. The theme is played again and again, each time in its entirety but each time illuminating some new, often unexpected aspect of its potential. Variation themes require only a single motive which may be expanded, condensed, elaborated, and so forth. With each repetition, the original material remains identifiable and whole.

In sonata form, two themes are contrasted at the outset, appearing initially in different keys; often these themes are somewhat fragmentary, or contain some discrepancy, discord, or incompleteness which leaves the listener wondering how the musical "problem" will be resolved. Sonatas require more than one piece of main material, because they employ a development section which relies on establishing new relationships between contrasting elements; in the development, the sonata's themes are broken down into more elemental parts which are combined with each other or transformed in unexpected ways. Unlike the

Table 1

Musical Techniques of Termination in Psychotherapy

Technique	Musical Description	Therapeutic Analog
Stinger	Brief exclamations without implication which punctuate an ending; often a single chord at the end of a short song	Word or sentence without implication punctuates ending of therapeutic segment (e.g., "OK," "Take care," "See you next week," "Goodbye")
Fade-out	Process is attentuated, often through lack of new material arising	Therapy gradually gets boring, runs out of steam; can result from therapeutic impasse; also can be useful way of gradually "weaning" fragile client
Slowdown	Gradual spacing out of the material	Usually done by spacing out treatment sessions; gives client chance to practice, gain confidence
Cessations	Abrupt endings after multiple repetitions of material	"Shock" ending can be useful with client who is using therapy inappropriately or is obsessively "stuck"
Multi-path	(Ambiguous) Several possible implications are stated but not resolved, with implications intentionally left hanging	Client left with paradox or "seed" images which are incomplete as treatment ends; client continues working-through after formal therapy is over
Transformation	Original material reappears but is altered subsequent to achieving resolution	Return in sonata form; useful for confirming conflict-resolution
Restatement	Original material reappears unaltered after it has been explored throughly from different perspectives	Return in variation form; useful for confirming "growth"
Transcendence	Original material is related to external references which go beyond the immediate form	Emergence of creative, new patterns beyond that directly relevant to therapy work (e.g, spirituality)

variation form, in which each appearance of the theme is recognizable as an elaboration of the original, sonatas' development sections juxtapose, contrast, and generally jumble up component parts of themes in the service of investigating them fully; although the resulting relationship of the material to the original theme is not always obvious, discrepancies are explored, and an attempt is made to *resolve* the discrepancies.

Whereas variation forms usually involve a somewhat stately pleasure at a progressive unfolding and exploration of the material, sonata forms usually involve a substantial amount of conflict and tension. This tension creates the possibility for eventual especially satisfying resolutions, enhanced by a recapitulation section which repeats the original material in a stable (congruent) version (that is, both of the original themes appear in the same, rather than contrasting, keys). On recapitulation, the old material is perceived differently, by virtue of all that has been learned and experienced during the development. Whereas development in sonata form depends on exploring discrepancies and incongruities, change in variation form is incremental, based on examining conformative relationships: *similarities* between successive versions are the subject of the investigation.

In therapy, various schools propose different forms of treatment that influence the kinds and degrees of change clients will undertake. Any therapy in which the client is encouraged to repeatedly elaborate on their experience while the therapist utilizes empathic mirroring or reflection, employs what is essentially a variation form. Whether the therapist is labeled Kohutian, Rogerian, or humanistic, the form of therapy involves exploration of clients' themes while cultivating an holistic appreciation of the incremental variations that occur, leading to gradual growth. In contrast, other therapies resemble sonata form in that they are essentially analytic: they take the client's material and explain it by breaking it down into smaller segments and contrasting it with other bits of material and experience. Both the interpretive psychodynamic schools and the cognitive and behavioral therapies employ an analytic methodology in which one component aspect of experience is contrasted against another: rational is contrasted with irrational thinking, anxiety-producing imagery is contrasted with deep muscle relaxation; present feelings are compared with early memories or wishes, all in the service of finding a resolution to a presenting symptom which is seen as having some discrepancy which must be explored. Within the family therapy field, a similar division exists between those schools which favor a holistic approach to experience (for example, Whitaker, 1979a, 1979b) and those which favor segmenting and punctuating components of experience to be contrasted against other components (such as Fisch, Weakland, & Segal, 1982; Minuchin & Fishman, 1981). Thus encouraging variation versus exploring discrepancy seems to be a distinguishing issue for many psychotherapies, although it should be noted that many other forms of both therapy and music exist.

Variation forms are essentially additive; their low degree of structure can be seen in the fact that there is no predetermined number of variations which must be accomplished, nor are there kinds of variations which are prescribed. Variation forms therefore lack internally-structured points of probable termination; you can basically add as many variations as you can think of (and as your listeners will tolerate), then stop.

Lacking an inherent stopping-point, variation forms often achieve closure through restatement: after the variations are completed the original theme is presented in its unadorned, unaltered form at the very end of the piece. The restatement thus juxtaposes the original material against what has changed. All the intervening variations thus function as departures from the theme; the restatement of the original theme at the end provides a return which establishes a sense of closure. Because variation forms achieve incremental changes through elaboration, rather than seeking resolution through analytically breaking down the material, variation forms are more "processive" and less "formal" than sonatas; change has involved expansion and elaboration, and closure is rounded by acceptance, and a sense of broadening, but not necessarily by a sense of resolution won after a hard-fought struggle. The sense of closure, while present, is not terribly strong, because there is a sense that there can always be more variations added or further growth at some later date.

A sense of higher closure depends on a greater amount of formal structure. In music, this is epitomized in the sonata form, which concentrates on exploring implications in a prescribed ordering of events (introduction, exposition, development, recapitulation) which leads to a special ending section: the coda. A coda is the very last statement of a musical composition, and takes the previous material and treats it from one last new perspective which, however, does not generate any implications or pathways for further exploration. The coda functions as a "last glance" at the material, seen from some distance, much as we might turn around and look at a city we are leaving when we are already some miles away from it. We can no longer do anything to change what has happened in the city, but our last view of it somehow encapsulates our experiences there. Codas offer one last departure from the expected to allow a return to the original material in full force; because this restatement of the original material is without implications or discrepancies, but is balanced and resolved, it lends a strong feeling of completion to the work. There are a variety of musical means one can use to evoke such nonimplicative closing statements. One way is to state the material a final time in a manner which appeared neither in the development section nor in the initial statement, but which is somehow complete in and of itself.

We have already mentioned how in time-limited therapies, the penultimate session often seems to "conclude" the treatment so that the very last session functions as an anticlimax. This tends to occur if therapist and client have strong expectations for an intense last session which never materializes. The alternative is to structure the very last session of a time-limited therapy as a coda. This is easier said than done: it may be difficult to provide a new perspective to the client in this last meeting which does not seem to open the door to further treatment. (In music, the coda often represents the very peak of a composer's inventiveness). On the other hand, when such new perspectives are attained in the final session, the client may appear transformed, as in the following example:

In one time-limited twelve-session therapy conducted by the first author, the client's presenting problem involved a pattern of being unassertive about her own wants and needs. She would please others excessively because she felt afraid that if she did not, people would abandon her; she also became anxious and guilty if she did something for herself, such as take a vacation or even go to a movie. All this was explored in some depth during the treatment, and the client made considerable gains. She became more assertive, more able to recognize her own wishes and act on them in appropriate ways. Termination, predictably, activated fears that by asserting herself within therapy she was "causing" herself to be abandoned by ending treatment. In the penultimate session she was able to grapple with her new-found ability to "go it alone without supports" if need be and treat herself well.

In the very last session, though, the perspective shifted. Rather than focusing on how others might abandon her, she was able to talk about how, fearing loss, she would protect herself from becoming close to people. She talked openly about how she felt close to the therapist and did not want to leave. This effected a deepening of the therapeutic work; we were able to discuss how we would go on remembering each other and acknowledge, with mutual expressions of appreciation, the value of what had been accomplished.

The client left in an emotionally-charged atmosphere of fondness, satisfaction, and sadness. I remained in the room a few more minutes, savoring what I thought was the end of the therapy. However, there was still a coda to come.

There was a knock on the door. The client came back in, stating she had left her keys behind. She picked up the keys, and said, "I guess I really don't want to leave, do I? (Long pause. Then she holds up her keys). But now I've got my keys. I can go now."

Silently, the client and I acknowledged the truth in both the literal statement and the metaphor.

On follow-up by an independent evaluator, the client was not only being more assertive, but was successfully engaging in more intimate relationships.

Conclusion

We hope that this foray into an aesthetic approach to psychotherapy will incite interest in what we see as the vast possibilities opened by such a perspective. When we approach psychotherapy from an artistic perspective, and treat psychotherapy itself as a kind of art, then the nature of experience becomes clarified: experience being inherently inchoate and ungraspable, it can nonetheless be realized through a medium of formal expression. We then become more aware of how formal and stylistic issues organize the content of psychotherapeutic experience. Our attention expands so we are no longer concerned just with interpreting *what* an experience is, but also with examining the "surface" issues of *how* the experience is. Examining this area offers insights into practical matters of technique, which we have illustrated by a literary analysis of beginnings and a musical analysis of endings in psychotherapy.

When we adopt an aesthetic perspective, we become concerned not just with accuracy but also with vision. When we do this, it is no longer sufficient to remain only in the pragmatic realm of *what* to *do* with a client, but also *how* to *be* with a client. This is not a question of turning mindlessly intuitive; the aesthetic perspective teaches us how to improve our methods of expression through rigorous analysis and mastery of techniques which pure pragmatics may ignore. Intuition, though, is also an important ability to develop for an artist, scientist, therapist, or client. A good mathematician gets a "feel" for how to approach a problem, then subjects that feeling to rigorous analysis. Therapists need a similar mix of structured rules and creative freedom. The different methods by which artists train artists to go beyond imitation into expressiveness could also be helpful in moving the training of psychotherapists beyond what is conveyed in a treatment manual; an aesthetic perspective can help direct us toward domains where intuition and creativity arise in the context of rigorous formal technique

Form and process, structure and content, thinking and feeling must all combine if we wish to create not only satisfying works of art, but also satisfying lives. Each of our client's lives, each of their stories, can be approached as a potential work of art. Good therapists exercise their craft by combining a knowledge of the structure of human experience with a creative intuition about finding the best processes to assist clients to shape the experiences of their lives into more fulfilling forms. But how do therapists or clients move from craftsmanship to art? Here Dewey (1934/1987) provides us with the wisdom of the aesthetic perspective, advising us that

> Craftsmanship to be artistic in the final sense must be "loving"; it must care deeply for the subject matter upon which skill is exercised. (p. 210)

It is not possible to apply creative techniques derived from aesthetics without critical judgment; the purpose of critical judgment, though, is to help us learn how to more fully *appreciate* a piece of art. This is the essence of psychotherapy: learning to appreciate our own and our clients' experiences every single moment, moment by moment. Such appreciation is the basic form of empathy we rely on for psychotherapy to exercise its healing art. In psychotherapy, the art we gaze at, listen to, and touch is not a museum piece but the basic stuff of our client's lives: the art of human experience.

References

Arendt, H. (1978). *The life of the mind.* New York: Harcourt Brace Jovanovich.

Bateson, G. (1972). *Steps to an ecology of mind.* New York: Ballantine Books.

Bateson, G. (1979). *Mind and nature: A necessary unity.* New York: E. P. Dutton.

Bloom, B. L. (1981). Focused single-session therapy: Initial development and evaluation. In S. H. Budman (Eds.), *Forms of brief therapy* (pp. 167–214). New York: Guilford Press.

Bohart, A. (1993). Experiencing: The basis of psychotherapy. *Journal of Psychotherapy Integration, 3,* 51–67.

Davanloo, H. (Ed.). (1978). *Basic principles and techniques in short-term dynamic psychotherapy.* New York: Spectrum.

DeShazer, S. (1985). *Keys to solution in brief therapy.* New York: W. W. Norton.

Dewey, J. (1934/1987). Art as experience. In S. Ross (Ed.). *An anthology of aesthetic theory* (pp. 205–224). New York: State University of New York Press.

Fisch, R., Weakland, J. H., & Segal, L. (1982). *The tactics of change: Doing therapy briefly.* San Francisco: Jossey-Bass.

Freud, S. (1963). The interpretation of dreams. In J. Strachey (Ed. & Transl.), *The Standard Edition of the Complete Psychological Works of Sigmund Freud (Vol. 5).* London: Hogarth Press. (Original work published 1900).

Gendlin, E. T. (1991). On emotion in therapy. In J. D. Safran & L. S. Greenberg (Eds.), *Emotion, psychotherapy, and change* (pp. 255–279). New York: Guilford.

Hatcher, S. L., Huebner, D. A., & Zakin, D. F. (1986). Following the trail of the focus in time-limited psychotherapy. *Psychotherapy, 23,* 513–520.

Horowitz, M., Marmar, C., Krupnick, J., Wilner, N., Kaltreider, N., & Wallerstein, R. (1984). *Personality styles and brief psychotherapy.* New York: Basic Books.

Hoyt, M. (1990). On time in brief therapy. In R. Wells & V. J. Gianetti (Eds.), *Handbook of the brief psychotherapies* (pp. 115–144). New York: Plenum Press.

Hoyt, M., Rosenbaum, R., & Talmon, M. (1992). Planned single-session therapies. In S. Budman, M. F. Hoyt, & S. Friedman (Eds.), *The first session in brief therapy: A book of cases* (pp. 59–86). New York: Guilford.

Kantor, D., & Lehr, W. (1975). *Inside the family: Toward a theory of family process.* San Francisco: Jossey-Bass.

Keeney, B. P. (1982). Not pragmatics, not aesthetics. *Family Process, 21,* 429–434.

Keeney, B. P., &. Spreckle, D. (1982). Ecosystemic epistemology: Critical implications for the aesthetics and pragmatics of family therapy. *Family Process, 21,* 1–19.

Keeney, B. P. (1983). *Aesthetics of change.* New York: Guilford Press.

Keeney, B. P. (1990). *Improvisational therapy: A practical guide for creative clinical strategies.* St. Paul, MN: Systemic Therapy Press.

Langs, R. (1976a). *The bipersonal field.* New York: Jason Aronson.

Langs, R. (1976b). *The therapeutic interaction.* New York: Jason Aronson.

MacLeish, A. (1976). *New and collected poems: 1917–1976.* Boston: Houghlin-Mifflin.

Mahoney, M., & Norcross, J. (1993). Relationship styles and therapeutic choices: A commentary. *Psychotherapy, 30,* 423–426.

Malan, D., Heath, E., Bacal, H., & Balfour, F. (1975). Psychodynamic changes in untreated neurotic patients: Apparently genuine improvements. *Archives of General Psychiatry, 32,* 110–126.

Mann, J. (1973). *Time-limited psychotherapy.* Cambridge: Harvard University Press.

Mann, J., & Goldman, R. (1982). *A casebook in time-limited psychotherapy.* New York: McGraw-Hill.

Meyer, L. B. (1956). *Emotion and meaning in music.* Chicago: University of Chicago Press.

Meyer, L. B. (1973). *Explaining music: Essays and explorations.* Berkeley: University of California Press.

Minuchin, S., & Fishman, H.C. (1981). *Family therapy techniques.* Cambridge: Harvard University Press.

Omer, H. (1993). Quasi-literary elements in psychotherapy. *Psychotherapy, 30,* 59–66.

Omer, H., & Alon, N. (1997). *Constructing therapeutic narratives.* New York: Jason Aronson.

Omer, H., & Strenger, P. (1992). The pluralist revolution: From the one true meaning to an infinity of constructed ones. *Psychotherapy, 29,* 253–261.

Rosen, C. (1972). *The classical style: Haydn, Mozart, Beethhoven.* New York: W. W. Norton.

Rosenbaum, R. (1988). Feelings toward integration: A matter of style and identity. *Journal of Integrative and Eclectic Psychotherapy, 7,* 52–60.

Rosenbaum, R. (1989, April). *Music and mind: Forms of stability, change, and integration.* Paper presented at the symposium of the Fifth Annual Conference of the Society for the Exploration of Psychotherapy Integration, Berkeley, CA, USA.

Rosenbaum, R. (1990). Strategic psychotherapy. In R. Wells & V. Gianetti (Eds.), *Handbook of the brief psychotherapies* (pp. 351–404). New York: Plenum Press.

Rosenbaum, R., Hoyt, M., & Talmon, M. (1990). The challenge of single-session psychotherapies: Creating pivotal moments. In R. Wells & V. Gianetti (Eds.), *Handbook of the brief psychotherapies* (pp. 165–192). New York: Plenum Press.

Rothenberg, A. (1992). Form and structure and their function in psychotherapy. *American Journal of Psychotherapy, 46,* 357–382.

Russell, R. L., & Van den Broek, P. (1992). Changing narrative schemas in psychotherapy. *Psychotherapy, 29,* 344–354.

Sampson, H. (1976). A critique of certain traditional concepts in the psychoanalytic theory of therapy. *Bulletin of the Menninger Clinic, 10,* 255-262.

Schafer, R. (1981). *Narrative actions in psychoanalysis.* Worcester, MA: Clark University Press.

Shapiro, D. (1965). *Neurotic styles.* New York: Basic Books.

Shectman, F. (1986). Time and the practice of psychotherapy. *Psychotherapy, 23,* 521–525.

Sifneos, P. E. (1987). *Short-term dynamic psychotherapy: Evaluation and technique.* (2nd ed.) New York: Plenum Medical Book Co.

Sontag, S. (1966). *Against interpretation, and other essays.* New York: Farrar, Straus & Giroux.

Spence, D. F. (1982). *Narrative truth and historical truth: Meaning and interpretation in psychoanalysis.* New York: W. W. Norton.

Strupp, H., & Binder, J. (1984). *Psychotherapy in a new key: A guide to time-limited dynamic psychotherapy*. New York: Basic Books.

Sullivan, H. S. (1954). *The psychiatric interview* (H. S. Perry & M. L. Grave, Eds.). New York: W. W. Norton.

Talmon, M. (1990). *Single session therapy: Maximizing the effect of the first (and often only) therapeutic encounter*. San Francisco: Jossey-Bass.

Watzlawick, P., [Bavelas] Beavin, J. H., & Jackson, D. D. (1967). *Pragmatics of human communication: A study of interactional patterns, pathologies, and paradoxes*. New York: W.W. Norton.

Whitaker, C. (1979a). The importance to the family therapist of being impotent. In *The best of the family, 1973–1978*. New Rochelle, NY: The Center for Family Learning.

Whitaker, C. (1979b). On family therapy (Interview with Bruce Howe). *Pilgrimage: The Journal of Existential Psychology, 7*, 107–114.

White, M., & Epston, D. (1990). *Narrative means to therapeutic ends*. New York: W. W. Norton.

CHAPTER EIGHTEEN

Action Stories

Ilene Ava Serlin

Growing attention is being paid to the use of narratives for healing (Feinstein & Krippner, 1988; May, 1989, Sarbin, 1986). However, these narratives are usually verbal, and the stories they tell come from the oral tradition.

The predominance of verbal narratives reflects a culture in which the word and the eye take precedence over the body and intuitive ways of knowing. The postmodern information explosion has increasingly reduced human interactions to bits of information, to cognitive processes that parallel those of the computer. The image of the computer as a symbol for this postmodern situation tells us that it is information which is of top value. The information age brings a loss of the tactile dimension of life, a replacement of behavior by cognition, action is devalued. Psyche, understood as an interior event of habitual and somewhat changeable thought patterns, is no longer in our worlds, in the landscape, in social action. Psyche is not understood as speaking through action.

Yet narratives may be non-verbal as well as verbal. Actions tell stories; in the old days, we were told to judge people by their actions, or that actions spoke louder than words. We were taught that integrity meant a congruence between individuals' thinking, feeling, and action, or, as the Buddhists say, between body, speech, and mind. We also knew how easily words could cover devious intentions or behavior, and judged others' words by their "goodness of fit" with their behavior, how they "walked their talk." Finally, we may remember the early stories told to us by our mothers, not so much in the words or the storyline, but in the tone of voice, the cool hand laid on a brow, her silent presence. The psychological meaning was embedded in these tactile moments, much as Proust's memory was embedded in a madeleine cookie. The meaning of stories lies not just in their verbal content or storyline, but in the whole gestalt of context, atmosphere, and timing.

Yet most of us are not trained in the art of non-verbal storytelling. As children, we may have learned to mime, to mimic each other or our teachers. We may have learned the agility of acrobatics, to sense the communication in the teamwork of sports, to know which limbs can be trusted when climbing a tree. Children in other cultures, however, learn a great deal more about nonverbal behavior. For example, in Bali, children are taught specific dance forms at an early age, in which their parents use their own bodies to mirror and to shape the limbs of their children. Through these dances, and in the dances of other cultures, children learn important lessions about cultural symbols, values, and traditions.

Beyond the early experiences of play, and the often-dreaded gym class, most Westerners do not learn how to articulate their bodies with any of the sophistication with which they learn to articulate words. Yet the ability to be nonverbally articulate and communicative is teachable, and potentially available for everyone. For example, in my therapeutic work with cancer patients, with seniors in nursing homes, and with psychotherapy clients, I draw extensively from their behaviors to weave nonverbal narratives which are healing. Through movement, they express grief and loss, disconnection and blockage, but then the movement may also turn into joy, reconnection, and a renewed life flow. The stories of death and rebirth, descent into sadness and ascent into joy, and disconnection and reconnection, expressed through movement, are ancient and common to all humankind.

How can we describe these nonverbal narratives? As a dance therapist who was trained in movement notation, I have learned to recognize patterns of time, weight, space, and flow in a movement process. Like a good story, a good or healing movement pattern will have a clear beginning, middle, and end. Like good music, healing movement will have an inner logic, a flow of events which changes organically without being contrived. Good or healthy movement has the characteristics described by the Hungarian psychoanalyst Susan Deri (1988) as a good Gestalt, in which the parts fit together in a coherent and meaningful whole. This good Gestalt also describes a good life as set forth by Mary Catherine Bateson (1989) who uses the metaphor of jazz improvisation to show that the composition of a good life has harmony as well as some dissonance, balance as well as some asymmetry, and a beginning, middle, and end.

Continuing the metaphor of jazz improvisation, we can see that the compositional aspects of any art form, whether it be painting, music or dance, can be used to diagnose and also to help construct and reconstruct a healthy life. How would this process be described verbally?

Although movement speaks eloquently about a person's story, or about a group process, little of this communication shows up in the literature. Besides the usual pathologically-oriented phrases of the intake interview ("patient appeared dishevelled, twitched nervously," and so on), notes usually are not made of the nonverbal behaviors. In my breast cancer research group, for example, one woman began the group with shoulders rotated in, a sunken torso, arms close to her side, standing back away from the circle, and using a very limited amount of personal space (that is, her kinesphere). By the end of the group, she was standing straighter, had an expanded range of motion and interactive gesture, and was initiating movements. Group process observations might pick up the fact that she had worked through some of her initial anger and withholding, had begun to experience more trust, and was emerging as one of the group leaders. The research results might show that her anxiety and depression had decreased; neither report would note the story told in her action.

Why is there is such a lack of attention to the nonverbal story? The history of literacy in the West has emphasized the written text, with its dialogue between writer and reader. The text, with its prototype in the Torah, Bible, and Koran, emphasizes the written word. Movement behavior, or action, is not understood as a text which is a dialogue between a mover and a witness. How might movement be understood as a text in a way which might provide the foundation to understand the language and stories of the body?

In this chapter, therefore, I work with the idea of text to understand and interpret the language of movement. Once this foundation is provided, it is hoped that the language of movement may become more accessible and useful to the therapist who does not utilize dance and/or movement as modalities.

Action Language

As a movement therapist, I read body movement as the text through which the patient's mode of being is made manifest. If his (or her) movements are

Figure 1

meaningful, then how can he (or she) and I understand their meaning? Can we let the movement speak its own meaning, so that inappropriate metaphorical or symbolic structures are not imposed on it?

The popularization of body language has spawned a bewildering array of nonverbal languages. For example, we might imagine a group of clinicians interpreting the meaning of the movement moment in Figure 1. One therapist might point out the subject's "closed" versus "open" position; another might notice the timing, weight shifts, and phrasing; a third might see a boy developmentally fixed at his mother's knee" while a fourth might see prayers and rituals of transformation. Which one of these perspectives is real, or are they all contained in the movement? What criteria would guide a therapist's choice of focus, and what level at what moment is salient for the therapeutic process?

Kinesthetic Imagining

The process by which movement becomes a text which has a narrative form, literal and symbolic content, and meaning is one which I call kinesthetic imagining. Kinesthetic refers to the kind of perception which originates in moving muscles. It is compounded from the Greek word "kinesis" which means "perception." In the original root word, therefore, the combination of movement and perception was already present. Imagining is the process by which images are generated and formed. This understanding of imagining as an active process is based on Jean-Paul Sartre's (1968) definition of image as a "structure of imaginative consciousness" and on Edward Casey's (1976) description of imagination as a verb and a process rather than as a product or a thing. Put together, kinesthetic imagining is the process by which the perceptions arising from moving muscles generate and make explicit imaginative structures of consciousness.

As a narrative process, kinesthetic imagining gives form and articulation to events in time. Instead of beginning with the word, kinesthetic imagining begins with the concrete sensation of moving muscles. Moving muscles generate associated feelings, thoughts, and meanings which show up as embodied images. These embodied images flow into one another, creating a storyline or a dance. These dances speak about individual personality style and organization, about group dynamics, and about mythic patterns: they are nonverbal personal and collective mythologies (Feinstein & Krippner, 1988). As embodied narrative, kinesthetic imagining is a dynamic process by which people often compose themselves and form their lives.

The Lived Body

If Cartesian dualism has split cognition from body, then kinesthetic imagining must bring cognition and the body back together. The unity of cognition and body is what Merleau-Ponty (1962) called "incarnate perception" in which the self knows itself through actions experienced within a certain horizon. Perception is thus understood as a set of relations within the self, and between self and world. Perceptions viewed as patterns of relatedness are called "kinetic melodies." This description of image as patterned process contrasts with the traditional description of an image as a purely visual picture in the mind. An image is not a thing or an object, but a "visible of the second power, a carnal essence or icon of the first" (Merleau-Ponty, 1962, p. 164). An image is not a thing, but an active way of seeing, a paradoxical set of relations between the visible and the invisible which is rooted in the perceptions of a lived body. When reconnected to its ground in perception and body, an image is the embodied unity of vision and body.

If the moving group tells a story like an orchestra plays a melody, then the individual mover must be warmed up before he or she can make movement melodies, just as an instrument must be warmed up before it can play auditory melodies. A body warm-up is not a mechanical process, as is aerobic body conditioning, but it is intended to bring conscious perception to the body. Any one of a number of exercises might accomplish this, but all would bring awareness to the breath, to isolated body parts, and to the orchestration of body parts working together. Some people find it helpful to begin with closed eyes, to turn away from images of the outer world and to focus on inner or proprioceptive sensations. Turning inward can turn perception into insight.

After warm-up exercises in one class, a student wrote in her journal:

> I had no eyes, only senses. They were black eyes sometimes. Thankful to be a big moving mass; the burden of consciousness, too much relating to the world through the eyes.

A second student noted:

> I wasn't there. All the parts of my body were involved into twisting, contracting, stretching to explore the outside world. My body was a huge We which could see everywhere — my body was skin which could sense all over, my body was all ear which could hear every sound. My tongue was my whole body and I tasted the whole world. No intellectual feeling existed. I was not happy, unhappy, I just was.

Improvising with basic sensations of weight, a third student moved into images of a deep underworld and the formlessness out of which all forms arise:

> That may be why I chose to explore the Dark Goddess, who demanded the entire creative "eye" lurking in that vast, all encompassing darkness. I felt there was vision, but of a different order. The eye seemed to be part of the tissue of the stomach; the navel, at the center, was embedded within. It was recognizable only as impulse. ... a pulsing. It is a very deep wisdom ... untranslatable ... the dark source of all-there-is ... the dark material, formless, shapeless, from which everything is made.

Action Language

The descriptions above are all poetic, movement imagery, like verbal imagery, is a poesis, a "making." Most of our words used to describe movement experiences, however, are still dualistic, such as the static, objectified, noun form of the word "image." The task of finding an active embodied language has precedents in the psychoanalytic tradition. Roy Shafer (1976) claims:

> I have good reason, therefore, to say that my project of devising an action language to serve as a new language for psychoanalysis falls within the great and arduous tradition of systematic and clinically-oriented psychoanalytic thinking. (p. x)

How can action be a language or a text? Language, according to linguistic philosopher Paul Ricoeur (1976), can be characterized in three ways. First, language is not comprised of the isolated units of word or gesture which are the signs of semiotics, but is instead patterns of word or gesture with semantic referents and which are visible in the opening pictures. From these pictures, it can be seen that movement language is expressed as kinds of qualities, relations, and actions, that includes sense and form. Second, movement as language discourse occurs in interaction between mover and witness, and opens a shared world, an "ensemble of references opened up by every kind of text." A text mediates between writer and reader, speaker and listener, or mover and witness. Action language, which bridges inner sensation and outer form, into dialogue between mover and witness, is therefore a text. In traditional psychology, the spoken word is usually the text, action language adds another form of text in which images and meaning occur.

Just as a poem has metaphor and/or symbol, or levels of meaning, so a movement text has levels of meaning. And just as we have been taught in school how to analyze a poem, or just as clinicians are taught how to analyze levels of meaning in a dream, so we too can analyze levels of meaning in a movement text.

A text, according to Ricoeur (1976), is characterized by multiple levels of meaning, each of which corresponds to a kind of imagery. The first level is the teleological level. This level is characterized by movement which has a progressive forward direction, opening into consciousness and intentionality. Teleological movement is shown in Gestalt exercises, in which the person's intention is clear in the movement. There is a one-to-one correspondence between intention and action, in movements such as (I am) retreating, and (I am) advancing. The use of simile and irony often occurs in this level. For example, as one student moved with another, she discovered that the way they leaned into each other was like her relationship with her boyfriend. All of her issues about commitment, trust, and mutuality were evident in the movement, the movement was not her relationship with her boyfriend, but it was a simile for her relationship with her boyfriend.

The second level is the archeological level. Here, forward movement is contrasted by movements which stumble and fall, which forget and which pause. These are "depth" movements which move backward into time, and which speak of regression, death, desire, and unconsciousness. This kind of movement is shown in the following description of the mythological figure of Ereshkigal: "She is the root of all, where energy is inert and consciousness coiled asleep. She is the place where potential life lies motionless — but in the pangs of birth" (Perera, 1981, p. 32). Suzanne Langer (1953) calls the unity of force and meaning on the archeological level a symbol. This particular symbol is not a picture but is a "pattern of sentience" which is made up of feelings and emotions, shaped as complexes of tension, and formed as rhythm into streams of resolutions. Action, expressed in this way, does not "mean" or refer to something else, it is already symbolic. Jung (1953) also observed that a symbol is not merely a picture, but is an act, an attitude; what distinguishes a symbol is the observing consciousness of the observer.

The third level of movement text is the eschatological. The patterns of correspondence between implicit and explicit forms are expressed as ritual and sacred story, not necessarily in the one-to-one correspondence between action and meaning exemplified by metaphoric movement. For example, in the opening pictures, the joined hands and symmetrical bodies make the patterns explicit, as do the formal content of circles, spirals, and mandalas which appear spontaneously in groups of moving people. Further, sacred movement is marked by a particular quality of energy. It is visible and palpable as numinosity, as "authentic movement" in which the transcendent function bridges moving and being moved. Sacred movement requires a surrender of power, of ego, and toward faith to be moved, therefore, it can be the most transformative kind of movement.

Action language focuses, clarifies, differentiates, and describes the emerging kinesthetic imagery. Having students keep movement journals was part of their process as they learned to transcribe felt-images into words or drawing to move the images further. The stages of development include authentic movement, amplification, description, differentiation, and naming.

As one student moved, the following archetypal figure emerged:

> The strongest, most singular image I encountered during this class was a dance I call my Goddess dance which tumbled out of my body the way a shell rolls out of the sea. You selected special music [and] all my joints softened. Without taking a step I could feel the weight of my body making a hundred little adjustments, a tiny current of energy flowing through every pathway, down to the earth, up to the crown, back and forth ... Grecian vases showing women in tunics and sandals, their hair bound in fluttering chignons, a Botticelli painting of a soft-boned lady covered with tiny flowers and some gauzy gown; the Star card from the Tarot deck which shows a nude woman with a long round shape, her face hidden in a shadow. These images floated before me as I swayed to the music. Slowly, I started to walk.

> I was aware of the fleshiness of the bottom of my feet, how far I could "step into" them. Sometimes I was dancing with a veil, sometimes with a rope of flowers. I was with other women, one of several dancing. The dance took a serpentine shape, turning back and forth on a line with the feet barely leaving the ground, but the knees fluid. At certain points I knelt, but the motion was continuous. My arms would furl and unfurl, twine or curl, close to my body or reaching for a bud, or the hand of another to dance with me. After a while my face allowed the feeling of grace I felt to form a small smile ... all the regression this quarter was a molting to let this butterfly emerge. I was transported to another time

and place, where I can be connected to the numinous. I could wait there in rapture for a long time in contemplation of this image and how soothing it is for me. How like the tiny flower she held was the Woman I danced!

Action Hermeneutics

In traditional verbal psychotherapy, the meaning of an event comes through reflection, which necessitates a turning away from the world of action. Action is separated from meaning; in fact, action is often looked upon with suspicion as "acting out."

Action hermeneutics, on the other hand, understands action as a meaning-making activity. Movement, in other words, can help clarity being, intentions, and depth imagery. Exegesis is the theory of interpretation, hermeneutics is the art or methodology of interpretation. Exegesis tells us that a text has several meanings, that there is a surplus of meanings, and that these meanings overlap. Interpretation is "the work of thought which consists in deciphering the hidden meanings in the apparent meaning, in unfolding the levels of meaning implied in the literal meaning" (Reagen & Stewart, 1978, p. 98).

How are Levels of Meaning Revealed in Action?

In Figure 2, for example, there seems to be a middle point in the circle which is invisible and which unites the participants. The movement is spontaneous; no one has instructed them to form this configuration. Still, what does it mean? Analytically, we can speak about the height of the arms in relation to the shoulders, about the difference in levels among the movers, yet this does not tell us about their understanding of their experience. All the participants seem to be sensing their correspondence with each other, there is some sort of patterning visible. It is not that this pattern points to a meaning or a sign; it is the meaning. Action is meaning. Meaning does not lie behind the action, as in the Aristotelian sense of the meaning behind the plot.

Figure 2

This meaning is known in two ways, It is known indirectly, by observing and analyzing the patterns. It is also known directly, through the senses. I know the other and his or her patterning by feeling it in my own body, through empathy.

The two poles of discourse for a spoken text have been described by Ricoeur (1976) as event and meaning. What are the poles of discourse for a movement text? The two poles of discourse for a movement text can be understood as empathy and analysis. Empathy gives us the direct, connatural knowing, analysis gives us the observable. By maintaining the tension between the two, we can preserve the integrity of the text.

At the teleological level, the polarity of empathy and analysis becomes symbolic. Meaning, or the linguistic pole, is united with force, as instinct. Instinct is expressed symbolically through the body; bios and logos are brought together in symbol.

Symbolic discourse moves further at the sacred level into a polarity of form and power. Power begins with the experience of awe, of being moved. Power is expressed not through linguistic forms, but through aesthetic ones of time, space, weight, and direction. Power has nonlinguistic meaning:

> The preverbal character of such an experience is attested to by the very modulation of space and time as sacred space or sacred time which result and which are inscribed beneath language at the aesthetic level of experience, in the Kantian sense of this expression. (Ricoeur, 1976, p. 61)

What are these non-linguistic forms which inform power? These are aesthetic forms of timing, space and flow grouped into coherent phrases and lyrical lines of correspondence. At the sacred level, these patterns become "diverse ephiphanies [which] communicate among themselves, while at the same time they also refer to the divine immanent in the hierophanies of life" (Ricoeur, 1976, p. 61). Made up of rhythms, pulsations, and phrases, these non-lingustic patterns have also been called "the music of the spheres." They are sacred not because they inform, but because they are informed by, an intelligible cosmos:

> In the sacred universe the capacity to speak is founded upon the capacity of the cosmos to signify. The logic of meaning, therefore, follows from the very structure of the sacred universe. Its law is the law of correspondence. (Ricoeur, 1976, p. 62)

In Figure 3 we can see patterns of correspondence. The focus is not between two people, but it is among people in community and in active relationship to their world. The joined hands make the links explicit, but the implicit connection was already present. Another way of seeing the form here would be to see the circles, spirals, and mandala patterns

Figure 3

which groups of people seem spontaneously to form. Taking this body-in-action as a symbol for life-in-action, we might begin to perceive the changing shapes and correspondences around us. We might hear the phrasing of an ordinary conversation, see the compositional relationship between the way this car goes down the street and the way that cloud passes overhead. It is not the content that marks the sacred, but in the sense of wonder when patterns start becoming apparent everywhere, in daily life. It is not even so much a matter of what these patterns are, but *that* they are is the fundamental character of the sacred. Form and force come together, the universe is intelligible. The discourse of the cosmos is spoken both linguistically and non-linguistically (that is, aesthetically) as the poetics of action.

One student's images of the sacred in movement were:

> I felt the movement as circular as though it were a cog driving a wheel. The wheel was our circle, the cog was the driving force of our collective energy, expressed in movement. I closed my eyes and had a sudden feeling, expressed as a vision ... I was seated in a circle of women, wearing only waist-cloths and primitive wraps, all moving together with that same rhythmic quality ... The work we were doing wasn't particularly clear, nor was it particularly important ... it could have been washing clothes or kneading bread. ... The beauty of the moment was in the deep feeling of community and the repetitive physical exertion made easier through the sharing of the rhythm. I wished that we all could pick up what I was singing and join in, for the other group — the one in my vision was singing or chanting or keeping the rhythm — it was somewhere in the time when music was born. In this moment is joined the height of both individual and collective, personal journey and collective.

What Happens When All The Images Overlap?

This brings us to the realm of story. Meaning is now located in the transitions of one gesture to another, in the shifting grouping of movements, in the ordering of a beginning, a middle, and an end. The action narrative has a plot, not recognizable in its content but recognizable in its dynamic structure. The human need for meaning translates, in the active mode, into a need for form, for creating patterns of coherence. Intelligibility is sensed not by rational logic, but by a kinesthetic imagination.

Because meaning at the sacred level requires first a radical surrender to being moved, and second to a faith that events are unfolding according to their own logic, accessibility at this level involves the most fundamental possibility of transformation. The aeschatological level of action is more encompassing than is the archeological or the teleological. Language of intention or will has moved to language of revelation.

But the mixture of power and form is fragile. While we may see sacred inspiration here, we can also see the kind of pathologies which result when power is not matched by forming coherence. On this non-verbal level, patients may exhibit an inability to complete form, gestures may trail off without conclusion, action may be flat without "peaking" at the middle into a statement, or the person may leave at the wrong (that is, "inappropriate") time. The sense of time, space and phrasing is disturbed, or the person marches "to the beat of his or her own drummer." These patterns of pathology, expressed in action language, express themselves as styes which can be read as texts.

If the sacred makes itself manifest in certain patterns of myth or archetypal form, then ritual is the re-enactment of the story. Ritual moves us beyond the necessity of particular forms to a simpler sense of ritual action as discernable in daily life. This is action marked by power. This quality may not be recognizable in these pictures, for it is found in the quality or intensity of movement. A special intensity or efficacy marks these rituals, because they embody the interpenetration of force and meaning, inner and outer expression, and form and content. Here action is word, and discourse is act.

Conclusion

Thus ends our narrative about action stories. The way we move through the world tells a story about who and how we are. Making action narratives explicit, therefore, can have both diagnostic and treatment effects. It can help us clarify our intentions, mythologies, and patterns of relatedness, to perceive our coping as well as our defensive strategies. In addition, seeing the patterns in the process, weaving the parts together, and acting with integrity and congruence can bring the participants a sense of healing wholeness.

References

Bateson, M. C. (1989). *Composing a life.* New York: Atlantic Monthly Press.

Casey, E. S. (1976). *Imagining: A phenomenological study.* Bloomington: Indiana University Press.

Deri, S. K. (1988). *Symbolization and creativity.* New York: International Universities Press.

Feinstein, D., & Krippner, S. (1988). *Personal mythology: The psychology your evolving self: Using ritual, dreams, and imagnation to discover your inner story.* Los Angeles: Jeremy P. Tarcher.

Jung, C.G. (1953). *Collected Works of C. G. Jung.* Bollingen Series XX (Read, H., Fordham, M., Adler, G., McGuire, W., Eds., R. F. C. Hull, Transl.) Princeton: Princeton University Press.

Langer, S. K. (1953). *Feeling and form.* New York: Charles Scribner's Sons.

May, R. (1989). *The cry for myth.* New York: W. W. Norton.

Merleau-Ponty, M. (1962). *The phenomenology of perception.* (C. Smith, Transl.) New York: Humanities Press.

Perera, S. B. (1981). *Descent to the goddess: A way of initiation for women.* Toronto: Inner City Books.

Reagan, C. E., & Stewart, D. (1978). *The philosophy of Paul Ricoeur. An anthology of his work.* Boston: Beacon Press.

Ricoeur, P. (1976). *Interpretation theory: Discourse and the surplus of meaning.* Fort Worth: Texas Christian University Press.

Sarbin, T. R. (Ed.). (1986). *Narrative psychology: The storied nature of human conduct.* New York: Praeger.

Sartre, J. P. (1968). *The psychology of imagination.* New York: Washington Square Press.

Serlin, L. (1976-77). Portrait of Karen: A Gestalt-phenomonological approach to movement therapy. *Journal of Contemporary Psychotherapy, 8,* 145–152.

Serlin, I. (1995). Notes on the single woman: The Anne Sexton complex. In K. Schneider & R. J. May, (Eds.), *The psychology of existence.* (pp. 271–286). New York: McGraw-Hill.

Shafer, R. (1976). *A new language for psychoanalysis.* New Haven, CT.: Yale University Press.

About the Contributors

Stephan A. Anderson, Ph.D., is presently a Professor and Director of the Center for Applied Research in the School of Family Studies at the University of Connecticut. He teaches courses on family therapy, domestic violence, and family assessment, theory, and research. He also supervises students in the School's accredited marital and family therapy programs. Dr. Anderson is a Connecticut licensed Marriage and Family Therapist. Previously he served terms as the Dean of the School of Family Studies and as the Director of the Marriage and Family Therapy Program. He is the author of numerous professional papers and co-author of several books including, *Family Myths: Psychotherapy Implications* (Haworth Press, 1989), *Personal, Marital, and Family Myths: Theoretical Formulations and Clinical Strategies* (W. W. Norton, 1989), and *Family Interaction: A Multigenerational Developmental Perspective* (Allyn & Bacon, 2002).

Michael W. Barclay, Ph.D., is a clinical psychologist who specializes in the treatment of families, couples, adults, children and teens. He has provided workshops for therapeutic foster families and the practitioners with whom they work as well as on metaphors, narrative and dissociative disorders. Barclay has also lectured on existentialism in psychological theory and psychotherapy at Notre Dame. His publications include *The Interpretation of Infant Communication* (Psychosocial Press, 1999), "Metaphoric Truth and Narrative Structure: Implications for Understanding and Treating Patients Exhibiting Dissociative Phenomena," in *Broken Images, Broken Selves: Dissociative Narratives in Clinical Practice* (Brunner/Mazel, 1997), articles in such journals as the *Humanistic Psychologist, Journal of Phenomenological Psychology, Theoretical and Philosophical Psychology,* and *Theory and Psychology.*

Arthur C. Bohart, Ph.D., is a faculty member of Saybrook Graduate School and Research Center, an Emeritus Professor of Marital and Family Therapy at California State University in Dominguez Hills, and a Fellow of the American Psychological Association. He has coauthored a number of books including *Empathy Reconsidered: New Directions in Psychotherapy* (with Leslie S. Greenberg, American Psychological Association, 1997), *How Clients Make Therapy Work: The Process of Active Self-Healing* (with Karen Tallman, American Psychological Association, 1999), *Constructive and Destructive Behavior: Implications for Family, School and Society* (with Deborah J. Stipek, American Psychological Association, 2001), and *Foundations of Clinical and Counseling Psychology* (with Judith Todd, Waveland Press, 2005). He is also on the editorial board of the *Journal of Humanistic Psychology.* Among his research interests are relationships, empathy, self-healing and self-righting as well as "human" psychotherapy dealing with personal choice, values, life style, and authentic relationships.

Michael Bova, M.P.S., A.T.R., is the Director of the Community Lodge Program with Northeast Community Center for Mental Health/Mental Retardation in Philadelphia, and a psychotherapist in private practice. He is a faculty-in-training with the Consciousness Research and Training Project in New York City. Bova is also a Registered Art Therapist with the American Art Therapy Association. He was a research assistant at the former Dream Laboratory at Maimonides Medical Center in

Brooklyn, New York and on the faculty of the School of Visual Arts in New York City, the University of Bridgeport in Bridgeport, Connecticut, and an art therapist and supervisor at Bellevue Hospital Center's Division of Alcoholism in New York City.

Harold Roger Ellis, Ph.D., as a child played with a wide variety of kids born to turn-of-the-century immigrant families in the melting pot of the east Bronx in New York City. Their ethnic gangs teased and competed, but in a fun-loving way, and when it came time to be in elementary school little Harold chafed at the rigidity and, it seemed to him, arbitrary discipline of the authoritarian school principal and "monitors." He became a rebel and reduced a year of this servitude by getting straight As. Starting at age twelve, he attended high school and engineering college at night while working full time in many of the design, manufacturing, engineering, magazine/book editing, teaching, miltary, and communications areas of the local electronics world. During his four-year military hitch assigned to the flight crew of the Air Force's VIP transport plan in Europe, Ellis experienced that not only in dreaming, but in real life as well, the high and mighty and the low and mucky were little different: when the field was level, communication could be direct and cohesive. Back home he became an electronics importer while sporadically completing his engineering degree and raising a family. Still a rebel, he switched careers to work in counseling and rehabilitation while getting degrees and certifications in humanistic and professional psychology, education and philosophy (Columbia University and Union Institute), as well as in rehabilitation, training supervision, dance therapy, and has a life membership in the Art Students League. Ellis has kept a dream diary for forty years, and facilitated dreamsharing groups for thirty-five years in a wide range of venues. In 1989 he launched *Dream Switchboard,* a twelve-page quarterly national newsletter which encouraged the formation of self-help, no-fee, small on-going dreamsharing groups, and The Community Dreamsharing Network which recruits and sponsors new members. Although discontinued in 1994 due to severe accident, the Network was later restarted as a not-for-profit.

David Feinstein, Ph.D., a pioneer in bringing a mythological perspective to personal, organizational, and community change, is the Executive Director of Innersource in Ashland, Oregon. He is author or co-author of over fifty professional papers and three popular books: *Rituals for Living and Dying: From Life's Wounds to Spiritual Awakening* (with Peg Elliot Mayo, HarperSanFrancisco, 1990), *Energy Medicine* (with Donna Eden, Piatkus Press, 2003), and *The Mythic Path: Discovering the Guiding Stories of Your Past — Creating a Vision for Your Future* (with Stanley Krippner, Elite Books, 2007). Serving as both a clinical and community psychologist for over twenty-five years, he has taught at Johns Hopkins University School of Medicine and at Antioch College.

Arthur W. Frank, Ph.D., is Professor of Sociology and Adjunct Professor of Nursing at the University of Calgary in Calgary, Alberta, Canada. He is the author of *The Wounded Storyteller: Body, Illness, and Ethics* (University of Chicago, 1995), *At the Will of the Body: Reflections on Illness* (Houghton, Mifflin, 2002), which won the Natalie Davis Spingarm Writer's Award from the National Coalition for Cancer Survivorship, and *The Renewal of Generosity: Illness, Medicine and How to Live* (University of Chicago, 2004). He is an associate editor and frequent contributor to the journals *Body & Society* and *Health.* An international speaker, in 1998, he was a fellow at the Bioethics Research Centre, University of Otago, Dunedin, New Zealand, and in 1999 he was Visiting

Professor at the Centre for Values, Ethics and the Law in Medicine, University of Sydney, Australia.

Leslie Gray, Ph.D., is a Native American psychologist who has studied with medicine people and elders from various tribal backgrounds. She is President and Founder of the Woodfish Institute, has a private practice in San Francisco, and has lectured at various universities including the University of California-Berkeley, and the Institute of Transpersonal Psychology. Her work has been featured in such periodicals as *East-West Journal* and *ReVision Journal*, as well as in the books *Spiritual Dimensions of Healing: From Tribal Shamanism to Contemporary Health Care* (edited by Stanley Krippner, Irvington, 1992) and *Ecopsychology: Restoring the Earth, Healing the Mind* (edited by Allan D. Kanner, Theodore Roszak and Mary E. Gomes, Sierra Club Books, 1995). Dr. Gray advocates and embodies a vision of health care that integrates ancient and tribal healing practices with modern medicine. She consults with individuals and organizations on the practice of ecopsychology and holistic health care.

D. Corydon Hammond, Ph.D., A.B.Ph., is a past President of the International Society for Neuronal Regulation, a past President and Fellow of the American Society of Clinical Hypnosis, and the past Chair of the Board of Trustees of the ASCH Education and Research Foundation. Board certified in EEG and Quantitative EEG from the American Board of Electroencephalography and Neurophysiology, he works actively in the fields of neurofeedback (EEG biofeedback), quantitative EEG brain mapping, hypnosis, and sex and marital therapy. He has received a number of academic and professional awards, among them the Morton Prince Award for Distinguished Career Contributions to the Field of Clinical Hypnosis from the American Board of Psychological Hypnosis and the Society for Clinical and Experimental Hypnosis. Currently he is a full Professor of Physical Medicine and Rehabilitation and functions part-time as the Co-Director of the Sex and Marital Therapy Clinic, which he founded, at the University of Utah School of Medicine. His publications include *Clinical Hypnosis and Memory: Guidelines for Clinicians and for Forensic Hypnosis* (American Society of Clinical Hypnosis, 1995), *Memory, Trauma Treatment, and the Law* (with Daniel B. Brown and Alan W. Scheflin, W. W. Norton, 1998), and *Improving Therapeutic Communication: A Guide for Developing Effective Techniques* (Jossey-Bass, 2002).

Frederick J. Heide, Ph.D., is an Associate Professor at the San Francisco Bay campus of the California School of Professional Psychology. His work has been published in the *Behavior Research and Therapy, Journal of Consulting and Clinical Psychology, Psychophysiology*, and elsewhere. For his pioneering investigation of relaxation-induced anxiety, he received the Outstanding Research Contribution Award from the Association for Advancement of Behavior Therapy (AABT). Dr. Heide is also co-founder, former board president, and performer with the American Folklore Theatre, one of the nation's largest professional musical theaters presenting solely original work. He has written a dozen stage musicals which have been seen by over 100,000 people, including two shows with Second City Theater founder Paul Sills. He has also created two PBS-TV specials and a folk music CD. Recent activities have included an invited presentation in Australia and courses on improvisational acting for therapists at the Medical College of Wisconsin. He winters in Berkeley, California and summers on his farm in Door County, Wisconsin.

Sarah E. Holmes, Ph.D., obtained her doctorate from the Marriage and Family Therapy Program in the School of Family Studies at the University of Connecticut at Storrs. She has published in the *Journal of Feminist Family Therapy* and *Contemporary Family Therapy*.

Stephen R. Koepfer obtained a masters degree in Creative Arts Therapy from Hofstra University. He is an accomplished competitive martial artist with wins in Kung Fu, mixed martial arts, grappling and Tae Kwon Do, finishing as a finalist in the latter in the 1997 United World Championships. He is also a regular contributor to *Ultimate Grappling Magazine*.

Stanley Krippner, Ph.D. obtained his doctorate in educational psychology from Northwestern University in 1961. He is internationally known for his pioneering work in the scientific investigation of human consciousness, especially in such areas as creativity, parapsychology, and altered states of consciousness. Prior to joining the Saybrook faculty in 1972, Dr. Krippner directed the Dream Laboratory at Maimonides Medical Center in New York and was Director of the Child Study Center at Kent State University. He has served as President of the Association for Humanistic Psychology, the Association for the Study of Dreams, and the Parapsychological Association. He is also a Charter Member of the International Society for the Study of Trauma and Dissociation, as well as a Fellow of the American Psychological Association, the American Psychological Society, the American Society of Clinical Hypnosis, the Society for the Scientific Study of Religion, and the Society for the Scientific Study of Sex. In addition to over 500 articles, he has co-authored or co-edited a prodigious list of books on a wide variety of topics, among them: *Healing States: A Journey into the World of Spiritual Healing and Shamanism* (with Alberto Villoldo, Fireside, 1987), *Source: Visionary Interpretations of Global Creation Myths* (with Rowena Pattee Ryder and Ruth Inge-Heinz, Golden Point Productions, 2000), *Extraordinary Dreams and How to Work with Them* (with Fariba Bogzaran and Andre Percia de Carvalho, 2002), *The Psychological Impact of War Trauma on Civilians: An International Perspective* (with Teresa M. McIntyre, Praeger, 2003), and *The Mythic Path: Discovering the Guiding Stories of Your Path — Creating a Vision for Your Future* (with David Feinstein, Elite Books, 2007).

G. Frank Lawlis, Ph.D. is a fellow of Division 12 (Society of Clinical Psychology) of the American Psychological Association. He is the supervisory psychologist of American Mensa, a research professor at the Department of Rehabilitation, Social Work and Addictions at the University of North Texas, a medical expert for the U. S. Department of Health and Human Services and the author of a number of books including *The Cure: The Hero's Journal with Cancer* (Resource Publications, 1993), *Caregiver's Guide to the Cure* (Resource Publications, 1994), *Transpersonal Medicine* (Shambhala, 1996), *The ADD Answer: How to Help Your Child Now* (with Phil McGraw, Viking Books, 2004).

Robert A. Neimeyer, Ph.D., is Professor and Director of Psychotherapy in the Department of Psychology, University of Memphis, where he also maintains an active clinical practice. Since completing his doctoral training at the University of Nebraska in 1982, he has published eighteen books, including *Constructivism in Psychotherapy* (American Psychological Association, 1999), *Constructions of Disorder* (American Psychological Association, 2000), and *Meaning, Reconstruction and the Experience of Loss*

(American Psychological Association, 2001). In addition to editing both the *Journal of Constructivist Psychology* and *Death Studies*, he has authored over 200 articles and book chapters, and is currently working to advance a more adequate theory of grieving as a meaning-making process. In recognition of his scholarly contributions, he has been granted the Eminent Faculty Award by the University of Memphis, was made a Fellow of the Clinical Psychology Division of the American Psychological Association, and was given the Research Recognition Award by the Association for Death Education and Counseling.

Daryl S. Paulson, Ph.D., is the President and CEO of BioScience Laboratories, Inc., a medical/pharmaceutical product research firm. He has doctorates both in psychology and in Human Science with an emphasis on psychoneuroimmunology. Dr. Paulson served in the U. S. Marine Corps with infantry units of the 1st Marine Division. He was awarded the Navy Commendation Medal with the Combat V for Valor, the Vietnamese Cross of Gallantry, and the Combat Action Award.

Patricia Perrine, Ph.D., is an international workshop presenter and transpersonal psychotherapist. She is Director and co-founder of Dancing Mountain Therapy Associates. In her practice, she combines creative arts, sharing and ceremony to provide experiences of transformative learning for her clients. She is currently doing research for a book on the psychological uses of mask-making.

Susan Powers, Ph.D., is an experiential psychotherapist trained in Gestalt Therapy and psychodrama who is also a full-time faculty member at the Woodstock Academy in northeastern Connecticut as well as an adjunct faculty member at the University of Connecticut. She has conducted seminars on a variety of topics including fantasy and science fiction, developmental psychology and stress management. In addition she co-edited *Broken Images, Broken Selves: Dissociative Narratives in Clinical Practice* (with Stanley Krippner, Bruner/Mazel, 1997).

Rachel Naomi Remen, M.D. is the Founder and Director of the Institute for the Study of Health and Illness at Commonweal, a Clinical Professor of Family and Community Medicine at the Unversity of California-San Francisco School of Medicine. She has authored more than seventy book chapters and articles, and a number of important books including *The Human Patient* (Doubleday/Anchor, 1980), *Kitchen Table Wisdom* (Riverhead/Penguin Putnam, 1996) and *My Grandfather's Blessings* (Riverhead/Penguin Putnam, 2000).

Robert Rosenbaum, Ph.D., is a psychologist at Kaiser Permanente where he works in both the Departments of Psychiatry and Behavioral Medicine. He is active in the Society for the Exploration of Psychotherapy Integration, and particularly interested in the incorporation of aesthetic and spiritual dimensions to psychotherapeutic practice and mind-body medicine. He is a student of Sujun Mel Weitsman at Berkeley Zen Center and the author of *Zen and the Heart of Psychotherapy* (Taylor & Francis, 1999). He also studies Da Yen Qi Gong with Master Hui Lui and recently was certified by her to teach in that tradition. He has been Chief Psychologist at Kaiser Permanente and director of the doctoral training program at the California Institute of Integral Studies. As a Fulbright scholar, he taught psychotherapy at the National Institute of Mental Health and Neurosciences in Bangalore, India.

Susan W. Schwartz, Ph.D., is a psychologist whose life-long interest in healing — with foremost attention to the workings of spiritual energy — has led her to explore its phenomena in clinical, academic, and research contexts, across cultures. She obtained a masters degree from Harvard University and a doctorate from Saybrook Graduate School and Research Center. She has a psychotherapeutic and metaphysical counseling practice in Massachusetts, and is currently writing a book on experiential healing as process and outcome.

Ilene Ava Serlin, Ph.D. is a psychologist and a dance therapist. As a psychotherapist, educator, researcher, dancer and artist, she seeks to bridge art and science, mind, body and spirit. Her orientation is existential/phenomenological and Jungian/Transpersonal. A faculty member of Saybrook Graduate School and Research Center, she obtained a masters in Dance/Movement Therapy from Hunter College and a masters and doctorate in psychology from the University of Dallas. She serves on the editorial boards of *American Dance Therapy Journal*, *The Arts in Psychotherapy*, and the *Journal of Humanistic Psychology*. Recent research interests have included: the use of dance/movement therapy for the treatment of women with breast cancer, and the development of a body-image scale which combines women's descriptions of their own embodied experiences with a Laban-based movement profile.

Alan E. Stewart, Ph.D., received his doctorate in Counseling Psychology from the University of Georgia in 1994. He has since completed postdoctoral training in counseling and psychotherapy at the HUB Counseling Center in Tucker, Georgia and also completed research postdoctoral training in psychology at the University of Memphis. From 1997 to 2002, he was an Assistant Professor of Psychology at the University of Florida. He now works as an Associate Professor in the Department of Counseling and Human Development at the University of Georgia. His research interests include constructivism, death notification, vehicular crash psychology, Alderian psychology, and professional development.

David G. Vogel, M.A., lives with his partner, Ellen Ezorsky, and their children in Cambridge Massachusetts. In the time intervening from the writing of his chapter to its publication, he has survived both cancer and severe burns from a house fire. As a trauma survivor and a member of the Phoenix Society for Burn Survivors, he has benefited from the healing power of sharing and telling personal stories of trauma, loss, recovery, and triumph. At present, he consults in forensic psychiatry, teaches psychology part-time at Merrimack College, and works with psychiatric intakes and evaluations at Caritas Norwood Hospital.

Index